Selected Letters of W. D. Howells

Volume 3

1882–1891

William Dean Howells
1887

W. D. HOWELLS

Selected Letters

Volume 3: 1882-1891

Edited and Annotated by
Robert C. Leitz **III**
with
Richard H. Ballinger
and Christoph K. Lohmann

Textual Editor
Christoph K. Lohmann

TWAYNE PUBLISHERS

Boston

1980

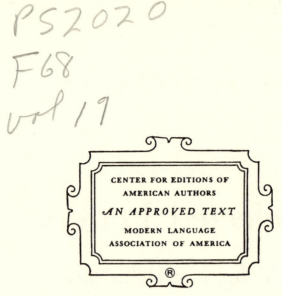

This volume of Selected Letters is also published as
Volume 19 of A Selected Edition of W. D. Howells

Editorial expenses for this volume have been supported by grants from
the National Endowment for the Humanities administered through
the Center for Editions of American Authors of the Modern Language Association

Published in 1980 by Twayne Publishers, A Division of G. K. Hall & Co.,
70 Lincoln Street, Boston, Massachusetts 02111

Printed on permanent/durable acid-free paper and bound in
the United States of America

First Printing

Library of Congress Cataloging in Publication Information

Howells, William Dean, 1837-1920.
Selected letters.

(A selected edition of W. D. Howells; v. 4, 9, 19)
Includes bibliographical references and indexes.
CONTENTS: v. 1. 1852-1872.—v. 2.1873-1882.—v. 3.1882-1891
1. Howells, William Dean, 1837-1920—Correspondence.
2. Novelists, American—19th century—Correspondence.
I. Arms, George Warren, 1912-
PS2020.F68   818'.409 [B]   78-27247
ISBN 0-8057-8529-9 (v. 3)

Acknowledgments

We are grateful for permission to print the letters in this volume, as given by William White Howells and the heirs of W. D. Howells. The following individuals and institutions have also permitted the use of letters in their collections: The Trustees of the Boston Public Library; Bowdoin College Library, Brunswick, Maine; The British Library Board; Brown University Library; Buffalo and Erie County Public Library; Mark Twain Papers, Bancroft Library, University of California (Berkeley); Miller Library, Colby College, Waterville, Maine; Columbia University Libraries; Cornell University Library; James Duncan Phillips Library, Essex Institute, Salem, Massachusetts; The Filson Club, Louisville, Kentucky; Folger Shakespeare Library, Washington, D. C.; Harvard College Library; Huntington Library, San Marino, California; Kent State University Libraries; University of Kentucky Libraries; William Salters Papers, Knox College, Galesburg, Illinois; Brotherton Library, University of Leeds (England); Miami University Libraries, Oxford, Ohio; Abernethy Library, Middlebury College, Middlebury, Vermont; New-York Historical Society; Henry W. and Albert A. Berg Collection and R. W. Gilder Papers, New York Public Library, Astor, Lenox and Tilden Foundations; Ohio Historical Society, Columbus; University of Pennsylvania Library; Allison-Shelley Collection, University Libraries, Pennsylvania State University; Princeton University Library; University of Rochester Library; Rutgers University Library; Sophia Smith Collection (Women's History Archives), Smith College, Northampton, Massachusetts; Hamlin Garland Collection and Willard S. Morse Collection, University of Southern California Library; Trinity College Library, Hartford, Connecticut; George W. Cable Collection, Tulane University Library; William Dean Howells Collection, Clifton Waller Barrett Library, University of Virginia Library; George N. Meissner Collection, Washington University Libraries; Western Reserve Historical Society, Cleveland, Ohio; Collection of American Literature, Beinecke Rare Book and Manuscript Library, Yale University; Mabel Loomis Todd Papers, Yale University; George Arms, Albuquerque, New Mexico; and E. N. Zeigler, Florence, South Carolina.

Richard H. Ballinger wishes to thank Texas A & M University for a research grant and the following individuals for assistance: Hung C. Yu, Sterling C. Evans Library, Texas A & M University, and Mrs. Randall Stelly, College Station, Texas. Robert C. Leitz wishes to thank The American Philosophical Society, the Trustees of Indiana University, and

Louisiana State University in Shreveport for research funds, and the following individuals for assistance: Professors Richard H. Ballinger, Harrison E. Hierth, and Parks C. Hunter of Texas A & M University; Professors Don L. Cook, Christoph K. Lohmann, and David J. Nordloh of Indiana University.

Contents

A Note on Editorial Practice

Two basic principles inform the treatment of the texts of the Howells correspondence which have been selected for publication in these volumes: one, the contents of the original documents are reproduced as fully and correctly as possible; and, two, all physical details of the manuscripts necessary for accurate reconstruction of the text are reported, though without encumbering the reading text itself. Consistent with these principles, the printed versions of the letters which form the body of these volumes retain the eccentricities of Howells' spelling, punctuation, and occasionally elliptical epistolary style, and are presented without such editorial appurtenances as brackets, arrows, virgules, and *sic*'s. The printed text is, insofar as possible, that of the finished letter, after Howells revised it either locally or generally by writing over, crossing out, and interlining. Howells' errors, except for inadvertent repetitions of words or syllables, are printed as they appear in the holographs, so long as the sense of the text can be discerned.

In accordance with the principle of reporting significant manuscript information, each letter is represented by a full itemization of cancellations, interlineations, the unusual placement of postscripts and marginal comments, and the presence of nonauthorial notes and comments believed to be contemporary with the composition or receipt of the letter, as well as of those editorial revisions necessary to insure comprehension. The reader should be aware, therefore, that some few words, letters, and marks of punctuation printed in this text are not in the original letters (or in transcriptions which have been employed when the originals are no longer extant or accessible). The full record of emendations, editorial comments, textual details, and Howells' revisions is provided in the Textual Apparatus, the introduction to which explains the symbols and abbreviations used to allow for the printing of the maximum of evidence in a minimum of space. Several exceptions, however, should be noted. Howells frequently failed to lift his pen when moving from one word to the next; thus, he often joined words that were not meant to be joined. Occasionally, though not always, he would repair such errors by separating these inadvertently joined words with a vertical line. Conversely, he sometimes lifted his pen while writing a single word, or he disconnected compounds that appear elsewhere as one word. In such cases, no notation of these irregularities has been included in the apparatus, while an attempt has been made, through comparisons among the letters, to render Howells' texts as nearly as possible in the form that he seems likely to have intended.

Given the wealth of references to personal and public events in the letters and the relevance of the letters to the shape and movement of Howells' career, annotation is potentially endless. The policy of these volumes is to present only the basic information which will make the context of the letters understandable and the letters themselves useful to both scholar and general reader. Annotation is thus restricted to explanation and clarification of references to people, places, events, literary works, and other such primary data. Interpretive comment is excluded.

Since the letters in this series represent only a portion of the extant Howells correspondence, it is also important that their relationship to each other and to letters not printed in these volumes be indicated. Cross references to other letters printed in the series simply identify correspondent and date: e.g., "Howells to Comly, 7 July 1868"; references to annotation accompanying letters add to this citation the specific footnote number: e.g., "Howells to Comly, 7 July 1868, n. 4." Manuscript letters not printed in this edition but cited or quoted are identified by correspondent and date, followed by the library location or collector's name in parentheses: e.g., "(MH)" for Harvard University or "(Ray)" for the collection of Gordon N. Ray.[1] Special collections within libraries are not indicated. When manuscripts of texts cited are also available in major printed collections (e.g., *Mark Twain–Howells Letters*), publication information follows the library symbol. Publication information appearing without notation of manuscript location should be assumed to designate texts extant only in published form. Quotations from letters in annotations follow the final, revised forms, and do not include a record of internal revisions. In addition, to avoid the proliferation of annotation, information necessary to the understanding of such quoted letters is provided within brackets at appropriate points within the quotations.

To further reduce the bulk and duplication of annotation, several other conventions have been adopted. People, events, and literary works are identified in footnotes at the points where their first significant mention appears in the whole series of letters. Further annotation of these same details is provided only where the context of a specific letter demands elaboration. The basic information can be located by using the indexes to the individual volumes or the cumulative index in

1. Libraries are indicated by the abbreviations detailed in *Symbols of American Libraries*, 10th ed. (Washington: Library of Congress, 1969).

the final volume of letters, where major references are distinguished by the printing of the appropriate page numbers in italic type. References to books give the year of first publication; however, books reviewed in dated articles should be assumed to have been published in the same year as the review, unless information to the contrary is provided. Whenever possible, references to books by Howells identify volumes published in "A Selected Edition of W. D. Howells," signaled by the abbreviation "HE" immediately following the title; references to works not available in this form generally cite the American first edition, which is identified by date of publication.

The editors have followed a consistent policy in the use of ellipses in quotations. If the first period is close up to the word preceding it, it stands for an end-of-sentence period in the original, with the omission following it. Thus, "invention.... develop" indicates that there is a period in the original after "invention," with the omitted portion of the text following it. However, "hereafter .... Good lord!" indicates that there is more text in the same sentence after "hereafter."

Titles of most secondary sources are given in full, but a number of them are cited so often in this series that the following list of short titles has been adopted.

Cady, *Howells*, I	Edwin H. Cady, *The Road to Realism: The Early Years, 1837–1885, of William Dean Howells* (Syracuse, N. Y.: Syracuse University Press, 1956)
Cady, *Howells*, II	Edwin H. Cady, *The Realist at War: The Mature Years, 1885–1920, of William Dean Howells* (Syracuse, N. Y.: Syracuse University Press, 1958)
Gibson-Arms, *Bibliography*	William M. Gibson and George Arms, *A Bibliography of William Dean Howells* (New York: New York Public Library, 1948; reprinted, New York Public Library and Arno Press, 1971)
James Letters	*Henry James Letters*, ed. Leon Edel, 2 vols. (Cambridge, Mass.: Harvard University Press, Belknap Press, 1974–1975)
Life in Letters	*Life in Letters of William Dean Howells*, ed. Mildred Howells, 2 vols. (Garden City, N. Y.: Doubleday, Doran & Co., 1928)

Lynn, *Howells*	Kenneth S. Lynn, *William Dean Howells: An American Life* (New York: Harcourt Brace Jovanovich, 1971)
Norton, *Lowell Letters*	*Letters of James Russell Lowell*, ed. C. E. Norton, 2 vols. (New York: Harper & Brothers, 1894)
Transatlantic Dialogue	*Transatlantic Dialogue: Selected American Correspondence of Edmund Gosse*, ed. Paul F. Mattheisen and Michael Millgate (Austin: University of Texas Press, 1965)
Twain-Howells	*Mark Twain-Howells Letters*, ed. Henry Nash Smith and William M. Gibson, 2 vols. (Cambridge, Mass.: Harvard University Press, Belknap Press, 1960)
Woodress, *Howells & Italy*	James L. Woodress, Jr., *Howells & Italy* (Durham, N. C.: Duke University Press, 1952)

C. K. L.

D. J. N.

I

The Independent Novelist

1 8 8 2 – 1 8 8 5

Introduction

THE first four years during which Howells worked without a regular editorial salary and had to depend on the income from his fiction alone were, all in all, considerably more successful than he had dared to hope. Although he frequently felt anxious about getting bogged down in his writing, Howells produced one major and three substantial novels, a volume of sketches, and a collaborative play. He became a familiar figure in English literary and cultural circles, partly through his new friendship with Edmund Gosse and partly as a result of the good offices of his old friend Henry James. During these years, furthermore, Howells established his connection with the House of Harper, beginning a prosperous author-publisher association that lasted in one form or other for the rest of his life, and provided him, during the second half of the decade, with a platform for advocating the principles of literary realism and social reform.

Howells had resigned the editorship of the *Atlantic* early in 1881 and made a contract with James R. Osgood & Co. for a fixed weekly salary in return for ten thousand royalty-free copies of each of his books. But it was by no means certain how the new arrangement would work out, particularly when in mid-November 1881 he fell ill with a fever brought on, as he wrote his father, by "long worry and sleeplessness from overwork . . ." (15 November 1881). After almost a month in bed, he decided to leave Belmont and move to Cambridge to be nearer to his doctor; his strength returned only slowly, and the decision was made to move once again, this time to 16 Louisburg Square, Boston, in January 1882. At the onset of his illness Howells had written only three quarters of *A Modern Instance*, but since its first installment had been printed in the December 1881 *Century*, he pushed on to complete the story even though he realized he had lost his grip on it. "I have made a long story of A Modern Instance," he wrote Charles Dudley Warner on 2 April 1882, "and I am just now slowly and painfully reaching the end. Since my sickness, I work with difficulty, and the result I fancy lacks texture."

A shadow had been cast over the Howells family by their older daughter's breakdown some time in the fall of 1880. Since Winifred's treatments had brought only limited improvement, it was thought that a European sojourn would do her good. This idea worked well with

Howells' plans for a series of sketches of Italian cities, and so the family sailed from Quebec on 22 July 1882, arriving at Liverpool after an agreeable eight-day voyage, and reaching London on the last day of July. There they were met by Henry James, who was helpful in finding comfortable lodgings for his American friends and introduced Howells to the proper London circles. Among the many English artists and literati whom Howells met, none turned out to be more important to him than Edmund Gosse, with whom he struck up an instant friendship that lasted for many years. Largely because of Gosse, the London sojourn was a busy and successful social season that left little time for work on *A Woman's Reason*, the novel Howells had begun several years before and now took up again as "Story No. 2" under his contract with Osgood.

The Howells family left London for Switzerland on 18 September 1882, settling near Villeneuve, on Lake Geneva. Life there was agreeable enough, even though it meant that the family had to learn French and put up with the rainy climate. But Howells enjoyed the lake and the mountains, the industriousness of the Swiss, and most of all the democratic spirit that reminded him of his native land. "It is curious," he wrote to his father on 7 October, "to find these French-speaking people such strenuous protestants and republicans, and so like ourselves in all religious and most domestic respects." Even though there were not so many social distractions as in London, Howells' work on *A Woman's Reason* progressed only "slowly and reluctantly," as he confessed to Henry James (4 October 1882). Once again, as so often before, he thought about writing a history of Venice, and he submitted to Osgood a sketch for "Story No. 3," a projected but never written historical romance. He still was convinced, however, that his proper calling was that of a novelist rather than a university professor; and for that reason, after consulting James Russell Lowell, Howells decided to decline the offer of an academic appointment he had received from the president of the Johns Hopkins University.

In early December 1882 the family moved to Florence, and Howells was back again in Italy after an absence of over seventeen years—a bitter-sweet experience for the middle-aged man revisiting the scenes of his earlier hopes and opportunities. "We are here in Italy again," he wrote Lowell in a somewhat melancholy mood, "in the old soft air, under the same mild old sky, out of which all snap and sharpness have gone as out of the mood of a man too much experienced to be eager about anything" (27 December 1882). These sentiments were soon to become the basis of Howells' characterization of Theodore Colville, the protagonist of *Indian Summer*, but for the time being *A Woman's Reason* still had to be finished and materials gathered for the sketches which were eventually to be collected in *Tuscan Cities*. This meant a busy travel schedule in the early months of 1883: two weeks in Siena, a few more in Florence, a month in Venice, ten days in Verona, and one in Milan. In early June the Howellses returned to London via Basle and Paris; but before leaving Europe altogether, Howells visited his father's birthplace in Wales, recording in two long letters his experiences in "Hay . . . on the banks of the pretty Wye . . . . [where] my great-grand-father once owned a flannel mill . . ." (21 June 1883). Finally, on 5 July, the family sailed from Liverpool, reaching Quebec on the twelfth and Boston three days later.

As Howells settled into his new home at 4 Louisburg Square, he could look back upon his European sojourn with only partial satisfaction. He had managed to complete *A Woman's Reason*, but he had neither written the sketches of Italian cities nor begun his next novel, as he had originally planned to do. He now set to work on *Indian Summer*, drawing on his recent experience of revisiting familiar Italian places. Work progressed so well that he finished the novel by late February or early March 1884. Meanwhile, "Story No. 3" for the *Century* was postponed partly because Howells took up a number of smaller pro-jects in the hope of providing additional income. In collaboration with Samuel Clemens he wrote a play, *Colonel Sellers as a Scientist*, which the two friends had discussed for several years; he produced the libretto for a comic opera, planned a translation of a German play for Augustin Daly, and thought about syndicating in the newspapers the rewritten version of an old play. But the hoped-for financial bonanza never became a reality, and by July 1884 Howells was working steadily on his third novel for the *Century*—his most ambitious fiction to date, *The Rise of Silas Lapham*.

The pressure under which Howells wrote this novel seems to have been conducive to his productivity. Richard Watson Gilder, the editor of the *Century*, wanted the first installment for the November number by mid-August, and he also pressed Howells for a paper on Florence. Yet Howells felt he could not do both without endangering the progress he was making on "the most recalcitrant of novels," as he called *Silas Lapham* in a letter to Charles Eliot Norton of 7 August 1884. Later that month, however, he was ready to send Gilder the first installment, and from then on, until he finished the novel in March 1885, his work went so well that he even found time to write "A Florentine Mosaic." One reason for his difficulties in getting the novel under way may have been the family's move to yet another residence, a house Howells had bought "on the water side of Beacon" (to Henry James, 22 August 1884)—the same location where Silas Lapham's ill-fated mansion was to proclaim its owner's newly achieved social status.

The failure of the publishing firm of James R. Osgood & Co. in May

1885 could have been a calamity for Howells, since he had an agreement for a fixed weekly salary. Though a new firm, Ticknor & Co., took over Osgood's contract with Howells and offered to publish his future books, he eventually signed with Harper & Brothers. Under the terms of this contract Harper had the rights to all of his writings, including one novel per year for serialization in *Harper's Monthly,* and Howells was to take charge of a new department in the magazine, to be called "The Editor's Study." The compensation was set at $13,000 annually, and there was opportunity for additional income from book royalties and other contributions to the magazine.

Before this new contract could go into effect, a remaining obligation under the old one had to be discharged. As Howells was working on the proofs of *The Rise of Silas Lapham* in the spring of 1885, he took up "the story of a country boy in Boston," which was eventually serialized in the *Century* and published in book form by Ticknor & Co. with the title *The Minister's Charge.* He had been thinking about this subject for at least two years and had written a draft of the opening chapters and a general outline of the whole novel in the winter of 1883-1884. The project was set aside for the composition of *Silas Lapham* until Howells needed some new literary material for an authors' reading in New York in April 1885 and decided to use the beginning of the story about the country boy. By June he was well under way rewriting the novel, focusing on the newly conceived theme of complicity; and seven months later Howells was able to report to his father that he was "nearing the end of my story, which has bothered me more than usual, and run to greater length than I expected. But 200 more pages like this ought to finish it" (23 January 1886).

Howells was right in his expectation that *The Minister's Charge* was just about to be completed. What he could not anticipate was that this first fictional treatment of the theme of complicity, and the reading of Tolstoy which had stimulated his interest in it, stood just at the beginning of a period of intense concern about social justice and the artist's role in advancing social reform. In the second half of the decade, the independent novelist, now in his full power as a critic and author of fiction, assumed a public voice and became the embattled spokesman of realism in literature and equality in the social system.

R. H. B.
C. K. L.

6 Garden st.,
Cambridge, Jan. 2, 1882.

My dear Fairchild:

We have, as you know, left Redtop for the winter, with the intention of getting into Boston, as soon as we can find lodgings; and I ought to tell you at this, the earliest practicable moment, that I have no expectation of going back to Belmont to live.[1] It is impossible to live there in the winter without suffering that I cannot meet, and the place is too expensive for me merely a summer residence; and indeed with the cost of a horse and man, and the extra cost of all the necessaries of life there, is too expensive at any rate.—But, now, my late sickness has left me with a weakened action of the heart that makes it useless for me thinking of ever walking up that hill for an indifinite time to come;[2] so instead of being able to retrench there at all, I should have to be at even greater expense, and perhaps keep two horses, so as to be invariably met at the station. I have thought these things all over carefully. We shall regret beyond expression to leave the place. First, of all we shall lose your neighborhood and that of your family which has become part of our life; and I shall disappoint *you*, who have meant so generously by me. Besides, we are deeply attached to the house, to which we have shaped ourselves and all that belongs to us; it is our ideal; we shall never have such another home. But it is of no use to dwell on this; you know how I must feel. Hereafter, we shall have to live in the city, and give up our dream of a country home.

There is *no* hope of my selling my Cambridge house; but I could make you a small payment on Redtop, without doing so,—say $2000 or $2500. I feel that I have formed obligations that do not allow me to leave the house on your hands; and I should at once ask you for a deed of it—if you had not asked me to agree, last summer, to sell the place back to you if ever I wished to part with it. I could only buy now with the hope of selling again as soon as possible; and in view of what you said I feel that you might not care to give me a deed.

I shall be very glad if you will write to me, and let me know your preference.

—Mr. Heath, of Ginn & Heath,[3] was anxious to hire the house furnished, if we went abroad, and may still want it. My furniture could remain till next July at least, when my present lease expires, and perhaps longer, if you wished.

Yours sincerely
W. D. Howells.

1. For an extended account of the Belmont period, see G. deB. Merrill, "Redtop and the Belmont Years of W. D. Howells and His Family," *Harvard Library Bulletin* 28 (1980), 33–57.

2. See Howells to W. C. Howells, 15 December 1881, n. 2; on 22 January 1882 (MH) Howells informed his father: "I am getting quite well again, and am fattening up, but not gaining much in strength."

3. Daniel Collamore Heath (1843–1908) left Ginn, Heath & Co. in 1885 to found the publishing firm of D. C. Heath & Co.

19 JANUARY 1882, BOSTON, TO JAMES R. OSGOOD

16 Louisburg Sq.,
Jan, 19, 1882.

Dear Osgood:

I have concluded not to write to Clemens. If he had applied directly to me for my opinion of his enterprise I should have felt free to give it; but if I did so without his asking, and merely by his permission, I should have the air of tutoring him, and he might justly snub me.[1]

The affair is his own, though I should regret its consummation (as I have understood it from you) beyond anything, still I cannot seem to volunteer any sort of interference.

If you have told Clemens I was going to write him, perhaps you had better send him this note.

Yours ever
W. D. Howells.

1. Howells is referring to a biography of Whitelaw Reid that Clemens thought of writing in order to get revenge on Reid for the New York *Tribune's* alleged crusade against him. Howells did not give Clemens his full opinion on the project, but in his letter to Clemens of 20 January 1882 (CU;*Twain-Howells*, pp. 385–86) he included a summary of this letter to Osgood. In his response of 28 January 1882 (NN; *Twain-Howells*, pp. 386–89), Clemens reported on the origin of the project and his decision to drop it after a careful search of *Tribune* files revealed little adverse criticism. Finally, on 31 January 1882 (CU; *Twain-Howells*, pp. 390–91), Howells revealed his immense relief upon learning that Clemens had given up the project.

Boston, Feb. 19, 1882.

Dear father:

The morning is dull and still, and I have been taking a long walk with John down by the wharves, to look at the shipping, which is perpetually fascinating to all of our blood.[1] John's only fault as a companion is that he talks too much, and wont leave me to my brown studies; but I suppose you would like this in him: I must have been too much the other way, when you used to take me walking as I now take him. He is a lovely fellow, however, and seems to grow sweeter and better all the time.—We are to have Boyesen in Boston for a course of Lowell lectures on the Iceland sagas; and I am wondering how I shall like him. He seems now, after leaving Cornell, to have got a professorship in Columbia college, New York city, where the full professorships are $7,500 a year; if he has one of these, he is lucky.[2] Harry James lodges quite near us,[3] and the other afternoon I had quite a long walk with him, talking literary shop, just as we used, ten years ago. It was a curious experience, both sad and pleasant: we scarcely seemed to have changed, in either our aims or methods; but I found my legs much older.—Winny is doing a great deal of gayety, this winter, and is enjoying it immensely. Of course, she enjoys it in a very Winnyish way, though. She reported that she had such a delightful time at her last party because a charming young man had talked to her about—J. Stuart Mill! Wasn't that a Bostonian pleasure? *Per contra*, the daughter of one of Elinor's rich cousins, from Troy, N. Y., going to school here, this winter, did not know that Longfellow was an American, and had never heard of Tennyson. At present, Pil is leading the family on art. She draws incessantly, and shows a great deal of imagination, as well as execution, filling sheet after sheet, with graphic dramas about princesses and fairies. All are well, & join me in love to all

Your aff'te son
Will.

1. The long walk indicates that Howells' health had improved since his report to his father on 12 February 1882 (MH): "I have had another week of retrogression; but this time from influenza, which we have all had very severely. In my weakened state such things take a deep hold of me; and I can't say that I have had a day of strong health since I fell sick in the beginning of November. I suppose I can't reasonably expect to 'feel well' till spring comes. But I am glad and grateful to be able to work pretty constantly."

2. Boyesen had been appointed professor of German at Columbia University in 1880.

3. Henry James resided at 102 Mt. Vernon Street on Beacon Hill.

2 MARCH 1882, BOSTON, TO ALFRED A. READE

Boston, March 2, 1882.

Dear Sir:[1]

If you will allow me to count myself out of the list of "great thinkers" and *very* "popular authors," I will gladly contribute my experience on the points you put. I never use tobacco, except in a very rare, self-defensive cigarette, where a great many other people are smoking; and I commonly drink water at dinner. When I take wine, I think it weakens my work and my working force the next morning.

Yours truly
W. D. Howells.

A. Arthur Reade, Esq.

1. Alfred Arthur Reade (b. 1851), British author, edited *Study and Stimulants: The Use of Narcotics in Relation to Intellectual Life, as Illustrated by Personal Communications on the Subject, from Men of Letters and Science* (1883).

2 MARCH 1882, BOSTON, TO WILLIAM C. HOWELLS

Boston, March 2, 1882.

Dear father:

I have just received Vic's and Aurelia's letters telling me that Sherman has written you of your possible removal.[1] I am in hopes that it may not come to this, and of course I shall do all I can to prevent it. What *can* be done, I have not a clear idea as yet, but the first thing of all is not to be discouraged. I do not know the politicians here; but I am going to spend Sunday with Mark Twain who is a great friend of Grant's, and can possibly get me access to him. I suppose Grant's influence would keep you in place. This is the only thing I can think of now; but something else may occur to me.[2] If the worst should come, I suppose it would not come till your commission expires in June, and this would give you time to form plans for the future. I have never heard what you expected to do in the event of your removal, and of course I can't suggest anything at present. But the thing now is to prevent your removal, if possible. If any idea occurs to you, I hope you'll let me know, at once.

We are all well and join in love to you all.

Your aff'te son
Will.

1. Before getting the letters from his sisters Victoria and Aurelia, Howells had received a letter dated 30 January 1882 (MH) from John J. Piatt, then a Washington, D.C., bureau editor for the Cincinnati *Commercial*, informing him that an Ohio congressman, probably Senator John Sherman, had suggested that W. C. Howells would likely be removed from his office, the U.S. consulship at Toronto. On 4 March 1882 Howells went to Hartford to visit Clemens, and the two later proceeded to New York to obtain General U. S. Grant's influence so as to avert such a development.

2. On 10 March (MH) Howells wrote his father from New York: "Clemens saw Grant to-day, on your affair, and Grant made a note of it, and said he would write to the President at once in your behalf. He told Clemens that the affair could be better arranged without our going to Washington. I presume that this will settle the matter, and you need have no further anxiety." This assessment of the situation proved to be correct. See Howells to W. C. Howells, 26 March 1882; *Literary Friends and Acquaintance*, HE, pp. 301–2; *Twain-Howells*, pp. 392–95; and *Life in Letters*, I, 308–10.

7 March 1882, Boston, to George W. Cable

> 16 Louisburg Square,
> Boston, March 7, 1882.

Dear Mr. Cable:

It must be for my sins that I have got too well to consider your kind invitation from the invalid's point of view; and I ought to shut my eyes to your temptation from any other.[1] Peach-blossoms! And here the snow-petals are all the flowers I see. Thank you and thank you again: if I could follow my wishes and my love of you, you should not wait for me long.— Yesterday I was at Mark Twain's and we read aloud from the Grandissimes—about the divine Aurore and the ineffable Inverarity.[2] What a lucky fellow you are to deserve your good luck in having such types to paint from, and how charming you make them. Clemens and I went about talking Creole all day,[3] as I did with my wife after reading the Gs.—I am sincerely glad you like my story.[4] I am doing my best to hide its faults from the reader, and I am very much in earnest about it every way.

> Yours cordially
> W. D. Howells.

1. After learning of Howells' "late serious illness," Cable, in a letter of 3 March 1882 (MH), invited Howells to visit him in New Orleans and "enjoy the absolute perfection of our spring."

2. For Howells' earlier praise of *The Grandissimes* and his and his wife's talking its dialect, see Howells to Cable, 2 October 1881.

3. Clemens had become a friend of Cable after their meeting in June 1881, but Clemens' opinion of him was to vary considerably through the later years. See *Twain-Howells*, p. 364 and passim.

4. After reading the early installments of *A Modern Instance*, which ran in the *Century*, December 1881–October 1882, Cable wrote in his letter of 3 March 1882 to

Howells: "I am thanking you daily for the lesson of Bart Hubbard, but I shall say nothing about that superb work, except to ask if you, also, do not think it—the whole story—your very best."

18 MARCH 1882, BOSTON, TO JOHN HAY

> 16 Louisburg Square,
> Boston, March 18, 1882.

My dear Hay:

It is so long since you wrote to me that I hope you think you owe me a letter. But this is not really the case. When your last came,[1] I was just crawling out of the bed where I had spent seven endless weeks, and I could only enjoy your letter and despair of answering it. That is often the effect of a good letter on me when I am in health; in fact, now when I am quite well again, and only two or three years older than I was four months ago, I begin with you on very small note, so that I can leave off at once when my courage gives out.

I will try to give you our *noticias,*[2] first. We are planning at present to go abroad in the beginning of July, with the intention of spending the next three months in Weimar or Baden-Baden, and then of going to Florence for the winter. I want to make a book for Osgood about the smaller cities of North Italy, and I expect to leave the family at Florence and wander about myself from Parma to Modena, Verona, Vicenza, Padua, Treviso, etc., and write about them as I did about Ducal Mantua.[3] Now what transport it would be if the Hays spent next winter in Florence, too! Is such a thing possible? Try to imagine it![4]—Well, Winny, who was down for nearly two years with nervous prostration, is now quite herself again, and Mrs. Howells is "usually well." The two younger children are in good state, and John is at this moment curled up on the lounge reading *Doctor Breen's Practice.* For this reason, if for no other, I could not have palpitating divans in my stories; my children are my censors, and if I wished to be wicked, I hope they would be my safe-guards.[5] A glance at the book shows me that John is deep in the love-makingest chapter. It was not written for children, but if a child may read it without harm, it seems to me something to be glad of. I am a great admirer of French workmanship, and I read everything of Zola's that I can lay hands on. But I have to hide the books from the children! I won't try to parry the kind things you say of my work: for I do work hard, and I know that I *aim* at the highest mark, morally and artistically. There I have to leave things to others. But your words gave me a delight and courage which, if there had been any decency in me, I should have confessed to you by telegraph rather than three months afterwards.

Harry James is spending the winter only a few doors from us.[6] (We left our country house after my sickness, and came into town.) I see him constantly, and we talk literature perpetually, as we used to do in our walks ten years ago. He is not sensibly changed, and, reflected in him, I find that I am not. He had a plan of travelling all about the country this winter and then of returning to England in April; but this has been broken up by the sudden death of his mother, and I doubt if he will stay continuously abroad again while his father lives.[7] He and his three brothers carried their mother to her grave; it was a most touching story, as he told it to me.

I have lately been at Hartford, and have seen a great deal of Mark Twain.[8] We confessed to each other that the years had tamed us, and we no longer had any literary ambition: before we went to bed we had planned a play, a lecturing tour, a book of travel and a library of humor.[9] In fact, he has life enough in him for ten generations, but his moods are now all colossal, and they seem to be mostly in the direction of co-operative literature.

Aldrich is busy on the *Atlantic* and is very fond of his editorial work. He hates writing, you know, and he likes reading and talking, and he spends six hours every day at the office where I used to put in a scant afternoon once a week. Whittier is visiting at the Claflins on Mt. Vernon street,[10] and with Aldrich in his old house on Charles st., we are quite a literary precinct. By the way, do you read Cable's books? They are delicious: there is no more charming creation in fiction than Aurora Nancanou in *The Grandissimes*. And Cable himself is the lovliest and loyalest ex-rebel that lives. He was at Belmont last spring and took all our hearts away with him.

I could go on writing for ever, if I had the wrist for it. But now, good-bye, with love from all of us to all of you. Try to see some way of meeting us in Europe.

Yours affectionately,
W. D. Howells.

1. The letter of Hay to Howells referred to is that of 31 December 1881 (MH), but on 30 November 1881 (MH) Hay had written to Howells, inquiring about his health and saying: " 'Dr. Breen' is the best yet, but the first part [*Century*, December 1881] of the 'Modern Instance' seems to me to have a closer grip of realism than anything ever done in America. I was reading it to Mrs. Hay the other night and kept thinking to myself 'How would this have struck me if it had been published anonymously?' We should have been crying out 'Here is the fellow who is to write a great American Novel at last.' "

2. Italian for "news."

3. For Howells' project, which eventually became *Tuscan Cities*, see Howells to Osgood, 6 November 1881. "Ducal Mantua" had appeared in the *North American Review*, January 1866.

4. In his letters of 30 November 1881 and 31 December 1881 Hay had inquired about Howells' European travel plans; and on 26 March 1882 (MH), in reply to the present letter, he wrote that he and his wife had made definite plans for a trip to Europe and a visit to Florence.

5. Howells' comments on dealing with sex in his works were occasioned by remarks in Hay's letter of 31 December 1881. While finding "excellent pages" in Alphonse Daudet's *Numa Roumestan* (1881), Hay decried its French salaciousness, quoting "Le Divan haletait encore." He further wrote: "Has it struck you yet that no man writing English writes a better story than you do—and that no man but Harry James stands in the same rank with you? Take the best Englishmen of the day & see where you can throw your hat through the holes in their work, and compare it, if you are capable of such a judicial task, with your own stories, or if that is beyond you, with James'. Between you and him I can make no comparison. You have chosen fields so different that there is hardly any rivalry. But the two of you are making permanent literature every line you write. I am not Chauvin as a general thing, but when I see the rottenness of the best French writing, and see the infection gaining the cleverest English—so that a proper young fellow like Mallock must write phallic romances to show he has read his Balzac as well as the rest, I can't help being a little proud that we have got two or three men still young, who can write a better style than any of these scavengers, and not require two ounces of red pepper to one ounce of meat, to make their writing palatable."

6. See Howells to W. C. Howells, 19 February 1882, n. 3.

7. Mary James had died on 29 January 1882. On 10 May, Henry James sailed for Ireland, en route to London. Later called back to America because of his father's serious decline, James arrived in New York on 21 December, too late for the funeral of his father, who had died on 18 December. See L. Edel, *Henry James: The Middle Years, 1882–1895* (Philadelphia: Lippincott, 1962), pp. 33, 41, 56–57.

8. See Howells to W. C. Howells, 2 March 1882, n. 1.

9. The play is identified by Mildred Howells as "Orme's Motor" (*Life in Letters*, I, 306, 312); according to *Twain-Howells*, p. 234, this was one of the early titles, along with "The Steam Generator," for a play eventually called *Colonel Sellers as a Scientist*. See *Literary Friends and Acquaintance*, HE, p. 289, for Howells' description of Clemens' plans for a lecturing tour (later called a "Circus" in Howells to Clemens, 18 April 1882) involving T. B. Aldrich, G. W. Cable, Clemens, and Howells. The proposed book of travel has not been identified. For *Mark Twain's Library of Humor* see Howells to Osgood, 17 April 1881, n. 4.

10. William Claflin (1818–1905) was governor of Massachusetts (1869–1871) and a member, U.S. House of Representatives (1877–1881). His second wife, Mary Bucklin Davenport Claflin (1825–1896), was the author of several books, including *Personal Recollections of John G. Whittier* (1893).

26 MARCH 1882, BOSTON, TO WILLIAM C. HOWELLS

Boston, March 25, 1882.[1]

Dear father:

I'm glad your consulate business is satisfactorily settled, and that your place is made sure while Arthur is in. I suppose it was Grant's letter that effected it; but it is pleasant to have Mr. Taylor show his good will, however late in the day.[2]

Our plans for the summer are not very clear, yet. We may conclude not to set up housekeeping again before we go abroad, which will be either in July or October, but to board in Lexington till we start. If we go by the Allen line from Quebec, we have thought of coming to you at Toronto for a good visit, and then going down the St Lawrence by boat; but probably this scheme will be changed many times. The only thing certain is the visit, which I can't yet fix the time for. We are all well except Elinor, who has her usual spring break-down.—Tom Watkins called the other night, and gave us news of you all.—I am hurrying forward my story,[3] and hope to have it finished by the 1st of May.—I have just heard through the publishers here that a complete edition of my books is to be published in Edinburgh, and that I am to receive copyright on them.[4]—I am going out to Cambridge this afternoon to Longfellow's funeral; the ceremony at the house is to be private; but I am asked.[5] It is awful to think of his lying there in that beautiful old house which he seemed to fill with his goodness. I can't reconcile myself to his death. I had the sad and curious fortune to ring at the door and ask how he was at almost the moment he died.

All join me in love to all.

> Your aff'te son
> Will.

I haven't yet read your pamphlet carefully; I will write of it hereafter.[6]

1. Evidence for the incorrectness of Howells' dating is given in n. 5 below.

2. "Mr. Taylor" was probably Ezra Booth Taylor (1823–1912), a Republican representative from Warren, Ohio, about fifty miles from Howells' early home in Jefferson, Ohio. Taylor was elected to fill the seat vacated when Howells' personal friend James A. Garfield resigned from the Congress in order to assume his new duties as president.

3. *A Modern Instance.*

4. The first of Howells' novels to appear under the David Douglas imprint was *A Chance Acquaintance*, published in June 1882. By the end of the year Douglas had issued eight Howells titles, the first in his American Authors series. See Scott Bennett, "David Douglas and the British Publication of W. D. Howells' Works," *Studies in Bibliography* 25 (1972), 107–24.

5. Longfellow died on Friday, 24 March 1882. According to Samuel Longfellow's *Life of Henry Wadsworth Longfellow* (1886), II, 473, the funeral services were held on Sunday afternoon, 26 March not 25 March, as the dating of this letter would indicate. Further evidence that the letter should have been dated 26 March is furnished by the fact that Howells usually wrote to his father on Sundays, and by the statement in Howells' letter of 2 April 1882 to Charles D. Warner that he had attended the service for Longfellow on last Sunday.

6. The pamphlet referred to here is perhaps *The Freewill of Man and the Origin of Evil* (1881). On 4 June 1882 (MH) Howells wrote to his father: "I have just been reading your lecture on Creation, which is admirably written, and which seems very true. Of course, there *is* no moral cause for creation except the Creator's need of expressing himself. If there is a break in your logic it is where you assume that Christ was God incarnate; there you ask us to believe rather than to reason with you. I don't say I think you wrong; I shall like to talk the whole matter over with you . . . ."

2 APRIL 1882, BOSTON, TO CHARLES D. WARNER

Boston, April 2, 1882.

My dear Warner:

It must be your remoteness that causes me to treat you with such indecency and ingratitude. Your kind and very welcome letter reached me in December, and if it had been written from Hartford I should at once have answered you, with thanks. But Munich—the distance daunted me.[1] You must be used to forgiving all sorts of unworthy people: try me.—Your letter reached me while I was still sick in bed (where I lay seven incredible weeks) and slowly convalescing. It was a time of great suffering to which variety of pain gave no charm, or even relief. I got well because there were no more things to have; but I was extremely sick—paying for a long immunity, and for follies of overwork committed in my anxiety to get off to Europe by the 1st of January. Now, if we sail by the middle of July we shall be content. I have made a long story of A Modern Instance, and I am just now slowly and painfully reaching the end. Since my sickness, I work with difficulty, and the result I fancy lacks texture. But I don't know. I'm certain, however that I feel much older than before, but I am glad to have got well on any terms. Winny, also, has got well, and we have all had a very comfortable winter in Boston. (I was brought down to Cambridge, so as to be near the doctor, and when I could go out we came into town.) The other children are well, but Mrs. Howells has her annual spring collapse. We expect Europe to reinstate her; but O my dear friend, how I hate to go! I would almost as soon spend a year in the Western Reserve. I loathe the idea of the voyage, and I despise the pictures and the scenery and the sunsets and the antiquity. But we going.—I was at Hartford not long ago, and cast a repining glance in the direction of your worse than empty house.

We are all feeling a personal loss in Longfellow's death. I was at the service in the house last Sunday, and it made my heart very heavy. What kindness, what goodness has gone out of the world!—Poor old Emerson was there, and twice he went up and took a long look at the face in the coffin: I wondered if he was perhaps trying to remember who it was. This afternoon Mr. Tom Appleton told me that Mr. Sam'l Longfellow was the family choice for a biographer.[2] I suppose our sketch must wait for that.[3] In the meantime there will be a great many studies and memoirs.— There is not a great deal to tell you in the way of news. Osgood is prosperous, and is shortly to make a voyage down to N. Orleans with Clemens, who means at last to make his piloting book.—I see Aldrich often, and he seems very happy in his Atlantic work, which I think he does with great credit to himself; but I believe he is writing nothing— not even the life of Willis.[4]—John Hay writes me that he goes abroad with his family in July, and we shall probably spend next winter in Florence together.—Mrs. Fields and Miss Deephaven Jewett[5] are going out in May—Mr. Fields's enterprise, I believe. Mrs. Howells joins in love to both of you, wherever you are.

Affectionately yours
W. D. Howells.

1. Warner, in a letter of 20 December 1881 (MH) from Munich, had expressed his grief on learning that Howells was very ill with a nervous disease brought on by overwork. See Howells to W. C. Howells, 15 December 1881, n. 2.

2. Thomas Gold Appleton was Longfellow's brother-in-law. Samuel Longfellow (1819–1892), clergyman, poet, and brother of Henry Wadsworth, edited the *Life of Henry Wadsworth Longfellow* (1886).

3. The sketch was a biography of Longfellow that Howells was to write for the American Men of Letters Series, published by Houghton, Mifflin & Co. and edited by Warner. However, his contract with James R. Osgood and a later contract with Harper & Brothers prevented Howells from writing books for other publishers.

4. Aldrich never wrote the biography of Nathaniel Parker Willis (1806–1867), the poet, playwright, and journalist. Instead, Henry A. Beers wrote *Nathaniel Parker Willis* (1885) for the American Men of Letters Series.

5. Sarah Orne Jewett, the author of *Deephaven* (1877), was a close personal friend of Annie Adams Fields.

8 APRIL 1882, BOSTON, TO THOMAS W. HIGGINSON

Boston, April 8, 1882.

My dear Higginson:

The Great Western March is expressive, but it isn't very taking, to my thinking;[1] I have tried to imagine something else; but with my Shakespeare Concordance at Belmont, I have but a feeble fancy. *The Land* and its *Finders* awkwardly suggests something. I have no books at all that will help me here; and I am very sorry, for you and Mrs. Higginson were so kind to me in my trouble.[2] The most I can do is to wish you luck.—I am glad to know that you like the story. As to that runaway marriage, I took legal advice: it's irregular but possible, and a point later on turns upon its irregularity.[3]

I heard of your accident only a day or two ago, and then I heard that it was not a serious matter.[4] Glad you're getting so well over it. My own health seems perfectly re-established.

Yours ever
W. D. Howells.

1. Higginson wrote Howells on 6 April 1882 (MH), asking him for his help in deciding upon a title for his series of papers on the history of America. Eventually

the series was called "A Larger History of the United States" and appeared in *Harper's Monthly* at intervals, August 1882–October 1883. Harper & Brothers published the collected essays in *A Larger History of the United States of America to the Close of President Jackson's Administration* (1886).

2. In the fall of 1881 Howells asked Higginson for his opinion on a title for his new novel, which was finally called *A Modern Instance*. See Howells to Higginson, 5 October 1881, n. 1.

3. In his letter of 6 April, Higginson declared *A Modern Instance* one of Howells' best works. He also asked Howells about the possibility of Marcia and Bartley getting married so quickly without going through the usual legal procedures: "I consulted a much-married New Hampshireman abt it & he said he had always had to get a certificate beforehand, as is necessary here in Mass. Your lovers were near the border between the two states of Mass & N. H. (as well as of singleness & matrimony), but could hardly be joined quite so easily in either as you imply. You might easily evade this (if I am right) by making the landlord town clerk & letting him provide the needed documents off hand."

4. Higginson's accident is unexplained except for his postscript to the letter of 6 April: "I am only slightly lamed; almost well."

18 APRIL 1882, BOSTON, TO SAMUEL L. CLEMENS

Boston, April 18, 1882.

You dear old fellow—

If you had given me time *I* should have written *you* a letter of humiliation and prayer; for I long ago learned (from Mrs. Howells) that I am to blame for everything; and I went to bed sick at heart, that night, wondering what I had done to spoil our arrangements, and going down among the lees and dregs of despair in self-accusation. But I'm glad you owned up, first; for now I can show your letter to Mrs. Howells and prove that *I'm* all right. But you arrogant and ridiculous boaster—did you think that *you alone* could manage a thing so complete as that?[1] No, sir; that failure bears the stamp of our *joint effort*, and deserves to be stored away with the Concord Centennial expedition.[2]—If General Grant had not been there to neutralize us, I think we should have had my father turned out of his place and imprisoned for life, when we went on to New York.[3] I used to tremble when I thought of our success in that matter. "Have we lost our cunning?" I asked myself. But I need not have been troubled; this last affair shows that *when there is no outside interference*, we cannot *fail* to fail.—I am sorry that Osgood is with you on this Mississippi trip; I foresee that it will be a contemptible half-success instead of the illustrious and colossal failure *we* could have made it. But we still have our chance in the Library of Humor, (unless Clark ties our hands) and what can we not hope from the Circus?[4]

—*Oh*, how I should like to be with Osgood and you! Give my love to the young willows (not widows) along the Mississippi shore, and good bye and good luck to you both.

Yours ever
W. D. Howells.

Mrs. Howells is off at Lexington. I'll send her your letter.

1. In a letter of 16 April 1882 (MH; *Twain-Howells*, pp. 400–2), Clemens apologized to Howells for some unintentional social discourtesy on his trip to Boston, 14–15 April. Mrs. Clemens added a postscript reiterating Clemens' regret.

2. See Howells to Aurelia Howells, 25 April 1875, n. 1.

3. See Howells to W. C. Howells, 2 March 1882, n. 1.

4. For the *Library of Humor* and the Circus, see Howells to John Hay, 18 March 1882, n. 9. In a letter of 19 April 1881 to Howells (MH; *Twain-Howells*, pp. 363–64), Clemens had proposed hiring Charles Hopkins Clark, managing editor of the Hartford *Courant*, to assist them with the *Library of Humor*. See *Twain-Howells*, pp. 398–99, for the procedure to be followed in this collaborative project.

21 MAY 1882, LEXINGTON, TO VICTORIA M. HOWELLS

Lexington, May 21, 1882.

Dear Vic:

We are just at the end of an easterly storm which has lasted nearly two weeks, and has obliged us to keep winter clothes and fires on and up. But now the sun is out again, and this sweet, quiet old town is looking its loveliest. I wish you and father could be here with us a while; but we shall soon be with you, now, and for a good, stout visit. I'm glad you look at our European vacation as merely an absence not longer than many others that take place between the times we see each other; for that, is all that we intend it to be. And I'm glad that you have that new hotel so near. Probably we shall only want one room; but it will be a good place to fall back upon with others of the family, if Henry wont stand us. We'll give you notice in good season of the exact time of our coming.[1]

We have moved nearly all our stuff out of the Belmont house, and stored it in Cambridge, and probably we shall not go back to Belmont to live, though we are not saying this generally.[2] When we come home, we may settle in Cambridge, or we may go to Boston to live; we are not decided. I have never been able to sell the Cambridge house, and consequently could not buy that at Belmont.[3] The Fairchilds were very anxious to have us spend such part of the summer there as we could, and so we have left things enough there to run the house for a few weeks in June.

We are all quite well, and join love to all of you.

Your aff'te brother
Will.

Why shouldn't Annie time her Quebec visit so as to meet us there before the steamer sails?

1. In a letter of 8 April 1882 (MH) to his father, Howells announced his plan to sail with his family on the *Parisian* from Quebec on 22 July, paying his father a visit at Toronto before sailing. At this time Howells' sisters Victoria and Aurelia and his brother Henry were living with his father. In a letter of 14 May 1882 (MH) to his father, Howells said that they expected to arrive in Toronto by 28 June.

2. At this time the Howells family frequently moved from one residence to another. Howells wrote to his sister Annie on 27 March (MH) from 16 Louisburg Square in Boston: "We may possibly be at Belmont from May 1st till October, but the probabilities are that we shall not open the house, but shall board some-where near Boston, and go abroad in July, to be gone a year." From late April through May the Howellses stayed in Lexington and then returned to Belmont until late June when they left for Toronto. See Howells to Clemens, 28 May 1882 (CU; *Twain-Howells*, pp. 403–4), and such letters as those to E. C. Stedman of 28 April (ViU) and to J. R. Osgood of 2 June (MH).

3. In a letter of 31 March 1882 (MH) to Charles Fairchild, Howells reported that he had declined an offer of $9,000 for his Cambridge house, since acceptance would have meant a loss of $6,000.

12 JULY 1882, TORONTO, TO JAMES R. OSGOOD

> *Consulate of the United States of America.*
> *Toronto.* July 12, 1882.

My dear Osgood:

I think No. 3 will be such a story as Mr. Alden wants; that is it will have to do with ordinary American character, though I hope to make the circumstances entirely "exceptional", and it will be as much a story of "American life and character" as the Lady of the Aroostook was. I have told you of my wish to contrast the nascent nationality of America and the dying nationality of Venice in the adventures of a young Puritan shipscaptain (I would make him the ancestor of Capt. James of the L. of the A.) who sails from Salem or Duxbury for Venice about the year 1790, and gets fallen in love with by a beautiful and noble Venetian. I mean that the affair shall "end up" well; and the story as it lies in my mind is a pretty and merry one, as well as romantic. It would be about the desired length. I have long wished to get on historic ground, and this gives me my chance.[1] This is about all I could say of the story at present; and of course I can't bind my self as to details of treatment, though I don't now think of anything exceptional in my conception of it.

I hope you wont let the negotiation go so far with Harpers that we cant let Smith have the story if he wants it at the same price. I feel a sense of allegiance to the Century, which has dealt so handsomely with us, and I suppose you share this feeling.[2] I have had another very friendly letter from Smith, in which he speaks of wanting me to do a "serial biography" for the Century.

I leave Toronto next Tuesday, and I suppose that I can hear from you here again if you wish to write immediately; and I can certainly hear from you at Quebec before the 22d. I shall call at the general delivery for letters in Quebec.

Yours ever
W. D. Howells.

1. Osgood, in his letter of 10 July 1882 (MH) to Howells, reported that Henry M. Alden had offered $6,000 for Howells' next story "provided it is not less than 120 pp. of Harper's Mag. . . . and that it 'shall be a story of American life and character with sufficient humor to meet popular requirement & having no such singularity of plot as characterized "An Undiscovered Country"—i.e. no plot based on exceptional or unusual manifestations of human character.' Of course he will trust all that to you, content with seeing only a sketch or outline, *à la Century*." In a letter of 17 July 1882 (MH) to Howells, Osgood wrote: "I am glad to learn from your letter of July 12 that you think No. 3 will answer the Harper conditions, and I suppose at the proper time you will send me a sketch of the story as I can show to Mr Alden, provided we decide to accept his offer." On 2 October 1882 (MH), Osgood asked for a sketch of the story as soon as Howells could send it in order to show it to Roswell Smith of the *Century* and to Alden. See Howells to Osgood, 16 October 1882, for Howells' fuller sketch of the plot of the story, which, however, was never written. Story No. 3 under Howells' contract with Osgood was ultimately *The Rise of Silas Lapham*. See *The Rise of Silas Lapham*, HE, pp. xi–xiii; and C. and R. Kirk, "Two Howells Letters," *Journal of the Rutgers University Library* 21 (1957), 1–7.

2. In his reply of 17 July 1882 Osgood wrote: "I feel as you do on the *Century* question, and I should not come to any final terms with Harper without some further talk with Smith. I did not bind myself to give him the chance at No. 3, and if he should not come to time very promptly and spontaneously I should think it right to change. And in some respects a change might be a benefit as widening the market and developing a new audience."

21 July 1882, Quebec, to Victoria M. Howells

Quebec, July 21, 1882.

Dear Vic:

I send with this a little "testimonial," which I hope you will accept in apology for itself, and for me, who intended to do something better at Toronto. My best love goes with it.

We are here in Quebec at last,—what is left undevoured by the hospitalities of the Count.[1] We had a very pleasant sail to Montreal, where the Annie family met us, and took Vevie, who was as good as could be all the time, and who called her mother "Aunt Lely" till she got used to her identity. Mole was on hand in great force, and the two funny litle things took each other round the neck in an affecting & dramatic embrace. Achille came as far as Sorel with us, where he hurried ashore in great precipitation—after which the boat lay there an hour.[2] Annie I found just as delightful as ever—there never was a more charming person; but she lets her children prey upon her. We had a good night, and in the morning at Quebec, I took a calash, and drove round hotel-ing. The Blanchard wouldn't do, and after going to the Albion, the Russell, & the St. Louis, and finding no rooms, we were glad to hide our diminished heads at the Lanes, after all.[3] We all took breakfast here, and in the forenoon Annie went with her tribe to the Mountains (perhaps because the mountains wouldn't come to her.) The Count's "attentions" began at once. He sent his *valet*, who took possession of our selves and our multitudinous trunks, with orders from the Count to pay everything. Then "his excellency" himself appeared after breakfast, and spent the whole day, driving, walking and dining with us, and in the evening went with us to the Stewarts, who asked us to tea.[4]—He was most affectionate in his inquiries about each of you, and he told me that father was "a man without a fault—without a fault." In fact that seems to be the universal opinion in Quebec, and you can imagine I don't dispute it. Father never seemed to me so dear and good as on this visit. We were a solemn party for a while after he went ashore at Toronto, and poor little Pil wept.

We are gradually getting into shape for the steamer; but it is an exciting and distracting time, and to-day we shall set our faces against all "attentions." I have scarcely had a chance to speak to Annie since we reached Quebec; but she and I are going to drive down to the steamer together to day.—Elinor's brother hasn't turned up yet, though I suppose he will be duly on hand.[5] I am writing this at five o'clock in the morning, the flies having started me out early; and all that wonderful Quebec landscape lies before me from the window.

I went onto the steamer yesterday with the Count, and saw our rooms again. They are very good; and the purser told me he expected that we would be in Liverpool a week after starting.

I will try to send home a line from Rimourski, where some mails go ashore.

With dearest love to father and all of you from us.

> Your aff'te brother
> Will.

Speak of me to Henry. I hope he's better.

1. See Howells to W. C. Howells, 4 August 1877, n. 2.

2. The W. D. Howells family left Toronto on the mail boat on 18 July, taking with them Annie Howells Fréchette's daughter Marie Marguerite ("Vevie"), who had been visiting her grandfather and aunts, one of whom—Aurelia—she called

"Aunt Lely." Upon reaching Montreal on 19 July, they were met by Annie, her husband Achille, and her son Howells ("Mole"). Achille stayed on board until reaching Sorel, about forty-five miles down the St. Lawrence River from Montreal.

3. After leaving Quebec, Howells wrote to his father in a letter marked "S.S. Parisian 3 hours down the River, July 22, 1882" (MH): "The Lanes would not take anything from us; and we felt very shabby for having treated them so cavalierly." See Howells to James, 26 August 1873, n. 8.

4. George Stewart (1848–1905) and his wife; for identification of the former see Howells to W. C. Howells, 2 June 1878, n. 2.

5. Elinor Howells' brother William R. Mead crossed on the *Parisian* with the Howells family (*Life in Letters*, I, 313). Another brother, Frederick G. Mead, came to say good-bye at Quebec but did not accompany them.

31 JULY 1882, LONDON, TO WILLIAM C. HOWELLS

18 Pelham Crescent, South Kensington
London, W. S. July 31,

Dear father:

You see by the address that we have arrived in London. We are safely and very comfortably housed in the lodgings found for us by Harry James, who met us at the station, and welcomed us to London in the kindest way.[1] We reached Liverpool at half past two on Sunday,[2] having made the quickest passage from Quebec on record. We were but 6 days 17 hours between Rimouski and Ireland, and only 4 days 19 hours from land to land. I posted to you at Liverpool the letter I had expected to send from Moville (Londonderry), for I learned that it was of no use to send it sooner. We staid overnight at the Northwestern Railway hotel, and started for London on the 11 o'clock train this morning. Great improvements have taken place in R.R. travel since I was here, and on applying for it, I got without extra charge, what they called a lavatory compartment—that is, a compartment from which opened a washroom and w.c. The place was marked with a placard "Engaged for Mr. Howells's Family," and we went swelling through England in fine style. I only wish you had been with us to enjoy the journey through this beautiful country! It is in the very prime of summer: they were making hay in the meadows; the wheat turning yellow; the waysides burned red with poppies; rooks were sailing every where, or strutting about over the grass; boys were bathing in the brooks, the canal-boats sluggishly creeping along, and the whole landscape was lovely and full of poetic association. I was continually reminded of the scenery between Martinsville and St. Clairsville:[3] the same rolling land; the same coal-smoked brick farm houses, the same woods free of underbrush. But it is of no use to attempt a catalogue of the charms of England; next summer, by this time, I hope we shall talk them over by the play of the sunset through the willow tree on your office-wall.—I believe I told you that the children profitted of the occasion to come out with the mumps on the steamer. They have nearly recovered, and are otherwise well, with enormous appetites. John has pronounced the English plums the best he ever tasted—and those enormous green-gages are certainly delicious. We have also had some gigantic goose-berries, which Winny admires exceedingly.—We are here for at least a fortnight, and perhaps for a month. In the meantime wherever we go, our address will be Gilligs American Exchange 449 Strand.

All the children join me in dearest love to all.

> Your aff'te son
> Will.

1. In a letter to Howells, 28 July 1882 (MH), James described the rooms which he had secured for the Howells family. "They are dearer than some & cheaper than others: *i.e.* 4 guineas ($21) a week for a drawing-room, dining room & three good bedrooms, in a quiet, salubrious, genteel, but unfashionable, situation." Besides helping arrange for the Howellses' accommodations, James also helped in securing a French governess and a tutor.

2. Sunday was 30 July.

3. Martinsville, Howells' birthplace, and St. Clairsville are located in Belmont County, Ohio.

1 AUGUST 1882, LONDON, TO EDMUND W. GOSSE

> 18 Pelham Crescent,
> South Kensington. August 1, 1882.

My dear Sir:

I found your very kind note at the American Exchange to-day, and I have to thank you for the acquaintance you give me.[1] I shall be only to glad to meet you and make it personal. We are very pleasantly lodged here, but our plans for staying in London are yet very uncertain. We only know that we shall stay till the end of next week, after which we may or may not go to Switzerland.

I shall try to find you at your office, and in the meantime my wife and I will be glad to see Mrs. Gosse and yourself.

> Very sincerely yours
> W. D. Howells.

1. In a letter of 26 July 1882 (MH; *Transatlantic Dialogue*, p. 92) to Howells, Edmund W. Gosse wrote: "My friend Mr. R W Gilder, of the 'Century' (of which I am the English representative) has encouraged, and indeed urged, me to thrust myself upon you, and take the liberty of an old acquaintance." This letter and Howells' response were the beginning of a long friendship well detailed in *Trans-*

atlantic Dialogue. On 2 August 1882 (MH; *Transatlantic Dialogue,* pp. 93–94) Gosse invited the Howellses to visit his home on Sunday, 6 August, with the Alma-Tademas and Henry James possibly also to be present. Gosse (1849–1928), poet and man of letters, was at this time employed as a translator to the Board of Trade but was also receiving recognition for his poetry and literary criticism. Lawrence Alma-Tadema (1836–1912), a naturalized British subject, was an artist elected to the Royal Academy in 1879 and knighted in 1899. His second wife was Gosse's sister-in-law.

5 AUGUST 1882, LONDON, TO JAMES R. OSGOOD

18 Pelham Crescent, South Kensington
London, S. W. August 5, 1882.

My dear Osgood:

I enclose the copy of my Niagara sketch.[1] It does n't seem to me any great things, as I read it over. I will *send* you one or two other copies for fear this should miss you.—I saw M. D. Conway yesterday. He is putting the last touches to his book about Concord and Emerson, which he has partly made from material given him by the family, and wholly with their privity. He says it is "not gossip" but is seriously and valuably reminiscential of the place and the man, both of whom he knew intimately at a very interesting time. He spoke of it to me as to an old friend, but I at once told him that I thought you would like to bring it out in America. Macmillans publish it here, and would publish there, but they agree with him that it would be better for him to have it with an American house. He and Holt have exchanged letters and in fact Holt has asked for it; but Conway would rather have it brought out in Boston, if it is practicable without aggrieving Holt. He will write to him, but in the meantime he wants to know if you will give him $1500 for the whole right of the book in the United States. I told him you would not like to vex Holt, and I have not committed you in any way: I only promised him that you would cable me Yes or No, care of Gillig.[2] It now occurs to me that if you are not willing to give that sum you could name a lower one for his consideration.—I think the subject of the book is a very good one, and Conway is so generally known, and has so many friends on the press everywhere that it's chances would be unusually good. Besides, it seemed to me in the line of biography you were working up, and might be a stepping-stone to the authorized life. But I haven't promised anything for you except the cablegram, and I don't urge the book on you; for of course the money asked is a good deal.—I'm having a good time. I lunch at the Savile Club to-day; and I've fairly swung into Story No. 2.[3]—Got a letter from Smith last night. He's still in Hamburg.[4]

Yours ever
W. D. Howells.

1. The sketch appeared as "Niagara Revisited, Twelve Years After Their Wedding Journey," *Atlantic*, May 1883. In his letter of 10 July 1882 (MH) to Howells, Osgood said of the piece that "it ought to suit the 'Alliance' capitally." The *Alliance* was a weekly journal published in Chicago. On 1 August 1882 (MH; *Life in Letters*, I, 315–16) Howells replied: "I have finished the Niagara sketch, and I shall send it to you, after getting it put in type, on Saturday. It is not a 'story' though it is largely fictitious . . . . My wife, after being ashamed of our getting $500 for it, now thinks we ought to have much more! Such is the effect of prosperity on the female mind." Later, on 23 November 1882 (CLSU) Howells wrote Osgood that he would prefer to have the Niagara sketch appear in the *Atlantic*, since *Their Wedding Journey* had originally appeared there. But then he added a postscript: "On second thoughts, I don't send the Niagara. If it had gone to the Advance [sic; i.e. *Alliance*], all well and good; but I don't care, just now, to challenge criticism by an inferior thing in a prominent place. *Please don't sell it to anybody.*"

2. Moncure D. Conway's *Emerson at Home and Abroad* was published in America by J. R. Osgood & Co. (1882), and the first British edition was brought out by Trübner & Co. (1883).

3. Story No. 2 was *A Woman's Reason*, serialized in the *Century*, February–October 1883, and published the same year in book form by J. R. Osgood & Co. An early title for this story was "A Sea-Change," and Howells had written the early chapters in the spring of 1878.

4. Roswell Smith was vacationing in Germany.

26 AUGUST 1882, LONDON, TO EDMUND W. GOSSE

18 Pelham Crescent,
August 26, 1882.

My dear Gosse:

I send you the last no. of A M. I.,[1] and you will see that it is not a thing to make a presentation copy of. Let me have it back (to keep my set whole) at your convenience, and when D. Douglas issues the book about Sept. 30,[2] I will give you a copy with my name written all over it.

I had such a lovely time last night that I would now like to cut the ties of a husband and father, and come to live with you. Is there not some law or privilege by which you could adopt an elderly foreigner of failing intellect? I would do chores about the house, run of errands, tell Theresa stories, and make myself generally useful.[3] Think of it seriously: I mean business.

Yours ever
W. D. Howells.

1. Howells apparently sent proof copy of the final installment of *A Modern Instance*, which appeared in the *Century*, October 1882; Gosse responded on 30 August 1882 (MH; *Transatlantic Dialogue*, pp. 96–97): "The end of A Modern Instance is superb. You draw your threads together with extraordinary skill. The old judge remains the most striking character all through, but all is strong & consistent. The railway journey is admirable: your journeys are always good. Perhaps Ben is made a little needlessly repulsive when he comes back? That is the only thing

which jars on me. I think you colour what he would feel a little from the old conventional water-colour paint-box of what people should feel. Marcia going west is at once an epitome of and a commentary on her whole character. A M. I. is altogether the greatest work of fiction that America has given us since the death of Hawthorne. I am quite sure of that."

2. David Douglas of Edinburgh published a two-volume edition of the novel. See *A Modern Instance*, HE, pp. 464–65.

3. Theresa, born in 1877, was the Gosses' eldest child. In response to Howells' offer, Gosse wrote in his letter of 30 August: "You shall be welcomed, oh! how gladly, into the Home of the Gigglers. In that home there are no chores to be done, & no errands to be run. It is giggling and making giggle from morning to night."

1 SEPTEMBER 1882, LONDON, TO SAMUEL L. CLEMENS

London, Sept. 1, 1882.

My dear Clemens:

You ought to have been yesterday with Osgood, Hutton[1] and me at Oxford. We started with the intention of coming back on a Thames steamer. Of course we failed in that, but what I was thinking was that if you were along, you could have kept us, with my help, from getting to Oxford.[2] We had a beautiful time in that beautifulest of old towns, and almost walked our legs off seeing it. We stopped at the Mitre tavern, where they let you choose your dinner from the joints hanging from the rafter, and have passages that you lose yourself in every time you try to go to your room. But you have been there.—We *did* do a few miles of the Thames, in a sort of big steam launch, and if it had not rained all the way, and Osgood hadn't had the rheumatism, and another fellow the diarrhoea, we should have enjoyed it. We came pretty near it, as it was.

We are in the prettiest and comfortablest kind of lodging in South Kensington (address me care American Exchange, however) where our five rooms with private dining-room and exquisite feed cost us only $50 a week (we paid $75 for *two* rooms in Boston) and here we expect to stay a month longer.[3] We have seen lots of nice people, and have been most pleasantly made of; but I would rather have you smoke in my face, and *talk* for half a day—just for *pleasure*—than go to the best house or club in London. And yet some of these people are delightful—Boughton,[4] for example, and Alma Tadema, above all. *What* a good fellow Tadema is! And I am sending you a card by a wonderful painter, Herkomer,[5] who is going to America next month.—John Hay has been here, and Mrs., and they are coming back in a day or two. Couldn't you and Mrs. Clemens step over for a little while? Warner lunched with us on Tuesday, and is to return from Scotland for a big dinner that Osgood gives next Thursday—W., Gen. Hawley, John Hay, Boughton, Aldrich, Tadema and W. D. H.[6] How does that strike you as a time?—The children and Mrs. Howells are enjoying themselves immensely, and all three of the chicks are keeping diaries. John's is worth reading: he's developing quite a style, and *sees* with eyes all round his head.

Mrs. Howells sends her love to both of you, and rejoices with me that you are so well out of that terrible scarlet fever peril. We quaked for you when we heard what was the matter with your children.

Did you ever hear from the Madison Theatre Mallorys?[7]—I suppose Clark has the consumption again: I don't get any material from him for the Library of H.[8]

Yours ever
W. D. Howells.

1. Laurence Hutton (1843–1904), an author and New York drama critic, later became associated with the house of Harper and wrote the "Literary Notes" for *Harper's Monthly* (1886–1898).

2. This is a continuation of Howells' private joke with Clemens about their failure in joint enterprises. See Howells to Clemens, 18 April 1882.

3. The rooms were secured by Henry James. See Howells to W. C. Howells, 31 July 1882, n. 1.

4. George Henry Boughton (1833–1905), a painter, although born in England, lived in New York State (1834–1860) before settling in London in 1861.

5. Sir Hubert von Herkomer (1849–1914), a painter, was born in Bavaria, spent six years of his boyhood in Cleveland, Ohio, and lived in England from 1857 to his death. In a letter of introduction, 28 August 1882 (MH), to Charles Fairchild, Howells recommended Herkomer as a "great painter" and "a Western Reserve boy." He added: "He has a notion of getting at American types,—especially financial heads, and I have hoped that you might help him to see the men in Boston who have done great things in money."

6. According to Osgood's letter to Howells of 3 September 1882 (MH) the dinner was to take place "at Hotel Continental No 1 Regent St., at 7 o'clock on Thursday" 7 September. Other guests, besides those mentioned by Howells, were Henry James, Edwin Booth, Laurence Hutton, Moncure D. Conway, W. Mackay Laffan, Clarence King, and Bret Harte. See *Twain-Howells*, p. 414, and Howells to Gosse, 9 September 1882. William Mackay Laffan (1848–1909), born in Ireland, had been an art and drama critic for the New York *Sun*. At this time he was the London representative for Harper & Brothers and English agent for the *Sun*. He became publisher of the *Sun* in 1884.

7. The Madison Square Theatre in New York was owned by George Scovill Mallory (1838–1897), a clergyman, and his brother Marshall H. Mallory. Clemens had approached them with the idea of a play coauthored by him and Howells. See Howells to Hay, 18 March 1882, n. 9. In a letter to Howells of 24 July 1882 (MH; *Twain-Howells*, pp. 411–12), Clemens wrote: "Those godly thieves of the Madison Square have not written me, but no matter about that: you write the play & send it along—there's plenty theatres beside the Madison, & I'll not sell it for nothing, be sure of that. And if the Madison should bid & buy, I will see it that they don't play any of their religious games on us."

8. See Howells to Clemens, 18 April 1882, n. 4.

18 Pelham Crescent
South Kensington, S.W. Sept. 2, 1882

Dear Mr. Waldstein:[1]

Your very kind note came just as I was setting off for Oxford on Wednesday, and I had no time to consult with Mrs. Howells. She is afraid now that she will not be able to avail herself of your offer, but I shall be very glad to come, if you will let me, some day week after next. Say Wednesday—or rather, Thursday? I wish I were to come in November;[2] but by that time we shall be in Venice.

I cannot tell you what pleasure it has given me that you have so perfectly understood poor Marcia, and my intention in her.[3] So many readers detest her; but to my mind she had a generous soul with limitations that appeal only to my pity. Thank you again and again for what you say of the story. But I feel guilty in having claimed even a little of your attention from the pursuit in which you are doing our name honor.[4]

Yours cordially
W. D. Howells.

It would give us so much pleasure if you could drop in any day at one o'clock and lunch with us!

1. Charles Waldstein (1856–1927), later Sir Charles Walston, an archaeologist, born in New York City and a graduate of Columbia University, was a lecturer on classical archaeology and reader in Greek art at Cambridge University in 1882.
2. In a letter of 29 August 1882 (MH), Waldstein invited Howells and Mrs. Howells to visit him in Cambridge, both then and at a later date in November, when he was presenting a production of Sophocles' *Ajax*. For the visit on 13 September, see Howells to Norton, 14 September 1882.
3. In his letter of 29 August, Waldstein commented on *A Modern Instance*: "...it is not only the central figure, 'the weak character strongly drawn' which attracts me; but also the other characters: the *Justice* in the depiction of the central female figure, worthy of sympathy though *trying* to live with, needing a character strong in virtue & in self-abnegation, but just the figure to bring out (not by mere commonplace contrast of strength) the weakness of the other." On 3 September 1882 (MH) Waldstein renewed his invitation to the Howellses and continued his analysis of Marcia Gaylord: "Marcia appears to me to have a large soul, too large & strong in its native power for the circumstances of her childhood & home education. They do not favour its normal growth & throw it out of balance. This you fully indicate, & her failings thus only call for sympathy & pity. . . . [¶] Marcia to me has been the *perfectly individual* drawing of of [sic] a broad modern type abt. whom I have reflected much in connexion with Women's education." Waldstein theorized the result if he should have the conduct of Marcia's education and could train her "to direct by intellect her emotions & set both together at times against her feminine constitutional weakness—What a splendid woman she will make!—for she has the stuff of which great women (& also great men) are made, a great power of loving, much cardiac vitality. But the very fact that, not through her own fault,

but through the natural & social surroundings her soul has not been allowed thus to develop, constitutes the tragic element. This is to me as tragical as any catastrophe between the individual & society translated into the sphere of Kings & heroes & & [sic] coupled with the downfall of states & the slaughter of men. It *is* a modern instance."

4. Howells felt that Waldstein, an American by birth and education, was bringing honor to the American name by his work at Cambridge University.

9 September 1882, London, to Edmund W. Gosse

18 Pelham Crescent,
Sept. 9, 1882.

My dear **Gosse**:

With the divination of a St-dm̄-n,[1] I know that ever since I have not answered your letter, you have been saying to yourself, "The super-sensitive H. cannot bear the slightest criticism. Here I have been travelling on the praises of his stupid story ever since he came to England, and at the slightest hint of a conventional color-box in his luggage, he goes off in a rage and wont write to me."[2] I own that the thing has that look, and yet it is only an appearance. The truth is I have been growing very old since you went away, and I am actually writing this with spectacles. This approach of age warns me to be off from London before I am too superannuated to travel; and we all start for Switzerland on the 18th. I shall not see you again, therefore, till next Spring, and that grieves me, for I love you. But we have enjoyed too much here, and I must go somewhere else to be a wiser and more industrious man, or else the Century will not get its novel for next year.[3] I have written but a hundred pages of it in six weeks, and I have had such a good time that I have been unable to do so much even as kill a consumptive girl, or make a lover homesick enough to start home from China and get wrecked on an atoll in the South Pacific: he is still shamelessly hanging around Hong-Kong, and I have thrown away no end of geography and geology on his atoll. As long as I dine out four times a week, he will not budge; and I am resolved to try what effect a Swiss pension will have on him.[4]—By the way, I wish you had been here to dine with the herd of Yankees whom Osgood managed to scare up one night in London. What do you say to Aldrich, Harte, Hay, Clarence King, Charles Dudley Warner Edwin Booth and W. D. H. meeting together at the Hotel Continental? We wanted you; and the only other Englishman we had was a Dutchman—Tadema. We had a famous time; and the enemy was represented by Laffan, who has just come over to replace Bowker.[5]

Last Sunday we went down to Stoke Poges, and viewed it in the pleasant light of your Gray.[6] Mrs. Howells has read scarcely anything else since I brought it home; and she has goaded me to desperation with quotations from it; but she was so handy that day with them that I forgave her. It was a heavenly day, and never to be forgotten. What a lovely, lovely place that little churchyard is!—A Boston man returned a copy of Shakespear once with the remark that he did not believe there were ten men in the State of Massachusetts who could have written that book; and for my part I remember few churches in Ohio at once so old and so picturesque as that at Stoke Poges. I admit as much as that.— We are going to be under the wing of Mdlle E. Colomb,[7] Le Clos, pres Villeneuve, Vaud; but if you have a moment for me, write me in care of Gillig's American Exchange 449 Strand.

Mrs. Howells joins me in cordial regards to both of you.

Yours ever
W. D. Howells.

1. This appears to be an allusion to a misunderstanding between E. C. Stedman and Gosse, which was caused by a somewhat ill-tempered note from Gosse reminding Stedman to finish an article on the younger British poets. See *Transatlantic Dialogue*, pp. 82–83.

2. See Howells to Gosse, 26 August 1882, n. 1, for the comment on *A Modern Instance* and Howells' coloring "a little from the old conventional water-colour paint-box of what people should feel."

3. *A Woman's Reason.*

4. On 10 September 1882 (MH) Howells wrote to his father: "... we are going to cut short our stay in London where I find myself too subject to hospitality to be able to work." He added in his letter of 17 September 1882 (MH) to his father: "I should have liked to stay longer in London; but I found society and sight-seeing fatal to work, and I shall not leave Switzerland till I have finished my story, which begins to push me somewhat."

5. See Howells to Clemens, 1 September 1882, n. 6. Richard Rogers Bowker (1848–1933), London representative for Harper & Brothers (1880–1882), became editor of *Publishers' Weekly* in 1884 and was the author of numerous books.

6. Gosse's *Life of Thomas Gray* (1882) in the English Men of Letters Series.

7. See Howells to W. C. Howells, 24 September 1882, for Howells' description of Mlle. E. Colomb, proprietress of the Swiss pension where the Howells family were to stay.

14 SEPTEMBER 1882, LONDON, TO CHARLES E. NORTON

London, Sept. 14, 1882.

My dear friend:

I am so bad a correspondent, that I seize myself in both hands at this last moment before leaving England, and send you any sort of line lest I should send you no sort. We have had a most charming sojourn here, and though every body says everybody is out of town, we have met all kinds of desirable people. I must name Burne Jones[1] first among these:

he came to a dinner with us at the Tademas, before I had the chance of making his acquaintance through your letter; and I had enough talk with him to feel his gentle and exquisite spirit, which had already delighted me in his pictures at the Grosvenor and the Royal Academy. I made interest with him at once by boasting you my friend, and he was full of affectionate questions about you, and self-reproach that he had not written you. I had not the courage to send a letter of introduction to any such fairy as a real nobleman, and your letter to Lord Reay[2] awaits delivery till our return to England in the spring. So does that to Morley,[3] who has been out of town. I have seen Lowell many times,[4] and have found him sweetly and beneficently unchanged. Mrs. Lowell is astonishingly well.—H. J., Jr., has been an adoptive father in housing and starting this orphan family in London.[5] Just now he has gone to France.

Two heavenly days—one in each place—I have passed in Oxford and Cambridge: in the latter only yesterday. Winny and I were the guests of Doctor Waldstein, who says his place there corresponds to yours in the *real* Cambridge. He and Mr Colvin the curator of the Museum were full of knowledge and praise of you.[6] I dined "in hall" in Waldstein (King's). I met one of the Darwins (the non-American-travelled one)[7] at Waldstein's rooms, and seemed to be in some sort at home among those people. But the strongest illusion of all was when we came to the Cambridge horse-cars. They are not so good as ours; but upon the whole their gardens and buildings are better—or at least *older*.

We start for Switzerland on Monday, and expect to spend two months by the lake of Geneva before going on to Italy.

Mrs. Howells and all the children join me in love to you all.

Yours ever
W. D. Howells.

1. Sir Edward Coley Burne-Jones (1833–1898) was an English painter who specialized in medieval and mythical subjects.
2. Donald James Mackay (1839–1921) was the eleventh Lord Reay. He lived in London until 1885, when he became governor of Bombay (1885–1890).
3. John Morley (1838–1923); see also Howells to Curtis, 23 April 1879, n. 2.
4. J. R. Lowell was the United States minister to England (1880–1885). In two letters to Howells, 7 August 1882 (MH) and 10 August 1882 (MH), Lowell invited Howells to dine with him and indicated that he would soon be visiting with Elinor and Winifred Howells also.
5. See Howells to W. C. Howells, 31 July 1882, n. 1.
6. See Howells to Waldstein, 2 September 1882. Sidney Colvin (1845–1927) was then director of the Fitzwilliam Museum at Cambridge (1873–1885). Later he became director of the British Museum (1884–1912).
7. It is difficult to determine which Darwin it was that Howells met. It was most likely one of Charles Darwin's sons, George Howard (1845–1912), Francis (1848–1925), Horace (1851–1928), or Leonard (1850–1943). All of them were at Cambridge in 1882.

24 SEPTEMBER 1882, VILLENEUVE, TO WILLIAM C. HOWELLS

Le Clos, Villeneuve,
Vaud, Switzerland. Sept. 24, 1882.

Dear father:

Your letters to me and to John have come since we arrived here, and we are in possession of reasonably late news from you. The promptness of everything is really surprising—so much greater than when we were in Europe before. But they have still a vast deal to learn of us, especially in railroading and in sleeping-cars. We took the bed-wagon (as the French call it) at Calais, having crossed very comfortably at Dover, and found it but little bigger and better than an ambulance. To satisfy the supposed passion for privacy it was cut up into half a dozen state-rooms with four berths in each, crosswise of the car, and outside of these an aisle ran the length of the sleeper. It was badly hung, and swayed and jolted as our cars did before we had the Miller platform.[1] However we got thro' to the Swiss frontier by daylight, by way of Amiens and Rheims, and then worked on through Berne and Lausanne by three in the afternoon. We are delightfully placed here, within a stone's throw of the Lake Leman and within two minutes' walk of the Castle of Chillon, round which we all rowed in a boat yesterday. We are with the Swiss lady to whom Edward Eggleston recommended us before we left Toronto, and we find ourselves very comfortable. It is a distinct pleasure to be in a Republic again; the manners are simple and un-ceremonious as our own, and people stand upright in all respects. The many resemblances to America constantly strike one; and if I must ever be banished, I hope it may be to Switzerland. These are my first im-pressions; I may change my ideas later.—We have already entered upon a severe campaign against the French language, but as yet without much method, though we hope to begin with that to-morrow, when Winny and Pilla expect to enter a girl's school, and due provision is to be made for John and the rest of us. Mademoiselle is the only one in the house who speaks English beside ourselves.[2] She is a jolly old maid of forty; and she has with her Mme. Grenier, her widowed cousin, and Mme.'s son and daughter, all nice, cultivated, friendly people, with whom we are obliged more or less to speak French. It is rough, but it is wholesome. After some terrific bouts with them, in which I trample accent and syntax into one common pulp, I stop and literally pant for breath.[3]

We are all very well, in spite of the cold rainy weather.—How good Henry's joke on the piper was. Perhaps after all, *he* will be the great humorist of the family. We unite in love to each of you.

Your aff'te son
Will.

1. A truss suspension system developed by Ezra Miller (1812–1885), the American inventor.

2. In his letter of 9 September 1882 to Gosse, Howells gave the name of the Swiss proprietress of the pension as Mlle. E. Colomb. See also Howells to James, 4 October 1882.

3. Howells published his impressions of Switzerland in "A Little Swiss Sojourn," *Harper's Monthly*, February–March 1888.

4 OCTOBER 1882, VILLENEUVE, TO HENRY JAMES

> Le Clos, près Villeneuve,
> Vaud. October 4, 1882.

My dear James:

We have now been rained in here two weeks; but the damp air is so good, and the lake and mountains so amiable that we are hardly even impatient with our imprisonment. If you happen to know the region, you can place our pension very near the Hotel Byron, and realize us on the right in going toward Montreux. Le Clos was formerly the country place of the family of Mlle Colomb, who were substantial people of Vevey, of the Brahminical caste. The house is full of old books, and smells equally of them, and the three cats and big dog which M'lle keeps. She is intelligent, witty, and I think one of the very most sensible people I ever saw: she has sense enough to be a man. Her cousin, Mme. Grenier (*veuve*) and Mme. Grenier's son and daughter are our fellow-boarders: the mother is one of those exquisite persons, who keep a pretty gentleness and a young habit of blushing, far into their gray hairs; the daughter is *jolie* (she gurgles it far down in her throat) and the son goes a great deal to the chase, and speaks Italian with me. We all struggle with French, the children more or less hopefully; and though I say it, we are an interesting household. I consider myself, especially fictionable, and I am sorry you are not here to study me in the character of a thoroughly bourgeois American: a man who had once some poetical possibilities, but who finds himself more and more commonplace in surroundings that twenty years ago appealed not in vain to something fine in him. I daily put on more *sitzfleisch*,[1] and feel hopelessly middle-aged, when I meet the pretty girls walking up from Chillon to gather the crimson leaves of the Virginia creeper, which hangs its splendor from all the walls here. Somewhere, deep within my awkward bulk, I know that I am as young and stylish and slim as any of them, but I know also that I don't look it.—England seems an age away, and of all that happened during our seven weeks in London, I remember your kindnesses most distinctly. I think you did not realize how good you were to us; but we did. The day we left we had a note from your brother, and I was very sorry we should not have seen him.—I am working hard at my story here, which takes shape very slowly and reluctantly. I shall never again I hope, attempt to finish a thing so long thrown aside.[2] All the family join me in love to you.

Yours ever
W. D. Howells.

1. German for "extra pounds from lack of exercise."
2. Howells had begun *A Woman's Reason* in 1878; see Howells to Gosse, 9 September 1882, for comments on the slow pace of his work on the novel.

7 OCTOBER 1882, VILLENEUVE, TO WILLIAM C. HOWELLS

Le Clos, Octr. 7, 1882.

Dear father:

I am writing you Saturday night, instead of Sunday morning as usual, because I must work at my story[1] to-morrow in order to be able to go to a little town on Monday, where there is to be a church-fair, and where I shall see some primitive Swiss life. It is curious to find these French-speaking people such strenuous protestants and republicans, and so like ourselves in all religious and most domestic respects. I wish you were here so often, for I am sure you would be interested intensely in this wise, good little country. Sometimes I think that what the Swiss do not know and do, is hardly worth while. For instance, they have a State fire-insurance; every one is *obliged* to insure, and the State promptly pays all losses. Education is compulsory, and stated examinations are held to *see* that every one can read and write.—Certain things, like growing fruit, cord-wood, etc., are "confided to the public faith," and whoever steals these is punished with double severity. The pasture lands are held in common; and the profits from cheese and butter are equitably apportioned by the commune among the people.—They are very hard workers, and few of them are "pretty to look at," but what sensible and decent people they are!—The children are making great advances of a good kind. They are not only getting a great deal of French, but they are drawing and journalizing with the greatest diligence. I could not wish them to be more alive to their opportunities. We have received your letters—yours, Aurelia's and Annie's, and we send love to the whole batch of you. Tell Annie, please, that I saw Millet, the painter, (to whom I gave Achille a letter) just before I left London, and he expressed the greatest interest, and said that whenever Achille came to New York, he would do all he could to forward his objects. Tell Vevie that Untle Will would lite to give her a *what* and a *tiss* both at once. We don't any of us forget her, and I don't think Pilla forgives her for coming to

Toronto and putting her nose out of joint with her aunt Lelie, "before she had got used to her."[2] She still drops some resentful allusions to the fact.—Elinor wonders wrathfully why you, father, never answer any of her letters, and I guess you had better up and write to her, sometime, instead of to me. She and the children will write soon and atone for my epistolary dryness.

Your aff'te son
Will.

1. *A Woman's Reason.*
2. See Howells to Victoria Howells, 21 July 1882, n. 2.

16 OCTOBER 1882, VILLENEUVE, TO JAMES R. OSGOOD

Le Clos, près Villeneuve,
Vaud, Switzerland, Oct. 16, 1882.

My dear Osgood:

Yours of the 2d is just at hand. The matter of the Venetian papers I have already fully written you about, and I have a clear understanding now that I can give them to Harpers if I like.[1]

I have already sent them—the Century people,—the first installment of the story, of which I have changed the title; I now call it "A Woman's Reason" which fits it far better than the other name.[2] I am having it stereotyped at Edinburgh, according to my last understanding with you, and I have sent it to New York in print. I will follow rapidly on with the copy, so that they need not be anxious.

—My notion for No. 3, is the adventures of young American skipper or supercargo who goes to Venice with his ship about the close of the last century, from Plymouth, or Salem, or perhaps Boston. I suppose him to be a man in whom the puritan tradition strongly lingers, and who is thoroughly characterized by the colonial civilization of his time, but whose blood is warm enough to be stirred by the love affairs that await him in the capital of the dying Republic. It is the year 1794 or '95, just before Venice falls, and I imagine a typical epoch of corrupt gayety, with masking six months of the year, and all manner of lively times; and one of my objects would be to contrast the new republic with the old, in the heart of the fresh young Yankee who finds himself in the midst of these scenes. As nearly as I can see the story now, the love-making is to be rather complicated: a splendidly reprehensible illus-trissima is to make rather fierce advances to him, while he is really taken with the young girl who becomes his wife. All is to be strictly within the bounds of honesty; and I think the story can be made very sweet and pretty for the mere novel-reader, while those who care for the deeper drift will be interested in the studies of the time and place, and their contrast with the New England life at both ends of the story: I should begin it and end it in Boston. I can't be more explicit about the plot, now; but this outline will give an intelligible notion of it, I hope. I have long wished to touch historical ground in my work, and here I shall do it. After all, any editor would have to trust me for the character and quality of the story, and let what I have done be a guaranty for what I shall do. I may change very considerably when I get to work on the story, but I give this sketch as it now lies in my mind. I choose a captain or supercargo for my hero, because that is the kind of American who would then probably find himself in Venice; and because the commercial American was then venturing abroad with the energy of the young Republic boiling in him.[3]

I'm glad the Modern Instance starts off so well, and I hope it will fulfill all your expectations.[4] Any characteristic reviews will be welcome.

Conway's *will* was good.[5]

All the family join me in regards. Remember me to all the people at 211.[6]

Yours ever,
W. D. Howells.

1. The Venetian papers, a revival of a plan for a history of Venice, were never written. See Howells to Warner, 17 March 1874, n. 2. The proposed history later reappeared in H. M. Alden's letters of 3 October, 11 October, 26 October 1899, and 25 January 1900 (all MH) to Howells, in which he proposed serial publication in *Harper's Monthly* prior to book publication by Harper & Brothers. See also Howells to Smith, 19 November 1882.

2. See Howells to Osgood, 5 August 1882, n. 3.

3. See Howells to Osgood, 12 July 1882, n. 1. Though Howells seemed anxious to explore the possibilities of historical romance, his enthusiasm for this type of novel waned; the work he describes here was never written. For his later criticism, see "The New Historical Romances," *North American Review* 171 (December 1900), 935–48.

4. In his letter of 2 October 1882 (MH) to Howells, Osgood reported that *A Modern Instance* was to be published as a book on 6 October "with good prospects."

5. Conway's "*will*" was probably a graceful and humorous testament delivered as a speech at "the Osgood dinner" on 7 September. See Howells to Clemens, 1 September 1882, n. 6.

6. 211 Tremont Street, Boston, was the address of James R. Osgood & Co.

17 OCTOBER 1882, VILLENEUVE, TO SAMUEL L. CLEMENS

> Le Clos, Villeneuve,
> Vaud, Switzerland, Oct. 17, 1882.

My dear Clemens:

What you want to do is to pack up your family, and come to Florence for the winter. I shall have my story as good as done when I get there early in December, and shall be ready to go to work with you on the great American comedy of "Orme's Motor" which is to enrich us both "beyond the dreams of avarice." It's fate needn't rest with the Madison Squarers.[1] We can get it played. We could have a lot of fun writing it, and you could go home with some of the good old Etruscan malaria in your bones, instead of the wretched pinch-beck Hartford article that you're suffering from now. I know Mrs. Clemens would like to come; and Osgood could collect that royalty for you in H., on your book.[2] If you come, you need not kill Clarke; you could bring his material with you.[3]

We are having a good, dull, wholesome time in this little pension on the shore of Lake Leman, within gunshot of the Castle of Chillon; but a thousand jokes rot in my breast every day for want of companionship. Think of a country where they are so proud of their manure heaps that they plait the edges of the straw that sticks out. John and I make the most of each other; but he finds me poor company, and the fact is his perpetual questions pall upon me.

We have now been here a month, and we have not spoken to an American soul, and to but one English, and that was a she-soul. Think of the amount of talk that must be bottled up in us! And the capacity for listening that I must have acquired. It is a great opportunity for you. Besides, nobody over there likes you half so well as I do.—We are about three miles from Montreux, a little place full of half-sick, indigent English and predatory Russians, and it is worth the voyage across the Atlantic to see the gloomy splendor with which they stare at and wont speak to one another in the street. Sometimes I'm a little down-hearted, but I always cheer up when I go to Montreux.—In London, Hay and King went to hear Bret Harte read a comedy he has been colaborating with a Belgian lady.[4] He has turned the "Luck" of Roaring Camp into a girl, and brought her to Paris, with all his Californians, where she has adventures.

All the family join me in love to yours.

> Yours ever
> W. D. Howells.

1. See Howells to Hay, 18 March 1882, n. 9, and Howells to Clemens, 1 September 1882, n. 7.

2. Clemens suspected that the American Publishing Co. had not paid all royalties due him on *The Prince and the Pauper*. See *Twain-Howells*, p. 416.

3. See Howells to Clemens, 18 April 1882, n. 4.

4. Madame Van de Velde was the wife of a Belgian diplomat in London; a close friend of Bret Harte, she translated some of his stories into French. Their collaborative play was never produced. John Hay and Clarence King were part of the American literary circle in London. See *Twain-Howells*, p. 416.

26 OCTOBER 1882, VILLENEUVE, TO EDMUND W. GOSSE

Villeneuve, Oct. 26, 1882.

My dear Gosse:

It is a proof of my continued youthfulness, I suppose, that I had begun to be afraid something in my letter had offended you; but take it as a proof also of my anxious affection: your letter came just in time to save me from writing to ask you what the matter was.[1] The joyful rebound of my spirits at once enabled me to think out the philosophy of my story and though it is not much of a philosophy, I have it hard and fast. Thank you for all your kind offers in regard to desolate islands:[2] I have started my man away from his atoll in an open boat, and he is to be presently picked up by a whaler. I think you will be amused by my instinctive efforts to *realize* a desolate island, and the hero's recognition of the stale and hackneyed character of the situation. My great helper has been Dana in his Coral Islands. Is the Mr. Gosse whom he quotes possibly your father?[3] When I came upon the name, I felt almost as if you were a partner of my enterprise. I wish you *would* send me those blue-books: my present hero is a well-principled person, but the trade of novel writing is so corrupting that before I have done with it, I am sure that I shall invent some young man who will at least *wish* to visit all the worst places in Hong Kong.[4] And wont you kindly send me the October Century? I can't "seem to" get hold of it. (I don't know why I should continue to heap up all these obligations: it must be just to see how many I *can* carry.)

This country life in Switzerland is immensely interesting, with astonishing flashes of resemblance to that of New England, which must come from the common Calvanism and Republicanism. There is nothing lacking here but the comfort of some one (why not *say* Gosse?) to talk the queer things over with. John and I walk about a good deal, and we row a little on the lake; but outside the house I will own it is not exciting. Within it is rather interesting, and if I were a truly unprincipled person,—as I sometimes wish I were, instead of this wretched halfway affair—I should scoop nearly everybody into my notebook. But I have a conscience: I may want to come back.—I forgive Mrs. Gosse for anticipating my intention in regard to those little books, but I shall certainly not forgive anyone else.[5] The only thing left for me to do now is to *write* you a whole new series.—After sending you my letter, I read your Gray,[6] and I was delighted with it. You have done a difficult piece of work with the most charming skill, and with an unfailing delicacy and *precision* of appreciation. I am glad that you are going to edit Gray's works, for now I shall read *them*. All the family send cordial regards to Mrs Gosse and yourself. Please tell Theresa that Mildred has drawn me a book full of animals in Swiss costumes.

> Yours ever
> W. D. Howells.

1. Howells is referring to his letter of 9 September to Gosse and to Gosse's response of 12 October 1882 (MH; *Transatlantic Dialogue*, pp. 99–100).

2. Gosse had written on 12 October that he expected an answer from Howells only if "...I can get you any books about reefs or coolies, or send you anything you want for yr novel [*A Woman's Reason*]."

3. James Dwight Dana, *Corals and Coral Islands* (1872); Gosse's father was Philip Henry Gosse (1810–1888), a naturalist who authored *The Ocean* (1844), *A Naturalist's Sojourn in Jamaica* (1851), and other books dealing with nature.

4. In his letter of 12 October Gosse wrote: "If you are really writing much about Hong Kong, you had better let me send you some blue-books lately published here, on the atrocious tyrannies of the local police, quite a Zolaesque study of the life in the low quarter of the town. But perhaps your hero is careful not to get into bad company, and keeps his ethics gilt-edged till he is thrown up upon the atoll." According to Gosse, he sent Howells a blue-book, but Howells was so scandalized by its contents that he did not acknowledge receiving it: "Usually so precise, he surprised me by giving no sign of having received this scabrous treasure. Being pressed, he admitted that he had received it, but that it had horrified and disturbed him so much that he had burned it, and had put away from him all thought of writing about Hong Kong" ("The Passing of William Dean Howells," *Littell's Living Age* 306 [10 July 1920], 99).

5. Mrs. Gosse had presented her husband with a birthday gift of the 1882 editions of *The Lady of the Aroostook, Their Wedding Journey*, and *A Counterfeit Presentment and The Parlour Car* (in one volume), published by David Douglas, Edinburgh.

6. *Life of Thomas Gray*.

16 NOVEMBER 1882, VILLENEUVE, TO EDMUND W. GOSSE

> Villeneuve, Nov. 16, 1882.

My dear Gosse:

The American Exchange promised to send me the Century, but it has not done so, and I must ask of your charity to send me the November number so that I can see what the deuce I have been saying of Dickens and Thackeray:[1] when I come back to England, in the spring I will re-imburse you for the small expenses I beg you to make for me, and will still hold myself your debtor for your kindness. I can't intelligently take hold of a matter which you say has interested the London newspapers, for I can't remember just what I wrote, though it must have been what I thought. But I always thought myself quite unapproached in my appreciation of the great qualities of Dickens and Thackeray, and I can hardly believe that I have "arraigned" them. I suspect that no Englishman could rate them higher than I do. If I had the grudge to monarchies which you suppose, both those authors must have fed it fat, for I learned nothing but democracy from them. But you really can't think me so pitiful as to judge men's art by their political opinions or conditions: if that were the case what should I have to say of Shakespeare or Cervantes, whom I quite prefer to Milton or Landor? Why should I think Tourguénief the master of his art, and the first of all novelists, within his range?—When I have seen the Century, and my offense in it against the great Shades, T. and D., I hope you will let me talk to you further about them: I fancy we shall not disagree at all. As to the two little Substances, H. & J., the former is now getting his desert in the American press for presuming to have a mind (which he had forgotten) about D. & T., and the latter has had no praise troweled upon him by American critics hitherto, but rather shovels and pitchforks full of blame. But I dare say this "will all come out right in the end." Only if the time and chance ever came together, I should like to say my say about the art of Dickens and Thackeray in full.[2]

—We are thinking of setting our frost-bitten noses southward. The snow is getting lower and lower on the mountains, and this afternoon when I walked out into their lordly presence, their breath cut cold across my cheeks, with a real wintry touch. The sight is lovelier and grander than I could describe; but one of the fine things about it is the effect of the pines, whether lightly powdered and etherialized by the snow far up the heights, or, farther yet, climbing in long black files along under the cliffs, or grouped in dark masses at the edge of sloping fields of snow. And the chalets, wading in the drifts of the mountain pastures are not bad, either.—But the weather here below is awfully cold and wet. We shall stay, I suppose, for a fortnight, yet, and then go to Florence.

I am glad and grateful that you have been so kind to Miss Preston.[3] She has gone back to feudalism in religion without affecting my regard for her, and may do so in politics on the same terms, if she likes. If she turned out a duchess in disguise I should still be friends with her, as I should with you my dear Gosse, if some apostate Jew some day got you made a peer.[4]

Yours ever
W. D. Howells

1. Howells, in "Henry James, Jr.," *Century*, November 1882, wrote: "The art of fiction has, in fact, become a finer art in our day than it was with Dickens and Thackeray. We could not suffer the confidential attitude of the latter now, nor the mannerism of the former, any more than we could endure the prolixity of Richardson or the coarseness of Fielding. These great men are of the past—they and their methods and interests...." In a letter of 8 November 1882 (MH; *Transatlantic Dialogue*, pp. 102–3) to Howells, Gosse wrote: "So you have demolished poor old Dickens and Thackeray, have you? Well, I am glad I was born in the good old times when they were thought good enough for week-day reading." Gosse also included the following poem:

Motto for the American Critic.

Ho! the old school! Thackeray, Dickens!
Throw them out to feed the chickens.—
Ho! the new school! James and —————
Lay the flattery on with trowels.
(Doggerel by a candid friend.)

A letter from Howells to Gosse appears to be missing from the correspondence, since in a letter of 14 November 1882 (MH; *Transatlantic Dialogue*, pp. 103–4) to Howells, Gosse wrote: "I was quite ashamed, when your lovely letter came, to think that it had been crossed by such a flippant one of mine. But I dare say you did not regard my impertinence. The newspapers here have been discussing your arraignment of Dickens and Thackeray very warmly, though in almost every case in a very courteous spirit towards yourself. I think, to speak of the matter quite soberly, that it is our tendency to overrate these writers from national partiality, just as it is your tendency to underrate them for the same reason.... I think I shall always do battle with you on your favourite literary stand-point, that the intellectual product of a democracy must be finer than that of a monarchy. I am sure the inmost reason of your dislike to Dickens and Thackeray is that they flourished in a corrupt and pestilent royalty."

2. This statement in a garbled form and some other quotations from this letter appeared in "Literary Gossip," London *Athenaeum*, 25 November 1882, p. 700. See *Transatlantic Dialogue*, p. 41, n. 104.

3. Harriet Waters Preston (1836–1911) was an author and translator; a number of her articles and book reviews appeared in the *Atlantic* when Howells was its editor. In his letter of 8 November 1882 (MH) Gosse called Miss Preston "most charming," and in his letter of 14 November Gosse wrote: "We are very much obliged to you for introducing Miss Preston to us. We like her extremely: but I wonder that you do, for she is not at all *democratic*!"

4. Probably an indirect reference to Benjamin Disraeli (1804–1881), prime minister of Great Britain (February–December 1868 and 1874–1880).

19 NOVEMBER 1882, VILLENEUVE, TO ROSWELL SMITH

Villeneuve, Nov. 19, 1882.

My dear Mr. Smith:

I was very glad to get your letter of the 2d, which came to hand yesterday; for though I had written fully to Mr. Gilder in regard to the Johns Hopkins affair, I had some lingering doubts as to whether I had not seemed wanting, in my note to you, in due appreciation of his friendly interest.[1] But that is now all settled, and we can let J. H. take care of itself for the present. What chiefly moved me in your letter was the postscript, endorsed by Mr. Gilder which could not have been more important if it had been a lady's.[2] Your saying, apropos of the Lexington paper, that you wished you could have for the Century something like a history from me, jumped with the temptation which is becoming poignant with me again, to write a popular history of Venice from the Bostonia-Chicago-New York point of view.[3] I do think that I could make a new thing in history, and something that would be thoroughly intelligible to all your readers and thoroughly interesting. I do not know whether Osgood and you have made affairs yet for my third novel; but that need not concern the history; it will be rather in the line of it, since the scene is to be in Venice at the time of the decadence. Probably, when I shall have written that third story, I shall not feel like spinning my bowels into another romance, were I ten times the spider I am; and probably I *shall* feel like writing the history. I should want to read a year for it, and then I could give it to the press as my pen ran. I should like Mr. Gilder and yourself to talk it over with Osgood: you would all have to consider that for two years' work, I must have "the grand cash." The work was something that I wished very much to do for the Atlantic at one time; I even collected some material for it, but I found that I had not the time to read for it, and edit the magazine, and so I gave it up.[4]

I suppose you will have seen that I have stirred up the English papers pretty generally by what I wrote of Dickens and Thackeray in my paper on James. I don't remember just what I said, but so far as they have quoted me, I stand by myself, and should only wish to amplify and intensify the opinions that they object to. I knew what I was talking about, and they don't know at all what they are talking about.

I am glad that A Woman's Reason pleases you, so far. I find it as I go on, a most difficult and delicate thing to handle, but I hope to make it justify itself. I don't expect everybody to agree with it, but I shall try to interest everybody, and to give them something to think about. If the perplexities of the story cause me to modify the plan of the Italian papers I will let you know: in any case I shall have work cut out for Mr. Pennell when he comes.[5] In about a week we shall start for Florence, and I hope there to finish the story by January. But if I don't, how would you like, instead of the Minor-City series, a series of semi-historical studies of Florence and the formerly dependent cities of Pisa, Siena, etc.?—which I could gather the material for without interrupting my work on the story.[6] That series might have a more continuous interest than the other. I suggest it as something that I might wish to turn to in extremity.

I wish you would kindly have the *Century* mailed to me direct from New York, c/o Gillig's Exchange 449 Strand. I don't see it, now, without troubling Gosse for it.

Mrs. Howells, after an attack of erysipelas, finds herself very well here. She joins me in regards to Mrs. Smith.

Remember me cordially to Mr. Gilder.

Yours sincerely
W. D. Howells.

1. In a letter to Howells of 7 October 1882 (MH), Richard W. Gilder reported giving Howells' name to President Gilman of Johns Hopkins University upon Gilman's request for a suggestion "of some person who would profess literature as an art, to their students." He further wrote: "They would be very much pleased to be able to look forward to your permanent connection with the Institution as Professor of Literature, but they think it best to suggest a temporary arrangement to last for a year or two, such arrangement, to be for one, two, or three months, during a single year, or during two years." In his reply to Gilder of 24 October 1882 (MdBJ), Howells wrote: "... I cannot think of the experimental lectureship .... I am too old to attempt a new line of work at my own risk. If the University could propose two or three years' salary in full, with the quality and authority of professor from the beginning, that would be something to consider; but I could not come 'on liking.' " Smith, in his letter to Howells on 2 November 1882 (MH), mentions that he talked about the Johns Hopkins position with Osgood, who "quite agrees with me that if you took to that sort of thing it might be made a source of income and a help rather than a hindrance in your literary work." See also Howells to Gilman, 3 December 1882. Daniel Coit Gilman (1831–1908) was president of Johns Hopkins University (1875–1901).

2. The postscript of Smith's letter reads: " 'Lexington' in Longman's Magazine is capital. I wish the world could get a History or Biography from your pen, and that The Century could be the medium of its publication." Then, added in Gilder's hand: "*So do I*—R. W. G." Howells' "Lexington" appeared in *Longman's*, November 1882.

3. See Howells to Osgood, 16 October 1882, n. 1.

4. See Howells to Warner, 17 March 1874, n. 2.

5. Joseph Pennell (1857–1926) was sent by R. W. Gilder to illustrate Howells' articles on Italian cities for the *Century*. In a letter of 21 June 1882 (MH) to Howells, Pennell described himself and said that he would meet Howells "in Rome or at some other point" in November.

6. Howells wrote the "semi-historical studies" of Florence, Pisa, Siena, and other Italian cities. These sketches appeared in the *Century*—"A Florentine Mosaic" (February, April, June 1885), "Panforte di Siena" (August–September 1885), and "Tuscan Cities" (October 1885)—and were illustrated by Joseph Pennell and later published in a single volume, *Tuscan Cities* (1886). In a letter to Howells of 6 December 1882 (MH), Smith indicated his eagerness for Howells to write the semi-historical sketches and said: "This brings the whole thing up on a higher plane than simple sketches of the minor Italian cities, and introduces the historical element which we think you will do most admirably."

3 DECEMBER 1882, VILLENEUVE, TO DANIEL C. GILMAN

Villeneuve, Dec. 3, 1882.

My dear Mr. Gilman:[1]

I do not know what to say in answer to your most kind and gratifying letter of the 14th ult., and I feel the disadvantage of trying to talk the matter over with you at this prodigious distance.[2] I am afraid in the first place that you do not know how rich and various are my disqualifications for such a position as that you offer me; and I am most anxious, before the negotiation goes farther, to be perfectly frank about them. I have a literary use of Spanish, French, German and Italian, and I have some knowledge of the literature and the literary history of those languages; but I have not a *scholarly* acquaintance with them, and could not write any of them correctly, not even Italian. Greek literature I know only by translations, and not fully; under *peine forte et dure*,[3] I might read Latin. As to English literature, why of course I know it in a sort of way, but rather in the order and degree of preference than thoroughly and systematically. And I do not even know our own language scientifically,—that is from the Anglo-Saxon up; and I might often be unable to give a philological reason for the faith that was in me.

Nevertheless, I do feel strongly and deeply, the art of literature, and I believe I could make others feel its beauty and importance. I have fancied myself confronting a class of young men,—and also young women,—and I have thought that I should begin by making each one tell me what he had read, in whatever language. Then I should inquire into his preferences and require the reason for them. When I had acquainted myself fully with the literary attainments and opinions of the class and come perfectly into *rapport* with them, I should want to see their work, to criticize it with them and correct it—not in detail but "by sample." All the time I should be giving illustrative readings and lectures, which would be rather to the point of what we were doing than in any order of time, or critical or historical sequence. Often I should read a poem, or an essay or passage from a novel or history, and prove to them—for such things are perfectly susceptible of proof—why it was good or bad; but I should always give them the first chance to analyze: I should seek at every step to make them partners in the enterprise, and not treat them as bottles to be filled with so much literary information and opinion. Sometimes I should turn to one literature and sometimes to another; if a new book were making much talk, I would read it and talk about it with them. In every way I would try to emancipate them from the sense of drudgery, and yet teach them that work—delightful work—was perpetually necessary in literary art as in every other. My idea is that the sum of this art is to speak and to write simply and clearly, and I should labor in every way to make them feel that this was also to write beautifully and strongly. Is any such system or no-system practicable with you? I could not and would not *teach* by any sort of *text-book* in any branch.

Now, how much of my time must I give to such work? How many hours a week?

I am by trade and by affection a writer of novels, and I cannot give up my trade, because, for one reason, I earn nearly twice as much money by it as you offer me for salary. But I feel the honor and distinction of being connected with such an institution as yours, and I own that your offer tempts me.

Yours sincerely,
W. D. Howells.

P.S. If it were at all possible to leave this matter open till my return next August, it would be best. I don't see how we can arrive at each other's ideas clearly and fully by letter.

1. See Howells to Osgood, 16 and 24 December 1882, n. 1.
2. In a letter of 14 November 1882 (MH) to Howells, Gilman regretted that Howells regarded the offer of a temporary position at Johns Hopkins University as a way of putting him on trial; Gilman felt rather that it was a chance for Howells to try the position. He requested Howells' "assent to a nomination for a Professorship of Literature, for three years,—at a salary of $5000-per year, the appointment to begin with our next academic year." In a postscript he added: "Your proposed *idea* of the work of a professor we should be very glad to see."
3. French for "great and painful exertion."

16 AND 24 DECEMBER 1882, FLORENCE, TO JAMES R. OSGOOD

4 Piazza dell' Independenza.
Florence, Dec. 16, 1882.

My dear Osgood: (*See postscript*)
I send you my letter to President Gilman, and when you have read it, I wish you would kindly forward it.[1] I don't think that the place will come to me, after all; and if it did, I doubt greatly if I should find pleasure or profit in it. That is, I'm afraid it would interfere with my writing quite as much as editing the Atlantic did. You say nothing of the magazine scheme we have often talked of together, and I suppose you have given it up;[2] but I am glad that you look forward to some renewal of our relations.—If this professorship affair falls through, as I expect it to do, I should rather not leave Boston, to which I am now so thoroughly "wonted." Your letter is most kind in every way, and I hope

you will approve of mine to President Gilman. I have tried to be perfectly honest with him.

I'm glad that No. 3 goes to the Century; and I suppose you can readily make it right with the Harpers. I wish you would find out from Gilder when he wants to begin No. 3, for after I have finished No. 2, I should like to switch off, and do the Italian Cities before beginning a new story.[3] I find the strain of working out plots and characters amidst new and distracting scenes, is awful; and I would like to postpone the commencement of the new story till I get home next autumn. I can do this if he need not start it in the magazine till say July or August 1884.

How goes the new book? Has it stopped selling? The skull-cracking (which is mitigated by distance, perhaps, and at least doesn't hurt much) ought to help it.[4]

Yours ever
W. D. Howells.

Dec. 24.

Since I wrote the foregoing, I have consulted Lowell in regard to the professorship,[5] and his mind, like my own from the first, is against it. I have therefore written, declining it. (*Please don't connect L.'s name with it*).

I have received a letter from R. S., allowing me to modify the Italian papers at pleasure, and wanting me to write him the Venetian history which I suggested in my letter of the 19th November, forwarded him through your hands. "Let us have the History of Venice, by all means, in due time, and we can talk about the grand cash, later on."[6] But this talk must come first, and I wish you and he could decide what you could jointly offer me for the history, to run a year or eighteen months. *No hurry.* Perhaps better see how the Florentine sketches turn out, first.

1. It is unlikely that Howells, at this late date, would have sent Osgood the letter to Gilman of 3 December. There appears to have been another letter, now lost, to which Osgood referred in his letter to Howells of 10 January 1883 (MH): "This morning I am in receipt of your letter dated Dec. 16 with postscript Dec. 24. I have forwarded the enclosure to Prest. Gilman as you request. I understand from the postscript, however, that you have written him another letter direct declining the professorship." On 28 January 1883 (MH) Howells replied: "I don't remember how I could have given you the idea that I had written to President Gilman directly about the Professorship. The only letter I wrote was the one I asked you to forward." These passages suggest the possibility that Howells wrote but never sent his letter to Gilman of 3 December 1882.

2. There are no references in letters of this period to the "magazine scheme," but in 1885 Howells and Osgood thought about publishing a magazine devoted entirely to fiction. See Osgood to Howells, 19 August 1885 (MH) and Alden to Howells, 9 September 1885 (MH).

3. No. 2 was *A Woman's Reason*; No. 3, originally a historical romance about Venice (see Howells to Osgood, 12 July 1882, n. 1), ultimately became *The Rise of*

Silas Lapham, Century, November 1884–August 1885. For the "Italian Cities" see Howells to Smith, 19 November 1882, n. 6. In a letter of 15 January 1883 (MH) to Howells, Roswell Smith wrote: "we are quite willing you should take all the time you want for writing novel number 3. We do not expect, or desire to begin it before Nov. '84.... We hope you will decide to give us the historical sketch of Florence and its dependent cities, instead of the sketches of the minor Italian cities, and we suppose that it will be the piece of work to be done next and before novel number 3."

4. On 12 December 1882 (MH) Osgood reported that sales of *A Modern Instance* were picking up again. The "skull-cracking" refers to attacks on Howells for his remarks on Thackeray and Dickens in his article on Henry James (see Howells to Gosse, 16 November 1882, n. 1). This criticism occurred in both British and American periodicals and newspapers and is mentioned in several letters to Howells: Roswell Smith's of 6 December 1882 (MH) and 11 January 1883 (MH) and R. W. Gilder's of 16 December 1882 (MH). See Cady, *Howells*, I, 218–21, and Lynn, *Howells*, pp. 269–71.

5. See Howells to Lowell, 17 December 1882.

6. Howells' quotation comes from Roswell Smith's letter of 6 December 1882 (MH); and on 15 January 1883 (MH) Smith wrote that it seemed best to Gilder, Osgood, and himself that the question of price for the proposed history of Venice wait until Howells' return.

17 DECEMBER 1882, FLORENCE, TO JAMES R. LOWELL

Hotel Minerva, Sta Maria Novella,
Florence, Dec. 17, 1882

Dear Mr. Lowell:

You have so often stood my friend that I easily forgive myself for troubling you about a matter which is troubling me a great deal. It looks like fortune, but who knows Fortune's real face? I am offered the Professorship of Literature in the Johns Hopkins University, and I am given to understand that I can make the place what I like. But I am forty-five, unused to personal influence and probably without the presence that would affect young people. I should have to unset and reset myself; I should have to rub up my general ignorance in all directions and try by some sort of swift magic to transmute it into general knowledge. I believe that I could give students ideas of literary art, and could criticise their work usefully, and this is what I am expected mainly to do. But I wished to ask of your experience how much of a distraction from my own literary work the contact with a class twice or thrice a week, and the inevitable preparation for the encounter, would be. Should I not be spoiling a fair-to-middling novelist in order to make a poor professor? I hate to leave Boston, and the notion of a new calling is a cold bath to my imagination. The advantages of the position are a salary that would keep the printer at bay, and leisure (I suppose) to do something besides novelling, if I ever felt inclined. I can only present my misgivings crudely and vaguely, but I know you can divine them, and I am sure you can trust me not to hold you responsible for any but a good result from your counsel.[1]

We are here, all very much flattened out by a change from three months of Swiss air to the mawkish tepidity of this climate; but we hope to get used to it.

Mrs. Howells commends herself to the kind remembrance of Mrs. Lowell and yourself, and I join her in hoping that you are both well and have not forgotten

Your aff'tionate
W. D. Howells.

1. Lowell replied on 21 December 1882 (MH): "If you are able now, without overworking mind or body, to keep the wolf from the door & to lay by something for a rainy day,—& I mean, of course, without being driven to work with your left hand because the better one is tired out,—I should refuse the offer, or should hesitate to accept it. If you are a systematic worker, independent of moods, & sure of your genius whenever you want it, there might be no risk in accepting.... [¶] A professorship takes a great deal of time, &, if you teach in any more direct way than by lectures, uses up an immense stock of nerves. Your inevitable temptation (in some sort your duty) will be to make yourself *learned*—which you haven't the least need to be as an author." Howells replied in a letter to Lowell of 27 December 1882 (MH; *Life in Letters*, I, 334-35): "Even if you had not advised me exactly as I wished, I believe I should have been grateful for your kindest of letters. It came in the morning, & in the afternoon I sent off my respectful refusal to President Gilman.... [¶] I think once I might have had the making of a scholar, even of a professor, in me, but it is too late now to inquire practically, and I should only have placed myself in a false position if I had taken the place; and should have known that I was suffering justly when the shame of my failure came. There is so much bitter in every man's cup, that whatever comes, I shall always be glad to have foregone that draught. I am not afraid of the future, as long as I can stand up to it; I have known smaller things than I know now, and I can go back to them without a pang, if need be, of which there seems no present sign."

12 JANUARY 1883, FLORENCE, TO JAMES R. OSGOOD

Florence, Jan. 12, 1883.

My dear Osgood:

I will try to put the Niagara Revisited into better form, and send it to you for Aldrich before long.[1] I am now on the home-stretch of A Woman's Reason, and I will finish that before attempting anything else.

I am sorry that Alden is vexed about not getting the story; but I don't care to see the correspondence, for I know that of course it must be from his misunderstanding of the matter.[2] It is quite indifferent to me whether he wants the Venice papers or not.[3] I find it difficult to warm up the old mood in which I used to write of Italy, and I can readily turn the result of my proposed sojourn in Venice to account in the way of fiction or history.

I enclosed you a letter to Pres't Gilman some days ago declining the Professorship.[4]

I'm glad the M. I. is starting up again.[5] Harpers sold 15000 of *Anne* by Miss Woolson. So Anne told me herself.[6]

Yours ever
W. D. Howells.

1. See Howells to Osgood, 5 August 1882, n. 1. In a letter of 12 December 1882 (MH) to Howells, Osgood reported that H. M. Alden had declined "Niagara Revisited" because "it appealed only (or rather chiefly) to the people who had read 'Their Wedding Journey,'" but that Aldrich had offered $300 for it.

2. See Howells to Osgood, 12 July 1882, n. 1. Osgood sold Story No. 3 (ultimately *The Rise of Silas Lapham*) to the *Century*, and H. M. Alden was disgruntled at not getting the serial story for *Harper's*, as Osgood wrote Howells on 12 December 1882, offering his correspondence with Alden. In subsequent letters the development of this matter can be traced. "I saw Alden of Harpers' Mag. the other day, and that affair is all right and pleasant, if his assurances may be accepted" (Osgood to Howells, 24 January 1883 [MH]). "You say nothing about the Harpers and their feeling. Did you succeed in bringing Alden to a better mind?" (Howells to Osgood, 28 January 1883 [MH]). "The Harper matter is all right now. I saw Alden at the Century meeting last month and we made our peace" (Osgood to Howells, 23 February 1883 [MH]).

3. See Howells to Osgood, 16 October 1882, n. 1.

4. See Howells to Osgood, 16 and 24 December 1882, n. 1.

5. In his letter of 10 January 1883 (MH) to Howells, Osgood wrote that *A Modern Instance* "is moving steadily though not very rapidly. We are now nearly through with the 7th thousand."

6. Constance Fenimore Woolson's juvenile book *The Old Stone House* (1872) had been published under the pseudonym "Anne March." Her novel *Anne* (1882) was published under her own name. Miss Woolson spent the winter of 1882–1883 in Florence.

28 JANUARY 1883, FLORENCE, TO WILLIAM C. HOWELLS

Hotel Minerva,
Florence, Jan. 28, 1883.

Dear father:

I let last Sunday slip without writing you, and as usual the week went by without my overtaking the neglected duty. It has been a very busy week of society, and I have had to do it all, for Elinor has been housed for the last ten days by a recurrence of the erysipelas in her nose from which she suffered in Switzerland; it's quite well now; but Winny is still half an invalid, and I get little or no help from her. I went with her to a large dancing party last Monday night, where she danced till two o'clock in the morning, and from which she has not yet recovered. I wish her to enjoy herself as other young girls do, but she has very little courage, and it is hard to know whether it is better to urge her or not.— During the rest of the week, I was out every night or afternoon but one; I find myself fatally well known, and I have a suspicion that my books have been at least heard of along with the British drumbeat. Of course it's a pleasure to have people wanting to see me, but it's a vain and empty one—the very most insubstantial of all pleasures, I think; and this is what I so long longed for! I have an apparently equal currency in English and American circles, here; and the other night I met a Berlin critic, who has written about my books, and who told me they were known to all the English-reading Germans.[1]—At the same dinner there was a young Englishman who had lived eight years in Canada, part of the time at Toronto, and who knew the Jarvises very well—a Mr. Grazebrook.[2]

The children, John and Pil, are getting on well, and John is finding great advantage from his travels. He really takes hold of everything in the most intelligent way, and makes a pretty full record, with pen and pencil, of what he sees. He tugs away valiantly at his Latin meantime. Pil has found a circle of little girls, and is very happy with them and her sacred subjects in art. We found yesterday that she had been treating the Resurrection of Christ: the tomb with the Angel and the Evangelist at the Door, and the Savior within. Her brain teems with these ideas.

Elinor is going to write you a regular volume of a letter soon. In the meantime I send this chip—dry and thin—with our joint love to all.

Your affectionate son
Will.

Better address all letters in care of Gillig's Exchange (American) 449 Strand London

1. The Berlin critic was presumably Heinrich Homberger. See Howells to Boyesen, 21 November 1878, n. 4.
2. The Jarvises and Mr. Grazebrook have not been identified.

5 FEBRUARY 1883, FLORENCE, TO WILLIAM C. HOWELLS

Florence, Feb. 5, 1883.

Dear father:

I was distressed to read of poor Sam's accident, in the Sentinel,[1] and I have written to him; but I suppose that in a time like this he will need some little extra comforts; and if you think so too I wish you would draw on J. R. Osgood & Co. for $50, and send it to Sam. I think it would be better to come as from you.

We were all at a masquerade carnival ball last week at one of the theatres, and last night we were to have gone to the great ball given by the Florentine nobility to the strangers; but Winny's strength failed her at the last moment. She is not so well as we hoped she would be; in fact she has rather lost ground since we came to Florence; so that next Sunday we shall go either to Rome or to Siena for a change, returning here for the month of March.

The masquerade which we attended was in a theatre; and in order to spur John up to some gayety his uncle Larkin[2] and I put on masks and dominoes and joined the party again. They all found us out except Winny who did not know us till we unmasked. By this time John was so stirred up that he wanted to spend the rest of the night in disguise. He is suffering from a combination of propriety and curiosity that makes him very amusing. But he is getting on well with his studies and is taking in education at every pore.

Except Winny we all keep very well; but we have no news. All join in love to all.

Your aff'te son,
Will.

1. The *Sentinel* of 13 January 1883 contains a report of Sam's having fallen from a hay wagon four days earlier, severely spraining his right foot and leg. "He has been suffering greatly from his wound," the account reads, "and may be laid up for some time."
2. Larkin G. Mead, Jr.

9 FEBRUARY 1883, FLORENCE, TO JAMES R. OSGOOD

Florence, Feb. 9, 1883.

My dear Osgood:

I have yours of Jan. 24, and I will try to tell you what my plans are, so far as I understand them. I have now made a pretty good study of Florence, which I shall return to complete in March, after having been to Pisa, Pistoja, Lucca, Leghorn and Siena and Areggo, the other Tuscan cities which I intend to include in the series.[1] We start on this round on Monday, and when we get back I expect to have my material well in hand; so that by the time we start for Venice the end of March, I shall be ready to work six weeks there, either on the Tuscan Cities or the new story (No. 3). I should perhaps prefer to begin on the Cities; but unless I can write those papers and get through my story by March 1st, 1884; I shall lose money on the work, for they pay me so much less than the story-writing: I had expected to sandwich them into a year's work on fiction. It may be, however, that I can work on them very rapidly, and so come out even; or perhaps I cannot get the story settled in my mind, and so w'd rather write them than lose time. I will be more definite about this later. If all things were equal of course I shd rather do the papers next.[2]

When at Venice I shall look up all the recent historical material; and as I do not expect to make a work of original research, I can write my history in America perfectly well. I now intend to return home in August (about the middle) and I *don't* intend to return to Europe *soon* again, if I can help it. At present I see no reason why we should not let the question of terms for the history rest awhile, or till we meet.[3] All that I wish you to keep in mind is that it will be two years' work for me, and that I can't undertake it unless I'm *well* paid.

As to the professorship I think very likely you're right in believing that if I could talk with Gilman I might think better of it. Perhaps we shall make some arrangement, after all. I haven't heard from him in answer to my letter.

Pennell is here, and I like him very much. He has gone to work on Florence, and I shall give him plenty of prints.[4] It is still rather cold for him to work out of doors.

Thank you for sending Wells the check.[5]—And don't think me inconsistent in first asking to do the papers on the cities, and then concluding that I must write the story first. It is something that I wished to be left free about, and I'm glad that your arrangements allow me to do as I like.

What about the Library of Humor? Is that wholly abandoned? Has any more material come from Clark?[6]

We have been tea-ed and dined to distraction.[7]

Yours ever
W. D. Howells.

P. S. I expect to get to England about the 2d week in June, and should be glad to find you there.

---

1. See Howells to Smith, 19 November 1882, n. 6. In a letter of 24 January 1883 (MH) to Howells, Osgood wrote: "And as to coming home: there is no need for hastening your return on account of No. 3. The Century has no intention of beginning its publication until late in 1884."
2. See Howells to Osgood, 16 October 1882, n. 1.
3. See Howells to Osgood, 16 and 24 December 1882, n. 6.
4. For preparing illustrations for *Tuscan Cities.*
5. Samuel Wells served as Howells' attorney in Boston.
6. See Howells to Clemens, 18 April 1882, n. 4.

7. In a letter of 14 January 1883 (MH) to William C. Howells, Howells wrote: "We are all getting on pretty well considering that we have had to do an amount of society since we came here that is absolutely enraging. Every moment of time, during the past week when I was not writing I was driving about with Elinor making calls and drinking tea with people I don't care for. But now we've put our foot down, and for this week at least the thing is at an end. I can't tell you how vexatious a burden this silliness has been in every way.—I am swinging along towards the close of my story [*A Woman's Reason*], and I hope to have it done in a fortnight, but I have run great risk of spoiling it by fooling round in society when I ought to have been thinking of it." See also Howells to Clemens, 10 February 1883 (CU; *Twain-Howells*, p. 425).

4 MARCH 1883, SIENA, TO WILLIAM C. HOWELLS

Siena, March 4, 1883.

Dear father:

I don't know exactly what to make of a letter of Vic's following yesterday, hard upon those you wrote reporting the satisfactory arrangement of your affairs at Washington: she speaks as if you might still have to give up your place on acc't of the separation of the house and consulate, and says you intend to go into Sam's farm. But perhaps she only wrote from some mood of temporary discouragement.[1]—We all rejoice in the grape-scissors, on which you ought to make money; when the models come, I'll see if it can be patented here. If you can get some man with capital to go in with you at home, I should think it would be better than to try to manage it yourself. By the way, Mark Twain has a taste for patent rights; and if he hasn't got too badly bit with some of his recent speculations he might like to take hold of your grape-scissors.[2] When you're ready it may be worth while to mention the matter to him.

We have no news beyond what Elinor has written. With love to all,

Your aff'te son,
Will.

1. The cause of W. C. Howells' recent concern appears in Howells' letter to his father, 14 January 1883 (MH): "Aurelia has written me about the worry you were feeling in regard to the visit of the Consulate Inspector and his subsequent letter about your having the house and consulate together. I suppose that long before this letter can reach you you will have ceased to care for the matter, and I am sorry that you should have worried over it at all. Their not replying to your letter means nothing but the brutal inattention with which consuls are always treated by the department; and I shouldn't dream of resigning, even if they cut off your whole allowance for office-rent. The place would still be a good one; and now that the civil service bill is passed, it will be yours, I suppose, for life."

2. Clemens was at this time trying to raise capital for the Paige typesetting machine, his latest speculation. In a letter of 12 August 1883 (CU) Howells asked Clemens if he wished to join in the promotion of the grape scissors, which Howells' father had invented and patented, and Clemens gave a conditional response.

The manufacturing and marketing plans are mentioned in several letters addressed to W. C. Howells, and on 17 December 1883 (MH) Howells reported that Charles L. Webster, Clemens' nephew, had put the scissors in the hands of a manufacturer who had agreed "to make several gross of the scissors, advertise them and put them in the trade, and then report...how they take." The manufacturer was Peter Lowentraut of Newark, New Jersey. Charles L. Webster (1851–1891), a husband of Clemens' niece, Annie Moffett, was employed by Clemens as an agent in 1881 and made manager in 1884 of Charles L. Webster & Co., the New York publishing company Clemens had established for publishing his books. See *Twain-Howells*, pp. 436–38, 920.

4 MARCH 1883, SIENA, TO CHARLES D. WARNER

Siena, March 4, 1883.

My dear Warner:

If I were not dead to shame I sh'd now be feeling a lively self-reproach for neglecting your kind letter so long. It reached me in the midst of a foolish round of "pleasure" in Florence which almost spoiled my business there, and has kept me hard at work here for the last month trying to "catch up." Siena is a good place to work, but that is the least of its merits. It is the most medieval town Ive ever seen, not excepting Quebec, and is almost as picturesque as Quebec. For the last three days, however, it has been giving us a tramontane[1] unexampled out of Hartford: it makes me feel as if I were at Mark Twain's with my handkerchief in my hand to keep those steel door knobs from snapping all my elictricity out of me.

But the cold pressure in regard to Thackeray and Dickens, which prevailed all over the region of my pericardium at the time you wrote, has quite passed away. I don't know how you ever got the notion that I was going to hurry to "explain" what I said, unless it was from that extraordinary and unauthorized statement in the Atheneum.[2] I wrote Gosse that when I got time I should like to say my say of D. & T.; but I am far too lazy and too busy to see the hour of doing it. Sometime I think it would be amusing to go over the whole affair, not omitting special consideration of the Quarterly Reviewer, who jumps up and down with rage.[3]

Our plans are to go to Florence again for three weeks, and then to Venice, where we expect to spend April and the greater part of May. (By the way I tried to see Mrs. Harris in Florence,[4] but she was not at home.) I hope to be writing there on my Tuscan cities, and to finish up the job by the time I get home at the end of the summer. If I were at leisure I should like extremely to see something of English society; but there is little hope of that, now. I shall go to some quiet place in

England, and work hard on the Italian papers. How would Oxford do? At Cambridge I know people.

The family are all enriching themselves in experience; but I think even the insatiate Mrs. Howells is nearly satisfied. John is going to Rome with Pennell (who is to illustrate me) but the rest of us joyfully refrain. The idea of the Colosseum makes me sick, and I am satisfied that the dome of the State House is good enough for me. I wish I could see it, this minute. John Hay and his wife were a week with us in Florence, and again in Siena. The young Baron Rothschild has taken a fancy to Clarence King (as if that man had not luck enough already!) and wants to live with him.[5] Mrs. Howells joins me in love to both of you.

Yours ever,
W. D. Howells.

1. Italian for "north wind."

2. See Howells to Gosse, 16 November 1882, n. 1 and n. 2.

3. The reviewer of "American Novels" in the *London Quarterly Review*, January 1883, had asserted that Howells simply "has no story to tell" and has no characters that are memorable. He felt that the narrative of *A Modern Instance* could be summarized in ten lines. "When an author has written half-a-dozen novels and a few odd plays, without the vestige of a plot in one of them, and not enough in all of them combined to make the foundation of a child's story, then it is quite obvious that a theory to account for and justify his style of art is no more than we have a right to expect."

4. Mrs. Harris has not been identified.

5. Howells' letter of 10 February 1883 (CU; *Twain-Howells*, p. 425) to Clemens indicates John Hay as the source of the story about King and Rothschild. Lionel Walter Rothschild (1868–1937), second baron, of the English branch of the great banking family, was a member of Parliament (1899–1910) and the author of a number of zoological treatises.

13 MARCH 1883, FLORENCE, TO THOMAS S. PERRY

Florence, March 13, 1883.

My dear Perry:

I am delighted to hear of the book, and I hope it will reach me while I'm still in Florence, so that I may be able to show it to Carl Hillebrand, whom I have met.[1] I have also met here Dr. Homberger, who wrote so kindly of my books in the *Rundschau* and the *Mag. für die Lit. des Auslandes*,[2] and I shall want to send him yours. I hope it will have the luck it merits, and I trust for your own sake that you have touched the British lion,—who seems to have been born, like Prince Leopold, without a cuticle,[3]—in such a way as to make him roar. It is only necessary to have insinuated that all English novels are not perfection. One of my London friends actually asked me if I didn't hate Thackeray and Dickens because they were English! But I don't consider the English clamor over that business so shameful as that of our own people, who are clearer-witted (really) and ought not to have been so stupid as to misunderstand what I really said in the paper on H. J.[4]

Your kind words are not the less welcome because—to my own surprise—I have been scarcely if at all troubled by the row about me, and have been chiefly vexed because it includes James.[5] As to what I've done in novels I'm not alarmed: my only trouble is about what I shall do hereafter.

We are back here after three weeks in Siena, which is a most fascinating old town, and medieval to the marrow of its bones. I think that there one really conceives of a little Italian Republic, and what it was like. When I fairly consider of it, I'm glad not to be a little Italian Republican. But all this remains for print.

I wish you could have scraped me up a little news, if there is any in Boston. We have done a great deal of society in Florence; but this time we shall keep out of it, partly because it interferes with the proper business of sight-seeing. I have been turning over a good many books, and putting myself in rapport with Italy again. But I'm not sure that it pays. After all, *we* have the country of the present and the future.

Yours ever,
W. D. Howells.

1. Perry's book was *English Literature in the Eighteenth Century* (1883). Karl Hillebrand (1829–1884) was a German journalist and historian.
2. See Howells to Boyesen, 21 November 1878, n. 4.
3. This reference remains obscure.
4. See Howells to Gosse, 16 November 1882, n. 1, and Howells to Osgood, 16 and 24 December 1882, n. 4.
5. In a letter of 27 November 1882 to Howells (MH; *James Letters*, II, 391–92) Henry James mentioned "the little breeze produced . . . by the *November* Century" and added: "You are accused of having sacrificed—in your patriotic passion for the works of H. J. jr—*Vanity Fair* & *Henry Esmond* to *Daisy Miller* & *Poor Richard!* The indictment is rubbish . . . . When I say 'you are accused' all I mean to allude to is a nasty little paragraph in the *World* which accuses Warner you & me of being linked in the most drivelling mutual admiration . . . ."

26 MARCH 1883, FLORENCE, TO WILLIAM C. HOWELLS

Florence, March 26, 1883.

Dear father:

Aurelia's long letter came to hand yesterday, and I was sorry to hear that any of you had been troubled by the newspaper assaults on me.[1] My work is no worse than it was when all those fellows were praising it, and this storm does not hurt me commercially; so I hope you wont pay any attention to it. Some time or other the tide had to turn against me, having run in my favor so long; and I am not in the least discouraged, any more than I was formerly encouraged. If I can be sure of health and quiet, I am not afraid of all the asses who have misunderstood what I said about Thackeray. A good deal of their clamor is spite, and much of it is, as you know, mere paragraphing. In the meantime, the *Revue de Deux Mondes*, of Paris, really the highest literary authority in the world, gives 20 pages to careful analysis and unstinted praise of my books.[2] But it is all nothing, one way or the other.

I am curious to know what you expect to do about Sam's farm. It seems a great pity that he should buy into any sort of printing business in Cleveland till he knew something practically about its value. But perhaps it isn't possible for him to get a situation without investing. I'm sorry for him, and for you; but it is no worse for you now than it was when you were supporting Sam out of the office.[3]

Our stay in Florence is drawing to a close, for before this reaches you we will have started for Venice. I suppose I shall settle down to work there for a while: because I have no time to lose, what with the Italian papers I'm to write, and the story which I'm to complete by the 1st of next March.[4]

—This is Easter, and it has been duly celebrated by Pillà and John. By the way John got back last Tuesday from Rome, where he had a good time, worthy of the old Romans, themselves. I suppose that no human boy ever saw more in a week than he did; and he has gained very much intellectually. As for Pillà, she simply draws from morning till night: we save her drawings; they are really wonderful.[5]

Winny is somewhat better; but she does no sight-seeing, and since we came back, we have done no society in Florence. We have a very pretty apartment, but Elinor and I have both suffered from terrible colds since our return. All join me in love to all.

> Your aff'te son
> **Will.**

Give our regards to the Griffiths. I shall write him soon.[6]

1. A reference to the critical storm caused by Howells' comments on Dickens and Thackeray.

2. "Les Nouveau Romanciers Américains," *Revue des Deux Mondes* (31 January 1883), by "Th. Bentzon," Mme. Marie Thérèse de Solms Blanc (1840–1907), a French novelist and critic, at the time Mme. Fentryn.

3. One of Howells' continuing burdens was his brother Sam's and his father's incompetence and financial irresponsibility. Undoubtedly Sam's farm had been largely financed by his father. Howells' letter of 1 April 1883 (MH) also reveals concern over his father's having told the State Department of his intention to resign

in June: "Of course you know the ground better than I do; but I had hoped that you would keep the Consulate as long as you could." And he added, referring to his father's plan to settle on a farm in Virginia: "I suppose the James River farm scheme is not a finality, and that one need not consider it too seriously, if Joe still has the Sentinel to sell as a preliminary. But it looks to me very much like a repetition of the happy experiment at Eureka, with your increased years, and Joe's invalidism to contribute to its success." Despite his son's warning, W. C. Howells did move to Virginia in late May or early June 1883, although not accompanied by Joe. See Howells to W. C. Howells, 3 June 1883, n. 2. Howells had very unhappy memories of the failure of his father's experiment in communal enterprise when the family lived at Eureka Mills. See Howells to W. C. Howells, 16 February 1873, n. 7.

4. For the Italian sketches, see Howells to Smith, 19 November 1882, n. 6. For the unwritten novel, see Howells to Osgood, 16 and 24 December 1882, n. 3, and *The Rise of Silas Lapham*, HE, pp. xi-xiii.

5. A selection of the ten-year-old Mildred's Italian drawings was published as *A Little Girl Among the Old Masters* (1883) with introduction and comment by Howells.

6. The Griffith family has not been identified.

3 APRIL 1883, FLORENCE, TO EDMUND W. GOSSE

Florence, April 3, 1883.

My dear Gosse:

"I am very guilty before you," as the people say in the translations of Tourguénief; but I will not also be tedious in apology. If I had written you as often as I wished to write, you would now be in possession of several volumes of my letters, in wh. I sh'd have committed myself in all sorts of ways.—We are again in Florence after three weeks in the Middle Ages at Siena, and we are finding our own era rather pleasant. Before we went we had called upon everybody, and now we have a good conscience in calling on no one. With little odds and ends of sight-seeing, and with a heavy cold apiece, four weeks have gone swiftly enough, and we are thinking even of setting our faces northward. I suppose we shall be a month or six weeks in Venice, where I must put in some hard work on my Tuscan Cities; and then we shall get back where you can "heave half a brick at me," if you like. Your notion of going down into some woods with me to see Thomas Hardy is something to my own soul's delight, and yet—I may as well be honest, for once—I may possibly have no time in England at all. I am torn between two homesicknesses: the longing for America, and the desire to stay in Italy. So I may bang about here, and then go home with a rush. Of course, London is the great world, and I would like to see more of it; but I can understand the case of Englishmen who are willing to live in Italy, and eke that of Americans. A friend of mine, a Cornell professor has just taken a villa outside of Porta Sta. Croce, for five years, and goes home to morrow to return with bag and baggage.[1] I drove out with him yesterday to see his villa: an absurdly beautiful splendid and historical affair which he gets *furnished* for £14 @ year! It is enough to make one forswear one's country. And then Florence is hardly a foreign city, if you seek its English or American life at all; but *as* a foreign city is full of literary advantages, wh. one hardly realizes without coming here. Why not colonize it? You get Hardy and Tadema and Thornycroft,[2] and some other literary fellows as good as yourself, and I will bring Mark Twain and Aldrich and John Hay, and Osgood shall come over and publish for us.—By the way, I heard with regret from Deschamps[3] that Tadema was not well, and that he was coming south for his health. Does that mean he is coming to Italy? I did greatly hope to see him again, before I returned to America, and I wish that it might be in Italy.

We have not met the Middlemores,[4] for they have been all the winter in Rome, where the Doctor warned us not to go with Winny. She has had in slight degree a recurrence of her nervous prostration, and he said she was almost sure to take the fever.—I enclose a fotograf of medallion which my brother-in-law, Mead, has made of me. I think it is an extremely good likeness. Mrs. Howells has no fotograf of herself; but if she ever gets one she will remember that you kindly askt for it.—How much we should both like to see you both again! You are London, you are England to us! You and the Tademas. Receive, my Gosse, what they call a stretto di mano,[5] down here, from your vero amico di cuore,[6] and with Mrs. Howells's love to Mrs Gosse, believe me

Affectionately yours
W. D. Howells.

1. The Cornell professor has not been identified.
2. William Hamo Thornycroft (1850–1925), a sculptor and intimate friend of Gosse.
3. Probably Pierre Charles Ernest Deschamps (b. 1821), a French bibliographer. Louis Henri Deschamps (1846–1902), French painter, is also a possibility.
4. Samuel George Chetwynd Middlemore was a British art critic; Maria Trinidad Howard Sturgis Middlemore was a collector of songs and legends. Howells had met them the previous year at the Gosses'.
5. Italian for "handshake."
6. Italian for "true friend of the heart."

5 APRIL 1883, FLORENCE, TO THOMAS R. LOUNSBURY

Florence, April 5, 1883.

My dear Lounsbury:

It was extremely kind and thoughtful of you to send me that friendly editorial from the Tribune; but I valued your letter infinitely more.[1]

I have known somewhat imperfectly that the scalping-knife of aboriginal criticism had been unsheathed for me; but I have not heard all the yells; and you give me the idea of something really blood-curdling. This is one advantage of distance: on most other accounts I think I would rather have spent the last year in America, for Europe is more interesting the first time, and I have had to unite Ethiopian servitude with Epicurean enjoyment: I brought a half-finished novel with me.[2] There is no danger of my answering the onslaughts upon my books, for God made me, if not wise, lazy, and I have undertaken already much more work than I like to do. Of course, some of the outcries have tempted me; they did invite response, I own, for they were very funny; but I have no time, and as you say they wont hurt me. There is only one man I'm afraid of: I know he lies in wait to write me down some day, and that he is capable of any sort of wrong: I refer to your poor, obliged friend W. D. Howells. As for the others, let them rage. I don't pretend that I'm not most humbly glad and grateful for any kindness that people feel for me on account of my books; I am so with all my heart, for every man feels his solitude in the world, and likes to hear that he has unknown friends. When the assurance of this kindness comes from such a man as you, there are no words to welcome it fitly.

I have read reviews of your Cooper, and I should like exceedingly to see the book;[3] but there is little hope of this till I am at home again. Warner wrote enthusiastically about the life; and I can fancy your enjoyment in treating so robust and vivid a figure. At the same time, I don't see how you got time for it.

Your question as to why I write no more of those little verses went to my heart. Once I thought my self a poet! Certainly my thoughts ran naturally in rhyme, and I do believe that I had formerly a pretty knack of just expressing a poetic emotion and then letting it alone. Sometimes I have hoped that when I got into quieter waters, and did not have to work so hard for my daily pound-cake, I might recover the spacious moods in which I used to do those things. But the time has not come yet. I wish it had, and I thank you for remembering that I *could* do them once.

This is a swash of egotism from beginning to end; but you boldly tempted me to talk about myself! If ever you get tired of the world and its pomps and vanities, go to Siena. That is the best thing left in Italy: it is the Middle-Ages a little shrunken in their shell, but the very Middle-Ages. We were there three weeks—worth our three months in Florence.

Yours ever
W. D. Howells.

1. Lounsbury's letter has not survived, but the friendly editorial was an article in the New York *Weekly Tribune*, 21 March 1883, defending James and Howells against the attacks made upon them because of Howells' praise of James in his article "Henry James, Jr." "The unfortunate remark about the methods of Thackeray and Dickens was mistaken criticism," the *Tribune* writer noted, "and we wish that Mr. Howells had not made it; but it will not bear the interpretation which many censorious persons have placed upon it, and it certainly does not account for the chorus of reckless denunciation which is suddenly raised against its author."

2. *A Woman's Reason.*

3. *James Fenimore Cooper* (1883), a biography in the American Men of Letters Series, which was edited by Charles D. Warner.

20 APRIL 1883, VENICE, TO JAMES R. OSGOOD

Venice, April 20, 1883.

My dear Osgood:

I found your letter of the 2d here this morning, and I had already heard from you in Florence about the time of your sailing. We expect to be in England just when you arrive, and I will send my address at once to Gillig,[1] and ask him for yours.—The Sleeping-Car makes a very pretty little book, and I hope it may do as handsome as it looks.[2] There is no hurry about Niagara Revisited; I can decide what to do with it when I see you.[3]—I'm sorry that A Mod. Inst. doesn't sell faster, and I hope that at least half your theory is right.[4]

By the way, did you every get a box for me, from Vevey, (in Switzerland), containing some antique pewter flagons and platters? It was sent last Dec., but you have never said anything of it, tho' I've twice specially enquired. I sent you the bill, to show at the Custom House. Perhaps it went to N. Y. *Please* look it up, and write me.

I think I shall certainly wish to write of Venice again; but it will be next year, after I've finished the third story.[5] I'm going to rush work on the Tuscan Cities, whilst I'm here, and hope to have finished the papers on Florence before I leave. That will let them run them in the magazine from November on.[6] Pennell got a letter the other day from the Art Editors of the C., telling him to get fotografs of old masterpieces, to be introduced as illustrations. I *don't want them.* I want life and character, past and present. I don't know anything ab't art and shall not avoidably speak of it. Do make them understand this, please. Mr. Gilder seemed to get my idea; but the Art Editors are all off the track.[7]

Venice is shabbier and gayer and lovelier than ever. There's a full moon to-night—But what's the use of trying to talk Venice to a man who's never been here?—When I first came out of the station on my arrival, I tho't I'd never been away. It's inexplicably, inconceivably the same. Now and then I run against an old fellow whom I knew, and they are all gray and fat.

Yours ever

W. D. Howells.

1. Gillig was the manager of the American Exchange in London.

2. In a letter of 28 January 1883 (MH) Howells suggested to Osgood that he publish in book form Howells' farce *The Sleeping Car*, previously printed in the 1882 *Harper's Christmas*. Osgood agreed to the proposal in a letter of 23 February 1883 (MH); and Howells, in a letter of 13 March 1883 (NNC) to Osgood, expressed the hope that his publisher would "do something delicate and pretty in the way of a cover for the 'Sleeping Car.'" In his reply of 2 April 1883 (MH) Osgood wrote: "We have published 'The Sleeping Car' which is well received. It is too early yet to judge of the sale, but it ought to prove a good summer-book. We sent you 6 copies the other day—I hope its Execution will please you."

3. "Niagara Revisited" was about to appear in the *Atlantic*, after considerable doubt on Howells' part where it should be published or whether it should be published at all. See Howells to Osgood, 5 August 1882, n. 1, and 12 January 1883, n. 1. Now arrangements for book publication were being made, and Howells had written Osgood on 13 March 1883: "I suppose we had better let Houghton & Mifflin add 'Niagara Revisited' to 'Their Wedding Journey'? If yes, you can so notify them." But on 2 April 1883 Osgood replied: "Of course we shall do whatever you wish about 'Niagara Revisited', but I don't quite see why you should give it to Houghton to be added to 'Their Wedding Journey'—certainly not without consideration. Why not keep it to make part of a new volume bye-and-bye? Cannot this matter rest until we meet?"

4. In his letter of 2 April 1883 Osgood commented: "'Modern Instance' has not quite reached 8000 yet, but is near it. It is a marvel that a novel so much talked about has not sold double that number: my only theory about it is that while everybody recognizes its strong qualities, the novel-reading class does not find it agreeable. 'A Woman's Reason' will suit them better."

5. The Venetian papers were never written; the "third story" was *The Rise of Silas Lapham*.

6. "A Florentine Mosaic," *Century*, February, April, and June 1885.

7. Richard W. Gilder had written Howells on 24 February 1883 (MH): "The Tuscan Cities idea is excellent; but I wish to explain about the *Art* side. The idea was that perons [sic] or events, or scenes named by you should be illustrated—Where convenient by the portraits by old masters, & their pictures. That is all." Alexander W. Drake was the art editor of *Scribner's* and its successor, the *Century* (1870–1916).

22 APRIL 1883, VENICE, TO WILLIAM C. HOWELLS

Venice, April 22, 1883.

Dear father:

I suppose this date must look as strange and as familiar to you as it does to me, and no doubt your mind will go back to the letters of twenty years ago which used to bear it. Probably no other place on earth —or in the sea—has changed so little during that time as Venice; and when I stept out of the station the other afternoon, it seemed as if I had never been away. As yet I have met few people whom I knew, but gradually I shall look them up. We visited our old home in Palazzo Giustinian yesterday, and found it turned into glass-works—beads, mosaics, etc.; but Casa Falier is still used as a tenement, and we hope to show Winny the room where she was born. The city seems to me a little shabbier than it used to be, and the ragged and dirty poverty that one sees everywhere is disheartening. But they say there is more commerce than formerly, and that the fortunes of the place are reviving. As yet they are not visible to the naked eye. John went with me on a walk back of Rialto today, and was dismayed by the misery and squalor everywhere. Around the Square of St. Mark's there is a little galvanic gaiety, and we do not let Winny go away from that. As yet, she is in a romantic rapture with the place. The sea-air does her good, and the novel beauty fills her romantic soul. I begin to understand what an intensely poetic nature she has, and that she suffers, or enjoys as her poetic sense is starved or gratified. It appears now that she cared nothing for Florence, while Venice is a constant delight to her.

This afternoon we went out to the Armenian Convent, and saw our dear old friend Padre Giacomo.[1] I had Pilla and John with me, and they both fell in love with the place and with him. When he came to the cloisters, he stooped down and put his arm round Pilla, and said, "This is a part of the Convent where we never allow ladies: what are you going to do?" She hung her head and he gave her a little hug: "You must say, But I'm only a little girl," and then he took her hand and led her into the forbidden bounds. He gave her a book about the Armenian rite, and she is reading it so as to be able to draw Armenian saints.

We expect to be here a month, so as to let me get fairly to work on my Tuscan papers,[2] and to let Winny have the benefit of the sea-air whilst it seems to be doing her good. Before we left Florence she was losing the habit of sleep, but here she sleeps eleven hours at night.

The town is very full of strangers, and one meets English and Americans at every step in the Piazza. For me it is very strange to be here as a tourist, where I used to live, and I half-resent the anomaly. But I would live here again for four years on hardly any conditions short of owner-ship of the city—and then I should be afraid it would fall on my hands.

All join me in love to all.

Your aff'te son,
Will.

---

1. Padre Giacomo Issaverdanz was a brother in the Armenian convent at San Lazzaro and a friend of the Howells family. See Woodress, *Howells & Italy*, p. 157, and *Venetian Life*, pp. 194–206.
2. *Tuscan Cities.*

22 APRIL 1883, VENICE, TO SAMUEL L. CLEMENS

Venice, April 22, 1883.

My dear Clemens:

I enclose a letter just come from the Madison Sq. Theatre people, with a note which you can forward if you like.[1] If you can get the right terms from them, with absolute surety, as to pay in the event of success, it would be worth our while to give the month of October to working on that play. There is the making of a good comedy in it without any doubt—something that would run like Scheherazade, for A Thousand and One Nights. But they ought to be made to understand that we could not fool away a month's time for nothing: I for my part should want to be assured a Thousand Dollars, whether they ever put the play on the stage or not. Then if they did produce it, the grand cash should be ours. Please let me know whether you write them, and if you do, what, and with what result.

There was a Prince Edwards Island woman in our pension at Siena, who was of Sienese origin, and had returned to her native city after twenty years' misery in the British Provinces. She had brought from our hemisphere two books: the Bible and—Roughing It; which she appeared to think equally inspired and binding. When we told her that we knew you, the effect was much as if we had said we knew St. Mathew.

I give you the bare bones of a fact, on which I'll enlarge when we meet. She said she often took the book—Roughing It—and showed the pictures to her Italian friends.

You wont expect me to say anything about Venice, merely because I'm here, will you? The idea of being here is benumbing and silencing. I feel like the Wandering Jew, or the ghost of the Cardiff Giant.[2] I used sometimes to dream of having come back, but nothing was ever so strange as this reality, for it isn't strange at all—so far as I'm able to express it.[3]

Winny, who had been drooping in Florence, and getting so that she could not sleep, has recovered in her native air as if by magic; she takes the deadly romantic view of Venice, and doesn't hesitate to tell me that I did the place great injustice in my books. It is quite amusing. She thinks it is *all* beauty and gayety; but for my part, the poor old place is forlorner and shabbier than ever. I don't think I began to see the misery of it when I lived here. The rags and dirt I witnessed in a walk this morning sickened me.

All join in regards to you all.

Yours ever
W. D. H.

1. On 6 April 1883 (CU) M. H. Mallory had written to Howells that a letter to Clemens had brought no response and that he would greatly prefer to arrange the matter entirely with Howells. He added: "Frankly, I need, and am anxious to attach your name to the Madison Square Theatre. I say 'need' because I am trying to keep only American plays on my stage and so need American writers, 'anxious' because not only had your name been partially announced, but I must see my way ahead. There is no doubt I can pay you as much as or more than you ever received for any literary work." Clemens forwarded Howells' letter, adding that he wished to wait with the play until Howells' return from Europe. See Howells to Clemens, 1 September 1882, n. 7, and *Twain-Howells*, p. 431.

2. According to legend, a farmer near Cardiff, New York, had dug up a giant petrified man in 1869.

3. Howells drew on this experience in his characterization of Colville in *Indian Summer*, just as Winny's romantic view of Venice, mentioned in the next paragraph, went into his presentation of Imogene Graham in the same novel.

20 MAY 1883, VERONA, TO WILLIAM C. HOWELLS

Verona, May 20, 1883.

Dear father:

I don't wonder you complain of the dryness of my letters: they are so dry that they bore me in the act of writing them; and I should think that you would be almost glad to get none at all. But Elinor will write in a few days, and at Venice she did write a long letter; only she wrote it to Annie instead of you. Perhaps Annie sent it to you.—We left Venice on Friday, and we expect to be here till next Thursday at least,[1] and then push on to Paris, reaching London about the first of June. We have nearly made up our minds that as it is impossible for me to write when we are travelling or briefly sojourning, it will be better for us to go home a month sooner; but we haven't changed our passage yet. When we reach Boston I will settle the family, and as soon as I have got a grip on my winter's work I will come to see you in your sunny Southern home.[2] I suppose I shall have to ride up to your gate on a clay-bank horse, and wait in the saddle till you come out with a cob-pipe in your mouth, and call off the dogs, and ask me if I won't 'light. Of course you'll call me Stranger, and I dare say we shall both feel strange enough.—I am answering your letter of April 29, and I shall send this to Joe, not knowing how else to reach you, in this rapid march of your events. I have no doubt you will be very comfortable and happy in Virginia, and I have great hopes of the grape-snuffers as a source of ways and means for you.[3]—Just what my own business future is to be after March 1, '84, I don't know till I see Osgood. He is to meet me in London at the end of June, and then we shall have a talk.—In the meantime we are here in Verona, after a thoroughly idle month in Venice, as far as I was concerned. But it did Winny a great deal of good, and I saw a sort of life there that I never dreamt of—a social life. I told you of the **Crown Princess of Germany,** in my last.[4] On Tuesday Winny and I went on board an **English** steamer where the Princess of Montenegro, the **Princesses Windisgratsch,** the Countesses Mocenigo, and half a dozen other "thrones, principalities and powers,"[5] who had read Venetian Life, had been asked to meet me. It was all very droll. Winny was magnificently dressed, and beat all the crowned heads at a game of tossing quoits into a bucket.

—I wish you were here to look out with us on the rushing Adige, or I were with you to gaze upon the placid James—I don't care much which. All join me in love to all.

**Your aff'te son
Will.**

1. Howells left Venice on 18 May 1883, expected to remain in Verona until 24 May, but did not leave until 29 May.
2. See Howells to W. C. Howells, 26 March 1883, n. 3, and 3 June 1883, n. 2.
3. See Howells to W. C. Howells, 4 March 1883, n. 2.
4. At the request of Katharine Browne, the wife of the prominent American lawyer Causten Browne, Howells attended a reception on 5 April for the German Crown Prince Frederick William and his wife, Victoria Adelaide Mary Louise (1840–1901), the oldest daughter of Queen Victoria. See Katharine Browne to Howells, n.d. (MH), and Howells to W. C. Howells, 6 May 1883 (MH; *Life in Letters,* I, 341–42).
5. Windischgrätz and Mocenigo were Austrian and Venetian noble families, respectively. For the quotation, see Milton's *Paradise Lost,* bk. 3, l. 320.

3 JUNE 1883, PARIS, TO WILLIAM C. HOWELLS

Paris, June 3, 1883.

Dear father:

We left Verona on Tuesday, and after a day in Milan, came on to Basle in Switzerland, where we spent Thursday and Friday nights. It is a beautiful city, full of shade, and pleasant looking homes; but our hearts were all sick for Italy. Elinor and I have quite changed our minds about the Italians: we now think them not only very sympathetic and brilliant, but really and thoroughly good-hearted. Their patriotism is something pathetic, and they make daily sacrifices for their country that render all we do for ours ridiculous in comparison. We miss their gentleness, their sweet manners, their daily kindness, and I suppose we are going home more or less spoiled, in this respect. After Verona, Boston! What a contrast! But Boston it must be, and we all recognize that the right thing is the best.—Yesterday we started from Basle at 9.15 and reached Paris at 7.30. It was a very quick run, and we only made some half-dozen stops, so that we were very tired when we got here. Paris is very full, on acc't of the races, and we tried at two hotels before we got in. But we are very comfortable, now, at the Hotel de Rivoli, opposite the Tuilleries Garden, and we expect to stay here a week. Then we go to London, *and sail July 5,* having succeeded, after all, in getting our passage changed from August.—We found our friend Mrs. Fairchild and her children here,[1] and Pil and John are very happy. Winny continues pretty well, and I think we shall all enjoy Paris.

There isn't much news to write you, and I have such a broken up mind about your whereabouts that I should hardly know how to write it if there were.[2] I will send this letter to Joe, and I hope it wont reach you in Virginia on as hot a day as it leaves me in Paris.

All join me in love to all.

Your aff'te son,
Will.

1. Howells' Belmont neighbors, 1878–1882.
2. According to Mildred Howells, her grandfather "first hired a farm in Goochland County, and in 1884 he bought one at Westham, Henrico County, on the James River near Richmond, where with characteristic optimism he planted a vineyard, peach and pear orchards, and made a carp pond. The farming part of the venture proved a failure, and he retired with his family to Jefferson, Ohio." See *Life in Letters,* I, 340.

21 JUNE 1883, HAY, TO WILLIAM C. HOWELLS

Swan Hotel,
Hay, June 21, 1883.

Dear father:

You see I have kept my promise at last, and am here in your birthplace.[1] I came down this morning from London thro' lovely English country—Swindon, Gloucester, and Hereford—and among the first low hills of the Welsh border. The Hay lies in the lap of these, on the banks of the pretty Wye, a shallow stream, turbid with recent rains. It is made up chiefly of low, stone houses on winding, crooked streets, with here and there a handsomer and larger dwelling. Hay Castle, where I have been to call for information about the local births and deaths, is a fine old Norman pile, just back of the town. But I will send you a pamphlet giving you all the history and topography, and will come at once to business. In the bookstore where I stopped to buy it, I told the wife of the owner that my great-grandfather once owned a flannel mill here,[2] and she said, "O, then this must be the place," and when I returned later, her husband took me back of the store up into the old factory, which you'll be amused to know is now a printing-office—book and job in a small way. It has deep stone walls, and is very strongly built, but is not of imposing size: about as big as your Toronto house. Mr Harden thinks there could never have been power looms in it.—His wife told me that this inn was kept by people of the name of Howells, and though I had taken a room at the other hotel, I came here on that account. I have my doubts of the bed, but one must do something for one's ancestors, and the landlady is a very nice and pleasant old body, with whom I've had some talk. Her husband, John Howells, died last year; they were first from Peterschurch, near here, but have been a long time in Hay. She says she remembers your Aunt Swetman very well: a spry, sharp little old lady, who lived and died a Quaker; some of her children and grand-children, the Trustils are still in the region.[3]—In the churchyard I find the graves of three of our name, and Watkenses *galore*, but so far I haven't found your grandfather's last resting-place. The Quaker chapel here was torn down only last year, but it had no churchyard. Canon Bevan,[4] of the Castle, has promised to look up the records with me to-morrow, and then I shall write you again, and in the morning, I'm to interview a very historical barber,[5] who is said to embody all the information about the past of the town and its inhabitants. So far, our ancestry does not impress me as so splendid as our posterity will probably be. It seems to have been a plain, decent, religious-minded ancestry enough, and I wish its memory well, but I'm glad on the whole not to be part of it— in fact to be above ground in America. Our landlady's daughter, by the way, has just gone out to Paisely in Ontario, with her husband, to farm. At Hay there is apparently no sort of manufacturing business, now; and the bridge-keeper told me the farms were not very rich. But it is neat, and looks not unprosperous—it looks more like an Ohio river town than anything else I can compare it to; and the drunkards on the street don't detract from the resemblance.

The people are very familiar; they bow to the stranger, and they speak upon small provocation; two of them have wished to sell me things on the streets; and the grocers' windows are full of American canned goods. Living is said to be very cheap, and if you find Virginia too dear, perhaps you will come here.—I please myself with the notion of writing my first letter to you in your latest home, from your earliest, and I hope my letter wont spoil everything by going astray.—I left the family well this morning in London, where I am almost consumed with engagements. Last night as I was quietly getting into bed came a card from Lady Rosebery for her reception and a letter from the Lord Chancellor's daughter asking me for Friday night, as her father "would be glad to make my acquaintance."[6] The night before, Lowell took me to Gladstone's reception and next week he dines me to meet swells, who it seems wish to see me.[7] Of all vanities these are the hollowest, and

I contrive in every possible way short of rudeness to avoid them; they make me acutely miserable.—But thank goodness we sail the 5th of July!—We got your first Virginia letter yesterday, and I'm delighted that you're so happy. Love to all.

Your aff'te son
Will.

1. William Cooper Howells was born in Hay, Wales, a small town on the Wye River. He was brought to the United States in 1808 by his father, Joseph Howells, who had textile mills but left them to go to the United States to seek new opportunities. See *Life in Letters*, I, 1–2, 343; Cady, *Howells*, I, 1–5.

2. Howells' great-grandfather was Thomas Howells.

3. Aunt Swetman and the Trustils have not been identified; nor have the dead Howellses and Watkenses mentioned in the following sentence.

4. William Latham Bevan (1821–1908) held the living of Hay, Breconshire (1845–1901) and was canon residentiary of St. David's Cathedral (1879–1893).

5. Mr. Games, who is mentioned in the following letter.

6. Lady Rosebery was Hannah de Rothschild (d. 1890), daughter of Baron Nathan Meyer de Rothschild of Mentmore, Buckinghamshire. She married Archibald Philip Primrose, fifth earl of Rosebery (1847–1929). Sophia M. Palmer, in a letter to Howells of 20 June 1883 (MH), mentioned Lady Rosebery's card and said that Lowell had promised to bring Howells to her place next Friday (22 June) to meet her father, Roundell Palmer (1812–1893), lord chancellor (1872–1874, 1880–1885) and first earl of Selborne. The trip to Wales prevented Howells from accepting the invitation.

7. In a letter of 19 June 1883 (MH) to Howells, Lowell invited him to dine on 26 June and reported having sent *The Undiscovered Country* to Lord Dufferin. Frederick Temple Hamilton-Temple Blackwood (1826–1902), first marquis of Dufferin and Ava, was a distinguished British diplomat and administrator. In a later letter, also dated 19 June 1883 (MH), Lowell issued another invitation: "I am dining tonight at 59 Portland Place, if you will come thither in a hansom at 10.30 & send up your name to me I will take you on to the Gladstones, who have a reception tonight."

24 JUNE 1883, LONDON, TO WILLIAM C. HOWELLS

Upper Bedford Place,
London, June 24, 1883.

Dear father:

I will resume the story of my explorations in Hay. The morning after I wrote you there, I had, to begin with, a breakfast at the Swan, of bacon, and fresh trout from the Wye. Then I went out and pumped Mr. Games, the barber, to the tune of tuppence for putting my razor in order. He remembered your Aunt Swetman, and showed me the "ironmonger's" close by where she kept her drapers' shop. He told me further that your grandfather had three mills: one where the printing office is, one "just above the Blue Boar" inn, and one "down on the Bank" (of the Wye.)

I heard later from the bookseller that the Blaneys, who kept the last, probably had some of their manufactures to sell, and I went to see. I found a quaint stone pile of buildings in a weedy enclosure on the slope by the river, and in a sort of little shop by the mill door a very friendly and sensible old woman. Dear, dear! And was I the son of that Mr. Howells? No, his great-grandson. "Well, sir, is the very spot; he built this mill his self, sir, and we had an old Weaver—his name was Prosser, sir, who remembered him well, sir, and used to be always talking about him." But Prosser had been dead two years, and I turned to and bought from her a woollen bed-cover, which is woven and dyed like a very heavy shawl, and which I'm going to give you as a memento of the place. Mrs Blaney showed me the mills, and from the antiquity of the machinery, I should say the bed cover might have been woven on the looms your grandfather set up there. "Many a time 'e's trod this path, sir," she said, going to open the door. From the mill she showed me that we stood in the corner of three counties: Brecon, Hereford and Glamorgan; and a lovely, mildly picturesque region it is, all about. The Blany mill isn't very prosperous, since Mrs Blaney's "master" or husband died: an exemplary man, by her accounts; but she keeps up the business,—carding, dying, spinning and weaving bed-covers, coarse shawls, linsey-woolsy, and Welsh flannels, a bit of which last I got you for a specimen.—At 12 o'clock I kept my appointment with Rev. Canon Bevan of the Castle, and after showing me over the fine old house he went with me to the church and examined the record there. But as our people were quakers, there was no record of their births or deaths. Every one to whom I mentioned them, said, "Oh, the quaker Howellses!" and then spoke of the Swetmans and Trustils. The tradition of Thomas Howells was perfect, even to his going to America and returning;[1] but I could nowhere find his grave, nor learn certainly whether he died in Hay. The little rose-embowered post office is kept in the house where your Aunt Swetman lived.—I had an hour at Hereford, on my way up to London, and I drove through the town to see the cathedral. The verger showed me the seat in the choir where the minor canon, Rev. Edward Howells, sat.[2] "Many's the 'alf crown I've 'ad from 'im, sir."

I found the folks all well in London, when I got back from my pilgrimage, and now we are all eager for our departure on the 5th of July.[3] We go to Quebec—our passage having been engaged in April. All join me in love to the family.

> Your aff'te son
> Will.

1. There was a tradition in the Howells family that Thomas Howells had made a trip to America. See *Life in Letters*, I, 1–2, and Lynn, *Howells*, pp. 14–15.

2. The Reverend Mr. Edward Howells, minor canon of the cathedral at Hereford, has not been further identified.

3. In a letter of 15 July 1883 (MH) to his father, Howells wrote: "We arrived at Quebec Friday night [13 July] on the *Parisian*, which left Liverpool eight days before."

26 JUNE 1883, LONDON, TO EDMUND W. GOSSE

> 51 Upper Bedford Place,
> June 26, 1883.

My dear Gosse:

Mr. Brownell called last night while I was immeritoriously banqueting with you immortals, but he left no address.[1] If he is the sort of discouraged and isolated man that I have inferred from talk of yours, I sh'd hate extremely to seem indifferent to his acquaintance; and this is to beg his street and number of you.

What a charming night that was, last night! Du Maurier and Hardy went most to my heart (you and Thornycroft were there already) but I felt that after all I had only shaken hands with Hardy across his threshold. What a world of delightful people, and only one little life to go round them all with![2] There seems to be a mistake somewhere: perhaps it's mine in not making sure of passing a leisurely eternity with you and your friends.

Woolner is a fine old head.[3]

> Yours ever
> **W. D. Howells.**

1. William Crary Brownell (1851–1928), American critic, lived abroad, mainly in Paris, during 1881–1884. He was an editor and literary adviser to Charles Scribner's Sons (1888–1928).

2. Gosse invited Howells on 9 June 1883 (MH) to dine at the Savile Club on 25 June: "I have asked W. Black, Dobson, Thornycroft, du Maurier, Brander Matthews & a few others to meet you." William Black (1841–1898) was a Scottish journalist and novelist. Henry Austin Dobson (1840–1921) was an English poet and man of letters; like Gosse, he was for many years employed by the Board of Trade. George Louis Palmella Busson Du Maurier (1834–1896) was an English artist and novelist. James Brander Matthews (1852–1929) was an author and playwright and professor of literature (1892–1900) and dramatic literature (1900–1924) at Columbia University. For the meeting between Howells and Thomas Hardy, see Florence Emily Hardy, *The Early Life of Thomas Hardy, 1840–1891* (London: Macmillan, 1928), pp. 208–9.

3. Thomas Woolner (1825–1892) was an English sculptor and poet.

4 JULY 1883, LONDON, TO "MY DEAR SIR"

> 51 Upper Bedford Place
> July 4, 1883.

My dear Sir:[1]

I hope you wont find it necessary to treat me in your sketch in any sort as a "phenomenon"; my want of schooling was fairly supplied by the studies I pursued by myself, and whatever I have done of fine or good is the result of a life-long passion for literature and of hard work. Every man works into himself through others: Heinrich Heine, Thackeray, & Tourguènief are the writers who have helped me most. Perhaps I may say that my grandfather did not go to America to "better his condition," for he was very well to do at home, but from a love for Democracy, which the Quakers have been the only people ever to realize in their lives, and in the hope that in a new country amid fresh opportunities, he could more fully realize his religious ideals. He became a leader in Methodism; my father, by a natural reaction, a Swedenborgian.

My mother was of Irish and Pennsylvania German origin.

> Yours truly,
> W. D. Howells.

1. Neither the correspondent nor the sketch subsequently referred to has been identified.

6 JULY 1883, MOVILLE, IRELAND, TO JAMES R. LOWELL

> *Allen Line Steam Ship*
> Moville, July 6, 1883.

Dear Mr. Lowell:

I gave Gosse a note of introduction to you, mindful of the kindly feeling you expressed for him, and of his advantage. In this I hope I did not presume too far, and that I am not wrong in asking you to remember him in connection with the Lowell Lectures.[1]

But if I were capable of shame I should blush to ask anything of you after all your unasked kindness.

The Johns Hopkinses are after me again tempting me to try it for a year![2]

All the family join me in love to you and Mrs. Lowell.

> Yours affectionately ever
> W. D. Howells.

How delicious your speech at the Irving dinner![3] Every phrase melted on my tongue.

1. Howells wished to help Gosse secure an appointment to deliver a course of lectures with the title "From Shakespeare to Pope" at the Lowell Institute of Boston. The Institute was established by the will of John Lowell (1799–1836), manufacturer of cotton textiles, to provide free or low-cost lectures in various branches of human knowledge. Augustus Lowell (1830–1900), also a manufacturer of cotton textiles and cousin of J. R. Lowell, was at this time the single trustee of the Institute. Howells' efforts to secure for Gosse this series of lectures at the Institute and at other places were ultimately successful, although not without difficulties and disappointments. See Howells to Gosse, 9 December 1883, 2 January 1884, and 23 March 1884.

2. The proposition of a professorship at Johns Hopkins had first been made in the fall of 1882; see Howells to Smith, 19 November 1882, n. 1. President Gilman apparently urged the matter again during a meeting with Howells in London in June 1883, and for a while Howells was tempted by it. See Howells to Hay, 30 July 1883. But by mid-October he had decided against it, writing his father on 14 October 1883 (MH): "the place would take more of my time than the salary would justify me in giving, and that was the end of it."

3. A large public dinner was given on 4 July 1883 for the British actor-manager Henry Irving (1838–1905) at St. James Hall in London, prior to his departure on a professional tour in the provinces and the United States. Lord Houghton proposed a toast to "Literature, Science, and Art," and among those who responded was Lowell.

30 JULY 1883, BOSTON, TO JOHN HAY

Boston, July 30, 1883.

My dear Hay:

I am ashamed that with all your trouble and ill-health you got in before me with a letter.[1] We have been two weeks in Boston, in a frenzy of house-hunting, and so there is a little more excuse for me than usual; but not excuse enough. The rest must come from your familiar kindness. It truly grieves me to hear the bad report you give of yourself; but I am not surprised, for I expected something of the kind from what you have undergone. What can a friend say to you that will seem least futile and insulting? I wish you better with all my heart.

How good you always are about what I write.[2] But I don't like your undervaluing *The Bread-Winners*.[3] I saw that story in MS. and it strikes me as even more fascinating in print. I thought—but probably I was mistaken—that the description of the heroine's pull-back had been toned down, and some physical sense of her thereby lost. But the story reads very evenly, and if it is a new hand, more power to it I say.[4] I see it already well-spoken of by the press. The relation of the heroine, with her robust romance of marrying a sick man, to the pale, thin Azalia, strikes me as uncommonly good.

I haven't yet read all of James's paper, but what he said of Warner's theory of fiction was all gospel.[5] As to *Numa*, I don't think it perfect, and its bad art in one respect arose from the bad French morality.[6] Think of a mother, who in order to reconcile her daughter to her husband's falsehood, cold-bloodedly tells her, with the father's consent, that her idolized father had also been false. It's atrocious.

We had a lovely time in England, where the hospitalities of London pressed us hard. I could have boarded around for a year on the invitations I had in a fortnight. Certain little books seemed to be known in quarters where their author never expected to find them; and from the bookstalls he had to turn his modest eyes away. I could celebrate at length, but you won't care. Something that happened to me may interest you: President Gilman of Johns Hopkins renewed that offer to me with such kind insistence and concession that I am presently much tempted to go to Baltimore three or four months of the winter. It will depend upon whether the President and I can come to an understanding about the time and length of time. We have all come home in pretty good trim, though Winny is not quite well yet.

We join in love to all of you.

Yours affectionately,
W. D. Howells.

1. Hay had written Howells on 27 July 1883 (MH): "I have been very miserable for a week or so—unable to walk, with that obscure malady which inspires contempt and rage in every doctor I have seen. I have no pain, & no interruption of any function. But I cannot walk ten rods and am drunk as a lord all the time without hilarity or rum."

2. In the same letter Hay said: "I have just finished this month's instalment [*Century*, August 1883] of *A Woman's Reason*. It is incomparably good. You satisfy absolutely both Warner's & James' definition, (vide. Jame's [sic] *Daudet*) you *do* entertain, and you *do* represent life." Warner's definition was contained in his article "Modern Fiction," *Atlantic*, April 1883; James's in his article "Alphonse Daudet," *Century*, August 1883. Also see n. 4, below.

3. Hay's anonymous novel, *The Bread-Winners* (1884), appeared serially in the *Century*, August 1883–January 1884, and Howells reviewed it in the same magazine, May 1884. In September 1882 Howells had read the manuscript and enthusiastically recommended it to T. B. Aldrich for publication in the *Atlantic*. Aldrich agreed, but with the condition that Hay reveal his authorship. Hay refused to do so and gave the novel to R. W. Gilder of the *Century*. See W. R. Thayer, *Life and Letters of John Hay* (Boston: Houghton Mifflin, 1916), II, 8; and Howells to Hay, 7 January 1884.

4. In their correspondence Howells and Hay maintained the pretense that they did not know the author of *The Bread-Winners*. It is so consistently maintained that there is some question whether Howells knew the author's identity; however, in a letter of 2 September 1882 (MH) Hay authorized Howells to communicate "the guilty secret" to Aldrich, and the context suggests this is a reference to the secret authorship.

5. James, in "Alphonse Daudet," argued "that the main object of the novel is to represent life." He disagreed with C. D. Warner's idea that the novel should, above all else, entertain.

6. James considered Daudet's *Numa Roumestan* "a masterpiece; it is really a perfect work; it has no fault, no weakness. It is a compact and harmonious whole." For Howells' earlier comments on French salaciousness, see Howells to Hay, 18 March 1882.

2 AUGUST 1883, BOSTON, TO CHARLES D. WARNER

Boston, Aug. 2, 1883.

My dear Warner:

Yes, I am here,—dodging the sun, it is true, but jumping at public honors wherever I suspect them to be lurking.[1] We arrived on the Parisian at Quebec, July 12th, and since the 15th we have been here in a passion of house-hunting: not even a friend of the ideal novel could imagine anything like it. But it seems to be all coming to an end, this morning, though it may be all just beginning. The family are really pretty well: Winny is better, and Mrs. Howells is a fountain of energy, on which I am the weary, weary ball, perpetually tost into the air.

I wish with all my heart I might see you, for I too have many things to say. Probably we shall meet in October if not sooner, for I'm coming then to see Clemens. I understand how perfectly you are tied for the present; but I rejoice that it's business and not malaria that has you in its grip. It really seems too good to be true, your luck in getting well. I am very well, and so full of material that I wonder I don't crack open on the back. Think of having all your material stopped up in you by incessant travel for nearly six months![2] You wouldn't like it yourself.

Yours ever
W. D. Howells.

The Invasion of England was mighty funny, and good.[3]

1. In a letter of 30 July 1883 (MH) Warner asked Howells' whereabouts and mentioned a New York *Tribune* notice of Howells "as moving about the shady sides of Boston streets, dodging the sun and public honor."
2. Even though Howells' writing was no longer stopped by "incessant travel," he had some difficulty in working again. An undated letter (MH) from R. W. Gilder, but written before 14 August 1883, welcomed Howells home and added: "Mr. Smith had dropped me a hint about your new Italian idea." The remainder of the letter indicates that Howells had expressed some doubt about the suitability of the Florentine papers and had suggested that the Pennell illustrations made in antici-pation of them might instead be used for a new story—presumably *Indian Summer*, laid in Florence. See *Indian Summer*, HE, pp. xi-xviii. Gilder thought that the pictures might seem incongruous with the story and suggested that if Howells found the papers a "burden," William J. Stillman might write them. On 14 August 1883 (MH) Gilder placed the Pennell cuts at Howells' disposal and suggested James as a possibility for writing the Florentine papers. Howells also mentioned his diffi-culties in letters to his father: "I'm very rusty about my work, and I must get something in the way of a story started—and well started—before I leave home" (26 August 1883 [MH]). "I have done nothing but begin stories, and tear them up, after I had written fifty or sixty pages on each. Now at last it seems as if I had got something practical started, though I scarcely dare speak loud about it" (un-dated fragment; ca. 9 September 1883 [MH]).
3. "The English Volunteers During the Late Invasion," *Century*, May 1883, was Warner's humorous but fundamentally serious treatment of the reaction of English critics to "the 'invasion' of 'American Literature in England.'"

5 AUGUST 1883, BOSTON, TO WILLIAM C. HOWELLS

Boston, Aug. 5, 1883.

Dear father:

Your long and satisfactory letter came during the week, when we still tormented with trying to find a house. We have got one at last—4 Louisburg Square,—and hope to be living in it by the middle of the week; but you had better still address me at Osgood's. The house is a pleasant, old-fashioned one, and is "furnished," so that we shall not have to get out all our things from their place of storage. As soon as our tenant leaves the Cambridge house in the spring, we hope to get that ready for occupation, and to get into it to "roam no more."[1]—I am glad you are so cheerful about Virginia: it's certainly much more important that you should like it than that W. D. or Howell Howells should.[2] I may possibly get down to see you in September; but I can't promise now. Meantime I do think that $5500 for a farm of 145 acres, near no better market than Richmond, is a monstrous price. Don't buy till you've rented the place awhile, for you may be very sure you can't sell again except at a loss.[3]

You will have received before this reaches you, I hope, a valise, which I sent you on Friday, by Adams Express, containing the Hay bed-spread, the Roman blanket, etc. Please acknowledge it at once, so that we may be at rest concerning it. At Hay many persons spoke to me of Wm. Hooper, who, you say has your clock.[4] His address is Falmouth, England, and a letter would readily reach him there.

I think of no news to write, and so send the family love to you all, including the Annie-bodies.

Your aff'te son
Will.

1. See Tennyson's "The Lotos-Eaters," line 45.
2. In a letter of 25 July 1883 (MH) to his father, Howells wrote: "Howell Howells .... does not like Virginia, soil, flies, climate or people and he does not paint your Arcadia in the most pleasing colors." Howell Howells has not been identified.
3. See Howells to W. C. Howells, 3 June 1883, n. 2.
4. William Hooper has not been identified.

15 September 1883, Boston, to William H. Ward

4 Louisburg Square,
Boston, Sept. 15, 1883.

Dear Mr. Ward:[1]

If you have no one else in mind to write about Mr. Maurice Thompson's Songs of Fair Weather I should like to review the book for you over my own name; I would make about two of your columns.[2]

—I feel that I am doing you a favor in telling you that Mr. T. S. Perry (author of "English Literature in the Eighteenth Century") has very nearly ready a paper on the Russian novelist Tourguénïef, which I think you could get.[3] Mr. Perry, by his thorough acquaintance with the subject is pre-eminently qualified to write on it; and he is better equipped for general criticism than any other man in the country.

Yours sincerely
W. D. Howells.

1. William Hayes Ward (1835–1916), Congregational clergyman, Orientalist, and author, was associate editor (1868–1870), superintending editor (1870–1896), and editor (1896–1913) of the New York *Independent,* a weekly magazine.
2. "Maurice Thompson and His Poems," *Independent,* 4 October 1883.
3. "Ivan Tourguéneff," *Independent,* 4 October 1883.

18 September 1883, Boston, to Samuel L. Clemens

4 Louisburg Square,
Sept. 18, 1883.

My dear Clemens:

Osgood gave me your MS.[1] to read last night, and I understood from him that you wanted my opinion of it. The opening passages are the funniest you have ever done; but when I got into the story itself, it seemed to me that I was made a fellow-sufferer with the Sultan from Sheherazade's prolixity. The effect was like that of a play in which the audience is surprised along with the characters by some turn in the plot. I don't mean to say that there were not extremely killing things in it; but on the whole it was not your best or your second-best; and all the way it skirts a certain kind of fun which you can't afford to indulge in: it's a little too broad, as well as exquisitely ludicrous, at times.

You're such an impartial critic of your own work that I feel doubly brutal, and as if I were taking a mean advantage of your magnanimity when I fail to like something of yours. But I fail so seldom that I have some heart to forgive myself. At any rate I feel bound to say that I think this burlesque falls short of being amusing. Very likely, if you gave it to the public, it might be a great success; there is no telling how these things may go, and I am but one poor, fallible friend of yours.

You are back in Hartford again, and I mean to see you there before long on my way to visit my father in Virginia.[2] Mallory of the Madison Sq. Theatre has asked me to meet him here on Thursday and talk play. Perhaps I shall have something to report.[3]

You're all well enough to stand the shock of our united affection, I hope.

Yours ever
W. D. Howells.

1. The "1002d Arabian Night" was never published, perhaps partly because Clemens saw the validity of Howells' criticism. The "certain kind of fun" mentioned in this letter is an oblique reference to Clemens' use of a narrative frame in which King Shahriyar is placed in bed with Scheherazade. See *Twain-Howells*, p. 442.
2. Howells did visit his father in Virginia, but he saw Clemens on the return trip to Boston. A letter of 12 October 1883 (MH) to his father speaks of his returning home the night before, of his unsuccessful search in New York for a Mr. Barrett (a patent agent), and of Clemens' favorable opinion of the grape scissors.
3. Howells was probably negotiating about *Colonel Sellers as a Scientist*.

24 SEPTEMBER 1883, BOSTON, TO EDMUND C. STEDMAN

4 Louisburg Square,
Boston, Sept. 24, 1883.

My dear Stedman:

I have been reading your paper on Longfellow[1] with a curious "angenehmer Schmerz,"[2] for I lived over the whole course of my liking for the verse and the man as I read. I believe I should on the whole rate him higher than you do; with all his simplicity (and even superficiality as regards passion) he was such a *great* artist. I think that whoever else of our day shall live to aftertimes he is *sure* of surviving. Those later sonnets!—I don't dispute your estimate, and your criticism has a reverent beauty that I should not know how to praise aright.

You remember, you dear, good fellow, that I too was once a poet![3] That is very good of you—very friendly and sweet! It made me wish to see you and thank you.

I hope you are well.

Yours sincerely
W. D. Howells.

1. "Longfellow," *Century*, October 1883.
2. Howells took the phrase, "pleasant pain," from Heine's *Reisebilder*.

3. In his article on Longfellow, Stedman had included Howells among the Cambridge "poets and scholars" who had helped Longfellow in his translation of Dante. On 8 October 1883 (MH) he commented on Howells' particular regard for Longfellow: "I well remember that he was your first & last love, how much in sympathy you two were in your tastes & studies, & what a paper you wrote on him—I think in the *No. Am. Review?*—As for remembering you as a poet: 'tis only by your reiterative and, truth to say, incremental persistence that you have made me think of you except as a poet, scholar, essayist. These you were born; the novelist came out of you, like the Testamental spirits, by prayer and fasting,—a resultant of your determination to express yourself (as is both wise and right) after the creative usage of the age." Stedman was referring to Howells' "Henry Wadsworth Longfellow," *North American Review*, April 1867.

4 NOVEMBER 1883, BOSTON, TO WILLIAM C. HOWELLS

4 Louisburg Square,
Boston, Nov. 4, 1883.

Dear father:

I had expected to go to Hartford yesterday, but I decided to stay till after election, and vote against Butler, for the canvass is very close, and this State was once lost, you remember, by one vote.[1] As soon as I have voted on Tuesday, however, I shall go to Hartford, and then I shall be able to write you something about the scissors. Clemens has not written to me, because, as I suppose, he has been expecting to see me.[2] If he doesn't wish to take hold, I think there will be no trouble about disposing of the invention. I spoke of it to Ammon, Osgood & Co.'s traveller, who owns a large grape-farm near Cleveland,[3] and he says it is a great thing, and that if it were only in the market now, it could be largely sold for this year's work in Northern Ohio. He understood its capabilities at once. Clemens will have found out where and how and for what price the scissors can be made, at any rate.

So far as I can judge, your idea of buying that farm for $5000 near Richmond is a good one.[4] I like the notion of the vineyard being started on it. Joe writes me that he is still anxious to get on a farm. I'm afraid he's not coming here, after all, this fall, and so I sha'n't have a chance to talk with him. It would be very nice if he could settle near you.

There is a little family news. Elinor, who has been suffering from her back, ever since I got home, is much better, and Winny is well enough to go to parties—which is something.

Tell Annie I hear nice things about Achille from all my friends in New York. He seems to be greatly liked. I believe he has now met everybody but Laffan, of those I introduced him to.[5]—I got a letter the other day from Rev. Sabin Hough, asking me to make the religious tendency of my novels "so strong that nobody could mistake it."[6] I told him that would be invading *his* province.

—I almost forgot about the persimmons. They were five days on the way, and I had them carried straight to the swill barrel. All ᴡʜat beautiful fruit was soured, and smelt like get-out. You did your part kindly and well; but the express company swindled me. The failure was so complete that it amused me.

All join in love to you all.

Your aff'te son,
Will.

1. Benjamin F. Butler (1818–1893) was at this time seeking reelection as governor of Massachusetts on the Democratic ticket. He was defeated by the Republican candidate, George Dexter Robinson (1834–1896), who served as governor 1884–1886.

2. Clemens and Howells were still trying to market the grape scissors W. C. Howells had invented. Howells presumably went to Hartford on Wednesday, 7 November. See *Twain-Howells*, p. 448.

3. John Henry Ammon (1840–1904) became a partner of J. R. Osgood & Co. in 1880, serving primarily as a traveling representative in the West; in 1885 he became head of the Harper & Brothers publishing department.

4. See Howells to W. C. Howells, 3 June 1883, n. 2. After his visit with his father in Virginia in early October, during which his father's plans were probably discussed, Howells wrote on 12 October 1883 (MH): "Don't buy a farm in a hurry! *Come up and see us before you decide anything.*"

5. In his letter of 12 October 1883 to his father, Howells wrote: "Lunched with Achille in N. Y. He is well, and homesick; but greatly encouraged about his work, which was praised by the teacher, the first night, and made the text of his whole lecture."

6. The Reverend Mr. Sabin Hough has not been identified.

19 NOVEMBER 1883, BOSTON, TO SAMUEL L. CLEMENS

Boston, Nov. 19, 1883.

Dear Clemens—

I enclose a scrap or two from a newspaper with valuable suggestions for Sellers inventions. I have just been talking with Mrs. Howells about when I can go to Hartford for the revision, & I have about concluded to postpone it till I can see a week clear before me. The trouble now is that I am so tired—actually brain-weary—with our work on the play already that I couldn't do anything on it that wouldn't hurt it for five or six days at any rate.[1] Then Cable comes here to read next Monday, & in decency I ought to be present.[2] By the first of December Arnold is to be here again with a lecture that he has several times told me he has put me into, & so I ought to be on hand to hear that.[3] I don't believe, therefore that I can get to Hartford with a solid week before me & a good conscience behind me till two weeks from to-day. But the time needn't a moment of it be lost. We are perfectly sure to make that play just what you want it & you can push on the negotiations with Raymond on that understanding. As soon as you have the type-writer copy complete, send it to me & I will doctor all the dialogue except the Sellers speeches. When we meet we can go over them together & my corrections, & decide about them.

I have been about half dead to-day from eating & laughing yesterday. I hope that having got rid of me, you got safely off from the Aldriches. That was a terrible moment, yesterday when she consented to let you go to Norton's with me, & never did a wish fulfilled bring me so little joy.[4] None but the pitying angels will ever know what Mrs. Howells said to me when she got me out of doors. She began by saying that I was always very lenient to *her* when she committed a blunder, & so she was not going to be hard on me. But I think the enormity of my crime must have grown upon her as she painted it to me. At any rate I never wish to be *spared* again.[5]

This is done on the new type writer I told you of. You see how distinctly it writes. I can use it with a fair degree of speed, & I shall give it fair trial. I have hired it for a month, paying $10 which goes as a payment on the machine if I keep it. It is only to cost $40 in all.

Mrs. Howells sends her love with mine to all your house. Pilla is very anxious to go back with me & see your girls. Tell Clara not to neglect that calf.[6]

Yours ever
W. D. Howells.

1. Howells apparently went to Hartford on Wednesday, 7 November, and worked with Clemens on *Colonel Sellers as a Scientist* until his departure on Thursday, 15 November.

2. In a letter of 23 November 1883 to his wife, Cable wrote: "At 5 P. M. Howells called. Oh! what a gentle, pleasant soul he is!" See Lucy L. C. Biklé, *George W. Cable* (New York: C. Scribner's Sons, 1928), p. 109. On the day of his successful reading (Monday, 26 November 1883), G. W. Cable wrote to his wife, mentioning a visit by Howells: "he was a little anxious about me, inasmuch as I took tea with him & his family (nobody else) last night & felt so unwell after attending church with him that he required me to stay all night at his house. [¶] Howells seems to be a most lovable man . . . . Tomorrow afternoon Howells gives me a big reception . . ." (Biklé, p. 111).

3. In a letter of 11 November 1883 (MH) to his father, written from Hartford, Howells said: "I am going up to Boston on Thursday [15 November], so as to breakfast with him [Matthew Arnold] at Aldrich's, and perhaps have him to some sort of doings at our house." Arnold did not accept Howells' invitation. See also *Twain-Howells*, pp. 449–50, and *Literary Friends and Acquaintance*, HE, pp. 272–73.

4. Apparently Clemens was in Boston on 17–18 November, and he and the Howellses visited the Aldriches. The difficulties in the relationship between Clemens and Lilian Aldrich began with their first meeting in 1868. See *Twain-Howells*, p. 450.

5. The nature of Howells' faux pas remains unclear, but it could conceivably refer to Howells' plan to take Clemens to the Nortons, having claimed his friend's company the previous evening. That Clemens and Howells were in each other's company on Saturday evening is suggested by the following letter of 17 November 1883 (Arms), which has hitherto not been printed:

My dear Clemens:

When I supposed you were coming to us I engaged to take you out to Cambridge this (Saturday) evening to see my play at a friend's done by children. If you can go, come to 4 Louisburg Square by a quarter to eight, and let me know, anyway.

Yours ever
W. D. Howells.

The play may have been *The Register*, which first appeared in *Harper's Monthly*, December 1883; the friend's house was probably Norton's.

6. See *Twain-Howells*, p. 450. Clara Langdon Clemens (1874–1962) was the only child of Clemens to survive him.

21 November 1883, Boston, to William C. Howells

4 Louisburg Square,
Boston, Nov. 21, 1883

Dear father—

Annie's letter about her proposed visit here came this morning, and pending Elinor's answer please tell her that two weeks from next Saturday, the date she names, is exactly the time when we should like her to come. We shall all be at home, and able to devote ourselves to her and Achille, to say nothing of Mole and Vevie.

I am waiting till you have time to tell me something more about the place you are going to. Do write me fully someday. I suppose you will soon be settled in it. While I was at Hartford, Senator Hawley told me that a great new city was springing up with Western speed at Newport News, where a great harbor for European steamers was to open, and railroads were building. I suppose you know all about it, however. Clemens's nephew who has the grape scissors in charge,[1] did not get to Hartford before I left. As soon as he reports, I will write you. Of course it is too late to do anything this year except see about the manufacturing. I forgot to tell you that I called upon the people who wrote you about the scissors from Boston. They seemed decent and honest; they said they would have liked to take it up and sell territory for you, but they were now pushing some other patents and could not. I left my name and will see them again if the affair with Clemens should fall through, which I don't at all expect.

Elinor has been afraid that perhaps John wrote you a letter that made you think he was conceited. He isn't at all so, but is a very simple, modest boy. Just now, however he is very full of his school, and perhaps he talkt too much of what he was doing. But I dare say you understood all that.

I have been writing this on a new kind of type-writer that I've taken on trial. I can use it about as fast as a pen, & write a much better hand with it. The machine weighs six pounds, & with a platen six inches square it prints perfectly, a system of parallel movements bringing the right type always into position. The type are India rubber. At present I'm greatly pleased with it.

Our great excitement, just now, is Pil & her wonderful book.[2] All Boston is talking of it, & with bated breath. The first edition is exhausted, & I have ordered another thousand. Pil keeps on playing paper dolls & prisoner's base. We don't let her see any of the notices or letters that we get about the book. All send love to all of you.

> Your aff'te son,
> Will.

1. See Howells to W. C. Howells, 4 March 1883, n. 2.
2. *A Little Girl Among the Old Masters*, with drawings by Mildred Howells and introduction and comment by W. D. Howells, was published in Boston by James R. Osgood & Co. on 15 November 1883.

27 NOVEMBER 1883, BOSTON, TO WHITELAW REID

> 4 Louisburg Square,
> Boston, Nov. 27, 1883.

My dear Reid:

I wrote you on Friday, enclosing the Tribune notice of A Little Girl among the Old Masters.[1]

I have not to complain that your critic ignored the qualities of childish fancy that alone gave the book a right to be, and that he treated the little drawings as if I had assumed them to be works of art; but I do complain that he spoke of it in terms singularly wounding and insulting to me. An outrage was offered me in the house of my friend; I have appealed to him for some sign of regret that this should have happened, and he treats my appeal with silent contempt.

There has never been anything but kindness between you and me; you have done me more kindnesses than I have ever thanked you for, because I could not seem to ask you for others.

You have to blame yourself in the past if your present attitude astonishes and hurts me.[2]

> Yours sincerely
> W. D. Howells.

1. In his letter of 19 November 1883 (DLC) to Reid, Howells enclosed a clipping of the *Tribune* review of Mildred's book, and added: "Perhaps I am wrong in

objecting to this paragraph, in which I am called a showman and my little girl is compared to a dancing dog." The complete text of the review in the *Tribune* of 19 November 1883 follows: "This is a curious production. A little daughter of Mr. Howells, possessing natural artistic tendency was inspired by the European galleries to make a number of quaint and clever but of course childish imitations and travesties of the old masters. The father of this ten-year-old genius has had these tender essays at art reproduced in a permanent form, and has himself undertaken the office of showman. Criticism of such a volume is naturally out of the question. Dr. Johnson's remark upon the dancing dog is inevitably recalled to mind. 'It is not,' said the doctor, 'that the animal dances well. The matter for surprise is that he should dance at all.' The text of Mr. Howells is pleasant enough reading, and the plates are not seldom amusing."

2. On 1 December 1883 (DLC) Howells wrote Reid again, responding to an apparent apology offered by Reid: "It is all right. I do not care whether we agree about the paragraph; if you regret my being hurt by it; that was all I could wish you to say, and you have said it fully and generously. Good-bye to the whole matter!"

9 DECEMBER 1883, BOSTON, TO EDMUND W. GOSSE

4 Louisburg Square,
Boston, Dec. 9, 1883.

My dear Gosse—

I waited a month or two for the decision of the autocrat of the Lowell Lectures, and then addresst him a modest reminder of our joint existence. The effect was the letter which I enclose. Upon the whole this experience of mine with Mr. Augustus Lowell is the most disagreeable that I have had since I past the age of being justly snubbed for poverty and obscurity. I don't know what he may finally conclude upon, but I can't conceal that I have very little hopes. It is a real grief and disappointment to me, for I had counted very confidently upon having you here, and I am afraid that I must have a very fraudulent appearance to you.[1]

I wonder if you have ever got two notes that I sent you to 29 Delamere Terrace? I wrote you directly after I reacht home, and then a month later about the lectures; but I have not had a squeak from you in response, and I can't console myself with the hope that you were abroad, for Brunetta writes me from Verona that you have not shown yourself there.

We are having Matthew Arnold rather intensely. His lectures in Boston at least have been a great success. I only heard that on Emerson, which seemed to me just and good: I never was too fervid an Emersonian, liking my poetry and philosophy best without conundrums. There were 500 people to hear him, who paid $2 apiece for the privilege. I have twice been his commensal, and like him. I don't know whether he quite makes us out; he seems at times rather bewildered, and I don't wonder.[2] I found America changed even in the year I was gone; it had grown more American, and I with my crimson opinions was scarcely more than of a dull purple in politics and religion. I put it extravagantly, but there is some truth in what I say.

James Bryce is also here, and him I *do* like. Irving I am to meet twice at least; he's just come to Boston.[3]

I'm far into the heart of a new story,[4] the idea of which pleases me greatly. It is that of a man whose youth was broken sharp off in Florence twenty years ago, and who after a busy newspaper life in our West, fancies that he can resume his youth by going back to Italy. There he falls in love with a girl young enough to be his daughter. It is largely a study of the feelings of middle-life in contrast with those of earlier years.

Entre nous—I have just finisht writing a play with Mark Twain, from which I hope big money.[5] It seems to me now at least very droll. We have the notion of doing half a dozen, with always the same character for protagonist, whom we wish to make the American mask—like Pantalone for Venice, Stenteretto for Florence, etc.

I met Harriet Preston the other evening, and had a long Gosse-sip with her. She is gone back to England already, and will give you all my news, with all my heart.

Now write and give me yours, individually and collectively!

Mrs. Howells is not very strong this winter, but is overpowering in her regrets for London. She and the children join me in love to Mrs. Gosse and yourself.

Yours ever
W. D. Howells.

1. See Howells to Lowell, 6 July 1883, n. 1. On 9 September 1883 (NjR; *Transatlantic Dialogue*, pp. 122–23) Howells wrote Gosse that he had seen Augustus Lowell several times but without success. Howells had hoped that enlisting J. R. Lowell's support would secure the appointment for Gosse, but on 20 December 1883 (MH; *Transatlantic Dialogue*, p. 129) Gosse wrote: "You will be disgusted to hear that I never saw Lowell. I sent him your letter, & got a polite note back asking me for a date ten days ahead. This I was obliged to decline, for I was just starting for Switzerland, & I have not heard again."

2. See Howells to Clemens, 19 November 1883, n. 3. Besides breakfasting with Arnold at Aldrich's, it is possible that Howells dined with him at Holmes's on 28 November or some time during Arnold's stay in the home of Charles Eliot Norton, 1–5 December. See *Letters of Matthew Arnold 1848–1888*, ed. G. W. E. Russell (New York: Macmillan, 1895), II, 260.

3. James Bryce (1838–1922), British historian, statesman, and diplomat, was the author of *The American Commonwealth* (1888). Howells met Henry Irving, the English actor, during Irving's American tour with the Lyceum theater company.

4. *Indian Summer* had apparently been offered to *Harper's Monthly* as early as October 1883, but H. M. Alden insisted on a synopsis of the story before he would commit himself. On 17 March 1884 (MH) Alden returned the manuscript of "September and May" (an earlier title) and expressed his delight about it.

5. That Howells' work on *Colonel Sellers as a Scientist* had been finished somewhat earlier is indicated by his letter of 6 December 1883 (MH) to Osgood, asking for the return of the Sellers play before Sunday (9 December).

2 JANUARY 1884, BOSTON, TO EDMUND W. GOSSE

4 Louisburg Square,
Boston, Jan. 2, 1883.[1]

My dear Gosse:

Your letter came day before yesterday, and this morning came your notice of Pilla's book in the Pall Mall.[2] In the first place I didn't dream of your writing of it at all, and then for you to write of it in *that* way—it toucht her mother's heart and mine more than I can tell you. The review was copied entire into a Boston paper which I don't see, and all our friends had read it before we had;[3] imagine our astonishment at finding one of the little drawings actually reproduced in your review! We *yelled* with joy when we saw it. And your kind words—*basta*! I am *used* to being treated better than I deserve!—Since you have taken an interest in the little book, it seems due to you to say that if we had not known the child's unspoilableness we should not have ventured upon it. I don't think any one could be less conscious of it than she. At first she was very proud of having made a book—as a book, merely; but she never was in the least "set up" with any one's praise of it, nor vain of her little skill, which we ourselves feel is probably an efflorescence of her childish spirit, with no sort of future before it. If it should come to anything it will not be through any prompting or petting of ours. The book has been quite successful: 2000 were sold here, fifty copies being sent to Trübner's in London. It has earned her $1000 which shall be for her *dot*, or for her schooling if ever she wishes to study art.

I wish you *had* told me about your American edition of the Seventeenth Century poets![4] Can't you still be served in regard to it? I thought Osgood was to publish it?

You may be sure that I for one American was ashamed of our silly and impertinent interference with justice in O'Donnell's case.[5] I think no man should be hung; but that man was a cruel and pitiless assassin, and rightly suffered under the law. If he had been a man of any other nationality Congress would not have dreamt of interfering; how then can I explain that this Irish forcing of our national action appeared merely grotesque to us? Congress is "Democratic": by seeming to befriend O'Donnell it could capture Irish votes for its party; and by making a Republican president its instrument it could foist any disagreeable consequences upon us.

It is all part of our "joke"; come over and try to understand it. The joke is not such a bad one in the long run.—I don't despair yet of the Lowell Lectures:[6] when they are secured, I will get Congress to instruct the President to ask the British Government *why* my friend Gosse cannot have three months' leave.

We had a stand-up lunch party this afternoon to entertain Stillman,[7] an old friend of ours who dined us last winter in Florence. It makes the round world seem no thicker than a map to meet at this rate on both sides of it.

Our good and delightful Henschel is going back to London in the spring. Perhaps he will carry with him the libretto of an opera by me, for which he wishes to make the music.[8]

I amuse myself, in my new story,[9] with the figure of a New England hill-country minister who has gone out to Florence, to spend his last days. His Unitarianism had frayed out into a sort of benevolent agnosticism before he left home, and in a fur-lined coat, over a *scaldino*[10] he shudders at all he left behind in Haddam East Village. He has deliberately proposed to die as far away from the lingering puritanism and winter of his native hills as he can; and he thinks that Savonarola made a great mistake in trying to kill the Carnival.

—Mrs. Howells and I are going up into the hills to-morrow, for a little change and a great deal of snow. Before we go we join in love to Mrs. Gosse and you.

Yours ever
W. D. Howells.

Love to the Tademas too.

1. Howells obviously misdated this letter.

2. Gosse's review of *A Little Girl Among the Old Masters* appeared in the *Pall Mall Gazette*, 20 December 1883; it expressed a generous admiration for the little volume, concluding that Mildred's "sketches were thoroughly worth presenting to the public, especially as they drew forth so many delightful pages from her father, and they are not childish in drawing beyond the wont of artistic childhood." Gosse also wrote Howells on 20 December 1883 (MH; *Transatlantic Dialogue*, p. 127), stating: "It seems rather absurd that I, who have never taken my pen in hand yet to review you, should review your child. But is hardly a review, merely a word of greeting...."

3. "A Tiny Artist," Boston *Daily Advertiser*, 1 January 1884.

4. Gosse, not knowing that Henry Holt, the American publisher of his poems, would be offended, had agreed to let Osgood publish *Seventeenth Century Studies*. As a result, the volume was not published in America until 1897 by Dodd, Mead. See *Transatlantic Dialogue*, p. 119.

5. Patrick O'Donnell, who claimed to be an American citizen, was convicted of murdering James Carey, an Irish informer, on the British ship *Melrose*, 29 July 1883. Because of public pressure, James R. Lowell, the American minister to England, requested in the name of President Chester A. Arthur that O'Donnell's execution be delayed so that the prisoner's counsel, Roger A. Pryor, could present points of error alleged to have arisen during the trial. The request was denied, and O'Donnell was hanged on 17 December 1883. On 20 December Gosse wrote: "I hope America is not going to sink into the Greater Ireland. We have been grieved over here at your government's weak interference about the murderer O'Donnell."

6. See Howells to Gosse, 9 December 1883, n. 1.

7. William J. Stillman, whom Howells had met during his Venetian years, was special correspondent for the London *Times* (1877–1898).

8. Georg Henschel (1850–1934), a German-born conductor, composer, and singer, wrote the music to *A Sea Change, or Love's Stowaway*, and Howells wrote the libretto. The opera was completed in 1885 and published in *Harper's Weekly*, 14 July 1888 and supplement.

9. *Indian Summer.*

10. Italian for "warming-pan."

7 JANUARY 1884, BOSTON, TO JOHN HAY

4 Louisburg Square,
Boston, Jan. 7, 1884.

My dear Hay:

Let me tell you at once that we have scarlet fever in the house, so that although I write at the bottom of it, and poor John lies at the top,—not very sick—you may burn this letter as soon as you please, if you think it necessary, on account of your children.

I think the storm about your friend's book is flurry which will pass, and let justice have a chance later.[1] Of course I know the annoyance he must feel; but you can tell him from me at least that I don't think any less of his work because it is being jumped on. Maud Matchin will live because she *does* live, and he has added a type new, true and difficult to draw, to our own fiction. If I were to make any printed defence of his book I should insist that it courageously expressed a fact not hitherto attempted; the fact that the workingmen *as* workingmen are no better or wiser than the rich *as* the rich, and are quite as likely to be false and foolish.[2] It certainly didn't strike me that the author was assailing them as a class. I still think that the result of the murder is too little moralized: it ought to be shown (not in words) that Sleeny was a homicide who would probably beat Maud, and that she was a huzzy who would deserve it; that they were bad and *bound* to be wretched. I would not have let her face wear any "happy" look, the slut! That is the grand literary and artistic shortcoming of the story; if I had been proof-reading for the author I should have markt what I thought some minor ones. Some of the things about the story are preposterous—as for example that Maud is made miserable because she was found poor, and Farnham made happy because he was found rich. She is supposed to have been virtuous because she told him she would only be his wife! In her heart she was just as ready to be his harlot if she could make sure of as much money and splendor. I've no patience with such twaddle. It is as well, perhaps, that the author suppressed the dedication, for it would have got me in for more fight than I've leisure for; I certainly should have spoken out, if I had been hit along with him.

We got your very kind note about Pilla's book from New York, and your praises were most grateful to both of us.[3] It has had a very fair little success, and would have had more if there had not been a very long break between the two editions. We had not forgotten the interest you and Mrs. Hay took in the little drawings, and counted on your liking the book. Of course, it was something hazardous, as concerned Pilla; but we knew her unspoilableness. The only ugly thing said of the book was in the *Tribune*, where there was a little paragraph as mistaken in point of view, as it was insulting in terms.[4] But Reid expressed his regret to me about it, and so it's all right, as far as he's concerned.

Mrs. Howells distractedly joins me in love to you both.

Yours ever,
W. D. Howells.

1. *The Bread-Winners* by Hay; see Howells to Hay, 30 July 1883, n. 3 and n. 4. Near the beginning of his review of Hay's novel (*Century*, May 1884) Howells wrote: "From the first it was noticeable that the criticism it received concerned the morality of the story, and even the morality of the writer, rather than the art of either, and, on the whole, we do not see why this was not well enough. It was, we think, a wholesome way of regarding the performance . . . ."

2. In the published review Howells elaborates this point, showing that in the novel working people, as a class, are neither praised nor condemned: "the author of 'The Bread-winners' meant no more nor less than to tell the truth about them; and if he has not flattered the likeness of his workingmen, he has done the cause of labor and the cause of art both a service . . . . When they will not work, they are as bad as club men and ladies of fashion, and perhaps more dangerous. It is quite time we were invited to consider some of them in fiction as we saw some of them in fact during the great railroad strike."

3. Hay had written Howells on 4 December 1883 (MH), praising *A Little Girl Among the Old Masters*.

4. See Howells to Reid, 27 November 1883.

21 JANUARY 1884, BOSTON, TO CHARLES E. NORTON

4 Louisburg Square,
Boston, Jan. 21, 1884.

My dear Norton:

Thank you for the books—especially Valery.[1]

Here is a letter from Padre Giacamo whom I shall be careful to assure of your initiative in an attempted benefaction which I'm afraid is going to be merely a benevolence. So far I have received but one gift for the Convent—$5.00, and from your discreet silence I fancy that you may not have got even so much.[2]

Mr. Gilder writes me from the Century that they hope to make use of "Mr Harrison's phenomenal power of observation and reporting before long." I suggest to him through you now to write out the experiences of a practical humanitarian as he has known them, or—*Giving: when it Helps and when it Hurts.* He can make something very valuable on the subject. An excellent subject also would be the Religion of the Average Rural Yankee.[3]

—John is up, and we are applying the materials of the old fashioned theology to his sick-room.[4] We all cough. Perhaps it was so much brimstone that fastened consumption on New England.

Yours ever
W. D. Howells.

1. Possibly Antoine Claude Pasquin (1789–1847), author of travel books on Italy who used the pseudonym "Valery."

2. In a letter to Howells, 4 January 1884 (MH), Padre Giacamo Issaverdanz thanked Howells and Norton for their efforts in trying to raise funds for restoring the monastery of St. Lazzaro, which had been destroyed by fire. Howells and Norton placed a notice in the Boston *Transcript*, 18 December 1883, requesting charitable contributions; and Norton wrote Howells, 22 January 1884 (MH), that he had received only a one-dollar contribution from John Holmes.

3. Gilder's letter has not been located, but the reference is evidently to Jonathan B. Harrison, whom Howells at one time called "a man . . . full of good works." See Howells to Norton, 29 August 1880. There are no articles by Harrison in the *Century*.

4. In a letter to his sister Aurelia, 13 January 1884 (MH), Howells described the process of purifying the room in which John Howells was sick with scarlet fever: "When John has 'peeled,' the room where he lies must be fumigated seventy hours with brimstone, and all the rest of the house at least five hours. This is to destroy the 'germs' which the doctors think *may* exist, and if they *do* exist, *may* carry the infection. I chafe and rage in vain . . . . The whole thing will, in money, cost me three or four hundred dollars; and the first time Pilla goes into a horsecar she may take the disease, after all."

15 FEBRUARY 1884, BOSTON, TO SAMUEL L. CLEMENS

Feb. 15, 1884

Dear Clemens:

This didn't go last night, and this morning I have your two letters about Goodwin.[1] I see that he wants the name of the character changed. The more I think of that, the more I feel that it would be useless. It would still be Sellers, and the change of name would make men and newspapers mad to no purpose.

I confess that it would be extremely distasteful to me to have my name connected in any way with Goodwin's. I was willing to consent if he went about under the wing of a respectable hen like the Madison Square management; but I cannot stand the thought of him "on his own hook." His name has been connected with low flung burlesques, and his family appear before the public habitually in nothing but stocking; at Montreal

I saw him in a play so indecent that I was obliged to leave the theatre with Mrs. Howells.[2]

You will say that Raymond is as great a blackguard, or greater. This may be true, but Raymond is identified with Sellers—not an ignoble figure. Decent people throng to see him, and no bad smell attaches to him out of the profession. It would be one thing to let him or some perfectly unknown man have the play, and quite another to let G. have it.

You may have reasoned it out in another way. If you have don't let me stand in your road. The life of the play is Sellers, and Sellers is yours. Pay me a sum outright for my work, when you've arranged with G., and let the play go to the public as yours solely and entirely; no one knows yet that I've helpt you.

It's only just to Webster to say that Mallory thought of Goodwin himself, and mentioned him; Webster didn't mention him at all to Mallory, although he had done so to me. He saw M. only in my presence.

Yours ever
W. D. Howells.

Then why not Cullington?[3]

W.D.H.

1. Only one of Clemens' letters about Nathaniel C. Goodwin, a popular actor, is extant. Clemens had written Charles L. Webster on 2 January 1884, instructing him to negotiate with Goodwin or Jimmy Lewis to play Colonel Sellers if Raymond would not pay $400 per week for the play. See *Twain-Howells*, p. 462.

2. Goodwin and his wife, Eliza Weathersby Goodwin, acted in plays that were occasionally billed with minstrel shows, but there is no evidence that they played the second-rate theaters. Only three days later, on 18 February (MH; *Twain-Howells*, pp. 473–75), Clemens wrote Howells that he had broken off negotiations with Goodwin, even though he disagreed with Howells' idea that the "Madison Square management" would provide respectability. The Madison Square Theatre was managed by George S. and Marshall H. Mallory.

3. Written above the dateline of this letter, this question refers to a newspaper clipping pasted at the top of the first page: "Mr. John T. Raymond was too ill to appear in Toronto on the 1st inst., and Mr. William Cullington played Col. Sellers very acceptably." Cullington was a famous actor on the New York stage. See *Twain-Howells*, p. 473.

23 MARCH 1884, BOSTON, TO EDMUND W. GOSSE

Boston, March 23, 1884.

My dear Gosse:

You will be thinking me very remiss, but I have not really been so. On the contrary I have been diligently working up a boom for you in the lecture-field.[1] I am sorry to say that the boom is not yet satisfactory. You realize that your Lowell course will give you only $750 or £150. I wrote to the Johns Hopkins people for their $1000—£200 course; they replied offering you $300—£60 for six lectures. I have again written Dr. Gilman that he promised you the $1000 at my lodgings in London, and I hope to bring him to reason. Mrs. Fields has applied to the Cornell University for their $600 course, and I have urged on Mr. Lowell that you ought to have the full course of twelve lectures for $1500.[2] Something will come of it all; and I am rejoiced that you wish to come. I will write you as soon as I hear from the various people. I like your subject, and I think Lang's title, "From Shakespear to Pope," excellent.[3] Remember to save yourself work on the lectures, if they run beyond six (as they must to justify you in coming) by leaving space for copious selections and extracts. The more desultory you can make them, after a first sharp outline, the better.

Mrs. Howells joins me in love to both of you, and hopes of seeing you here, our guests.

Yours ever

W. D. Howells.

I've finished my novel and am writing Georg Henschel (Tadema's friend) the libretto for a comic opera.[4]

1. See Howells to Lowell, 6 July 1883, n. 1.
2. Howells wrote Mrs. James T. Fields on 15 February 1884 (CSmH; *Life in Letters*, I, 360). Augustus Lowell was trustee of the Lowell Institute.
3. Andrew Lang (1844–1912), a poet, critic, and friend of Gosse, had proposed this title for Gosse's lecture series; it was eventually also used for the book. See Gosse to Howells, 8 March 1884 (MH; *Transatlantic Dialogue*, p. 134).
4. The novel was *Indian Summer*; the comic opera was entitled *A Sea Change, or Love's Stowaway*.

4 April 1884, Boston, to Charles L. Webster

Boston, April 4, 1884.

Dear Mr. Webster:

I am perfectly willing that Raymond should have the play on the terms suggested.[1] He has not seen the piece, and I do not know where he is. He left Boston last Saturday night. It should be stated to him in opening negotiations that Mr. Clemens has concluded to do so and so; for I told him it was useless for him to propose $250 a week to Mr. Clemens.

If Mr. Clemens is disabled, or in trouble, or has some unknown offence with me, I can understand his preferring to write to his friend by the hand of his agent; but not otherwise.[2] I am, of course, always glad to hear from you personally.

Yours sincerely
W. D. Howells.

1. Raymond wrote Howells, 28 March 1884 (NPV), that he could not produce *Colonel Sellers as a Scientist* for a year because of other commitments. He then continued as follows: "I will give you two hundred and fifty $250 dollars per week for the play and if only acted a portion of the time the sum to be one seventh for each performance *less* than a week." Howells then wrote Clemens on 29 March 1884 (NPV; *Twain-Howells*, p. 481): "I believe that unless Raymond's present play fails during the season we shall never get more than $250 a week from him. If we cannot make up our minds to take that—and I do not at all urge it—I propose that we shall simply change the name of Sellers throughout our play, and let the Madison Square people try it if they will on its own merits." Even though Howells and Clemens eventually agreed to Raymond's offer, the actor-producer finally rejected the play because its authors refused to make the revisions he requested.

2. Clemens forwarded to Webster Howells' letter of 29 March, instructing him to answer it and indicating that he was willing to go along with anything. Howells obviously felt that Clemens had snubbed him by having Webster answer his letter, and so Webster immediately wrote to Clemens urging him to smooth Howells' ruffled feelings. See *Twain-Howells*, pp. 481–82.

6 APRIL 1884, BOSTON, TO WILLIAM C. HOWELLS

Boston, April 6, 1884.

Dear father:

I am glad to hear that all is going so well with you since your return, though you say nothing about the fish-pond or the clear title—the things in which I am perhaps mainly concerned.[1] I hope you will not fail to have both.

The last week has been one of extraordinary work with me. I wrote the whole of the last act of my libretto—which alone would be as long as The Register, and which includes some ten or twelve songs.[2] The thing is now done, and ready for the composer.

Raymond has made an offer for the Sellers play and will probably get it; though he will not be able to bring it out till a year from now.[3]

I am getting out a little volume called Three Villages, to include my studies of Lexington, Shirley (the Shaker Village) and Gnadenhütten.[4] I think you will be interested to read the latter over again. In the proof it seems to me very good.

The children are about their usual tasks and pleasures. Friday night John and Pil went to a fancy children's ball: John as a 17th century nobleman in pink and silver, and Pil as a little Swiss peasant girl. You can't think how charming they lookt. Pil might have stepped right out of a vineyard at Villeneuve—only in that case she would not have been so clean.

We are still agitating the house question, and still halting between Boston and Cambridge.[5]

All are very well and join me in love to you all.—The arrowheads were enormously appreciated.

> Your aff'te son
> **Will.**

1. W. C. Howells had visited his son in Boston some time in March; the fish pond (apparently a project to raise fish for commercial purposes) and clear title refer to the father's farm propery in Virginia.

2. The libretto was for the opera *A Sea Change, or Love's Stowaway*, with music by Georg Henschel. Howells' farce, *The Register*, was first published in *Harper's Monthly*, December 1883, and issued in book form in 1884.

3. See Howells to Webster, 4 April 1884, n. 1.

4. *Three Villages* was published by James R. Osgood & Co. in 1884. The three sketches were originally published as follows: "Lexington," *Longman's*, November 1882; "A Shaker Village" (retitled "Shirley"), *Atlantic*, June 1876; and "Gnadenhütten," *Atlantic*, January 1869.

5. Howells and his family were residing in a rented house at 4 Louisburg Square in Boston. In August 1884 Howells bought and renovated a house at 302 Beacon Street in Boston.

10 APRIL 1884, BOSTON, TO SAMUEL L. CLEMENS

Boston, April 10, 1884.

Dear Clemens:

It is all perfectly true about the generosity, unless I am going to read your proofs from one of the shabby motives which I always find at the bottom of my soul if I examine. But now, it seems as if I were glad of the notion of being of use to you; and I shall have the pleasure of admiring a piece of work I like under the microscope.[1]

I'm very much interested in your report of Webster's scissor contract. Of course if the thing succeeds it will be a nice, sure thing for father.[2] I am not certain that it ought to be made for an unlimited time.

I'm curious also to know what Raymond will do about the play.[3] He struck me as much more of a man intellectually than I had supposed him. Very likely he will toss the whole thing overboard. At any rate I prefer not to hope.

I've just finished my libretto—two weeks work.[4]

> Yours ever
> W. D. Howells.

1. Howells had agreed to read the proof sheets of *Huckleberry Finn*. Having been given free rein by Clemens, he edited the entire book in typescript and, in addition, read many of the galley proofs. See *Twain-Howells*, p. 494.

2. Though Wiss of Newark, New Jersey, had originally been contracted to manufacture the "Howells Grape Gatherer," the lure of greater profits caused Howells and Charles L. Webster to switch manufacturers to Lowentraut of Newark, a company that would sell the grape shears as well as make them. Howells was satisfied with the Lowentraut negotiations that would allow William C. Howells to receive ten per cent of the jobbing price of the shears, $1 for the japanned version and $1.25 for the nickle-plated model. See Howells to W. C. Howells, 21 April 1884 (MH). However, as time passed and more details of the marketing were discovered, Howells became less satisfied with Lowentraut's slipshod handling of his father's product. In a letter to Joseph A. Howells, 11 May 1884 (MH), Howells recommended that his brother "take hold of the thing" and be paid Lowentraut's commission.

3. *Colonel Sellers as a Scientist.*

4. *A Sea Change, or Love's Stowaway.*

16 APRIL 1884, BOSTON, TO EDGAR W. HOWE

Louisburg Square
Boston, April 16, 1884

Dear Sir:[1]

I wish to thank you for the copy of your "Story of a Country Town," which you sent me, and for the very great pleasure I have had in reading it. Consciously or unconsciously, it is a very remarkable piece of realism and whether it makes you known now or not it constitutes your part of the only literary movement of our times that seems to have vitality in it. I have never lived as far West as Kansas but I have lived in your country town, and I know it is every word true, down to the perpetual Scriptural disputes of the inhabitants. Fairview and its people are also actualities, which even if I had never seen them—and I have—your book would persuade me of. Such people in the story are excellent, all natural and sentient, except the last half of your Jo, who slops into sentimentality and driveling wickedness, wholly unworthy. Biggs is delightful, and all his household. John Westlock is a grim and most pathetic tragedy; his wife moves me less, but she is alive, too. I have no time to specify, and I don't know how to tell you of the impressions of simple, naked humaness that the book gives me. It has many faults, as any fool can show you, but be sure that you have written so good a book that it will be hard for you to write a better. I am afraid that you will never write another so sincere and frank. I wish I could see you; but upon your honest piece of work I give you my hand with my heart in it.

Yours truly,
W. D. Howells.

Have you read Zola or Tourguenieff? Will you send me your fotograf?[2]

1. Edgar Watson Howe (1853–1937), editor and owner of the Atchison, Kansas, *Daily Globe* (1877–1911) and *E. W. Howe's Monthly* (1911–1937), is remembered chiefly for his naturalistic novel, *The Story of a Country Town* (1883). In "Two Notable Novels," *Century*, August 1884, Howells expressed at greater length many of the same sentiments about Howe's novel as in this letter.

2. Howe replied to this letter on 7 May 1884 (MH), writing in part: "The letter and the picture came to hand, and I am very proud of both. I can only hope that in the future I may prove worthy of your good opinion. . . . When I get out my writing at night now, it is with a view to satisfying Howells and Clemens rather than the public." Howe's great appreciation for Howells' good opinion of his fiction was conveyed in two later extant letters, 28 July and 27 November 1884 (photocopies at MH). See also James B. Stronks, "William Dean Howells, Ed Howe, and *The Story of a Country Town*," *American Literature* 29 (1958), 473–78; and Calder M. Pickett, *Ed Howe: Country Town Philosopher* (Lawrence: University Press of Kansas, 1968), pp. 73–75.

30 APRIL 1884, BOSTON, TO WHITELAW REID

4 Louisburg Square
Boston, April 30, 1884.

My dear Reid:

Would you like a little paper from me—about a column and a half—on Two Plays which I saw in New York? The plays are May Blossom and Dan's Tribulations,[1] and I should try to show that the latter was the spring of a new drama, and the former the dregs of stage-playing. The paper would be signed and would be such as the Century would give me $100 for.[2]

With kindest regards to Mrs. Reid,

Yours ever
W. D. Howells.

1. *May Blossom*, a romantic drama by David Belasco, played at the Madison Square Theatre, 11–12 April 1884; *Dan's Tribulations*, a dramatic musical by Edward Harrigan and Tony Hart, played at the Theatre Comique, 7 April–31 May 1884.

2. An undated letter from "D. N." to Whitelaw Reid (DLC) comments on Howells' proposed review: "Miss Hutchinson thinks the paper would be read with interest, & would be worth the money. M[r]. Bowers thinks it would be absurd for Howells to write on a subject on which he is not an authority when Winter, who is an authority, could do it so much better. And further that a man must be an idiot who looks upon 'Dan's Tribulations' as the opening of a new drama. [¶] My own opinion is that Howells would be read but that as a dramatic critic he is not worth $15 a column." Ellen Hutchinson was art editor for the New York *Tribune*, but Mr. Bowers and "D. N." have not been identified. William Winter (1836–1917) was drama critic and an editor of the *Tribune* (1865–1909). Howells wrote Reid, 5 May 1884 (DLC): "Not hearing from you at once, I offered the paper to the Century; but to tell the truth, my humor has cooled, and I do not think I shall write it at all . . . ."

12 MAY 1884, BOSTON, TO JAMES R. OSGOOD

4 Louisburg Square,
Boston, May 12, 1884.

Dear Osgood:

I suppose you will see Mr. Alden in New York, and I wish you would tell him that I have had it in mind to answer his last letter ever since I came away. In that he said that he would like to reconsider the plan of my story if I would make more of the hero and heroine;[1] and I could easily do this, for I never meant to make what he seemed to think I would—that is, something farcical or comical. In the first place, I don't believe in heroes and heroines, and willingly avoid the heroic; but I meant to make a simple, earnest, and often very pathetic figure of my country boy, whose adventures and qualities should win him the reader's entire sympathy and respect. It seemed to me that I had indicated this purpose both in my opening chapters and my sketch, but I must have failed, since Mr. Alden understood something so different. Nothing in a story can be better than life, and I intended to make this story as life-like as possible. But I look at life as a very serious affair, and the tendency of the story would be to grow rather tragical than comical. I do not see how I could re-write the plan so as to present to Mr. Alden's mind the image of a more considerable hero; I can only give him the assurance that he will be anything but a trivial or farcical figure. If he wishes to reconsider the idea with this light upon it, and this assurance I shall be glad to write the story to his order, and keep his wish in mind; but neither you nor I wish him to take it with a faltering faith in my ability to make it important and attractive.

Perhaps you will show him this letter. He appeared to think that I had some poet *manqué* like Gifted Hopkins in mind;[2] but I had nothing of the sort. I believe in this story, and am not afraid of its effect before the public.

Yours ever
W. D. Howells.

1. Neither H. M. Alden's letter nor Howells' "plan" for *The Minister's Charge* (1887) has been located. However, an entry in Howells' "Savings Bank" notebook (MH) indicates his early conception of the story: "Barker from thinking how S. depresses & J. elevates him, dimly conceives of the notion of elevating others. (Complicity). In this way he is to escape from all that's sordid in his own life." And several pages later, this further entry appears: "*Conclusion of L. B.* Bromfield Corey to Sewell. 'Why, all our aristocracy began so. In three generations his descendants would have been an old family on Commonwealth Ave., with country house at Beverley, and would have left Mrs. Sewell out when they asked you to dinner. Any Irishman would make a better and easier living off his farm.' " A letter from Howells to Osgood, 29 April 1884 (MH), suggests that Howells was interested in

serializing his new novel in *Harper's Monthly*: "It has occurred to me that it might be as well to wait a few days, and see whether Mr. Alden may not write me again in regard to the story. We can lose nothing by delay, and if he applies again it will put us in a better position. I will be guided by your judgment." It appears that Howells' refusal to go along with Alden's suggested changes was the reason for the eventual publication in the *Century*, February–December 1886. See also *The Minister's Charge*, HE, pp. xi-xvi.

2. Probably a reference to Lemuel Hopkins (1750–1801), one of the Connecticut Wits.

14 MAY 1884, BOSTON, TO BELTON O. TOWNSEND

4 Louisburg Square,
Boston, May 14, 1884.

My dear friend:

It was extremely pleasant to see your handwriting again, and to know that you still valued our old relation. But I cannot mar the recollection of that by praising your volume of verse, which is as wholly bad as a thing of the kind can be.[1] I regret that you have printed it, and since it can only do you harm with those who do not know the good work you have done in other directions,[2] I desire the smallest possible currency for it. You must forgive my frankness: I should have been less than your friend if I had forborne.

I hope your brother, of whom we saw only too little, is well. Remember us all kindly to him, and believe me

Yours cordially
W. D. Howells.

1. See Howells to Townsend, 19 December 1874, n. 1. On 30 August 1884 (E. N. Zeigler) Howells tried to soothe Townsend's hurt feelings: "If I wounded you, you must forgive me; the thought of giving pain to any one is intolerable to me, and I have truly liked and respected you in spite of what I consider still the error of publishing your poems. I should be wronging you very cruelly to praise them; but I like you so much,—you seem to me so true and good and brave a spirit—that I wish with all my heart I could praise them." See also Howells to Clemens, 26 May 1884 (CU; *Twain-Howells*, p. 489).

2. See Howells to Garrison, 25 April 1877.

19 MAY 1884, BOSTON, TO JOHN AUGUSTIN DALY

Boston, May 19, 1884.

Dear Mr. Daly:

I will naturalize that German comedy for $2000 cash on delivery of the MS., if it is to appear *without* my name.[1] If you want my name with you, you must pay me much more.[2]

Yours sincerely
W. D. Howells.

1. Daly had written Howells on 11 February 1884 (MH) that he would be "only too glad to do a work of yours suited to my company." Apparently Howells submitted *A Counterfeit Presentment*, which Daly rejected on the grounds that it was "too *neat* for popular representation." As an alternative he sent Howells a copy of *Hunting a Wife*, a German comedy he wanted Howells to translate. See Daly to Howells, 13 May 1884 (MH).

2. Daly responded to Howells, 21 May 1884 (MH): "I have never paid a sum down to authors for plays since I have been in the business . . .— [¶] I am willing to give $150 per week—if your name is attached & you make the piece fit the company." Though Daly proposed to Howells on 28 May 1884 (MH) that he would be glad to give one of Howells' plays or adaptations during the 1885–1886 season if it were ready in time, he never produced any of Howells' dramatic works.

20 MAY 1884, BOSTON, TO EDMUND W. GOSSE

4 Louisburg Square,
Boston, May 20, 1884.

My dear Gosse:

I rejoice with you, with all my heart, on your appointment which I suppose is almost the pleasantest thing that could happen to you.[1] I can imagine you there in that beautiful old town, in some college with a "back" as lovely as one of Watteau's women,[2] and if I could envy you at all, I should envy you that fate. But I can't envy you; I shall only love you the more the luckier you are.

I have been reading your 17th century poets since I came home from New York and enjoying every word: perhaps we can get up a "boom" for the book here on your appointment.[3]—I am very glad that this will not prevent your coming here. Maybe we shall receive you at our own house in the *real* Cambridge, which is, you know, a suburb of Boston.— Tell Tadema that Henschel and I are working together at a comic opera (the libretto is done) which is to be bro't out here this fall, and we hope in London.[4] Henschel's music is lovely.

My wife joins me in love and rejoicing.

Yours ever
W. D. Howells.

1. Gosse wrote Howells, 7 May 1884 (MH; *Transatlantic Dialogue*, pp. 140–41) that he had been appointed to the Clark Lectureship in English literature at Trinity College, Cambridge University. He felt that his new position would "justify you a little,—with your American friends,—in your too generous estimate of me."

2. Antoine Watteau (1684–1721), a French painter, was famous for his innovative treatment of landscape backgrounds in portrait paintings, the best known of which is "Rosalba Carriera" (1721).

3. *Seventeenth Century Studies*.

4. See Howells to Gosse, 2 January 1884, n. 8.

8 JUNE 1884, BOSTON, TO WILLIAM C. HOWELLS

Boston, June 8, 1884.

Dear father:

I let John write the last letter for me, being occupied with the making of the prompt-book for my opera. I believe we have told you that it has been taken by the Bijou theatre here.[1] They will produce it the day after Blaine's defeat,[2] and if it succeeds, it will be a very nice thing for me. But I have made my fortune in the theatre too often to be elated at this chance.

Talking of fortunes makes me think of grape scissors. You mustn't suppose I'm neglecting the matter. I'm looking after it most vigilantly; but there seems to be a hitch somewhere in Lowentraut.[3] He reported the batch ready for stamping three weeks ago, but they are not yet finished. Joe and I have got everything in train for advertising and selling.

The Blain nomination is a great pill, here. I dined Friday night with four Republicans, and was the only one who wouldn't say he was going to vote *against* Blaine. They think he is flashy, ambitious and selfish, and will get us into trouble with other powers to make a showy administration. I don't know. Do you?

The summer has got here in full force, at last, and we've been frying for the last four days.

We shall probably stay in town till after Class Day, to give Winny her chance at the students. Then we shall break for the country somewhere.

All join me in love to all.

Your aff'te son
Will.

1. George H. Tyler (d. 1884), general manager of the Boston Bijou Theatre Company, first wrote Howells on 11 April 1884 (MH), expressing his interest in acquiring the rights to *A Sea Change, or Love's Stowaway*. In his letter to Howells of 16 April 1884 (MH), Tyler proposed to pay Howells $100 per week while the opera was being performed or three percent of the gross receipts for the production rights in the United States and Canada.

2. James G. Blaine had been nominated for president at the Republican national convention in Chicago. He lost to Grover Cleveland in the general election on 4 November 1884. Throughout the campaign Howells waivered in believing Blaine's assertion of innocence in a financial scandal that broke in 1876. He wrote to W. C. Howells on 21 September 1884 (MH): "After convincing myself that Blaine is not a rogue at all, I have at present great difficulty in arriving at the conclusion that he is not too great an ass to be President." Nevertheless, Howells' strong Republican sympathies outweighed his doubts, and he voted for Blaine. See also Howells to Clemens, 10 August 1884, n. 8; Howells to Perry, 15 August 1884; and Howells to W. C. Howells, 19 October 1884, n. 2.

3. See Howells to Clemens, 10 April 1884, n. 2.

18 June 1884, Boston, to Richard W. Gilder

Boston, June 18, 1884.

Dear Mr. Gilder:

Thank you for both your kind notes.[1] I meant to sign the O. Letter.[2] How would you like one—or a short paper—on Marital Suffrage, advocating more or less mock-seriously, the disfranchisement of all celibate persons, and the confinement of the franchise to husbands and wives?[3]

I can give you the first Florentine paper in October.[4]

Yours ever
W. D. Howells.

1. Gilder wrote to Howells on 13 June and 16 June 1884 (MH). In the earlier letter he mentioned negotiations with J. R. Osgood for some stories by Howells on nine subjects specified in a list Gilder could no longer locate; in the second letter he listed the six stories he wanted to publish in the *Century*—"The Mercy of God," "New Leaf Mills," "God Does Not Pay Saturdays," "The Area of Calamity," "John Borden's Chance," and "A Voice & Nothing More."

2. Gilder wrote Howells on 2 June 1884 (MH), thanking him "for the Open Letter on the two fictions." He was probably referring to "Two Notable Novels," *Century*, August 1884, in which Howells reviewed Edward Bellamy's *Miss Ludington's Sister* and Edgar W. Howe's *The Story of a Country Town*. On 16 June, Gilder wanted to know whether the review was to be signed, since Howells had failed to indicate his choice in reading the proofs.

3. The proposed paper on "Marital Suffrage" was never published.

4. "A Florentine Mosaic." See Howells to Smith, 19 November 1882, n. 6.

Ca. 20 June 1884, Boston[?], to Hugo Erichsen

1 Daytime; forenoon.[1]
2 Generally not—almost never.
3 No.
4 None.
5 Two or three; sometimes four.
6 I am lazy, and always force myself more or less to work, keeping from it as long as I can invent any excuse. I often work when dull or heavy from a bad night, and find that the indisposition wears off. I rarely miss a day from any cause. After my early dinner I read, correct proof, walk about and pay visits. For a lazy man I am extremely industrious.

W. D. Howells.

1. The listed numbers indicate Howells' response to questions contained in the letter given below, in which Howells had inserted numbers (here shown in square brackets) in order to facilitate his reply. Since Dr. Erichsen's printed letter is dated 14 June (NHi), it is likely that Howells responded about 20 June 1884 from Boston, his residence at the time.

Detroit, June 14 1884

Dear Sir:

At present I am engaged in collecting material for an interesting book, to be published under the name "The Methods of Authors." As its title indicates, it will contain the mode or way of working of writers in all parts of the world. I trust that it will not only be interesting, but also useful to authors themselves. Please inform me of your own method. [1] Do you prefer daytime or the night? [2] Do you make an outline, a skeleton of your work first? [3] Do you use stimulants when at work, as wine, coffee or tobacco? [4] Have you any particular habit, when at work? [5] How many hours a day do you spend at the writing desk? [6] Did you ever force yourself to work when not having an inclination to do so? Please answer these questions and communicate to me such other matters connected with the subject as you may think of.

Respectfully yours,
Dr. Hugo Erichsen,
11 Farmer Street, Detroit, Mich.,
United States of America.

Erichsen included the material Howells sent him on his working habits and added some material not furnished by Howells in his book *The Methods of Authors* (1894), pp. 95–96.

31 JULY 1884, WOLFEBOROUGH, NEW HAMPSHIRE, TO RICHARD W. GILDER

Wolfeborough, N. H.
July 31, 1884.

My dear Gilder:

I hardly know what advertising material to give you about the story.[1] It will involve more interests, I find, and be more of a love story than I expected, but the main idea of a rude, common, unrefined nature, holding out against a temptation which must beset many business men and accepting ruin rather than inflict it, remains the same. The story opens with an interview by Bartley Hubbard, in which the hero's history and character are outlined. The scene is always in Boston, except at the close, when it will be somewhere in Northern New England. I can't think what else to say. As to the illustrated papers, the first will sketch the opening of a winter in Florence, as I saw it.[2] I expect that it will be very desultory. Something like my Italian Journeys.

I hope to see you at Marion next week, early.[3]

Yours ever
W. D. Howells.

I wouldn't give this idea away.

1. Gilder wrote Howells on 25 July 1884 (MH): "Could you kindly send me some rough notes describing your novel—and the Italian series—that we can make use of in writing our prospectus." The novel was *The Rise of Silas Lapham*, which

was published serially in the *Century*, November 1884–August 1885, and in book form by James R. Osgood & Co. in 1885.

2. "A Florentine Mosaic."

3. Gilder was vacationing in Marion, Massachusetts.

7 AUGUST 1884, BOSTON, TO CHARLES E. NORTON

Boston, Aug. 7, 1884.

Dear friend:

Your kind and tempting note happens to find me here, while the family are at Kennebunkport, and it is a real grief to me to forego the pleasure you offer.[1] I long to see you, and talk over the lovely time which you must have had in England.[2] I too have seen the Mother of Harvard in beautiful Oldest Cambridge and I could sympathize intelligently with all your reminiscences.[3] It seemed to me such a fit thing that you should go there on the mission that took you: no one could be more acceptably American among gentle Englishmen.

Well, the worst for me is that I cannot come, for I am not alone presently sorrowing over the most recalcitrant of novels,[4] but I am promised long ago for the only days I can give this summer to some friends at far Campobello.[5] Winny will feel the same regret that I do when she knows what she has lost. With her love to Liby,

Yours affectionately
W. D. Howells.

1. Apparently Norton had invited Howells and Winifred to attend the Ashfield Academy dinner on 22 August and to spend that week with the Norton family.

2. Norton had spent six weeks in England as Harvard's representative at the tercentenary of Emmanuel College at Cambridge.

3. See Howells to Norton, 14 September 1882.

4. *The Rise of Silas Lapham.*

5. The friends Howells visited in Campobello, New Brunswick, are not identified. Howells wrote W. C. Howells on 23 August 1884 (MH) that he spent "four days at Campobello" to fill an engagement of Winny's, partly. Howells felt that the strange new scenery he saw there "is all material for the future, I suppose, but in the meantime it isn't favorable to writing." The Campobello setting was used in *April Hopes*, on which Howells began work in the spring of 1886.

10 AUGUST 1884, BOSTON, TO WILLIAM C. HOWELLS

Boston, Aug. 10, 1884.

Dear father:

I came down here last Monday, to put the house in order—or rather my books—leaving the family at Kennebunkport, Me. (I seem to have written you all this before.) And here I have been hard at work, and lonesome of course. There is not only nobody else in the house, but nobody else that I know sleeps in town. Altogether the effect is queer. There are miles of empty houses all round me. And how unequally things are divided in this world. While these beautiful, airy, wholesome houses are uninhabited, thousands upon thousands of poor creatures are stifling in wretched barracks in the city here, whole families in one room. I wonder that men are so patient with society as they are.[1]

Aurelia's letter came Thursday, and I was glad that the poor child was pleased. Tell her not to be restricted by any suggestions of mine in the use of the money.[2] You must be patient about my not bringing many of the family with me this fall. It is a long journey, and neither Elinor nor Winny is quite strong enough for it. I am sorry you are so far off, but that can't be helped. I will do the best I can. It's pleasant to know that you're arranging your house to suit you.—Lowentraut sent an inquiry for the shears from some one in Bridgeport, which I forwarded to Joe—the first he's had. L. has behaved badly about finishing them up in time. If they succeed we must get some one else to make them.[3]

With love to all,

> Your aff'te son
> Will.

1. These thoughts on the inequity of society are reflected in chapter 14 of *The Rise of Silas Lapham*, where Bromfield Corey, according to the earliest version of the text, speaks of dynamiting the empty residences of the rich. See *The Rise of Silas Lapham*, HE, pp. 194, 384–87.

2. Howells had written his sister on 1 August 1884 (MH) from Wolfeborough, New Hampshire, suggesting that she take her father to the seaside at Newport News, Virginia, for a "free and unhurried" day or two of vacation. Howells enclosed five dollars with his letter, which was in addition to ten dollars he had sent her the previous day in a letter to his father.

3. See Howells to Clemens, 10 April 1884, n. 2. On 31 July 1884 (MH) Howells had given his father a summary of the dismal state of affairs in respect to the grape-shears venture: "You cannot be more vexed about the scissors than I am. I suppose Joe has thirty dozen, for they were shipped to him six weeks ago. The remaining half of the sixty dozen, Lowentraut has been delaying in spite of all the urging I could bring to bear.... I'm afraid Lowentraut is a rascal, and that he's delaying purposely. I suppose he's vexed at my taking the management from him."

10 AUGUST 1884, Boston, to Elinor M. Howells

> Boston, Aug. 10, 1884.

Dear Elinor:

I shall not come up till Tuesday, on account of business.[1] I found here a letter from the Englishman who dramatized A Foregone Conclusion, saying that he had given the play for this country to the Mallorys and they would communicate with me.[2] It was a very nice letter, and asked my sanction and revision of the play. Friday, Mallory wrote asking where they could see me, and he is coming here to-morrow, with the play, which they wish me to work over.[3] I think the affair important enough to stay over for. Wouldn't it be funny if I should have *three* pieces running, this winter?[4]

Yesterday I almost killed myself putting the rest of the books up. The labor was immense and brought on an attack of diarrhoea. But that seems stopped now, and I shall be careful. You mustn't wonder if I haven't done much since I've been here. The fact is, I've been sick nearly the whole time, and several days I only went out of the house to meals, having a bad "pain across me" most of the time. O dear! If I could only get a little real rest. What a pulverized summer! I shall bring the trunks and all your things. Love to the children.

Your
W. D. H.

1. Elinor and the children were vacationing in Kennebunkport, Maine.
2. William Poel (1852–1934), an English actor and dramatist who worked mostly in amateur productions, wrote Howells, 23 July 1884 (MH), that he had written an adaptation of *A Foregone Conclusion* called *Priest or Painter*, which played at the Royal Olympic Theatre in London, 11 July 1884. See W. J. Meserve, *The Complete Plays of W. D. Howells* (New York: New York University Press, 1960), p. 314. Poel further noted: "...Dr. Mallory, proprietor of the Madison Square Theatre in New York, who was present at the performance here, has proposed to communicate with you on the subject [of writing revisions] and is taking out with him a copy of the play." Poel's real surname was Pole.
3. George S. Mallory. For Howells' earlier dealings with the Mallorys see Howells to Clemens, 1 September 1882, n. 7.
4. *A Sea Change, or Love's Stowaway, Colonel Sellers as a Scientist,* and *Priest or Painter* were the three dramatic works.

10 AUGUST 1884, BOSTON, TO SAMUEL L. CLEMENS

Boston, Aug. 10, 1884.

Dear Clemens:

If I had written half as good a book as Huck Finn, I shouldn't ask anything better than to read the proofs; even as it is I don't.[1] So send them on; they will always find me somewhere. I'm here in town for the present; but I'm going to Kennebunkport where the family are on Tuesday, and then to Campobello, N.B. Back to Boston the last of the month.

I see that the circus has been finally reduced to Cable and you.[2] That is right. The public wants to hear both of *you*; but I should have been a drag.

That *was* funny about the Mark Twain fotograf and the sick women's comprehensive censure of authors.[3] I'm looking up, for my new story, facts about the general lack of literature in people, and I asked the teacher of a first-class ladies' school here how little literature a girl could carry away from her school.[4] "Some go barely knowing that Shakespeare was an Englishman. One who had read all the 'love-part' of your [my][5] novels, did n't know that you were an American or a contemporary. We have to fight in eight months against fifteen or twenty years' absolute ignorance of literature."

I've got a mighty pretty house here on the water side of Beacon st.,[6] and Mrs. Howells wants Mrs Clemens and you to consider yourself engaged for a visit to us when my opera[7] comes out in November.

> Yours ever
> W. D. Howells

What I want to do is to vote for Clevelands *widow*. She's the one who ought to be elected.[8]

1. Three days earlier, on 7 August 1884 (MH; *Twain-Howells*, pp. 497–98), Clemens had written Howells: "I have no doubt I am doing a most criminal & outrageous thing—for I am sending you these infernal Huck Finn proofs—but the very last vestige of my patience has gone to the devil . . . . Now you're not to read it unless you really don't mind it . . . ."
2. See Howells to Clemens, 18 March 1882, n. 9.
3. Clemens recounted these two humorous episodes in the postscript to his letter of 7 August. One anecdote concerned a salesman of actresses' photographs who did not recognize the name Mark Twain and asked "Where does she play?" The other anecdote was about a woman, who in reference to Howells, James, Whitman, and Swinburne said: "they're all alike—when you've read one, you've read 'em all!"
4. See *The Rise of Silas Lapham*, HE, pp. 112–15.
5. Howells' brackets.
6. 302 Beacon Street.
7. *A Sea Change, or Love's Stowaway.*
8. Because of the attacks by the "Mugwumps" on J. G. Blaine, the Republican nominee, his supporters sought to blemish the personal character of Grover Cleveland, the Democratic nominee. In July 1884 it was revealed that eight years earlier Cleveland had engaged in a liaison with Maria Halpin, a widow who bore Cleveland's illegitimate child. Clemens supported the "Mugwumps" while Howells supported Blaine.

15 August 1884, Kennebunkport, Maine, to Thomas S. Perry

Kennebunkport, Me., Aug. 15, 1884.

My dear Perry:

The charges against Blaine are denied by men in whose candor and judgment I have much greater faith than I have in Schurz's:[1] for example, Judge Hoar and Wm. Worth Phelps,[2] not to name others; and Blaine himself denies them. I do not believe them; and it is not true that Blaine is supported by the worst of both parties. He is supported by many of the best men I know.

The charges against Cleveland I *must* believe, because with ever so much sophistry and shuffling his friends admit that he has a son by a woman not his wife.[3] This may not be the worst thing in the world for him; but neither is it the worst for her, then. Yet you propose to place one paramour at the head of the nation, while you would not admit the other paramour to your house even as a servant.

This injustice insults my sense of right and wrong none the less but all the more because this is the attitude of society generally in regard to the paramours.

I will tell John that I voted for a man *accused* of bribery, and that I would not vote for a man *guilty* of what society sends a woman to hell for.

Politician for politician, self-seeker for self-seeker, I prefer a Republican to a Democrat; and I will not vote a party into power which is composed of all that is retrograde and savage in our politics, and which has betrayed every trust honest men have reposed in it.

Yours ever
W. D. Howells.

1. This letter was an answer to Perry's letter of 12 August 1884 (MH), itself a response to an earlier letter by Howells, in which Howells asserted that he would vote for Blaine. Perry told Howells that he felt Carl Schurz's speech in Brooklyn, New York, on 5 August 1884, was "a presentation of the facts [against Blaine] that yet awaits an answer & will long await one." (For the complete text of the speech, see the New York *Times*, 6 August 1884.) Perry further argued that Blaine's dishonesty as a public servant was a worse thing than Cleveland's private licentiousness.
2. Probably Ebenezer R. Hoar (1816–1895), judge in the Massachusetts court of common pleas (1849–1855) and the Massachusetts supreme court (1859–1869). William W. Phelps (1839–1894), U.S. representative from New Jersey (1873–1875; 1883–1889), wrote a letter to the New York *Times*, 27 April 1884, defending Blaine's stock transactions.
3. See Howells to Clemens, 10 August 1884, n. 8.

22 AUGUST 1884, KENNEBUNKPORT, MAINE, TO HENRY JAMES

Kennebunkport, Maine, Aug. 22, 1884.

My dear James:

It is very good of you to write me when I've so long owed you a letter,[1] and to make my buying a house "on the water side of Beacon" the occasion of forgiving my neglect. The greatest pleasure the house has yet brought me is this; but it is a pretty house and an extremely fine situation, and I hope it is not the only joy I shall have from it.

I have spent some desolate weeks in it already, putting my books on their shelves, while the family were away at mountain-side and seaside,[2] and I can speak confidently and authoritatively of the sunsets from the library-windows. The sun goes down over Cambridge with as much apparent interest as if he were a Harvard graduate: possibly he is; and he spreads a glory over the Back Bay that is not to be equaled by the blush of a Boston Independent for such of us Republicans as are going to vote for Blaine.—Sometimes I feel it an extraordinary thing that I should have been able to buy a house on Beacon str., but I built one on Concord Avenue of nearly the same cost when I had far less money to begin with.[3] In those doubting days I used to go and look at the cellar they were digging, and ask myself, knowing that I had had barely money to pay for the lot, "*Can* blood be got out of a turnip?" Now I know that some divine power loves turnips, and that somehow the blood will be got out of the particular turnip which I represent. Drolly enough, I am writing a story in which the chief personage builds a house "on the water side of Beacon," and I shall be able to use all my experience, down to the quick.[4] Perhaps the novel may pay for the house.

I am just back from a visit of a few days at Campobello,[5] which is so far off that I feel as if I had been to Europe. It is a fashionable resort, in spite of its remoteness, and I saw many well-dressed and well-read girls there who were all disposed more or less to talk of you, and of your latest story, A New England Winter.[6] Generally speaking I should say that its prime effect had been to imbue the female Boston mind with a firm resolve to walk on the domestic roof at the first opportunity. The maiden aunt gives universal satisfaction, especially in her rage with her nephew when he blows her a five-fingered kiss. I myself having the vice of always liking you, ought perhaps to be excluded from the stand, but I must bear my witness to the excellence particularly of some of the bits of painting. In just such a glare of savage sunshine I made my way through Washington street in such a horsecar as you portray, the day I read your advance sheets. Besides that, I keenly enjoyed those fine touches by which you suggest a more celestially difficult and evasive Boston than I ever get at. The fashionableness which is so unlike the fashionableness of other towns—no one touches that but you; and you contrive also to indicate its contiguity, in its most etherial intangibility, to something that is very plain and dully practical. It is a great triumph which Pauline Mesh embodies. The study pleases me throughout: the mother with her struggles—herculean struggles—with such shadowy problems; the son with the sincere Europeanism of an inalienable, wholly uninspired American. As for the vehicle, it is delicious.

I don't know whether I've bragged to you of all the work I've done the past winter. One piece of it was an opera which Henschel set to music, and we had a contract with the Bijou Theatre for its production in November. The other night the manager with whom we contracted, in trying to get aboard his yacht in the fog, fell and fractured his skull, poor man. He died, and with him our legal hold upon a potential fortune. I dare say the Theatre will still want it;[7] but I wait the return of the puissant Osgood, who put our contract through before knowing.— The Madison Square people have bought the London dramatization of A Foregone Conclusion, and have sent it to me for revision.[8] As yet we have not got beyond the point of my having refused to do it for next to nothing. Sometime, when we meet, I will tell you how those gifted brothers led me on protesting over the same path you trod to the same flowery pitfall with another play.[9]—I really begin to admire them; they are masters of no common skill.

We are expecting the Gosses at our house early in December, and have plans for making them like the country, which ought to succeed at least so long as they are in it.

Before Perry went away for the summer I saw him very often. Since that time we have developed into political enemies: men to whom the private vices of Cleveland and the civic crimes of Blaine are reciprocally virtues of the most pleasing complexion.[10]

There is no literary news to give you in this dull season, at this little seaport, where loverless maidens superabound in the hotels and the rowboats on the river in such numbers as would furnish all the novelists with heroines indefinitely. The family joins me in love.

Yours ever

W. D. Howells

1. Howells' letter was in response to one from James, dated 31 July 1884 (MH), in which he comments on his present condition: "I am at the present moment what I imagine you most naturally suppose me to be—a battered relic of the London Season. It is fortunately over, & I possess my soul once more. I have tried hard to lead a quiet life, but have succeeded only in being infinitely interrupted & distracted. Moral—I shall next year seek safety in absence."

2. Wolfeborough, New Hampshire, and Kennebunkport, Maine.

3. The house at 37 Concord Avenue was constructed in 1872–1873.

4. *The Rise of Silas Lapham.*

5. See Howells to Norton, 7 August 1884, n. 5.

6. James's story appeared in the *Century*, August–September 1884. One of the characters, Miss Lucretia Daintry, a Boston spinster, demonstrates her spirit of Yankee independence by inspecting the roof of her house with the man who had come to repair it: "She had walked all over it, and peeped over the cornice, and not been in the least dizzy; and had come to the conclusion that one ought to know a great deal more about one's roof than was usual."

7. Meserve notes that the Bijou later lost interest in *A Sea Change, or Love's Stowaway* because of the difficulty and expense of staging the production. See *The Complete Plays of W. D. Howells* (New York: New York University Press, 1960), pp. 270–71.

8. See Howells to Elinor Howells, 10 August 1884, n. 2.

9. Howells was probably referring to James's dramatization of "Daisy Miller," which the Mallory brothers encouraged him to complete, only to reject it when finally done. See L. Edel, *Henry James: The Middle Years, 1882–1895* (Philadelphia: Lippincott, 1962), pp. 39–40. For Howells' dealings with the Mallorys in connection with the production of *Colonel Sellers as a Scientist*, see Howells to Clemens, 1 September 1882, n. 7.

10. See Howells to Perry, 15 August 1884.

7 SEPTEMBER 1884, BOSTON, TO WILLIAM C. HOWELLS

302 Beacon st.,
Boston, Sept. 7, 1884.

Dear father:

I have been at home during the past week, and I expect the family about Wednesday. The week has been the hottest of the summer, but to-day we have the east wind and are all right again. As soon as I got home I enquired about the price of grapes, and found that only fancy kinds were selling for 5 or 6 cents, with the prospect of lower prices. So I saw at once that it would not do for you to ship them to this market.

I have not much news of any kind. As usual I am at work, and am about half way through the novel that begins in the November Century.[1] My affairs with the stage are in a mixed condition. Three weeks ago it seemed probable that I should have three pieces running: the comic opera, the Sellers play, and the revised dramatization of the Foregone Conclusion (first brought out in London this summer.)[2] But the operatic manager was killed, the Madison Square people who have the dramatization have not come to terms yet, and Raymond will probably not give the farce till Spring. So my fortune is not yet made. Perhaps it never will be; but I shall not lose heart, for all that.

The election is going very queerly, but I think Blaine will get it. The bolters here are very bitter.[3]

With love to all

Your aff'te son
Will.

1. *The Rise of Silas Lapham.*

2. *A Sea Change, or Love's Stowaway; Colonel Sellers as a Scientist;* and *Priest or Painter.*

3. The "bolters" were the "Mugwump" dissidents in the Republican party.

19 OCTOBER 1884, BOSTON, TO WILLIAM C. HOWELLS

302 Beacon street,
Boston, Oct. 19, 1884.

Dear father:

Your last letter, which I had been a long time waiting for, went to New Bedford on its way to Boston, for reasons of its own. It was very plainly directed. I was glad to hear that you were all better than your crops; and to get that amusing and miraculous flash from Henry, about the lack of woman's nursing, etc. How small the difference in his poor bewildered brain must be from any other!

I do not know that I have a word of news to send you back. It has been an intensely busy month with me, for besides having to help settle the house, I have been writing almost double quantity on some papers about Florence for the Century, keeping on my mind the stress of the unfinished novel which I have had to postpone for the time.[1] But I have nearly pulled through, and next month, with my little outing with you, and my lighter work, I hope to breathe freer. I trust that poor Joe— who has been under the weather—will be sure to meet me.

I am much perplexed, politically. When I read Blaine's letters, I see no wrong in them, though they are not very inspiring, but when I get them rearranged by the Independents, I am quite bewildered.[2] He has been most foully outraged, however, by the publication of his private, business correspondence, and that makes me indignant. It looks now, as if he would be elected.

All are well, and join me in love to all of you.

Your aff'te son
Will.

1. "A Florentine Mosaic" and *The Rise of Silas Lapham.*
2. Howells is referring to a series of letters by Blaine to Warren Fischer in which the suspect business practices between Blaine and the Little Rock & Fort Smith Railroad were revealed. These letters were made public in 1876 by James Mulligan and resurfaced during the 1884 presidential campaign. On 16 April 1884 Blaine wrote another letter to Fischer, giving instructions to write a letter publicly exonerating him of any wrongdoing in the railroad scandal. The contents of this letter were also revealed in the newspapers even though Blaine had asked Fischer to destroy it. Howells had written to John Hay, 17 September 1884 (typescript copy at MH): "I used really to think—or rather to take it for granted—that there must be something compromising in the Fisher [sic] letters. Since I bored myself to read them I am astounded at their innocence, their blatant and foolish innocence."

9 NOVEMBER 1884, BOSTON, TO WILLIAM C. HOWELLS

302 Beacon st.
Boston, Nov. 9, 1884.

Dear father:

This is cold weather for people of our politics, with no good prospects of a thaw. I have done what suffering I could, and now I'm lying back, and letting things take their course. A great cycle has come to a close; the rule of the best in politics for a quarter of century is ended.[1] Now we shall have the worst again. Well, patience! It can't be so bad as it was before the war.

As soon as I hear that Joe has started for Virginia I will start too, and I hope we shall all have a good, quiet time together. I am feeling fagged with the last year's work, and shall be glad of a complete rest. If it were of any use to repine I should have to lament the total failure of some enterprises, but I am still fairly prosperous, and I hope we shall be able to see our way through all the clouds.—The family are well, and join me in love to all. Except that Uncle Joe's Corinne[2] paid us a little visit lately, I have no news.

Your aff'te son
Will.

1. Grover Cleveland had just won the November election, thus bringing to an end the Republican domination of the presidency, which had lasted since the election of Abraham Lincoln.
2. Joseph Howells (1814–1896) was the brother of W. C. Howells; Corinne's relationship to him is not known.

24 DECEMBER 1884, BOSTON, TO EDMUND W. GOSSE

302 Beacon st.
Boston, Dec. 24, 1884.

Dearest Gossy:

The children are busy trimming their Christmas tree, and all our hearts go out in self-satisfied compassion towards you poor things. We have missed you terribly; and like the prisoner who was liberated after many years of confinement, we long for our bondage again.[1] (There is no extra charge for this figure.) Boston still palpitates with you, and the weather has come on with a snow storm which you ought to have seen. But no doubt you prefer basking on the Battery in New York. Three letters to-day and three yesterday came for you and were promptly forwarded. They seemed to be mostly English.

Do be very nice, and tell all about Mrs. Bryant Godwin if you meet her, and what she says of "R. S. connected with the C."[2] Also, any other social adventures that befall you. I wonder if your host will play a simple American citizen's Christmas, or something medieval,—baronial. In either case, give him my love, and good wishes, for he is heartily worthy.

The Tavern Club men think the Gosse dinner was the pleasantest they have yet had, and the spotted baby has covered you with glory.[3]

Mrs Howells has been sending you laurels plucked from various boughs, and there are but a few sprigs of parsley left me to glean. But the Perrys were talking you over with me, and they said—*he*, mostly— "And isn't *Mrs.* Gosse nice, too! I liked *her.*"—I saw the good little Doctor[4] on the street, but avoided his eye: I could *not* stand any more praise of Gosse from him.

I've been working like a beaver since you left, and am getting Silas well on to disaster. He is about to be "squeezed" by a rail-road, in a trade.[5]

I do wish you could both see the brave old Boston in this snow. It's superb.

Mrs. Howells says "Mrs. Proudie's regards to Mr. Pepys." I don't know what it means.[6] Sass, probably.

All the family join me in love to both of you.

Yours ever
W. D. Howells.

1. The Gosses stayed with Howells from 30 November until 19 December 1884. Gosse was visiting Lawrence Barrett in New York during the Christmas holiday.

2. "Mrs. Bryant Godwin, mother of Miss Nora Godwin, a young American whom the Gosses had twice entertained in London shortly before their departure, had written to Mrs. Gosse . . . to complain that her attempts to get in touch with Mrs. Gosse had been 'frustrated by the refusal of Mr. R. Smith (connected with the Century) to give me your address.' The joke . . . was that Roswell Smith owned the *Century*." See *Transatlantic Dialogue*, p. 158.

3. The Tavern Club dinner in Gosse's honor and with Howells presiding was held on 18 December 1884. The allusion to the "spotted baby" is probably in reference to a toast or a joke of Gosse's at the dinner.

4. Oliver Wendell Holmes.

5. See *The Rise of Silas Lapham*, HE, pp. 271–80.

6. Elinor Howells appears to have referred to herself as Mrs. Proudie of Trollope's Barsetshire novels and to Gosse as the diarist Samuel Pepys.

18 JANUARY 1885, BOSTON, TO WILLIAM C. HOWELLS

Boston, Jan. 18, 1885.

Dear father:

I suppose you have Annie and her children with you now, and are in the full enjoyment of them. Will you tell Annie that I got her lovely letter, and will write to her soon. We could n't arrange to meet her in New York, and in fact I must not think of leaving this desk again till my story is finished.[1] I have had to interrupt it with a good many things; but I hope another month will see it ended.—I want very much to have you pay us another visit, this spring, father. But we wont ask you to come in March again. We shall want to have you early in May, after you've got your spring planting done, and the abominable spring weather here is settled. Do you think you can manage it?—Have I told you about the flocks of wild ducks that visit the waters behind our house on stormy days? This morning, three large birds, as big as turkeys, which must have been some sort of fish-hawks, were sailing over the river; and there is always a great variety in the feathered life.—Would you care to see the volume of the elder James's "Literary Remains" which has been published?[2] It contains his autobiography, and I have been reading it with great interest. I could send it if you wished.—I don't know who else could have written that scrap about me from the St. Paul paper, but it doesn't sound exactly like Joe.[3] Elinor was greatly pleased with it. I am thinking seriously of doing a lecture for delivery next winter, and an Agent whom I've consulted thinks I would have a very good success.[4] In the meantime the work I have laid out for this year is appalling when I look at it in bulk. But it's surprising how much you can do, if you do something every day.—I hope you'll take up your memoranda again, father, and continue them. Perhaps the James book will stimulate you. I'll send it. Tell me how you are getting on. Have you seen a doctor about that trouble of yours? With united love to all,

Your aff'te son
Will.

1. *The Rise of Silas Lapham.*
2. William James, ed., *The Literary Remains of the Late Henry James* (1884).
3. Neither the "scrap" about Howells nor the "St. Paul paper" has been identified.
4. Howells did not undertake lecture tours until a dozen years later. In 1897 and 1899 he lectured under the management of James B. Pond (1838–1903), the manager of many of Clemens' lecture tours. See also Howells to Clemens, 5 May 1885.

8 March 1885, Boston, to William C. Howells

Boston, March 8, 1885.

Dear father:

I have had a letter from Joe this week, in which he speaks of being well again, and of having succeeded in keeping the county-seat at Jefferson. I dare say he suffered from the excitement of that question, which it would have been disastrous to have had settled in favor of Ashtabula.—Tell Annie that Mr. Chaplin[1] is coming here today with a few others to lunch with Charles Egbert Craddock,[2] the writer of the Tennessee mountain stories. Every one supposed him to be a big Tennessee man, but he turns out to be a little, frail girl, a cripple, whose name is Miss Murfree. There has been great astonishment at the fact, and Chaplin gives up going to Osterville to meet her.[3]—You say nothing in your last about your memoranda, but I hope you're thinking about them. We all want you to repeat that visit, this spring, which we enjoyed even more than you did. I shall arrange for it in good time.—There is not much news, except the old story of hard work.—This ice field back of our house has broken, and we see the clear water again in patches, so that we feel that spring is coming "slowly up this way."[4] All join me in love.

Your aff'te son
Will.

1. Perhaps Jeremiah Chaplin (1813–1886), minister and Boston literary man, who wrote, among other works, biographies of Charles Sumner, Galen, and Benjamin Franklin.
2. Mary Noailles Murfree (1850–1922), a local color fiction writer from Tennessee, wrote under the pseudonym of Charles Egbert Craddock. As editor of the *Atlantic*, Howells had published several of her stories; and in later years he discussed some of her fictions, beginning with *The Prophet of the Great Smoky Mountains* (1885) in "Editor's Study," *Harper's Monthly*, January 1886, where he commented: "Through such work as hers and Mr. [G. W.] Cable's the South is making itself heard in literature after a fashion likely to keep attention as well as to provoke it. These writers, while they study so carefully the actual speech and manners of the people they write of, still permit themselves a certain romance of motive . . . ." For accounts of Howells' meeting Miss Murfree at Thomas B. Aldrich's dinner party see E. W. Parks, *Charles Egbert Craddock* (Chapel Hill: University of North Carolina Press, 1941), pp. 124–25, and "Howells' Meeting Miss Murfree," *Literary News*, April 1885, the latter reprinted from the Chicago *News*.
3. Osterville is located on the south shore of Cape Cod, Massachusetts.
4. See S. T. Coleridge, "Christabel," line 22.

9 MARCH 1885, BOSTON, TO EDMUND W. GOSSE

> 302 Beacon st.
> Boston, March 9, 1885.

My dear Gosse:

I don't know which has more touched my heart, your letter or your present. I read Pastor Fido long ago in a dear little copy in vellum, for which my friend Dyer gave me in exchange, very much against my will, his Omar Khayyam, and I had remained inconsolable till your gift came. Think of having that loveliest bit of Unreality in the first edition, a Venetian edition! I am more than grateful—I am forgiving.[1] I almost freely pardon you from this hour for having scalped me on our glove trade. As soon as I set eyes on those seal-skin gloves of yours, I said to myself, "This simple islander does not know the value of seal-skin gloves on the mainland. Come, let me get the better of him." Hardly had you turned your back on Boston when your gloves, for which I had given a beautiful pair of beaver gauntlets and a collar, began to go to pieces on my hands. Then we examined them and found by the figures inside that you had given seven and sixpence for them. Was this right, was it kind— to lay for the American in his lair, and do him under his own roof? Come and live among us! You are worthy! You need not take out naturalization papers; I will tell them this little story at the polls, and they will let you vote anywhere! Perhaps I shall send you those fotografs when I have quite digested the glove-trade; I find the Pastor Fido a famous stomachic.

We are just now in an excitement as great as the Gosse boom at its wildest, about Charles Egbert Craddock, the author of the Tennessee mountain stories, who has turned up in Boston, a little *girl-cripple*, not so big as Pilla. She visited Aldrich first, and as soon as he could get his breath, he sat down and wrote me asking me to meet "Craddock" at dinner! He had Holmes and Barrett too, and he simply revelled in our successive gasps. Now, Craddock (Miss M. N. Murfree) is being lunched, (here yesterday) dined, receptioned and breakfasted from one end of Boston to another. She has a most manful and womanly soul in her poor, twisted little body. Her stories are extraordinary; but I dare say you know them.

I'm afraid poor Barrett is going to lose his daughter—the next oldest, *not* Milly.[2] She was taken here last week with peritonitis, and there is scarcely a hope of her recovery. It will be terrible for them all. Her mother was in New York, but came on, on Friday.

I am delighted that the American foray turned out so well, money wise.[3] It's too bad you couldn't have had more time. You might as well have carried home three times as much. You ought to write a popular lecture and make the grand lecturing tour.

The Museum people found it too expensive to produce the opera.[4] There is a *chance* that it may be given in New York. My father's affairs in Virginia are going somewhat better; I hope to run down to see him during the spring.

Our teapot was stirred to its depths by the Birdseye sacrilege,[5] but public feeling is rapidly reconciling itself. Even a sacrilege does not hold us long. Of course, nobody of any sense supposed James *meant to mean* the venerable Miss P.—S. Lapham is finished, and I am hammering away at my Italian papers for the Century.[6] "R. Smith, connected with the Century magazine"[7] is in town, and called upon us yesterday. In the dearth of other topics he spoke occasionally of the periodical. Of course he was kind to your memory.—Gosse, I suppose I shall never have as good a time again as I had with you. You just suited my complaint. Those laughs at nothing, those senseless giggles, what intellectual pleasure ever equalled them? When shall I see your like again? Never!— We "some talk" of taking the Old Manse in Concord for the summer.[8] Hey? All of us join in love to both of you. My wife ardently awaits your wife's report of all your adventures.

Your affectionate
W. D. Howells.[9]

1. Gosse wrote Howells, 15 February 1885 (MH; *Transatlantic Dialogue*, pp. 164–66), that he was sending him a copy of G. B. Guarini's *Il Pastor Fido*, which Howells had read in Venice twenty years earlier. Louis Dyer, Howells' friend, was a classics teacher at Harvard.

2. Mary Agnes Barrett, Lawrence Barrett's second oldest daughter.

3. According to entries in his pocket diary, Gosse earned £466.3.9 for his American lecture tour, although in his 15 February letter to Howells he reported earning £498. See *Transatlantic Dialogue*, p. 134.

4. Because of a lackluster "orchestra reading" of *A Sea Change, or Love's Stowaway*, on 27 January 1885 at the Boston Museum and the elaborate staging required for the opera, Roswell M. Field, manager of the theater, decided against producing it. Howells, discouraged that his opera would not be produced in Boston, wrote Osgood, 5 February 1885 (MH), asking him to see if it could be staged in New York; if it could not, Howells concluded, "let us publish the confounded thing and be rid of it."

5. In his letter of 15 February Gosse wrote: "James has been dismayed to be told, first by Lowell, next by me, and next by a quite independent third witness, that everybody in Boston will take his Miss Birdseye [in *The Bostonians*, the first chapter of which had appeared in the *Century*, February 1885] for a portrait of Elizabeth Peabody. Is there a stir about it?" Elizabeth Palmer Peabody (1804–1894) was a prominent transcendentalist and Nathaniel Hawthorne's sister-in-law.

6. "Panforte di Siena," *Century*, August–September 1885, and "Tuscan Cities," *Century*, October 1885.

7. See Howells to Gosse, 24 December 1884, n. 2.

8. Emerson and the Hawthornes had lived in the Old Manse in Concord, but there is no evidence that Howells ever rented the place.

9. Because Howells had mistakenly addressed the envelope to "Edward Gosse, Esq.," Gosse underlined "Edward" and wrote in the margin: "Oh! Oh! Very well! Walter Deloraine Howells! or is it Welch Deceiver Howells?"

13 MARCH 1885, BOSTON, TO JOSEPH W. HARPER, Jr.

302 Beacon st.
Boston, March 13, 1885.

Dear Mr. Harper:

I think the high contracting parties to the treaty which our friend Fairchild has negotiated may now fitly recognize each other, and I wish to say how extremely gratifying the result is to me.[1]

Aside from the substantial advantages, in which I shall do my best to make you an equal sharer, I prize the personal relations, and the fulfillment of a wish which dates, in such form as it could honestly assume at the time, from the beginning of my acquaintance with you.

Yours sincerely
W. D. Howells.

Of course, if J. R. O. & Co. are only in a trance, poor fellows—But Fairchild has sufficiently conditioned us.

1. Charles Fairchild had been conducting preliminary negotiations with Harper & Brothers for the publication of Howells' works in the event of the failure of James R. Osgood & Co. Though other publishing firms offered to accept Howells' works once Osgood failed (see Howells to Ticknor, 10 June 1885), he remained faithful to his tentative commitment to the Harpers. For Howells' agreement with Harper & Brothers, see Howells to Osgood, 14 October 1885, n. 1.

27 MARCH 1885, BOSTON, TO JAMES PARTON

302 Beacon st.
Boston, March 27, 1885.

Dear, dear friend:

How *much* good your letter did me! Even now, after the second reading, I want to cry over it. Thank you and all of you, with my best love.[1]

—Ah! The expenses! I am on the fire, and I *must boil*. But as yet I like the boiling—and somehow, somehow, I hope to be lifted off before I begin to burn the empty brain-pan. I have had a frightful year of work: since last March I have written one opera-libretto, one novel (Silas) five Italian papers, for the Century and two farces for Harper.[2] I must give my daughter her chance in this despicable world,—where

I'm so much better for having had none; I must get my boy through school and into college,—where I'm so much wiser for not having been! It's the pleasures and follies that we pay dearest for.[3]

I put all my sense into my novels—I keep none for myself.

Yours ever,
W. D. Howells.

I wish I could see you and talk with you sometimes.

1. Parton's letter to which Howells was responding is not known to be extant, but Parton wrote Howells, 6 April 1885 (MH), deploring the lack of adequate financial reward to authors because of the absence of an international copyright agreement; then he continued: "Your works are so thoroughly wrought out to the last comma and the last page, that they must come out of your vitals. So far, I can truly say, that you show no sign of fatigue, but every sign of growth; and as long as you enjoy the boil, all is well."

2. Howells is referring to *A Sea Change, or Love's Stowaway*, *The Rise of Silas Lapham*, "A Florentine Mosaic" and "Panforte di Siena" (the essays on Italy were issued in five installments), "The Elevator" (*Harper's Monthly*, December 1884), and "The Garroters" (*Harper's Monthly*, December 1885).

3. Parton replied to this comment on 6 April: "learn to be a Yankee, and admonish your son to be a miser of the New Hampshire type: 'Be mercenary, boy, and rule the earth.' Speak roundly to him."

5 MAY 1885, BOSTON, TO SAMUEL L. CLEMENS

Boston, May 5, 1885.

My dear Clemens:

I am exceedingly glad that you approved my reading, for it gives me some hope that I may do something on the platform next winter. It *seemed* to me that I was making the audience understand, and with a little more practice and ease I believe that I could do what I want. But I would never read within a hundred miles of *you*, if I could help it. You simply straddled down to the footlights, and took that house up in the hollow of your hand and *tickled* it.[1]

I don't see how a *reasonably selfish* author could have refused to read there. Wasn't it our own interest we were promoting? Cable ought to have thought that his books were to gain as much as any one's. And Warner failed, too! Well, the show netted $1700, Lathrop tells me.[2]

I had to go out into the country just after the thing, and I left while you were still talking.

I guess Osgood's break is not a bad one,—not the worst, any way. If he can resume I suppose I shall go on with him; if not I shall lapse to somebody else. Fairchild thinks there wont be any loss. But in the meantime, till something is concluded, I am my own lord as well as master.[3]

It's all right about the Library of Humor copy. That is at Osgood's house, & I shall have it today.[4]

Yours ever
W. D. Howells.

1. In a letter of the same date (NN; *Twain-Howells*, pp. 527–28) Clemens congratulated Howells for his part in an authors' reading for the American Copyright League at Madison Square Garden on 28 and 29 April: "Heiliger Gott! but it was good reading. Far better than Cable could have done it—which is not much of a compliment, but it started honestly *out* to be a compliment. It had simplicity, sincerity, & absence of artificiality, in place of Cable's self-complacency, sham feeling & labored artificiality. Sincerity *is* a great & valuable thing in front of an audience." Howells read chapters from *Indian Summer* and an early draft of the opening chapters of *The Minister's Charge.* For Howells' lecturing plans later that year, see Howells to W. C. Howells, 18 January 1885, n. 4.

2. G. W. Cable had refused to participate in the authors' reading because of his wife's illness; but Clemens, in his 5 May letter to Howells, had vented his anger about what he considered Cable's mercenary motives, adding: "He is intellectually great—very great, *I* think—but in order to find room for this greatness in his pygmy carcase, God had to cramp his other qualities more than was judicious, it seems to me." G. P. Lathrop was the organizer of the event.

3. On 4 May 1885, two days after James R. Osgood & Co. had gone into receivership, the firm published and sent a letter to Howells (MH) and other authors, reminding them that it was forced to suspend payment, although it anticipated resuming normal relations shortly. For a detailed account of the reasons for Osgood's failure see Carl J. Weber, *The Rise and Fall of James Ripley Osgood* (Waterville, Maine: Colby College Press, 1959), pp. 205–24.

4. See Howells to Osgood, 17 April 1881, n. 4.

11 MAY 1885, BOSTON, TO CLARENCE C. BUEL

302 Beacon st.,
Boston, May 11, 1885.

Dear Mr. Buel:[1]

I am sorry that I can't consent to your friend's request, much as I should like to oblige him; but if he wishes to use the name, he can do so without my consent. A mineral paint firm in N.Y. objected to my letting Lapham's paint be driven out because it had been identified with theirs from the first, and they didn't want it superseded by "some *cheap mud*"![2]

Please communicate my desire to your friend with my kindest thanks and regrets. But I really wish he wouldn't.

Yours cordially
W. D. Howells.

1. Clarence Clough Buel (1850–1933) was an assistant editor of the *Century* (1881–1910). He wrote Howells, 9 May 1885 (MH): "A friend of my youth, Mr Frank B. Felt who is an officer of the Pullman Iron & Steel Co, writes me that he is also interested in a paint company and that you have sunk an imaginary shaft into their mine. He wishes to get even with you by jumping your claim to the name of 'Silas Lapham' which he would like to adopt as the trade-mark of 'a very superior quality of mineral paint' that they have just begun to manufacture."

2. Howells had received a cordial letter from A. K. Prince of the Prince Manufacturing Co. in New York City, 23 October 1884 (MH), admiring *The Rise of Silas Lapham*, "especially as it is such a very good description of our Prince's Metallic Paint," and inviting Howells to visit the company's operations in Pennsylvania. It is not known whether the same or another company objected to Lapham's paint being driven out by the West Virginia paint company. That circumstance comes to pass in chapter 26 of *The Rise of Silas Lapham*, which appeared in the *Century*, August 1885.

28 May 1885, BOSTON, TO J. H. HAULENBECK

> 302 Beacon st.
> Boston, May 28, 1885.

Dear Sir:[1]

I have received a letter addressed to W. *B*. Howells, which I suppose is intended for me, in regard to a story for your magazine. I think that I might be able, if I put unusual restraint upon the corrupt nature I have inherited from Adam, to keep within the line of strict morality which you prescribe, and I do not believe I should "offend the religious principles of any sect" of readers, except possibly the Sandomanians,[2] whom I always make a point of attacking in my novels.

But I am afraid I could not write a sensational story, without touching upon morality or religion. Hitherto I have avoided offence of this kind by being very tame and commonplace, and I am too old to run risks.

You are very kind to ask me to write, and I am sorry that I cannot.

> Yours truly
> **W. D. Howells.**

Mr. Haulenbeck.

1. J. H. Haulenbeck was the publisher of *Godey's Lady's Book*. Since this letter was acquired from Howells' heirs, it is likely that Howells decided against actually sending it.

2. The Sandemanians were the American branch of the Glassites, an independent Presbyterian sect founded by the Scottish minister John Glass or Glas (1695–1773). Robert Sandeman was Glass's co-worker.

10 JUNE 1885, GREAT BARRINGTON, MASSACHUSETTS,
TO BENJAMIN H. TICKNOR

Berkshire House,
Great Barington Mass. June 10, 1885.

My dear Ticknor—

I had Mr. Sam'l Wells see Mr. Morse in regard to our legal status under my old agreement with J. R. Osgood & Co.,[1] but they do not seem to have reached daylight. There is reason, however, why I should now tell you that before you spoke to me I had agreed conditionally with another house for the sale of my stories in serial form, and expected also to place my books with it, in the event of Osgood's not going on.[2] The notion of your taking the business had not then been broached, and I did not take it into account in making my arrangement. It complicates matters, of course, and I do not yet know what is to be done. But I wish to advise you of the fact, and to assure you of my hearty wish for your prosperity, what ever happens to my books. You may be sure, also, that in any final arrangement I will not consider my own rights and interests alone.[3]

As soon as you can write me I shall be glad to hear from you concerning your plans and prospects. In the meantime I will ask you to consider this letter as between ourselves.

Yours sincerely,
W. D. Howells.

P. S. I should have told you just how I stood before, if I had felt quite free to do so; I strain a point now, in order that you may not count upon my books too confidently. I have already hinted an uncertainty in regard to them.

1. Samuel Wells (1836?–1903) was Howells' attorney; Robert M. Morse, Jr., was the legal assignee for the assets of James R. Osgood & Co.

2. See Howells to Harper, 13 March 1885.

3. Ticknor had written Howells, 1 June 1885 (MH), that a new firm, Ticknor & Co., was going "to purchase all the assets and assume and conduct the business of the late firm of James R. Osgood & Company...." Ticknor further told Howells that the new firm would like "to assume and perform the contracts existing between you and James R. Osgood & Company, including the payment in full of any royalties or other indebtedness that are now in arrears." On 20 July 1885 (copy, MH) Howells signed a contract with Ticknor & Co. The agreement provided for immediate payment to Howells of $1,730.77, plus weekly payments of $144.23, with the last weekly payment to be adjusted so that Howells would receive payment at the rate of $7,500 a year for the period 1 May 1885 to 1 March 1886, plus royalties due him. The agreement further provided for Howells to furnish six short stories (later replaced by *The Minister's Charge*) to the *Century*, the stories to be republished in book form by Ticknor & Co., and for Ticknor & Co. to publish in book form *Tuscan Cities* and to republish *The Rise of Silas Lapham*, *Indian Summer*, *A Modern Instance*, and *A Woman's Reason*.

12 JUNE 1885, GREAT BARRINGTON, MASSACHUSETTS,
TO AURELIA H. HOWELLS

Berkshire House,
Great Barrington, June 12, 1885.

Dear Aurelia—

I enclose a postal order for $15, which I should have paid for your pongee, if you had preferred it. It is made payable to father, but it is yours to keep or give him as you like.

In his last letter he speaks of exhaustion from his work. *Is it necessary that he should work at all?* If it is merely pottering about at light jobs that he would rather do than be idle, I am willing; but if he is working, at his time of life, to save the hire of a hand, I want to pay for the hand and have father stop. Please tell him so at once, and say that I shall feel badly if he does not accept my offer. *When is he coming to see me?* I wish he would come at once. We are here in a pleasant little hotel, in the loveliest village of the Berkshire Hills, and we could make his visit pass very agreeably. John or I would meet him at the depot in Jersey City, when he arrived from Richmond, and then he would have only three hours' ride to this place. He might be able to buy a ticket in Richmond for Great Barrington Mass., (Housatonic R. R.) but at any rate he would have no trouble.[1] Do write me something definite about his coming. All join me in love.

Your aff'te brother,
Will.

1. Howells wrote W. C. Howells, 24 May 1885 (MH), that he and his family were going to Great Barrington on 1 June and would spend the entire month there. Although in that letter he also invited his father to visit them and suggested an itinerary similar to the one proposed to Aurelia, W. C. Howells did not make the trip.

17 JULY 1885, OLD ORCHARD, MAINE, TO CYRUS L. SULZBERGER

Old Orchard Me., July, 17, 1885.

My dear Sir:[1]

I thank you for your frank and manly letter.

I supposed that I was writing in reprobation of the prejudice of which you justly complain, but my irony seems to have fallen short of the mark—so far short that you are not the first Hebrew to accuse me of "pandering" to the stupid and cruel feeling against your race and religion. I will not ask you to read again, in the light of this statement, the passage of my story which you object to, for I have already struck it out of my book, and it will not re-appear. In that passage I merely recognized to rebuke it, the existence of a feeling which civilized men should be ashamed of. But perhaps it is better not to recognize all the facts.

Perhaps also you owe me an apology for making an unjust accusation. I leave that to you.[2]

Very truly yours,
W. D. Howells.

1. Cyrus L. Sulzberger (1858–1932), an editor of the *American Hebrew*, had written Howells on 12 July 1885 (MH), asking him to change a slur on Jews in the second chapter of *The Rise of Silas Lapham* before the novel was to be published in book form. Specifically, Sulzberger objected to two passages in a conversation between Lapham and his wife in which they discuss the drop in land value in the Nankeen Square area because Jews have moved in, and express the stereotype idea that all Jews are rich. See C. L. Sulzberger, " 'Silas Lapham' and the Jews," *American Hebrew*, 4 September 1885; G. Arms and W. M. Gibson, " 'Silas Lapham,' 'Daisy Miller,' and the Jews," *New England Quarterly* 16 (1943), 121; and *The Rise of Silas Lapham*, HE, pp. 383–84, which also cites Kermit Vanderbilt's treatment.

2. Sulzberger apologized in a letter dated 19 July 1885 (MH), but he added: "Still in justification of my own stupidity in missing the point of your irony I may say that Silas's admission that 'they' do depreciate the value of property when they get in—a fact concerning the financial accuracy of which I have some doubts—seemed to me rather as an endorsement than a rebuke of what you truly call the 'stupid and cruel feeling' against us."

19 JULY 1885, WELLS BEACH, MAINE, TO HORACE E. SCUDDER

Wells Beach, July 19, 1885.

My dear Scudder:

We left Old Orchard Beast yesterday on a parlor car, and worked down to Wells in the caboose of a freight train, from Kennebunk. Thank you for your friendly thoughtfulness;[1] but here we are in a clean, quiet hotel, with enough to eat, and heaven forbid that we should go away, even to Little Boar's Head. There are bores' heads enough here; the air is cool, and the society is of that plebeian easiness which suits best the vulgar humor of this family. If we go again, it will be to scale the loftiest tops of the White Mountains.

Pilla had a high time with Sylvia up to the last moment in Gr. Barr.[2] and they united in punching one of the foremost novelists of the country in the stomach as we journeyed to Boston. As the freedom of the child of another literary man I gladly permitted it.

Mrs. Howells joins me in love to you all.

Yours ever
W D Howells.

1. Scudder wrote Howells, 16 July 1885 (MH), from his rented vacation cottage, Little Boar's Head in South Hampton, New Hampshire, inviting him to join the Scudder family at this seaside resort.

2. Sylvia, one of Scudder's twin stepdaughters, stayed with the Howells family at the Berkshire House, Great Barrington, Massachusetts, in June.

4 August 1885, Wells Beach, Maine, to Thomas B. Aldrich

Wells Beach, Aug. 4, 1885.

My dear Aldrich:

You mustn't hope, after galling my pedant-pride through three pages, to soothe it by asking me a flattering question about an Italian superlative.[1] Italian I care nothing for, but my Russian I am proud of, and I think I know my Tourguénieff. However, I *am* glad you like Imogene,[2] for she seems pretty good to me, and I do value your good opinion. If I were to speak of her as a distinctively beautiful American, I believe I should say la Bella Americana, rather than bellissima, though I believe it's perfectly right to say that. I remember the Venetians used to speak of Mrs. Ruskin as la Bella Inglese,[3] as if she were so extremely; and it seems to me that the superlative would weaken the qualification.

We are off to-morrow morning for the White Mts.; but I hope to see you in Boston before the end of the month.

Yours ever
W. D. Howells.

1. Aldrich's letter, to which this is a reply, is no longer extant, but Howells had written Aldrich on 29 July 1885 (MH), sending him the conclusion of *Indian Summer*, which had just begun in *Harper's Monthly*.

2. Imogene Graham, the young American woman in *Indian Summer*.

3. Euphemia Chalmers Gray Ruskin (1828–1897), wife of John Ruskin.

9 August 1885, Bethlehem, New Hampshire, to Samuel L. Clemens

Ranlet House,
Bethelehem, N. H. Aug. 9, 1885.

My dear Clemens—

I was glad you could find it in your heart to write me that kind letter, for it did me a world of good.[1] What people cannot see is that I analyze as little as possible, but go on talking about the analytical school which I am suppose to belong to; and I want to thank you for using your eyes. I am in hopes you will like the story all through, though it is all a variation of the one theme.

Did you ever read De Foe's Roxana? If not, then read it, not merely for some of the deepest insights into the lying, suffering, sinning, well-meaning human soul, but the best and most natural English that a book was ever written in. You will find it in the Bohn library.[2]

I wish to goodness that you could take a week off and run up to this White Mountain village. I think the landscape would be a revelation to you, and if we were not always insulting our maker you would be amazed at the affront offered him by the ugliness of the little Yankee town dropt into the beauty of his everlasting hills.

We had a funeral service for Grant, here, yesterday, and all the time while they were pumping song and praise over his great memory, I kept thinking of the day when we lunched on pork and beans with him in New York,[3] and longing to make them feel and see how far above their hymns he was even in such an association. How he "sits and towers" as Dante says.[4]

Mrs. Howells sends love to both of you with me.

> Yours ever,
> W. D. Howells.

1. Clemens had written Howells on 21 July 1885 (NN; *Twain-Howells*, pp. 533–34) to say how much he liked *Indian Summer*, of which he had just read the second part (*Harper's Monthly*, August 1885). After explaining his boredom with the works of George Eliot, he commented on Howells' novel: "It is a beautiful story, & makes a body laugh all the time, & cry inside, & feel so old & so forlorn; & gives him gracious glimpses of his lost youth that fill him with a measureless regret, & build up in him a cloudy sense of his having been a prince, once, in some enchanted far-off land, & of being in exile now, & desolate—& lord, no chance to ever get back there again! ... you make all the motives & feelings perfectly clear without analyzing the guts out of them, the way George Eliot does."

2. Howells is probably referring here to the Standard Library edition of classic authors by the prominent English bookseller and publisher Henry George Bohn (1796–1884). In this collection, *Roxana* (1883) is the fourth volume of Defoe's works.

3. U. S. Grant died on 23 July 1885 at Mount McGregor, near Saratoga, New York. See Howells to W. C. Howells, 2 March 1882, n. 1.

4. This phrase does not come from Dante; it is cited from an unidentified source in E. A. Brigidi's *La Nuova Guida di Siena*, 2d ed. (1885), a work mentioned by Howells in *Tuscan Cities*. See *Twain-Howells*, p. 537.

---

11 AUGUST 1885, BETHLEHEM, NEW HAMPSHIRE, TO JAMES R. OSGOOD

> Ranlet House,
> Bethlehem N. H. Aug. 11, 1885.

My dear Osgood:

I shall be glad to know what the Harpers have to propose,[1] and I wish very much that J. W. H. Jr., would extend his vacation travel as far as this place. I go to Mt. Desert[2] to fetch Winifred away this p. m. but expect to be back by Friday or Saturday.

I am afraid the subject of that play is now so cold in my mind that nothing can revive it.[3] I am sorry; I wish I could have said this when you first spoke to me of it, but your enthusiasm kindled me a little and I fizzed. Now, I can't even fizz. I'm very much taken up with the new story,[4] which Gilder says I may run to the exclusion of the short stories, if necessary.

Yours ever
W. D. Howells.

1. Joseph W. Harper, Jr.'s letters to Howells in June and July 1885 indicate that both he and Howells were considering (independently of one another) schemes that would engage Howells' talents in magazine publication, and Howells sought Osgood's advice in dealing with Harper. Harper proposed that Howells contribute "a *feuilleton* for 'Harper's Weekly,' embracing current social, literary & artistic topics, with story & incident,—which we could illustrate in an open sort of way" (12 June 1885 [MH]). Harper's letters to Howells, 20 June 1885 (MH) and 1 July 1885 (MH), indicate that Howells' scheme was for a "Miscellany of Fiction," probably a quarterly, devoted entirely to fiction. Osgood wrote Howells on 6 August 1885 (MH) that he had discussed Howells' "magazine scheme" with the Harpers, that they were not enthusiastic about it but did wish to discuss it with Howells, and that J. W. Harper, Jr., wanted to arrange an interview with Howells. Whether any of these discussions actually occurred remains unclear, but on 9 September 1885 (MH) Henry M. Alden, editor of *Harper's Monthly*, wrote Howells, proposing that he "be associated with us in the editorial conduct of our Magazine" by placing him in charge of a new department: "We propose to discontinue our *Editor's Literary Record* & to substitute therefor a purely literary department—one that shall have a relation to the current literary movement (in America *& Europe*) corresponding to that which the *Editor's Easy Chair* has to the current social movement." This proposal was the basis of "The Editor's Study," which, as Alden put it in this letter, was to offer "an analysis of literary traits & tendencies" rather than mere book reviews.
2. Mt. Desert Island, Maine.
3. The play has not been identified.
4. *The Minister's Charge; or the Apprenticeship of Lemuel Barker*, *Century*, February–December 1886; it was published in book form by Ticknor & Co. of Boston in 1886.

11 SEPTEMBER 1885, BETHLEHEM, NEW HAMPSHIRE, TO
THOMAS C. DONALDSON

Bethlehem, Sept. 11, 1885.

Dear Mr. Donaldson:[1]

I send $10 towards Walt Whitman's buggy, with the understanding that it is not a critical endorsement of his poetry or his theory of poetry, concerning which I have many reserves;[2] and on condition that I do not appear in the list of subscribers.

The chief pleasure I have in this matter is your letter, reminding me of some one who knew me in my Columbus days. Your name comes back to me; but I am growing an old fellow, and don't remember every one.

I had a letter from father yesterday. He is now on a farm near Richmond, Virginia.

Yours truly,
W. D. Howells

1. Thomas Corwin Donaldson (1843–1898), a lawyer and close friend of Whitman in his later years, undertook a subscription campaign in August 1885 to buy the aging poet a horse and buggy so that he could continue to get out despite his increasing lameness. Such prominent men as R. W. Gilder, C. D. Warner, Clemens, Howells, Whittier, Holmes, and Edwin Booth were among those who made the ten-dollar contribution solicited by Donaldson. A phaeton, specially built for Whitman in Columbus, Ohio, was delivered to him on 15 September, together with $135.40 in cash, which remained from the contributions. See Gay Wilson Allen, *The Solitary Singer* (New York: Macmillan, 1955), pp. 522–23.

2. See Howells to Lowell, 6 November 1865; Howells to Stedman, 5 December 1866 and 29 April 1880.

12 SEPTEMBER 1885, BETHLEHEM, NEW HAMPSHIRE, TO
BENJAMIN H. TICKNOR

Bethlehem, Sept. 12, 1885.

My dear Ticknor:

You may be sure that I will consider your interests in the utmost degree practicable and consistent with my own in any arrangements I may make, hereafter;[1] and this from pure good will, for Mr. Wells has always instructed me that you did not inherit my contract with Osgood & Co., and I think you used his written opinion to that effect in settling with one of the banker-creditors of that firm.

I cannot tell yet—for I don't know—what shape my republications may take; when I do know you shall know it from *me,* and not from the newspapers.[2]

Osgood knew that the H.'s wanted my serial work; beyond this he had nothing to do with my affair. I think that I even heard first of their wish from another. In this matter he has faithfully considered you.

I hope to see you at the end of the week. We are all getting on famously.

Yours ever
W. D. Howells.

1. Ticknor, knowing that Howells was negotiating with Harper & Brothers, feared that his company would lose the republication right to Howells' works previously published by Osgood. One of the terms of Howells' contract with Ticknor was that Ticknor would pay 16⅔ percent royalty on republished volumes if Howells agreed

not to take over the continued publication of these works himself. If Howells chose to, he could include these republication rights and republication rights for future works in his contract with Harper. Ticknor all but begged Howells to continue his connection with Ticknor & Co. On 1 August 1885 (MH) he wrote: "Parting company with you will be a great sorrow to me, & I want to postpone the evil day as long as possible & gather all the crumbs that I may from your bounteous table in the meantime." And again on 10 September 1885 (MH): "...I understand of course that your stories go to H & Bro, serially & as books but I trust you will bear us in mind in whatever there may be beyond that...."

2. In his note to Howells of 11 September 1885 (MH), Ticknor enclosed the following newspaper clipping: "Mr. Howells may yet decide to stick to 'The Century' in spite of the tempting $10,000 a year offer of the Harpers. One of the members of that firm said on Monday: 'The report is substantially true, but the contract, although made out, is not signed yet, but we hope it will be.'"

13 SEPTEMBER 1885, BETHLEHEM, NEW HAMPSHIRE,
TO WILLIAM C. HOWELLS

Bethlehem, Sept. 13, 1885.

Dear father:

I suppose I shall write you next Sunday from Boston, for I expect to go back on Thursday.—The autumn is coming on gloriously here, and I wish you could see it. This is much more of a farming country than I supposed at first. High up here, 1500 above the sea, there is splendid wheat, which they're just now cutting, and densely heavy oats. But the winds make it cruelly cold in winter, though the snows keep off the deepest frosts. I've finished my sketch of log-cabin life, and hope to let you see it before it's printed.[1] The family are all well, and join me in love.

Your aff'te son
Will.

1. Probably "Year in a Log-Cabin, a Bit of Autobiography," *Youth's Companion*, 12 May 1887; published in book form as *My Year in a Log Cabin* by Harper & Brothers in 1893.

14 OCTOBER 1885, BOSTON, TO JAMES R. OSGOOD

Boston, Oct. 14, 1885.

Dear Osgood:

I return the contract with some slight changes and additions which Wells thought important, and I will sign it as soon as you send me a copy.[1] There is one point, which I had better speak of. How will the clause forbidding the use of my name editorially work with reference to the Mark Twain Library of Humor? Of course I can't tell when he will publish it; but if the house objects to my name on the title page, I will try to sell him the work I've done on the book, and let him have the sole glory.[2] You can explain the history of the thing.

Your letter of Monday was a great comfort, and yesterday's with that W. D. H. ad. confirms me in the hope of a continued Boston residence,[3] for some one here will want that young man.

> Yours ever
> W. D. Howells.

1. Howells, with Osgood's advice, reached a preliminary agreement with Harper & Brothers on 6 October 1885 and final agreement on or around 16 October. On 15 October (MH) Osgood sent Howells a copy of the contract with Harpers which contained all of Howells' recommendations. The final contract provided that Howells would receive $3,000 a year for his monthly columns for "The Editor's Study" in *Harper's Monthly*, and $10,000 a year for his other productions, including serial rights for one novel. Howells was also to receive 12½ percent royalty for book publication of his novels and fifty dollars per thousand words for additional matter contributed to *Harper's Monthly* and thirty dollars per thousand words for matter contributed to *Harper's Weekly*.

2. Osgood replied in his letter of 15 October that the Harpers preferred for Howells "to receive payment for your work done on the book and eliminate your name from it." See also Howells to Clemens, 5 December 1885, n. 1.

3. Howells wrote Osgood, 12 October 1885 (MH), beseeching him "*not* to say anything of my projected removal [from Boston] till it is nearer accomplishment, and beg the [Harper] Brothers and Nephews not to do so." Osgood responded on the same day (MH) that the Harpers "respect your desires in the matter. They have no disposition to 'Barnumize' you, or to do anything which will make you uncomfortable."

20 OCTOBER 1885, BOSTON, TO S. WEIR MITCHELL

> 302 Beacon st.
> Boston, Oct. 20, 1885.

Dear Dr. Mitchell:

I have talked with Dr. Putnam,[1] and understanding from him that there is not a crisis in Winifred's case, and that it would suffer nothing from the delay of a month or two, I wish to give myself this breathing space in regard to her. We are just going to take her into the country with us, where the conditions as to freedom and quiet will be infinitely better than here, and where she will continue under his treatment until he sees that she is getting no good from it. Then he will frankly tell me, and I shall turn to you. This conclusion—such as it is—is quite my own; Dr. Putnam, till I expressed a wish to go on for the present with him, did not suggest it.

—Last night I took up In War Time,[2] which I had merely run through before, and read it faithfully from beginning to end. To my mind there has seldom been a man in fiction so perfectly divined as Wendell. It is so true that I felt all the time you might have studied him from me; for I am a coward, and all kinds of a tacit liar—not because I don't love the truth, heaven knows, but because I'm afraid to tell it very often; perhaps I'm not quite so selfish as he. But the thing is done wonderfully— with neither harshness nor pity, merely justice. The whole book is balanced, and done *well*. I don't care for what people call "art"; I like nearness to life, and this is life, portrayed with conscience, with knowledge, both deep and quick, and with a most satisfying, self-respectful simplicity and clearness, which is the only "art" worth having.

Yours sincerely
W. D. Howells.

1. Probably James Jackson Putnam (1846–1918), a Boston neurologist who specialized in psychoneuroses.
2. Howells reviewed Mitchell's *In War Time* (1885) in the "Editor's Study," *Harper's Monthly*, January 1886, where he praised the "artistic quiet of the book" and the sympathetic and skillful characterization of a coward in Ezra Wendell: "It was a new thing to attempt to paint a cowardly nature like that; and it was no less the affair of a good art than of a humane spirit to do justice to the gentleness that goes with the timidity, the sensibility that accompanies the falseness, the goodwill that qualifies the selfishness."

26 OCTOBER 1885, AUBURNDALE, MASSACHUSETTS, TO EDMUND W. GOSSE

Woodland Park,
Auburndale, Mass., Oct. 26, 1885.

My dear Gosse:

Nothing could have been kinder or sweeter than that review of yours in the Pall Mall Gazette,[1] and I thank you for it with all my heart. It has been copied here far and wide; and now comes under cover from you the criticism of the Saturday.[2] I do not see how the greediest of authors could ask better things, and if you know the critic will you tell him that it is such a notice as I would have written myself. Truly there were just the things said there that I was aching to have said. Both of these reviews are far friendlier than most things on this side.—I wish I *were* going to London; but I have only come as far out as this on the Boston & Albany RR. (Wellesley College, with the heaven-kissing Hill in the gymnasium is but a station or two beyond.)[3] I have let the pretty house on Beacon st. because poor Winny is too poorly to do any society in it, and without that her mother and I have no heart for it. I suppose we shall stay here till March, and then I shall have two months in New York.

You'll have heard of my contract with the Harpers, which is incredibly advantageous for me; and I'm to do a department for them each month, about literature. Your lovely book is in my hands, and will be the text of one of the little papers.[4] Merely looking into it gives me a queer homesick longing for last winter. It *was* a pretty time, was n't it? We must have it again, some day. We are presently to dine Lowell at the Tavern Club,[5] and I wish you were to be there too!

Mrs. Howells joins me in love to Mrs Gosse and yourself.

Yours ever
W. D. Howells.

1. Gosse reviewed *The Rise of Silas Lapham* in the *Pall Mall Gazette*, 11 September 1885.

2. The author of the review of *The Rise of Silas Lapham* in the *Saturday Review*, 17 October 1885, has not been identified.

3. Lucille Eaton Hill was a teacher and director of physical education at Wellesley College for twenty-seven years, beginning in 1882. The reason for Howells' referring to her as "heaven-kissing" is not clear. See *Transatlantic Dialogue*, p. 163.

4. *From Shakespeare to Pope* (1885) was reviewed by Howells in "Editor's Study," *Harper's Monthly*, March 1886.

5. The dinner was held on 4 November at 1 Park Square in Boston.

28 OCTOBER 1885, AUBURNDALE, MASSACHUSETTS, TO EDWIN D. MEAD

Woodland Park Hotel,
Auburndale, Mass. Oct. 28, 1885.

Dear Eddy:

I am writing about a young fellow who develops a liberal theological tendency. What sort of books would he fancy, or begin reading? I mean what Unitarian doctrinnaires, essayists and divines?[1]

We are here for a great part of the winter, and have let the house on Beacon st. for six months. Come out and take lunch at 1, or dinner at 6.

Yours ever
W. D. Howells

1. Howells consulted with Edwin D. Mead while writing *The Minister's Charge* because Mead had studied for the Episcopal ministry (1875–1876) but withdrew because of his leanings toward Unitarianism and transcendentalism. The "young fellow" may have been Lemuel Barker; if so, Howells' conception of the character must have changed subsequently.

30 October 1885, Auburndale, Massachusetts, to Thomas S. Perry

Auburndale, Mass., Oct. 30, 1885.

My dear Perry:

Anna Karénina is a wonderful book.[1] I seem to live in it, I don't think it is so great as Tourguéniff's, but the subtlety of the observation in it is astounding, simply. The way the Karénine's passion is treated—I've only got through Part I—is a little superstitious? Or am I older than I was? That looks like the only bit of convention yet. But how good you feel the author's heart to be; and what a comfort, what a *rest* that is!

Yours ever,
W. D. Howells

Please let me have the English criticism again, with this letter.[2]

1. Howells reviewed *Anna Karenina* in "Editor's Study," *Harper's Monthly*, April 1886. "As you read on," he writes in the central passage of the review, "you say, not, 'This is like life,' but, 'This is life.' It has not only the complexion, the very hue, of life, but its movement, its advances, its strange pauses, its seeming reversions to former conditions, and its perpetual change; its apparent isolations, its essential solidarity."

2. Apparently Howells had sent Perry some English reviews of *The Rise of Silas Lapham*. See Howells to Gosse, 26 October 1885, n. 1 and n. 2.

18 November 1885, Auburndale, Massachusetts, to Helen Walter

Lee's Hotel,
Auburndale, Mass. Nov. 18, 1885.

Dear Madam:

I have written to the editor of the magazine, asking him to send you the advance sheets of my story, and I have no doubt he will do so.[1] We shall know of course that they meet only your eyes, and shall rely upon you to destroy them as soon as you have read them.

I cannot tell you how sincerely and humbly grateful I am to be the means of lightening the moments of sickness to you, and this book of mine will always have a peculiar interest to me because it has interested you at this time.[2]

My wife joins me in cordial regards and sympathy.

Yours sincerely
W. D. Howells.

Mrs. Meader.

1. In an earlier, undated letter to Howells (MH; *Life in Letters*, I, 374), Helen Walter of Milton, New York, writing under the pseudonym of "Elizabeth C. Meader," told Howells that she was an invalid whose death was imminent. As a final request she asked Howells if she could see the advance sheets of *Indian Summer* so that she would know the conclusion of the novel before she died. Though Howells' response was sympathetic, his publisher was skeptical. Before releasing the advance sheets, Osgood, J. W. Harper, Jr., and Alden decided that Alden should write "Mrs. Meader," explaining that because her request was so extraordinary, the advance sheets would be released only upon her physician's written confirmation of her illness. See Alden to Howells, 2 December 1885 (MH).

2. In a letter to Howells, 25 November 1885 (MH), "Mrs. Meader" apologized for the lie. She felt that Howells would see through the hoax, but his sincere and sympathetic letter convinced her that she should confess her fraud. At this point she also revealed to him her real name. Mildred Howells observes that her father drew upon this strange episode for his novel *Fennel and Rue* (1908). See *Life in Letters*, I, 374.

22 NOVEMBER 1885, AUBURNDALE, MASSACHUSETTS,
TO THOMAS R. LOUNSBURY

> Lee's Hotel,
> Auburndale, Nov. 22, 1885.

My dear Lounsbury—

By this time you are sick of the type-writer you wrote me on,[1] and are ready to learn that the true and only Mind Cure is the Hall Type Writer. I have used it off and on for a year, and it has cured me of the mind completely. Perhaps this is the reason why I was so completely taken in by your praises of Indian Summer. I said, "Here is a man who unites good taste with sincerity." If I was mistaken, forgive me. As you know very well, there is nothing an author will believe sooner than praise of his work; I suppose the most hardened Agnostic might be flattered into the belief that he was inspired when he wrote certain passages.

As to Ticknor & Co., I think they are on a pretty good basis, though I can't speak positively. Mr. Godfrey, the Co., has plenty of money, which he made by lumbering.[2] I have no doubt but they would be glad to have your book;[3] but I suggest that before doing any thing at all you write to J. R. Osgood, now with the Harpers,[4] and ask his advice. It will be worth having.

Mrs. Howells returns her compliments, and says to tell you that my daring that terrible day, left her for once with nothing to say. But it is a dangerous precedent. I feel that it will not "broaden down" in the right Tennysonian fashion.[5] Good heavens, I shudder in remembering it!

I knew that by this time they would have an original for Imogene[6] in Buffalo, and I hope she is a nice one, for I rather like her. To tell the truth, I like the story altogether, and I enjoyed doing it better than anything since A Foregone Conclusion. But our people now don't want one on foreign ground, and I shall hardly venture abroad again in fiction. It is very convenient, however; you can segregate your characters so nicely, and study them at such long leisure.

Let me hear from you again, if I can be of use, or even when you merely wish to pour your appreciation of my novels into a sympathetic ear.

Yours ever,
W. D. Howells.

1. Lounsbury's letter to Howells is not extant.

2. Ticknor wrote Howells, 1 June 1885 (MH), that the new firm of Ticknor & Co. would be "composed of Benjamin H. Ticknor, Thomas B. Ticknor, and George F. Godfrey, of Bangor."

3. It is not known for which book Lounsbury was seeking a publisher at this time; none was published by Ticknor.

4. After his business failure, Osgood became the Harpers' representative in London.

5. This passage remains obscure; but the Tennyson reference is to "You Ask Me, Why, Tho' Ill at Ease," lines 11–12.

6. Imogene Graham, in *Indian Summer.*

5 DECEMBER 1885, AUBURNDALE, MASSACHUSETTS, TO SAMUEL L. CLEMENS

Lee's Hotel,
Auburndale, Dec. 5, 1885.

My dear Clemens:

I have got Webster's check for $2000, but I have a difficulty about keeping it, which I must lay before you. If we have no definite plan for publishing the book, the money does not belong to me.[1] I do not believe the Harpers will consent to my name with another imprint willingly till it has been identified with theirs by several publications—that is, a year or two hence. You may not wish to wait so long, and I certainly could not ask you to do so. Is there not some one else whose name you could associate with yours on the title page? Or couldn't I reduce the number of selections from you so as to sort of fig-leaf your editorial nakedness? Or couldn't we get over it in some joking way in the introduction (which I'm to write) & say that the selections from you had been committed to your friend Howells, who had betrayed your confidence?— Wouldn't Uncle Remus,[2] for the other half of the $5000, or Warner, or Aldrich, or Cable, or Blaine, or Cleveland, or somebody, go on the title-page with you in my place? How would Beecher do?[3] Think the misery over again.

I'm more rejoiced than I can tell you at the gigantic triumph of the

Grant book. I should like to see you in these days of wild excitement. How you must smoke and swear![4]

I read your piece about the unsuccessful campaign[5] with the greatest delight. It was immensely amusing, with such a bloody bit of heart ache in it, too.

Yours ever
W. D. Howells.

1. Howells had written Clemens on 16 October 1885 (CU; *Twain-Howells*, p. 537), that since the Harpers did not want Howells' name to "appear except over their imprint," he would accept $2,500 for his work on the "Library of Humor." He proposed that since Clemens had already paid $500 on account, he could pay off the debt by sending a "check for $2000 more—just half the price agreed on for my co-operation . . . ." Clemens responded on 18 October 1885 (NN; *Twain-Howells*, pp. 538–39) that he would postpone publication of the "Library," and he asked Howells if he could defer payment of the $2,000 until January 1886. However, on 2 December 1885 (NN; *Twain-Howells*, p. 540) Clemens wrote Howells that he had instructed Charles L. Webster to send Howells the money. The book was finally published as *Mark Twain's Library of Humor* in 1887.

2. Joel Chandler Harris had published *Uncle Remus: His Songs and His Sayings* (1881) and *Nights with Uncle Remus* (1883).

3. Probably Henry Ward Beecher, whose most recent book was *Evolution and Religion* (1885).

4. *The Personal Memoirs of Ulysses S. Grant* had been published by Charles L. Webster & Co. in November 1885. Howells may have been referring to the disputes that arose when Vice-president Thomas A. Hendricks (1819–1885) died on 25 November, leaving no clear successor to President Cleveland and no legal process for selecting one.

5. "The Private History of a Campaign that Failed," *Century*, December 1885, recounts Clemens' hapless adventures as a Confederate volunteer in the Marion Rangers, a rag-tag organization that disbanded at the first real threat of meeting the enemy, a threat posed, ironically enough, by troops under the command of U. S. Grant.

19 DECEMBER 1885, AUBURNDALE, MASSACHUSETTS, TO GEORGE W. CURTIS

Auburndale, Mass. Dec. 19, 1885.

Dear Mr. Curtis:

I must thank you for the very sweet and gracious welcome you give me to the magazine.[1] I had hoped to steal in unobserved, but being so hospitably detected I feel ashamed not to have made my manners to the older denizens. Let this stand for something of the kind. You know how I have always liked your work in the Chair. For you to rise from it with an outstretched hand of greeting was—like you.

Very sincerely yours,
W. D. Howells.

1. Curtis had written a flattering welcome of Howells to *Harper's Monthly* in his column, "The Editor's Easy Chair," *Harper's Monthly*, January 1886.

26 DECEMBER 1885, AUBURNDALE, MASSACHUSETTS,
TO WILLIAM C. HOWELLS

Auburndale, Dec. 26, 1885.

Dear father—

The box of holly came Thursday, and was used not only to trim our own rooms but to share with the other boarders. The berries were greatly admired; but I found the holly leaves not of so bright green as that of the holly I saw in Virginia, or that they bring to market here from our South Shore coast. I suggest to the girls that for another year they use longer boxes, and put in larger boughs. They give too much for the money: 3 lbs. would be enough, and if they can add mistletoe it will be an attraction; it was very fashionable this year, and will be more so next.[1]

I'm rejoiced at their pleasing success, and hope the vine enterprise will turn out well.

You needn't worry about Sam;[2] Joe was to have seen him last night, and we shall try to study out something for him to do. His address at present is with Joe, who will forward letters; I don't just remember it.

I'm glad you're so very much better, and I do hope now that you will keep so. I hate to be scolding at any or all of you, as I seem to be always doing.[3] What you say of Henry's frequent seizures gives me great concern; but you don't say whether he still takes the bromide.

Charles Mead was here last night, and made kind inquiries after you all.—Tell Aurelia I *am* working steadily but not too hard. I dreamed of Vic last night, my dream running back to the cow hooking episode.[4] Give her my best love. I hope *that* cow is sold.

I'm so glad you are going to let the farm, and not have the worry. Better have all your contracts in writing, and properly drawn up so that you wont be either annoyed or cheated.

The children had a good Christmas, and mine was brightened by the cheerful accounts I had from you.

All join me in love,

Your aff'te son
Will.

1. Howells had written Aurelia Howells on 20 December 1885 (MH) that he was delighted with her enterprise of selling boxes of holly during the holidays and was especially pleased because she was able to use W. C. Howells' grape shears in cutting the plants.

2. In the same letter to Aurelia, Howells wrote: "I have had to send Sam some money again; he has lost his place, and says he can get nothing to do. I wrote to him to go into every place in Cleveland, that if I gave money, I preferred giving it to father."

3. Howells was concerned about his father's health and did not want him to continue farming. He wrote Aurelia on 20 December that he wanted their father "to sell all his horses but one, and let his farm . . . , keeping ample homestead grounds. Then he could sell his corn crop."

4. In October, Victoria Howells had been knocked down by a cow. See Howells to Aurelia Howells, 25 October 1885 (MH).

II

Literary and Social Reform

1886–1891

Introduction

In the years 1886-1891, when Howells was writing the "Editor's Study," he was often the focal point of public controversy. His advocacy of the principles of literary realism, hitherto primarily confined to book reviews and private correspondence, now offered a stronger and more widely perceived challenge to public taste and to the business interests of book and magazine publishers. What had been a matter of personal preference and individual suasion, turned into a literary movement in the late 1880s, with Howells as its chief spokesman. He also became increasingly perturbed and outspoken about social injustice and economic inequality; but even though his views were sometimes radical, his own life-style, as he remarked, fully appreciating the irony of the situation, always remained that of a comfortable man of the middle class. All in all, the battles Howells fought, instead of causing his physical condition to deteriorate and his productivity to diminish, seem to have given him the strength and energy that made these years the richest of his long career as an author.

The initial skirmishes were holdovers from a controversy that had begun in November 1882 when Howells published "Henry James, Jr." in the *Century*. His advocacy of the "new school" of writers, epitomized by James, and his criticism of the "old school" of Dickens and Thackeray infuriated especially the British critics. So when he began in earnest to wage the Realism War in his column in *Harper's Monthly*, many critics in England and America renewed their attacks on Howells. His iconoclastic comments on romantic fiction and his favorable reviews of such writers as Sarah Orne Jewett, Thomas Hardy, Emile Zola, Guy de Maupassant, Harold Frederic, Lafcadio Hearn, Juan Valera, Palacio Valdés, and dozens of others who adhered to the tenets of literary realism, although judiciously tempered by his own sense of tradition and propriety, were seen as threats to established literary taste, to public morality, and to the economic interests of those who profited from the popularity of romantic and sentimental fiction.

In his correspondence with many of these writers, Howells offered encouragement and praise for literary accomplishments of promise. Occasionally he made a blunt comment on either style or content, but these instances were rare, and one gets a sense that even unasked-for advice from so respected a source was generally accepted or at least seriously considered. This is true even for his correspondence with Henry James and Samuel Clemens, which is characterized by extensive critical comment and observation. Howells' letters to James are more congratulatory than those to Clemens, presumably because James had few supporters among the critics, and Howells felt a special obligation to sustain the spirits of his friend. "... I want to tell you now," he wrote James on 10 October 1888, "that I think your Partial Portraits wonderfully good work. It makes all my critical work seem clumsy and uncouth. Surely you were born with the right word in your mouth; you never say the wrong one any way.—Of course the beastialità will keep being said; but I think there is distinctly a tendency to a better sense of you here, if you really care for the fact." The letters to Clemens are robust in tone, sometimes chiding him for unnecessary crudeness in content and form, but praising him also for the charm and originality of his works and the incisiveness of his satirical pieces.[1]

The letters of this period also reveal Howells' varying response to the critical barbs aimed at him by his detractors. In the earlier phases of the extended controversy he seemed to take pleasure in verbal jousts; as he wrote Edmund Gosse on 24 January 1886, "it's fun, having one's open say again, and banging the babes of Romance about. It does my soul lots of good; and how every number [of the "Editor's Study"] makes 'em dance." But a year later his playful tone sobered, and he wrote his father that the criticisms of him that appeared in the newspapers were "inevitable, because I'm now something of a 'shining mark,' and because in fiction I've identified myself with truth and humanity..." (27 February 1887). As the years passed and the critical attacks on Howells became increasingly defamatory, he finally complained in the "Study" of their *ad hominem* style, but he did not shrink from any assaults on his literary theories. If anything, he became more confident of the correctness of his ideas.

In addition to formulating his concepts of literary realism, Howells discussed social and economic theories in his monthly column in such a way that attacks by his literary opponents often sprang from differences in social ideology as much as from contrasting concepts of fiction. He reviewed books on the social injustices of America's capitalistic society and commented on authors who offered remedies and radical alternatives to capitalism. Edward Bellamy, Laurence Gronlund, Sergei Stepniak, and R. T. Ely were among those whose books awakened Howells' social

---

1. Only a very small selection of Howells' letters to Clemens is printed in this edition because of the excellent earlier editorial work done by Henry Nash Smith and William M. Gibson in *The Mark Twain–Howells Letters* (Cambridge, Mass.: Harvard University Press, Belknap Press, 1960).

conscience. The most influential of all, however, was Tolstoy, whom Howells publicly proclaimed to be "the greatest living writer, and incomparably the greatest writer of fiction who has ever lived . . ." (*Harper's Monthly*, July 1887). He used both the "Editor's Study" and his correspondence to encourage others to read Tolstoy and to follow the principles of Christian Socialism in their own lives.

To give that advice to others, however, was one thing; to live up to it himself was quite another problem, as Howells unhappily came to realize. The simple, frugal, virtuous life was difficult to put into practice in an urban-industrial society, even if one had the will to give up the amenities of modern living. Thus Howells wrote to Edward Everett Hale that Tolstoy's "ethical books . . . have made me unhappy. They have shown me the utter selfishness and insufficiency of my past life, without convincing me that Tolstoi offers quite the true solution. . . . I'm afraid Tolstoi doesn't value amusement enough in a world that seems to get very wicked without it. I'm afraid also that this fear is a sneaking love of the world anyway in me" (28 June 1887). Despite these occasional doubts, Howells drew the moral strength from Tolstoy's writings that he needed to defend often unpopular positions, and he was quite sincere in telling his sister Annie that Tolstoy's fiction is "worth all the other novels ever written" (18 November 1887).

Perhaps the most controversial and unpopular cause that Howells took up was that of the Haymarket anarchists. For some time his view that a travesty of justice had been perpetrated in the trial and conviction in 1887 of the eight accused men remained private; he expressed these feelings in letters to his father and friends in journalistic circles. He corresponded with both George W. Curtis, editor of the "Editor's Easy Chair" column in *Harper's Monthly*, and John Greenleaf Whittier in hopes of getting their support for a plea of clemency, so that "the cruellest wrong that ever threatened our fame as a nation" (to Whittier, 1 November 1887) would be averted. But when all of these private efforts proved futile, Howells finally sent his friend Whitelaw Reid, editor of the New York *Tribune*, a letter for publication. Its appearance in early November 1887 led to expressions of ridicule in newspapers and magazines throughout the nation of Howells' leniency toward the men who, so it was claimed, had threatened the very existence of American democracy. When four of the anarchists were hanged, Howells wrote another, more stinging editorial letter to the *Tribune*, but he evidently never mailed it. Instead, he suggested an alternative publication to William M. Salter, a sympathetic Chicago clergyman, that would soothe his feelings of outrage: "a book embodying expressions of sympathy and protest . . . and a narrative of the efforts of the clemency committees" (20 November 1887). But even though Howells agreed to contribute a letter to such a book, Salter deemed the idea impracticable, and Howells refrained from any further public statements on the anarchists' behalf.

Howells' disillusionment with the outcome of the trial and with the moral state of the country found expression both in his letters and publications of this time. He increasingly became convinced that socialism would provide a sound foundation for the rectification of social injustices in America. "I incline greatly to think our safety and happiness are in that direction; though as yet the Socialists offer us nothing definite or practical to take hold of," he wrote his father on 22 January 1888. By July he had informed himself sufficiently about socialist ideas that he declared he would vote for "any candidate [in the presidential election] embodying my hopes of nationalizing the industries, resources and distributions of the country" (to W. C. Howells, 8 July 1888). Yet he was never able to affiliate permanently with the American section of the Socialist Labor Party, finding Tolstoy and the Christian Socialists more compatible with his convictions. He eventually summed up his views in a letter to Thomas Wentworth Higginson: "Tolstoi tells us simply to live as Christ bade us, socially and politically, severally and collectively" (28 September 1888).

The major fiction of this period demonstrates Howells' interest in examining contemporary social and economic problems from a distinctly egalitarian point of view. His portrayals of unequal economic and false social stratifications in *The Minister's Charge, Annie Kilburn,* and *A Hazard of New Fortunes* are of a piece with the expressions of concern in his letters. Such unpopular views caused the critics to comment with little enthusiasm on these novels. Howells' friends in New York and Boston, who usually wrote him letters of praise about recent publications, either refrained from comment on the fictions or criticized them for being "too predominantly *grim*," to use Higginson's phrase in a letter to Howells, dated 7 August 1888. Other critics were less polite and more vocal in their tirades against these scandalous novels with their socialistic bent. If Howells was at times troubled by his inclination "to sugar-coat" the "medicinal properties" of his novels, as he put it in a letter to Edmund Clarence Stedman (4 February 1888), his critics chided him for the bluntness with which he presented his social views. He was determined to show the lack of "complicity" or social involvement, the false compassion for the "commonplace people" among the aristocrats in American democracy, and the repression of the working class by the capitalist bosses. Clearly, as he remarked to Henry James, he was "not in a very good humor with 'America' " because "after fifty years of optimistic content with 'civilization' and its ability to come out all right in the end, I abhor it, and feel that it is coming out all wrong in the end, unless it bases itself anew on a real equality" (10 October

1888). In the same letter he continued with considerable irony: "Mean-time, I wear a fur-lined overcoat, and live in all the luxury my money can buy." That Howells was troubled rather than pleased with this discrepancy between his life-style and his convictions is quite evident, even though on 2 February 1890 he gave his father contrary assurances, writing that "it is a comfort to be right theoretically, and to be ashamed of one's self practically."

To the public contumely and the private sense of shame was added the experience of personal tragedy. Despite the prolonged European sojourn a few years earlier, restful summer vacations in the mountains and by the sea shore, and an almost constant monitoring of her health by parents and physicians, Winifred Howells deteriorated to the point where she was unable to make her debut in Boston society late in 1885. Howells, who had watched his sister Victoria die of malaria in December 1886, desperately tried to restore his oldest child's health by moving away from the rigors of social life in Boston to the more restful environments of Auburndale, Massachusetts, and Lake George, New York, and by forcing her to exercise and eat. The doctors treating Winny could find no physiological reason for her frail health, so they concluded it had a psychological origin. In September 1887 the Howells family moved once again, this time to Dansville, New York, the site of a sanatorium where Winny would be taken care of. But, becoming frustrated with the ineffectiveness of the treatments and their drain on his finances, Howells eventually placed Winny in care of a New York doctor and took her along to a villa the family had rented for the summer of 1888 in Little Nahant, Massachusetts. None of these measures brought improve-ment, as Howells explained to Edward Everett Hale: "after tormenting her all summer upon a theory of treatment, [we] find it probably all a cruel blunder, and are now hoping to get Dr. Mitchell to take her" (30 August 1888).

S. Weir Mitchell, the noted Philadelphia physician, at first seemed to have some success with his theory that strengthening Winny physically by means of force-feeding her would make it possible for him to treat her psychologically. By February 1889 her condition improved sufficient-ly, and Mitchell allowed her to convalesce at a rest home in nearby Merchantville. But on 2 March 1889, one day after Howells'fifty-second birthday, Winny unexpectedly died from "a sudden failure of the heart," as Howells wrote his father on 4 March. The loss crushed Howells and devastated Elinor, whose health, always fragile, became even more precarious for the rest of her life. His efforts to complete *A Hazard of New Fortunes* were futile, and nothing that he wrote during this period of extreme depression seemed acceptable. In a letter to his father, nine months after Winny's death, Howells confided: "I find myself in the strange mood of wishing to live only from moment to moment: to write, to read, to eat, above all to sleep and forget. I have no longer any objects in the world, any incentives beyond these. The finality seems forever gone out of earthly things" (24 November 1889).

Although Howells received solace and satisfaction from his other children—John was enrolled at Harvard and Mildred was achieving success in her art studies—he still sought escape from the thought of his dead Winny. He wrote three books, *The Shadow of a Dream, A Boy's Town*, and *An Imperative Duty*, after the family had moved back to the Cambridge area. He worked at his writing and became engrossed in his former activities—corresponding about politics and religion with his father, providing some financial support for his improvident relatives, worrying over the health of his aging father and retarded brother, encouraging young writers—in an effort to restore at least the semblance of normality to his anguished life. He and Elinor avoided society as much as possible, however, participating in events only insofar as was necessary to keep the children happy and to maintain professional relationships.

The nomadic existence of the family continued unabated. The return to the Cambridge area in May 1889 was probably motivated partly by the need for peace and security which they felt among such old friends as Lowell, Scudder, Norton, and Aldrich, and partly by the wish to be close to Winifred's grave. But in December of that year they moved to Boston; they spent the following summer in various towns in upstate New York and in Lynn, Massachusetts, before returning to the Bay City; and for the summer of 1891 they escaped for three months to Intervale, New Hampshire. Howells' most significant move, however, occurred in November 1891, when he decided to become editor of John Brisbane Walker's *Cosmopolitan Magazine.*

Howells had begun negotiating with Walker, a man of "strong socialistic tendencies," after having heard from Harper & Brothers that they did not wish to continue their contractual relationship with Howells beyond 1891, and after considering the possibility of editing a magazine for S. S. McClure, who had agreed to syndicate *The Quality of Mercy.* The agreement with Walker meant that the family had to move to New York, a rather pleasant prospect for Howells, who had become enthralled with the vitality and variety of the metropolis. As he wrote his father at this time: "Between the two cities [Boston and New York] I prefer New York; it is less 'dour,' and there is more for me to see and learn there" (18 October 1891). His instincts were right, as they had been twenty-five years earlier when he began his association with the *Atlantic* in Boston. New York was clearly becoming the center of literary activity and of the publishing business in America and therefore

seemed to be the right place for a man who hoped to use his new editorial position "to do something for humanity as well as the humanities"
(to C. E. Norton, 12 December 1891). What Howells did not fully
understand, apparently, was that such lofty goals could not long survive
in the age of mass circulation magazines; the *Cosmopolitan* could not
become what the *Atlantic* once had been, and instead of serving for
fifteen years, Howells quit his new editorial position after only six
months. The independent novelist, who had developed a distinct literary
credo and a principled though somewhat diffuse social philosophy,
could no longer bear the editor's yoke.

R. C. L.

C. K. L.

18 JANUARY 1866, AUBURNDALE, MASSACHUSETTS, TO SAMUEL L. CLEMENS

Auburndale Jan. 18, 1886.

My dear Clemens:

Pil and I had a delightful little visit with you's all, and got home well
worn out with pleasure.[1] I still grieve over the loss of your conclusions
about Daggett and Mackley,[2] which the Type Setter Committee cut
off.[3] But I hope some time to get 'em. That notion of yours about the
Hartford man waking up in King Arthur's time is capital.[4] There is a
great chance in it. I wish I had a magazine, to prod you with, and keep
you up to all those good literary intentions.

You are an awfully good fellow to talk with. I wish you were handier.

Pil will write to Susy.

With love to all

Yours ever

W. D. Howells.

1. Howells wrote about his and Mildred's visit to the Clemenses in his letter
to his father of 17 January 1886 (MH): "On Wednesday [13 January], Pilla and
I went to Hartford for a day to see Clemens and his children play in a dramatization of the Pauper & the Prince. The play was very pretty, but the broken-down
trains didn't bring us till it was half done. The delay served to bring out all
Pilla's sweetness and good sense. She quietly read through a novel that she had
brought, and then philosophically joked about our getting to Hartford in time
to see the curtain going down on the legs of the performers."

2. Rollin M. Daggett (1831–1901) was a newspaperman who had worked with
Clemens in Nevada on the staff of the Virginia City *Territorial Enterprise*. In
November 1885 Clemens had considered having Daggett's book on the Sandwich
Islands published by Charles L. Webster & Co. See *Twain-Howells*, p. 546. "Mack-
ley" was John W. Mackay (1831–1902); he was one of the discoverers of the Bonanza
mines in Nevada and controlled the principal mines on the Comstock lode.

3. Apparently during Howells' visit Clemens had been reminiscing about his Nevada days, when he was interrupted by some people with whom he discussed business matters relating to the Paige Typesetter, in which he had heavily invested for a period of five years.

4. It appears that Howells either read or heard Clemens talk about an early version of *A Connecticut Yankee in King Arthur's Court* (1889).

23 JANUARY 1886, AUBURNDALE, MASSACHUSETTS, TO WILLIAM C. HOWELLS

Auburndale, Jan. 23, 1886.

Dear Father—

Your nice long letter has come, and has given me great pleasure; for I see that tho' you are low spirited you are getting better. But you must not be low-spirited, either. Your affairs are now in much better state than has been the case since you went to Virginia; and you are in a way to rid yourself of all care. I am delighted to think that Lennox will take your farm,[1] for he seemed to me an honest man; *but have everything clearly in writing*; and if possible *take a low rent* rather than *a share in the crops*, which would keep you anxious and bothered the whole year. I urge you also not to furnish horses for working the place; you will be feeling all the time that they are abused. Now for the rest, try to ease yourself in mind and body. You will certainly not be allowed to suffer. You have your own immediate family all to yourself again, and in any exigency Joe or I would of course come to you. I hope you keep the entry stove well fired up, and I enclose something for that special purpose. Keep indoors, and try not to take cold. I wish you would write a full acc't of your case to Uncle Joe;[2] he is very skilful, & would prescribe something that would set you up again.

I enclose a letter from Robt. Clarke of Cincinnati, which tho' disappointing is very kind.[3] In my change of publishers I have not been able to arrange in the way I thought I might about your autobiography, but when I see the Harpers I will suggest the matter to them. I am now so pressed that I c'dn't prepare the copy, if it were accepted, but in the summer I hope for more leisure. Long before that time I expect to have seen you again. I am delighted that you intend to do something for Howe's history,[4] as soon as you're well, for it will keep you from brooding upon yourself.

You will be glad to hear that Winny is much better, tho' still far from active.

I am nearing the end of my story,[5] which has bothered me more than usual, and run to greater length than I expected. But 200 more pages like this ought to finish it. Then I shall feel like taking a little breath.

The family all keep well, and I suppose the air of this place is rather peculiarly good. Invalids are sent here from all about. Do you think you would be "game" to come up here next month for a little visit? You know how happy it w'd make us all if you could come.

I had a nice long letter from Annie the other day, and she suggested my making this invitation, which has so long been a standing one.

Joe writes me that Sam has found steady work again; so you need not worry about him. There is one thing that I want you to know, in connection with the little help I have been able to render you, and that is that Joe has probably done more, in ways that you're not aware of. He is a good and generous fellow, and he feels keenly his inability to be of service to you, moneywise, oftener.

All join me in love to all of your family.

> Your affectionate son,
> **Will.**

Tell Aurelia that we now think those shoes were mislaid or stolen when we were packing your barrel. Elinor is greatly obliged to her for taking so much trouble, and sorry for making it.

1. See Howells to W. C. Howells, 26 December 1885, n. 3. Lennox has not been identified.

2. Joseph Howells was a physician in Hamilton, Ohio.

3. On 6 January Howells had apparently written to Robert Clarke & Co., a publishing house in Cincinnati, suggesting that they bring out W. C. Howells' autobiographical reminiscences. In a letter to Howells of 20 January 1886 (MH) the publishers wrote that they "would like very well to give your fathers [sic] life and reminiscences to the public, but fear we cannot undertake it at present." In 1895, however, the company did publish the older Howells' *Recollections of Life in Ohio, from 1813 to 1840*, with an introduction by W. D. Howells.

4. Probably W. C. Howells had been asked to contribute to Henry Howe's *Historical Collections of Ohio...an Encyclopedia of the State: History Both General and Local, Geography with Descriptions of Its Counties, Cities and Villages, Its Agricultural, Manufacturing, Mining, and Business Development, Sketches of Eminent and Interesting Characters, etc., with Notes of a Tour Over It in 1886* (1889–1891).

5. *The Minister's Charge.*

24 JANUARY 1886, AUBURNDALE, MASSACHUSETTS, TO EDMUND W. GOSSE

Auburndale, Jan. 24, 1886.

My dear **Gosse:**

It was delightful to get your broken-spirited letter of Dec. 28, and all this sympathetic family joined in the laugh at your calamity.[1] We loved you, and for that reason we rejoiced to see you brought low. Pil was especially so charmed with the notion of your going down to Oblivion on the arm of Obloquy,[2] that she made a picture of you, at once, in the act. Mrs. Proudy was jubilant;[3] and I tried to affect a compassion which I didn't feel. The fact is that ever since I opened my "Study" in Harper's, the small fry of critics swarm upon me; and it was impossible not to be glad another fellow was getting it, too. Here is a paragraph about you for the March number, wh. I expect to put an end to our friendship, if you take it as wildly awry as the other people do the other things.[4]—But it's fun, having one's open say again, and banging the babes of Romance about. It does my soul lots of good; and how every number makes 'em dance! There has n't been so much honest truth aired in this country since Columbus's second mate shouted "Land, ho!" and Columbus retorted "What a lie! It's clouds."

I am pulling in from my long fictitious voyage;[5] and when the story is quite done—say March 1st—Mrs. Howells and I expect to go to Washington for a month or two.[6] I've a notion that W. would be a good place for us to live; but I'm not certain, yet.—We have read "Firdausi" aloud, and I am glad of the whole book.[7] I like the shorter and more familiar pieces best because they are more full of you.

All join me in love to Mrs. Gosse and yourself.

Yours ever
W D Howells

1. "I am in a mournful frame of mind," Gosse wrote on 28 December 1885 (MH), "for I have come in for a veritable vendetta of criticism...and my new books this winter have caught it from the crawling things of criticism." See *Transatlantic Dialogue*, p. 181.

2. Gosse noted in his letter of 28 December to Howells: "I really thought you were going to allow me to go down to Oblivion on the arm of Obloquy." He made this comment because there had been a seven-month gap between Howells' letter of 9 March 1885 and that of 26 October 1885.

3. See Howells to Gosse, 24 December 1884, n. 6.

4. Commenting on Gosse's *From Shakespeare to Pope* (1885) in "The Editor's Study," *Harper's Monthly*, March 1886, Howells expressed his pleasure at Gosse's charming and intelligent treatment of the minor English poets of the seventeenth century: "not to have been poets ought now to be a fine satisfaction to those poor seventeenth-century nonentities, if they could only know how exquisitely Mr. Gosse has employed their absence of poetic quality. We had almost said that this lack in his subject is necessary to show Mr. Gosse at his best, but we remembered in time his other *Seventeenth Century Studies* and his beautiful *Life of Gray*."

5. *The Minister's Charge*.

6. Howells first mentioned the idea of going to Washington, D.C., in a letter to Clemens, 11 December 1885 (NPV; *Twain-Howells*, pp. 544–45): "I don't know but we may go to Washington in February, for the rest of the winter. I think I might get the ground for a story, there." Howells, Elinor, and Mildred arrived in Washington on 26 February 1886 and resided at a boarding house at 1408 H Street.

7. *Firdausi in Exile and Other Poems* (1885). It was one of Gosse's works that had been harshly dealt with by the English critics, one of whom wrote in the *Pall Mall Gazette*, 14 December 1885: "Mr. Gosse, setting forth to be a poet, is lost in the modern throng of clever verse-writers."

28 JANUARY 1886, AUBURNDALE, MASSACHUSETTS, TO THOMAS S. PERRY

Auburndale, Mass., Jan. 28, 1886.

My dear Perry:

Don't come Sunday because there's to be someone else that day, and I want you all to myself. Can't you come Monday, if fine, and have a walk? Or foul, and a talk? Of course you're right: no one invented realism; it came. It's perfectly astonishing that it seems to have come everywhere at once, and yet not in England. They always had it there, though, and were ashamed of it.

Be sure to bring your manuscript, I want to hear it.[1]

This time I made the Study mainly about Tolstoi, Gogol, and Valdés.[2] But isn't it strange that in all this vast land there should not be one intelligent voice besides yours on the right side? How does history account for that?

Yours ever,
W. D. Howells.

1. Probably either "The Progress of Literature," in M. R. Gately's *World's Progress* (1886) or *The Evolution of the Snob* (1887). Howells commented on both in "Editor's Study," *Harper's Monthly*, December 1886.
2. See "Editor's Study," *Harper's Monthly*, April 1886.

3 FEBRUARY 1886, AUBURNDALE, MASSACHUSETTS, TO JAMES R. LOWELL

Lee's, Feb. 3, 1886.

Dear Mr. Lowell—

For *you*, after your journey to Washington, and all its glories and disgusts, to be first to write me of my new story[1]—But when were you *not* the first in kindness to me? There ought to be some way for me to get out the gratitude and affection I feel; but you are a great poet and you can imagine it. I will even try to learn the right use of prepositions and the signs of the future and the conditional.

My wife thanks you with me.

Yours sincerely ever
W. D. Howells.

1. The first number of *The Minister's Charge* had appeared in the *Century*, February 1886, and Lowell wrote Howells on 2 February 1886 (MH) that he thought the novel delightful even though Howells was guilty of misusing prepositions. Lowell jokingly added that he was ready "to get up a Society for the Prevention of Cruelty to Prepositions.... It will spare neither age nor sex, & will be happiest when dancing a wardance on the broken ties of friendship." Lowell had gone to Washington to testify in support of an international copyright agreement.

9 MAY 1886, BOSTON, TO JOHN HAY

302 Beacon st.
Boston, May 9, '86.

My dear Hay—

I'm sending you a copy of Tuscan Cities, which I've just got out of storage with a number of others; perhaps you never noticed the deeply veiled reminiscence of yourself towards the middle of Chap. XXII, p. 67.[1]

We have got back to our old ruts, and are jolting along in them, sick with regret for the airy paths of your sky. As usual, I'm beginning a story—this time for the covert discouragement of love-marriages, and the promotion of broken engagements.[2]

We had a pleasant time in Hampton and New York, but my heart untraveled fondly turns to Washington,[3] of which your kindness and Mrs. Hay's was so chief a part. My wife joins me in cordial regards to you both, and Pillà sends love to Helen.[4]

Yours ever
W D Howells.

1. The passage in "A Florentine Mosaic" reads: "when I drove up to San Miniato to 'realize' the siege of Florence ... I would far rather have been an unpremeditating listener to the poem of Browning which the friend in the carriage with me was repeating. The din of guns drowned his voice from time to time, and while he was trying to catch a faded phrase, and going back and correcting himself, and saying, 'No—yes—no! That's it—no! Hold on—I have it!' as people do in repeating poetry, my embattled fancy was flying about over all the historic scene .... It was prodigiously fatiguing...."
2. *April Hopes*, published serially in *Harper's Monthly*, February–November 1887, and in book form by Harper & Brothers in 1888.
3. See Howells to Gosse, 24 January 1886, n. 6.
4. Helen Hay (1875–1944) was John Hay's daughter.

23 MAY 1886, BOSTON, TO SAMUEL L. CLEMENS

Boston, May 23, 1886.

My dear Clemens—

I never read a more pathetic story than that you tell me of your mother.[1] After all how poor and hackneyed all the inventions are, compared with the simple and stately facts! Who could have imagined such a heartbreak as that? Yet it went along with the fulfillment of everyday duty, and made no more noise than a grave underfoot. I doubt if fiction will ever get the knack of such things. How could it represent them?

I'm worrying away at the start of a new story,[2] which I haven't fairly got on its legs after a month's trying. And to-morrow I have to switch off and do a "Study." What a fool I was to undertake that! But oh! how much better it all is than to be waiting for the axe to-morrow night![3] I would rather be the lessee of a theatre any time than the author of a new play.

Yours ever
W. D. Howells.

1. Clemens communicated to Howells on 19 May 1886 (NN; *Twain-Howells*, pp. 566–67) "a most curious & pathetic romance" about his mother, Jane Clemens, who at age eighty-two tried and failed to see a man with whom she had been in love as a young woman.

2. Probably *April Hopes,* though see Howells to W. H. Smith, 6 June 1886, n. 1.

3. *Colonel Sellers as a Scientist* was to have begun a two-week run at the Lyceum Theatre in New York on 24 May, but Howells and Clemens withdrew the play from production. See Howells to Clemens, 7 February 1890, n. 1, and *Twain-Howells,* pp. 558–59.

2 JUNE 1886, BOSTON, TO JAMES R. OSGOOD

302 Beacon st.,
Boston June 2, 1886.

My dear Osgood—

I have had two letters from you, and I have waited till I could give you some account of my stewardship in regard to the Longfellow portrait before writing you.[1] I have done what I could, without success, in the way of private applications, and have consulted with Wells about getting Appleton to subscribe.[2] He says A. has no money to give, and he was very discouraging about it generally. Millet[3] suggested applying to Class Secretaries, but W. said the Class Funds were for crackers and cheese. Anthony had thought of putting the picture at Doll's with subscription attached,[4] but most every one has now left town, and I was not sure you'd like the notion, especially if the plan failed. It occurred to me Sunday, however, that it might be well to hang the picture in Alumni Hall on Commencement Day, when the Alumni having dined might disburse. I went over to see Norton, and he consulted the College authorities. The Bursar wrote to him that the President thought it would be better to hang it in Massachusetts Hall. I enclose Norton's comment, and unless you forbid it, I will send the picture out to the Bursar.

If you approve, wont you get Lowell's leave to use some lines from his letter, which could be appended to the portrait?

I hope you are getting acclimated and otherwise reconciled.[5]

I have started in on a novel,[6] and I hope to get it well forward by the fall. I shall stay here all summer, and probably go to New York for the winter, though this depends somewhat on the family health. We all liked New York immensely.

My elder brother may turn up in London within a month; if he does he may like to shake your hand for me.

Yours ever
W. D. Howells.

1. Osgood owned a portrait of Longfellow by George Healy (1813–1894), an American portrait painter, which several admirers of Longfellow wished to buy for $1,500 to give to Harvard for display in Alumni Hall. Howells assisted in soliciting the subscriptions and notified Ernest Longfellow (1845–1921), the poet's son, on 23 May 1886 (ViU), that J. R. Lowell had already made a contribution to the subscription fund. The two letters from Osgood have not been located.
2. Samuel Wells, Howells' attorney, had probably approached Thomas G. Appleton, Longfellow's brother-in-law.
3. Francis D. Millet.
4. A. V. S. Anthony, while working for Ticknor & Fields, superintended the quarto illustrated edition of Longfellow's works. The plan was to display the portrait at Doll's picture shop, with a solicitation for subscriptions.
5. Osgood had recently begun his assignment as agent for Harper & Brothers in England.
6. Probably *April Hopes*, though see Howells to W. H. Smith, 6 June 1886, n. 1.

6 JUNE 1886, BOSTON, TO WILLIAM H. SMITH

302 Beacon st.,
Boston, June 6, 1886.

My dear friend[1]—

I have waited for the arrival of my brother Joe, in order to advise with him as to Sam before answering your most kind letter. We are both very grateful to you for keeping the matter in mind, but we don't think it advisable that Sam should come to New York or go to Texas. If there were anything in Northern or Central Ohio, however subordinate, it would be better for him. In fact it would be well for him at first to be under direction, till he had learned just what was wanted of him. I don't myself know what your work is; but I suppose it's news-gathering and despatching, which he should have a little time to catch onto. He can write fairly well, and has had newspaper experience in Cleveland. At present he's working at a comical wage in the Madison newspaper office, barely better than nothing; but he is in a position to wait for anything that may occur to you.[2] If you'll tell me a little what kind of work yours is I can judge better of his fitness for it.

—Your gossip about the national marriage was most amusing.[3] What a shabby-sentimental-brutal thing it all is! And then that harlot and her bastard in the background![4]

—Poor old Logan's speech was delicious. How we should have gone for it in the good old newspaper days! I couldn't help sending it to Mark Twain, whose comment please return.[5]

Joe is here on his way to England. He's all run down with dyspepsia, and goes out hoping to profit by the change and rest. He sails on the *State of Indiana* next Thursday, from N. Y., and will probably drop in to see you a moment.

I'm glad you approved of the Goethe paragraph.[6] It seemed true, to me.

With our united regards to you all,

> Yours ever
> W. D. Howells.

1. Howells' friendship with Smith went back almost thirty years to the time when they were both newspapermen in Cincinnati. Only a few days later, on 10 June 1886 (OCoO), he wrote Smith again, this time in connection with a novel that he was working on: "I'm writing a story which introduces a Cincinnati man—of good social standing, rich, well educated, travelled—come to New York, where he buys a house and settles down with with [sic] his family. Can you tell me, from your observation of Westerners in N. Y. whether they ever get to feel at home there, really? What are their amusements? How do they bore themselves? Are they clannish, and if so, where do they chiefly consort together." The "Cincinnati man" was probably to be a character in *April Hopes*, the basic concept of which Howells had developed in early May. See Howells to Hay, 9 May 1886. This speculation seems plausible in light of the comment about "throwing away two hundred pages of starts," in Howells' letter to his father of 27 June 1886. See *April Hopes*, HE, xii–xiv.

2. At this time Sam Howells was probably employed by the Madison, Ohio, *Index*, a small newspaper which Howells later bought for his brother so that he could settle down in a town only fifteen miles from Ashtabula. See Howells to W. C. Howells, 19 September 1886. It appears that Sam was seeking more lucrative employment as a reporter for the Associated Press.

3. On 2 June 1886 President Grover Cleveland married Frances Folsom.

4. A reference to Cleveland's former mistress and their illegitimate son. See Howells to Clemens, 10 August 1884, n. 8.

5. General John A. Logan (1826–1886) gave the main address at a Decoration Day ceremony at Grant's tomb in New York, 31 May 1886. Logan's speech lauded Grant as a great soldier and statesman. Clemens wrote Howells on 4 June 1886 (MH; *Twain-Howells*, pp. 570–71), about hearing a similar speech delivered by Logan in Chicago in 1879: "Three thousand people changed their attitudes every three-quarters of a minute under the unimaginable torture of that speech...."

6. "Editor's Study," *Harper's Monthly*, June 1886, contained a review of *Life and Genius of Goethe*.

27 JUNE 1886, BOSTON, TO WILLIAM C. HOWELLS

Boston, June 27, 1886.

Dear father—

I have not heard from you this week though I sent a telegram announcing Joe's safe arrival.[1] I suppose you are all well, and perhaps have Annie with you, and so have been taken up with her and her children. If they've come you must give them all my love. John and Winny are still with me here, but Elinor and Pil went into the country on Tuesday, to keep an engagement we had made for rooms.[2] Winny was to have gone with them, but was not quite up to it. She goes to morrow. John is about taking his Harvard preliminary examinations, and is working very hard.

After beating about for two months, and throwing away two hundred pages of starts, I've at last got started on a story that I think will bear my weight.[3] If it should break under me I don't know what I should do.

In these dreadful between times I get very low spirited and begin to be afraid there's no more work in me. I have run a long time; when will the pendulum begin wag without ticking, and then stop altogether? But as soon as I'm fairly off on a story I've no further trouble of mind about any thing but getting it forward in the right shape.

We have had cool, lovely weather this whole month. This morning I wish you could see how the water is tossed in the Charles behind my house, and the clouds are blown through the spaces of blue sky.

With love to all,

Your affectionate son,
Will.

1. Joseph Howells arrived in Glasgow ca. 23 June.
2. Elinor and Mildred Howells had gone to Sharon, Massachusetts.
3. See Howells to W. H. Smith, 6 June 1886, n. 1.

13 JULY 1886, BOSTON, TO CHARLES E. NORTON

302 Beacon st.
Boston, July 13, 1886.

My dear Norton:

You wont have thought me indifferent to your kindness. I've been trying to reconcile an acceptance of your invitation with a stern resolve to go nowhere this summer, but to sit here, and work with the unremitting industry of a hero rather than a writer of novels. However, I think that by the middle of August I shall be so sick of what I'm at, that I shall be only too glad to leave it and my question then will be whether I'm fit company for any one.[1] But I will throw myself on your charity, which I've known unfailing for many years.

Prof. Royce[2] has just left me, and except for one or two other Cambridge men the whole region is depopulated. I shall not try just this experiment again; it's too horribly lonesome. After I've done writing in the morning I don't know what to do; so I read, and I've read till I'm a mere encyclopedia of fiction. In these days I've actually read through Tolstoï's Peace and War. But that's a great book, great as well as big.

I want very much to see what you've been saying of Froude; tantalizing bits have come to me in the papers.[3]

I suppose you didn't see Grant Allen again.[4] He dined with me before he left Boston, and talked somewhat of coming to live in Concord.

My family are all at Sharon, except John who went off with one of his friends to the Adirondacks, after his preliminaries. Give my love to all your household and to Curtis.

Yours sincerely
W. D. Howells.

1. Norton had invited Howells to visit him at his summer home in Ashfield, Massachusetts. Howells accepted the invitation, arriving there 19 August and returning to Boston, 21 August.

2. Josiah Royce (1855–1916), the American philosopher who developed the philosophy of idealism, was, at this time, an assistant professor of philosophy at Harvard.

3. "Recollections of Carlyle, with Notes Concerning His 'Reminiscences'" by Norton was published in the New Princeton Review, July 1886. Norton criticized James Anthony Froude (1818–1894), a close personal friend of Carlyle, for publishing the personal memoirs of Carlyle, who had specifically stated in writing that he had not intended them for publication. Froude asserted his innocence by claiming Carlyle said that after his death his friend could do whatever he judged best with manuscripts of memoirs.

4. Charles Grant Blairfindie Allen (1848–1899) was a Canadian naturalist and novelist who lived in England. Howells had recently commented on the use of American idiom and dialect in Allen's novel, Babylon (1885), stating that his Americanisms are faulty and derivative. See "Editor's Study," Harper's Monthly, February 1886.

18 July 1886, Boston, to William C. Howells

Boston, July 18, 1886.

Dear father—

Elinor went back to Sharon yesterday, and I'm in the house alone again. Do you still think of visiting me this summer? After Annie gets fairly domesticated with you, couldn't you come? Perhaps we shall **not** be in Boston another year, if we arrange to take John abroad, and I should like you to get some pleasure out of this house before we leave it.

I've been reading the introduction to James's Literary Remains this morning—took it up quite accidentally—and have been greatly struck by his thinking. He makes you feel the race-unity, and perceive that there can be no personal hope or happiness opposed to it. His son, who edits the book seems to doubt whether he finds a warranty for all his philosophy in Swedenborg.[1]

I have no news. With love to all.

Your aff'te son
Will.

1. In the "Introduction" to *The Literary Remains of the Late Henry James*, William James sought to clarify his father's interpretation of Swedenborgian doctrines, defining it as "monistic enough to satisfy the philosopher, and yet warm and living and dramatic enough to speak to the heart of the common man."

23 JULY 1886, BOSTON, TO WILLIAM C. HOWELLS

Boston, July 23, 1886.
Dear father—

You certainly write me startling news, and it is a little odd to have one's opinion asked, and then told that you have concluded to act without it. But you know much better than I do whether Warren's place is worth yours. All that I could have advised—and I do this now—would have been that you should consult fully with Joe, before *passing any papers* with Warren.[1] *Keep his offer open* till you hear from Joe;[2] he will naturally suppose that you will wish to do so, and will wait, I dare say. If he wont I should feel a little anxious about the fairness of the trade.

Do I understand that you all mean to go back to Jefferson to live? The girls were so strongly opposed to it when we last talked the matter over. If you do, that is one thing, but if you contemplate this exchange with a view to acquiring property that would enable you to live in Richmond, or any other city, you would be doing a mistaken thing in which I could not feel it right to support you. I should feel very happy if you were going to be near Joe, in a comfortable house, and wholesome region, with ground enough to give Henry ample range; and it will be a pleasure to talk it all over with you when you come here.[3]

I'm glad Annie's with you at last. W. H. Smith wrote me of her passing through N. Y. Love to her and her children, with all the rest.

Your aff'te son
Will.

Remember, I only suggest your asking Warren to wait till you hear from Joe; if he *wont* wait, you must use your own judgment.

1. Warren has not been identified, but evidently he had proposed to exchange his Jefferson, Ohio, property for W. C. Howells' farm. Howells changed his mind and later approved of the proposed business arrangement. He wrote his father on 27 July 1886 (MH) that Warren's letter "seems very fair and honest; and I am glad that you have accepted his offer."

2. Joseph Howells, then regaining his health on a tour of the British Isles, was unavailable for consultation by his father. On his return trip to America Joe's ship "broke some part of her machinery, and had to put back" to Glasgow. See Howells to W. C. Howells, 14 August 1886 (MH). This event seems to have prefigured the incident of Jeff Durgin's return to America in chapter 14 of *The Landlord at Lion's Head* (1897).

3. W. C. Howells moved back to Jefferson in October 1886.

19 AUGUST 1886, ASHFIELD, MASSACHUSETTS, TO ELINOR M. HOWELLS

Ashfield, Aug. 19, 1886.

Dear Elinor:

I have your note of yesterday, and I shall willingly stay till Saturday morning, for the visit would have seemed to end rather abruptly.[1] They're all extremely kind, and I'm delighted with the whole affair. I like to see what I can of the Curtises, as well as the Nortons. Miss Curtis is a splendid girl.[2] She has read Winny's sonnet and admires it immensely—perfectly wonderful for a girl to write.[3]

The dinner went off very brilliantly—best speaking I ever heard.

I note what you say of the story,[4] and will carry it breath further, so as not to leave it uncertain.

Love to all.

Your
W. D. H.

Mrs. Curtis is deliciously determined and original. At tea he said to her, "Rest perturbed spirit!"[5] just as I do to you. They think very much as we do.

1. Howells was visiting Charles E. Norton for the occasion of the annual Ashfield Academy Dinner.

2. Probably Elizabeth Burrill Curtis (b. 1861), the older daughter of George W. Curtis.

3. Probably Winifred Howells' sonnet, "Past," *Century*, April 1886.

4. *April Hopes*.

5. *Hamlet*, I. v.182.

25 August 1886, Boston, to Gertrude Van R. Wickham

Boston, Aug. 25, 1886.

Dear Madam[1]—

I have no dog, and I am very much afraid of other people's.[2] In the chronic absence of the dog it is difficult even to send you his fotograf. I am heartily sorry I cannot be of use to you.

Very truly yours
W. D. Howells.

1. Gertrude Van Rensselaer Wickham (1844–1930) was the author of *The Pioneer Families of Cleveland 1796–1840* (1914) and a leader of women's groups in Cleveland. It appears that she was preparing a book or article on the dogs of famous Americans.
2. Howells considered it "essential to the study of my very morbid youth" to understand his obsessive fear of dogs and their association, in his mind, with hydrophobia. See *Years of My Youth*, HE, pp. 78–82.

31 August 1886, Boston, to Thomas W. Higginson

302 Beacon st.
Boston, Aug. 31, 1886

My dear Higginson—

Thank you for your friendly note. After your liking my story and my democracy, I ought to be willing you should dislike my literary creed, or my preaching it.[1] But I can't. I don't mind people's trying to raise apples and peaches, but I insist upon pears because now it is not "an apple year," and because all the peaches I taste have "got the yallers." They've run out.

To drop metaphor I mean that no reader of mine shall suppose that the true and natural way of writing fiction which is now universal, wherever the fiction is worth reading, is any longer to be taken on sufferance. It has come to stay.

I do a good deal of writing, but I fancy that like yourself I find a comfort rather than a hurt in it. I write three hours a day, and I sleep eight. This seems to make it safe to keep on.

Your ever
W. D. Howells.

1. Although Higginson's letter to which Howells is responding has not been located, it most likely commented on *The Minister's Charge*, of which seven installments had appeared in the *Century*, and on Howells' most recent "Editor's Study," *Harper's Monthly*, September 1886. In connection with a review of Dostoevski's *Crime and Punishment*, Howells made his famous comments about the peculiar

social conditions in America that were a result of its democratic system, and that made it appropriate for the American novelist to deal with "the more smiling aspects of life, which are the more American ...." "It is worthwhile," Howells continued his argument against the appropriateness of a tragic vision for the realistic novelist, "even at the risk of being called commonplace, to be true to our well-to-do actualities .... Sin and suffering and shame there must always be in the world, we suppose, but we believe that in this new world of ours it is mainly from one to another one, and oftener still from one to one's self. We have death too in America, and a great deal of disagreeable and painful disease ...; but this is tragedy that comes in the very nature of things, and is not peculiarly American, as the large cheerful average of health and success and happy life is. It will not do to boast, but it is well to be true to the facts, and to see that, apart from these purely mortal troubles, the race here enjoys conditions in which most of the ills that have darkened its annals may be averted by honest work and unselfish behavior." Because of his strong antislavery background, Higginson may have particularly objected to Howells' subsequent observation that even so dark a stain on American history as slavery was too remote to be the subject matter of realistic fiction.

2 SEPTEMBER 1886, BOSTON, TO CHARLES D. WARNER

> 302 Beacon st.
> Boston, Sept. 2, 1886.

My dear Warner:

Under my agreement with the Harpers, I can't write a book for any other publisher, and this cuts me off from attempting the Longfellow in your series.[1] It is a book which I should like some time to do, not only because I've promised it, but because I could paint the life of Cambridge in it so fully. But now, it's impossible. I'm too busy and too tired, as well as too tied.

—I've had glimpses of your "Pilgrimage" from month to month which delighted me;[2] but I'm waiting for the book. It keeps me jumping to read what *I* write for the mags., let alone my friend. Come over next year, and meet me in England.

> Yours ever
> W. D. Howells

1. Warner, editor of Houghton, Mifflin & Co.'s American Men of Letters Series, had written Howells, 1 September 1886 (MH), asking him to begin a critical exploration of Longfellow's "character and the significance of his literary performance in the time in which he lived in New England."

2. Warner's *Their Pilgrimage* (1887) was appearing serially in *Harper's Monthly*, April–November 1886.

Boston, Sept. 19, 1886.

Dear father—

Your last hospital bulletin was not cheering. When Achille went to bed with a chill in your postscript my own teeth almost began to chatter. I hope that you and Aurelia and Henry are taking quinine as a prophylactic. There's no other safety for you. In Florence everybody takes it who comes there—they have their choice between quinine and ague. As soon as the Fréchette children can travel I hope they'll start between chills, and that Annie and Achille will try what they can do to shake the first northern express off the track. Poor things—what a miserable visit it's been for them. I suppose it's the rainy weather that's developed all the malaria of your climate. Well, at any rate there's a fair prospect, if Warren comes on before frost, that he wont die of *consumption*.[1]

I suppose you know that I have bought the Madison Index for Sam.[2] I didn't wish to do so, I'll confess, but he was constantly asking me for money; I was paying his house rent; and I thought I had better give him this chance at self support. It's a very *good* chance, for the office is worth from $1000 to $1200 a year, and Sam's income jumps from $6 to $20 a week at once. He promises to put his girls to work in the office, and do the whole thing in the family. I shall be glad if he keeps half of his promises, but you'll not be surprised to know that I have no faith in them or him. I can only wait and see what new turn his incapacity will take.

We are gradually getting the family together in Boston, but Winny will stay in the country till November, I hope. Pil came home last night.

John has been using up the latter half of his vacation in preparing for examinations at the Technological Institute,[3] where he wishes to take the special course in Architecture, preparatory to going to the Beaux Arts in Paris. He has had three weeks to make up a year's work, and the most we can hope is that he will get in with conditions. He is facing life in a very manly way, and though he is a little foppish and worldly, he's thoroughly good. He had set his heart on going to Harvard, but he gave that up at our suggestion, with an ambition to begin work for himself as soon as possible. If it were not for Winny's ill health the children would be altogether a comfort. But we must not expect everything in this world—for fear we shouldn't get all of it.

With love to the patients in all the wards,

Your aff'te son
Will.

1. See Howells to W. C. Howells, 23 July 1886, n. 1.
2. See Howells to W. H. Smith, 6 June 1886, n. 2.

3. The Massachusetts Institute of Technology was at this time located in Boston, one block east of the Public Gardens. Building and Architecture was one of ten four-year courses offered by the institution.

12 OCTOBER 1886, BOSTON, TO ALBERT M. PALMER

302 Beacon st.,
Boston, Oct. 12, 1886.

Dear Mr. Palmer:[1]

I see by an "interview" with you that you propose giving my Foregone Conclusion about the middle of November. If this is true, will you kindly let me know the day? I should like to be present.[2]

The play was mentioned as "Priest and Painter." This was the name given by Mr. Poel to his version;[3] but as I have rejected all the characters and dialogue he added to my story, and given the play a totally new ending, according to my original conception, I would rather it were called *A Foregone Conclusion*, after the *novel*, or else, *Don Ippolito's Ordeal*. I hope you will be able to gratify me in this matter.

Yours truly
W. D. Howells.

1. Albert Marshman Palmer (1838–1905) was manager of the Madison Square Theatre in New York. He staged the first American performance of *A Foregone Conclusion* on 18 November 1886.
2. See Howells to W. C. Howells, 21 November 1886.
3. The Mallory brothers of the Madison Square Theatre had purchased the London version of the play from William Poel, but as staged in New York, it went by the same title as Howells' novel, *A Foregone Conclusion*. See Howells to Elinor Howells, 10 August 1884, n. 2, and Howells to James, 22 August 1884; also, for an account of other dramatic versions of the novel, see W. J. Meserve, *The Complete Plays of W. D. Howells* (New York: New York University Press, 1960), pp. 314–15. For a contemporary review, see the New York *Times*, 19 November 1886.

26 OCTOBER 1886, BOSTON, TO JAMES R. LOWELL

302 Beacon St.
Oct. 26, 1886.

Dear Mr. Lowell:

I must write and express my sympathy with you in the outrage you have suffered at the hands of a man who could have meant you no mischief, for that is not conceivable, under the circumstances. Your letter of protest and denial is perfect, for it is perfectly, miraculously, tempered, when the provocation to wrath must have been almost insupportable. It will suffice for your friends abroad, and here we forget everything in two days.[1]

I am glad you are in the country again:[2] I wish it were more home to you.

Yours affectionately
W. D. Howells.

1. The "outrage" that Howells refers to resulted when Julian Hawthorne, son of Nathaniel Hawthorne and literary editor of the New York *World*, published an interview he had conducted with J. R. Lowell, in which the recently retired minister to the Court of St. James expressed his outspoken views on English topics and personalities. The signed interview appeared in the *World* on 24 October. On 25 October the Boston *Advertiser* carried the letter that Howells mentions, in which Lowell denounced the opinions expressed in the interview and claimed to have been unaware that his words would be printed. Hawthorne responded to this letter in the *World* of 26 October, and his response elicited from Lowell a still stronger denunciation, which appeared in the Boston *Herald*. Hawthorne next wrote a long personal letter on 31 October. When he received no answer, the *World* printed on 11 November both the text of his letter and an editorial insisting that Lowell had known beforehand the use to which his remarks were to be put. See R. and C. Kirk, "Letters to an 'Enchanted Guest,'" *Journal of the Rutgers University Library* 22 (1959), 17–20; and George Knox, "The Hawthorne-Lowell Affair," *New England Quarterly* 29 (1956), 493–502.

2. Lowell had returned to America in 1885 after eight years abroad as U.S. minister to Spain and England.

31 OCTOBER 1886, BOSTON, TO WILLIAM C. HOWELLS

Boston, Oct. 31, 1886.

Dear father:

I was troubled not to get a letter from Jefferson last night;[1] but my latest news—Willy's[2] note of Thursday evening—was favorable, and I am making the most of that. You are passing through a very trying time, and I wish I could do something more than offer you my sympathy. I don't understand whether you and Aurelia are in your own house, or are still at Joe's. It was fortunate that your furniture came so promptly.—We are pretty well settled for the winter. Winny seems pretty well, and John is making splendid progress in the Institute of Technology; it's really the beginning of his professional studies. Pilla is studying with a painter, who comes twice a week to overlook her drawing. We had not meant to stay another winter in Boston, but the children's advantages are such that we decided to do so, and I think we have done well.—Unless Vic's sickness[3] should require me to come sooner, I now plan to be with you soon after Thanksgiving, when you will be settled and in running order, I hope. By that time, also, I shall have nearly finished the

story I'm engaged on,[4] and can take a little time with a quiet mind.—
Will you let me know if you and Henry are supplied with warm under-
clothing? Has he an overcoat?

All join me in love to both families.

Your aff'te son
Will.

1. Having sold his Virginia farm, W. C. Howells had recently moved back to
Jefferson.
2. William Dean Howells II.
3. Victoria Howells was suffering from malaria. She died 3 December 1886.
4. *April Hopes*.

7 NOVEMBER 1886, BOSTON, TO EDMUND W. GOSSE

302 Beacon St.
Boston, Nov. 7, 1886.

My dear Gosse:

I thank you for sending me your defense against the Quarterly.[1] You
need none with this family but we all thought your answer to the brutal
assault which we've not yet read admirable. I know the assault from
hearsay, Perry having told me how foolish and dishonest it was. The
feeling here is all one way. Aldrich says the close of your reply (the last
two paragraphs) is most masterly, and I think so too.

You will see in the December Harper how much I like your Raleigh,
but I must tell you personally that I found it only less delightful than
the Gray: that remains unapproachable.[2]

Last night I met the Creightons,[3] from your imitation-Cambridge at
Norton's, and Mrs. C. tried to make me jealous by pretending that you
giggled with her husband as much as you did with me. I was furious,
but I was too polite to show it.

The Middlemores are here and we are to give a large lunch for them
on Thursday.[4] The Hawthorne-Lowell interview has been a great
sensation here and there is no doubt but it was a most cruel betrayal. It
oughtn't to be regarded in England as representative of Lowell at all.[5]

The family joins me in love to Mrs. Gosse and yourself.

Yours ever,
W. D. Howells.

Mr. Edmund Gosse

1. John Churton Collins had severely criticized Gosse's *From Shakespeare to Pope*
(1885) in his article, "English Literature at the Universities," *Quarterly Review*,
October 1886. Gosse replied to this attack in the *Athenaeum*, 23 October 1886,

and sent privately printed copies of his defense to his friends. Collins (1848–1908) later became professor of English at Birmingham University.

2. Howells reviewed Gosse's *Raleigh* in "Editor's Study," *Harper's Monthly*, December 1886. Gosse's *Life of Thomas Gray* had appeared in 1882.

3. Mandell Creighton (1843–1901), an English theologian, was professor of church history at Cambridge (1884–1891) and bishop of London (1897–1901).

4. Samuel G. C. Middlemore, the English art historian, and his wife, Maria T. H. S. Middlemore.

5. See Howells to Lowell, 26 October 1886, n. 1.

16 NOVEMBER 1886, BOSTON, TO ACHILLE FRÉCHETTE

302 Beacon st.
Boston, Nov. 16, 1886.

My dear Achille—

I wish, with all my heart, that I could suggest something for your reading; but I'm really quite incapable of it. The strongest passages I ever wrote are the closing episodes of Chapters VII & VIII of A Modern Instance; but they shake my own nerves when I read them, and I don't believe other people would stand 'em.—My heart is in my mouth all the time at the reports from poor Vic,[1] though now she's apparently recovering; I have my bag ready packed to start for Ohio when they send. But if they don't send, and the hopeful condition continues, I shall go to N. Y. when they are to give my dramatization of A Foregone Conclusion, with Young Salvini as the priest.[2]

We are all getting on well, but shall be the better for any news you send us about your family.

John is studying architecture in the Technological Institute and Pil is drawing from casts.

Dearest love to Annie and the children, and Georgy,[3] who's now with you, I suppose.

Yours ever
W. D. Howells.

1. See Howells to W. C. Howells, 31 October 1886, n. 3.
2. Alessandro Salvini, son of Tommaso Salvini, the Italian actor. For Howells' comments on the production, see Howells to W. C. Howells, 21 November 1886.
3. Probably the daughter of Howells' brother Sam.

21 NOVEMBER 1886, BOSTON, TO WILLIAM C. HOWELLS

Boston, Nov. 21, 1886.

Dear father—

My last news from you was good, and I hope Victoria's recovery will be uninterrupted. Of course I can't understand at this distance how sick she may still be; but I hope she is now out of danger.[1] Under the immense relief of the hopeful reports from you all, I went to New York and saw the trial performance of my play at the Madison Square Theatre, on Thursday. The house was a splendid one, and the applause was incessant; it was a great success, I thought, but the newspapers, without a dissenting voice, pronounce the play bad.[2] What the managers will do with it, I don't know, and I'm not anxious; but I thoroughly respect the play. I'm very hard at work on my story[3]—the first for the Harpers under my contract—and I'm nearing the end of it.

I'm glad the package was suitable, and that the overcoat fitted Henry. Of course I had to guess at his size; but I put the coat on over my spring overcoat, and judged from that.

We are all well, and join in love to you all. Give our dearest love to Vic.

Your affectionate son,
Will.

1. See Howells to W. C. Howells, 31 October 1886, n. 3.
2. The reviewer of *A Foregone Conclusion* in the New York *Times*, 19 November 1886, acknowledged the audience's receptiveness to the play but concluded that the play was weak because of its lack of "variety of incident," lengthy conversations between two characters, weak characterization, and "no action to speak of." Although not very successful, the play continued to be performed for sometime. See W. J. Meserve, *The Complete Plays of W. D. Howells* (New York: New York University Press, 1960), p. 315.
3. *April Hopes.*

9 DECEMBER 1886, JEFFERSON, TO JOHN W. DE FOREST

Jefferson, Ohio, Dec. 9, 1886.

My dear De Forest:

Your letter was forwarded to me here where I came last week to the death-bed of my sister.[1] It was doubly welcome for the relief it afforded, and for the very great pleasure it gave me. Your praise is worth something, for it comes from skill and knowledge;[2] and oddly enough your name was at the point of my pen almost at the moment your letter came, for I had been mentioning your short stories among those which gave us Americans a sort of preeminence in that way. I hope what I said will meet your approval.[3] You are always very interesting to me as a man who did twenty years ago the kind of work which has just now gained full recognition. Miss Ravenel and Kate Beaumont[4] are as good pieces of realism as I know of—the latter, as I remember it, is worthy of the greatest novelist living in any country.—I am not trying to outdo you, as you may think, in civilities, I say what I mean. As to my own work, I believe I see rather more in Barker, of fruitful goodness and work than you do,[5] and I suspect I have a softer heart for the vulgarity of those poor, silly, common girls—especially 'Manda, in whom I think I struck a new streak.—I shall like to see what your aristocrat has to say of realism;[6] I know the kind of aristocrat in Boston who abhors it. By the way, I ought to tell you that it was your bold grappling with the fact of the robust love-making among three fourths of our nation that gave me courage to deal with it in Lemuel, and a Modern Instance. It's odd that no one touched it before you. But our life, as it differs from that of other nations, is as yet almost wholly untouched in our fiction. You I consider our earliest *novelist.*—I wish we might meet. In the meantime I thank you for your letter.

Yours sincerely
W. D. Howells.

1. Victoria Howells died 3 December 1886.

2. On 6 December 1886 (MH) De Forest had written Howells a long, detailed, and enthusiastic letter about *The Minister's Charge,* which was just completing its run in the *Century.* De Forest praised Howells' skillful characterizations and his courage in being an outspoken and uncompromising realist. "I admire, most of all, your honesty & courage. How dare you speak out your beliefs as you do? You spare neither manhood nor womanhood, & especially not the latter, though it furnishes four fifths of *our* novel-reading public. It is a wonder that the females of America, at least the common born & bred of them, do not stone you in the streets." In a later passage he refers to Howells' "martyr-like valor in standing to a true confession of" a realistic philosophy. However, toward the end of his long letter De Forest admonishes Howells that both romantic and realistic fiction "are equally allowable, & in a certain sense equally true. Each is the result of a selection; for we cannot tell the *whole* life, even of a country village; we must choose some characters for our painting, & shut our eyes to others. . . . Let each one select what he can best paint. But, returning to you & your work, I should advise you (I hope wisely) to go on with that kind of work. No one else, neither Jane Austen nor Henry James, has quite so pefectly depicted & so profoundly analysed, the nature of the vast substructure of humanity,—the immense majority,—the nineteen twentieths."

3. Discussing American short story writers in the "Editor's Study," *Harper's Monthly,* February 1887, Howells wrote that De Forest is "a novelist whose work has in some respects not only not been surpassed, but not approached, among us— a realist before realism was named, and an admirably equipped artist . . . ."

4. *Miss Ravenel's Conversion from Secession to Loyalty* (1867) and *Kate Beaumont* (1872).

5. De Forest commented extensively on Lemuel Barker, including these remarks: "endowed as he is with some genius, he is a kind of fool. He can't rise (except in mere fits of resultless longing) above his birth-line. He gets engaged, like a nigger

whitewasher, without a dollar in his pocket, to a girl as poor as himself & a hopeless invalid. He has no radical self-command & no effective forethought."

6. In De Forest's letter of 6 December, he mentioned an "old gent" in his last-written, never-published novel, *A Daughter of Toil*, who hated books written about common people.

15 DECEMBER 1886, BOSTON, TO CHARLES E. NORTON

Boston, Dec. 15, 1886.

Dear friend—

Your Carlyle volumes[1] came to me just as I had received a telegram summoning me to Ohio, where my eldest sister had lain very sick of malarial fever contracted in Virginia. She died, and in the sorrow and trouble that followed I couldn't find the moment and the mood together for thanking you. Even yet I haven't had a chance to look at the books; but I am going to read them, and in the meantime I send you mine.[2]

—I returned through New York, and laid before the Harper's our last-August notion of a Library of School Reading;[3] they were much struck with it, and called in their educational man,[4] who instantly approved and prophesied success, suggesting, however, the grouping of the subjects into fewer volumes. I think they will take up the project, and I hope you're still in the humor of it; for it wont be a great labor to make the books, and there'll be great use and a very pretty penny in it.

I hope soon to come out to see you.

Yours ever
W. D. Howells.

1. Probably C. E. Norton, ed., *Early Letters of Thomas Carlyle (1814–1826)*, 2 vols. (1886).

2. Howells probably sent *The Minister's Charge*, which had just been issued in book form.

3. Howells and Norton considered collaborating on a series of "Ashfield Readers" or a "Library of School Reading," a proposal that emerged during Howells' visit with Norton in August 1886. The project, however, did not materialize. Instead Norton later edited for D. C. Heath & Co. the *Heart of Oak* series (1893–1894), which he claimed would "offer a body of good literature and interesting reading for youth . . . ." See Kate Stephens, *A Curious History in Book Editing* (New York: Antigone Press, 1927), p. 57.

4. Abner Harper and J. C. Jones managed the textbook department at Harper & Brothers. See Eugene Exman, *The House of Harper* (New York: Harper & Row, 1967), p. 168.

18 DECEMBER 1886, BOSTON, TO RICHARD W. GILDER

Boston, Dec. 18, 1886.

Dear Gilder—

I return the note of Mr. Jester, who ought to be Mr. Sage.[1]

In all, I've had some forty or fifty letters about the story, which is selling next to Silas Lapham.[2]

I was amused at the promptness with which my name was dropped from among your "attractions"—the story not being even announced in the adv.s of your two or three last No.s. This is speeding the parting guest. A dieu![3]

Yours ever
W. D. Howells.

1. Mr. Jester has not been identified, nor is it known to what this comment refers.
2. The last installment of *The Minister's Charge* appeared in the *Century*, December 1886; the book, although it has an 1887 imprint, had already been issued by Ticknor & Co.
3. Howells, apologetic for his stinging words, wrote to Gilder on 22 December 1886 (Arms): "I am certainly sorry to have given you pain by a hasty self-betrayal, and all the more so because I see by the slip you send me that I was half-wrong as to my facts. But in the newspapers and the window-cards I saw no mention of the story, and I'll own it fretted me—not much, for if it had I shouldn't have mentioned it.... I have always felt deeply the intelligent kindness with [which] I have been treated by everybody in the Century office, and I am as loath as you could be to let our parting be any but the friendliest."

19 DECEMBER 1886, BOSTON, TO WILLIAM C. HOWELLS

Boston, Dec. 19, 1886.

Dear father—

I got your letter of the 15th, and I wished that I could have gone out to answer it in person, and give you what cheer there might be in good advice freely offered and general crossness. You may be sure that I think often of you in these days, and that I long to say something supporting and consoling. But you have had always the elements of self-comfort in you, and I know that you will be able to bear this trial as you have borné others.[1] For the poor girl who's gone I can't grieve; she seems enviably out of all trouble; and from where she now is she must see that the trouble to which she's left you is not hopeless. I speak to Aurelia as well as you; and I hope that you will both realize how much more you can be to each other than ever before. With Henry taken care of, and kept away from you in his turbulent moods, as I trust he is, you can have time to talk and read together. Aurelia can help you with those sketches you propose to write,[2] and should not let herself be taken up with daily cares. She can't escape them, of course, but she need not be frittered away by them.—We have no news. The children have written you during the week, and I don't know that I've anything to add, except that we're all very well. We expect to have a very quiet Christmas.

With love to you all

> Your aff'te son
> Will.

---

1. Howells is referring to the recent death of Victoria Howells.
2. Probably *Recollections of Life in Ohio, from 1813 to 1840*.

23 DECEMBER 1886, BOSTON, TO JAMES R. LOWELL

> Boston, Dec. 23, 1886.

Dear Mr. Lowell:

Your visit, the other day, gave me great pleasure, and when you were gone, Mrs. Howells and I had a half hour of pure exultation in the proposal you left me to think over. I have thought it over since, and it has grown more and more impossible for me to accept it. I am so much used to my present way of life that I could not change it for a new one with strange cares and responsibilities unless I felt far more sure of succeeding in it than I do.[1] Even to avoid failure I must work harder than you would believe, or than I am willing to do without greater faith than I have in my possible usefulness.

I do not believe any one could feel more deeply, more intimately the honor intended me; to remember that it was proposed to me by *you*, of all men, will be always the sweetest thing to me in my whole literary life.[2]

> Your grateful and affectionate
> W. D. Howells.

---

1. The proposal was the offer of the Smith Professorship of the French and Spanish languages and literatures at Harvard. See *Life in Letters*, I, 384.
2. Addressing Howells as "My dear Boy," Lowell wrote him on 24 December 1886 (MH; *Life in Letters*, I, 385–86) in order to express his agreement with Howells' refusal and to point out that the proposal was not his but Charles W. Eliot's; Lowell then continued: "I should have been mightily pleased to see you in my gown & so would Longfellow. When you talked to 'em about Chaucer, you would have had only to add a hood to it to give 'em as good a piece of realism as ever you could wish."

25 December 1886, Boston, to Henry James

302 Beacon St.,
Boston, Dec 25, 1886.

My dear James—

I'm ashamed to send you a type-written letter; but I'm almost obliged to do so, for my wrist has weakened again and my handwriting has gone all to pieces. This sort has at least the merit of clearness; and you can forgive something to mere modernity in me.—Your most kind letter from Milan caused great excitement and rejoicing in this family.[1] What could I ask more, even if I had the cheek to ask half so much? One doesn't thank you for such a thing I suppose, but I may tell you at least of my pride and pleasure in it. I'm disposed to make the most of the abundance of your kindness, for in many quarters here the book meets with little but misconception. If we regard it as nothing but an example of work in the new way—the performance of a man who wont and can't keep on doing what's been done already—it's reception here by most of the reviewers is extremely discouraging. Of all grounds in the world they take the genteel ground, and every

"Half-bred rogue that groomed his mother's cow,"[2]

reproaches me for introducing him to low company. This has been the tone of "society" about it; in the newspapers it hardly stops short of personal defamation.[3] Of course they entirely miss the very simple purpose of the book. Nevertheless it sells, and sells bravely, and to my surprise I find myself not really caring a great deal for the printed animosity, except as it means ignorance. I suspect it's an effect of the frankness about our civilization which you have sometimes wondered I could practice with impunity. The impunity's gone, now, I assure you.—But all this is too much about myself. The other day the Harpers told me they had a new story from you which they seemed immensely pleased with.[4] I understood that it was on international ground, and I was glad they seemed disposed to rejoice with me that it was so. I took occasion to say to them that I hoped you would never allow yourself to be disturbed there by any outside influence. It is pre-eminently and indefeasibly your ground; you made it, as if it were a bit of the Back Bay; and the character that must pass under your eye is increasingly vast in quantity. I feel myself a recreant in not yet having read your two last books; I now read a good deal for reviewing, or whatever my work in Harper may be called; and I leave the books till I have the occasion to talk of them. I know certain passages and characters in The Bostonians quite well, and I think Olive Chancellor miraculously good; but the Princess

Casamassima I don't know at all yet. Lowell goes about proclaiming it your best, and I've heard only good of it on all hands.—The furore caused by the Hawthorne outrage has pretty well died away.[5] It was a cruel atrocity, and all the more detestable because of that incurable single-heartedness of Lowell's, to which Hawthorne's treachery was inconceivable. A curious phase of the affair was that Hawthorne actually found credence for his version of it with some decent people; all the blackguards—and we've a lot of them—instinctively took sides with him.—I see Perry every other day, and we talk literature perpetually. Pellew[6] has come back to town, & I find him very interesting. He's a very able fellow, and distinctly a literary promise. Another man whom you will hear of is a Mr. John Heard, a Paris-born Bostonian, whose later life has been passed in Mexico; he writes equally well in French and English, and has contributed to the Revue Internationale of Florence.[7] These, with a young Russian, are the people I see most. Into Boston society I'm asked very little and go less. I would like to go oftener to Cambridge; but it's very far off; and I'm looking forward to our escape next summer to Paris, where John is to go on with his architectural studies in the Ecole des Beaux Arts if he can get in. He's a youth of parts, and has hitherto done what he's attempted. Just now, he's very much absorbed in his first dress-suit which he gets into every night after dinner for some social occasion.—We expect to be two years in Paris, and when we return, I hope that we can contrive to spend the year pretty equally between Washington and Cambridge. Certainly I think we shall always winter hereafter in Washington; if it hadn't been for John's going into the Tech.,[8] here, we should have been there this winter.—I see Aldrich more rarely than I should like, these days, for the comfort of mere old friendship is very great. —I'm sick of this confounded machine, and you shall have the rest through the pen.—Last summer, which I spent in my house, here, I went several times to see Grace Norton, always gay company, and full of the literary interest which I care for almost alone. She gave me news of you, and sometimes read passages of your letters, which always amazed me by their excellent abundance. How can you get time to write them? By the way I find your Little Tour in France[9] delightful reading: it's a more absolute transference to literature of the mood of observation than anything else that I know.

We have been having a decently merry Christmas, and the children have enjoyed it; but I notice a decadence from the more robust and resolute Christmas of the old Dickens days, when holly was such a panacea. If one came back to Boston fifty years from now I fancy he would find it even soberer than now on Christmas. That reminds me I shall be fifty my next birthday, the 1st of March. I've heard people say that they are not conscious of growing older; but *I* am. I'm perfectly aware of the shrinking bounds. I don't plan so largely as I used, and without having lost hope I don't have so much use for it as once. I feel my half century fully. Lord, how it's slipped away!—Our Winny, who's been ailing so long, seems at last to have got her feet on the rising ground again. I wish you would give all our loves to your sister, and give us some good news of her when you write. The family join me in affectionate regards to yourself, whom we count upon seeing next year. If this letter follows you to Italy, salute the Arno and the Grand Canal for me; the Tiber I don't feel quite up to. Salute also the Bootts and their Devoneck,[10] and believe me

Ever yours
W. D. Howells.

1. James' letter has not been located, but it appears to have contained some complimentary remarks about *The Minister's Charge*. He had briefly commented on the novel in "William Dean Howells," *Harper's Weekly*, 19 June 1886, where he praised Howells for the "art of imparting a palpitating interest to common things and unheroic lives.... Indeed, the only limitation, in general, to his extreme truthfulness is, I will not say his constant sense of the comedy of life, for that is irresistible, but the verbal drollery of many of his people. It is extreme and perpetual, but I fear the reader will find it a venial sin."

2. See Oliver Wendell Holmes, "Astraea: The Balance of Illusions," line 334.

3. The comments of the New York *Tribune* reviewer exemplify the personal slurs to which Howells here refers. Howells, the writer observes, "is perfectly at home in all the departments of a second rate hotel; and he knows horse-cars as if he had worn a bell-punch. His most affectionate care has been lavished upon the two shop-girls Statira Dudley and Amanda Grier. There is not a smirk on their silly faces, a twitch of their showy skirts, an inflection of their shrill voices, a horror in their grammar or behavior, which he has not studied with enthusiasm and reproduced to the life." For other reviews, see *The Minister's Charge*, HE, pp. xvii–xix.

4. Probably "Louisa Pallant," *Harper's Monthly*, February 1888.

5. See Howells to Lowell, 26 October 1886, n. 1.

6. For George Pellew, see Howells to Curtis, 3 March 1888, n. 1 and n. 2.

7. Heard has not been further identified.

8. Massachusetts Institute of Technology.

9. *A Little Tour of France* (1885).

10. Francis Boott, the American composer and friend of the James family, his daughter Elizabeth (1846–1888), and her husband, Frank Duveneck (1848–1919), an American artist, lived in Florence while James resided in Milan. James had met Duveneck in 1880 and considered him "much the most highly developed phenomenon in the way of a painter that the U.S.A. has given birth to." See Edel, *James Letters*, II, 280.

26 DECEMBER 1886, BOSTON, TO WILLIAM C. HOWELLS

Boston, Dec. 26, 1886.

Dear father:

I shall be relieved when you have finally made some permanent arrangement about Henry; in the meantime, it's gratifying to know that you and Aurelia no longer sentimentalize his case, but are willing to protect yourselves from his irresponsible violence. I earnestly hope that if John[1] is afraid of him, and will not help you manage him, you wont be slow in looking up some one who will.—This seems like Monday; Christmas having taken the place of the usual Sunday. It went off very well, and the children were happy, especially dear Pil, who does so much to give others pleasure. She labored for weeks with her pencil and needle; and she is always the most devoted creature. I suppose you don't know what a beautiful character the child has; but I know of no one equal to her, and she grows more beautiful every day. She and Lucia Fairchild[2] are great friends, and are both humorous and brilliant girls; I assure you their talk is worth listening to. Pil now takes her part in entertaining all our visitors, and she is so intelligent and well read that she can talk with the best; while she never loses her childish, utter simplicity.—Our flock of wild ducks, which I told you of, is here in full force this winter, and I think there must be more than a hundred of them in the water behind the house most of the time. It's a great pleasure to watch them.—I've done up James's book,[3] and I shall send it tomorrow; I'm sure you'll enjoy it. Send me a diagram of your library when you get it all arranged, and of the whole house; Elinor would like to see it. All join me in love to you both. Did Aurelia get the book Mrs Fields sent me for her?

Your aff'te son
Will.

1. John may have been the black servant to whom Howells alluded in an earlier letter to W. C. Howells, 12 December 1886 (MH). It appears that John was inadequate in dealing with Henry Howells and that someone else was hired by early January. See Howells to Aurelia Howells, 9 January 1887, n. 1.
2. Lucia Fairchild (1872–1924) was the daughter of Charles Fairchild.
3. *The Literary Remains of the Late Henry James.*

9 JANUARY 1887, BOSTON, TO AURELIA H. HOWELLS

Boston, Jan. 9, 1887.

Dear Aurelia:

I am glad you have that Miss Skinner,[1] for it seems the best arrangement you could make. You don't need an asylum nurse; and I *know* that she would be of no use, and would be very expensive. Such a thing isn't to be thought of; when Henry becomes very bad you must shut him up, and keep him shut up till he's better. There's nothing else for it.—I'm afraid that in my many talks on this subject, I haven't expressed the sympathy for *you*, Aurelia, that I've always felt and do feel. I don't believe in the family system with Henry, and never did; I think it's made him the horrible burden that he now is; but, you, I recognize all the time, are a good and unselfish woman—one of the best I ever heard of, and I do love and respect you most tenderly. I wish I knew how to let a little more hope and light into your life; but we all have our cares, and I see no one who is quite happy; perhaps you're as *happy* as any. We are glad that you have got the barrel at last, and that the things please you. The Paris garment is an outside spring and fall wrap; it belonged to Winny, and I'm sure it must be very becoming to you. I had to write to Sam quite peremptorily from here, to send you the barrel. Has he ever paid father that $5.oo he borrowed? Please tell me.—The winter is very hard, here, as it seems to be with you: snow and ice all the past month. I suppose you must often think of the mild Virginia winter; but you must remember the malaria behind it.—I must not forget to speak of that letter from Mulholland's sister:[2] it is most gratifying for us, and leaves father in just the right position; but it comes too late to "soothe the dull cold ear of death."[3]— Father seems to think that he enclosed his "letter to a cousin," but he did not. I should like to see it.—We are all well, and join in love to you all. I enclose a little belated Christmas for *you* with the love.

Your aff'te bro.
Will.

1. Miss Skinner has not been identified, but she may have been W. C. Howells' housekeeper; see also Howells to W. C. Howells, 26 December 1886, n. 1.

2. Mulholland's sister has not been identified. Her brother, John Mulholland, married Victoria Howells in 1883. When William C. Howells moved to Virginia, the Mulhollands followed. Their marriage was unhappy, and Mulholland deserted Victoria shortly after their move to Virginia. See C. and R. Kirk, " 'The Howells Family' by Richard J. Hinton," *Journal of the Rutgers University Library* 14 (1950), 19. Mulholland's sister probably wrote a letter of sympathy to the Howells family upon the occasion of Victoria's death. In 1888 Howells was asked by a Mrs. Macabey, the future mother-in-law of Mulholland in his second marriage, to write a character reference for Mulholland. Howells, in a letter to his father of 9 August 1888 (MH), noted that he wrote to Mrs. Macabey's minister, Mr. Hailey, "that we had no wish concerning Mulholland except to forget him; and that I could not re-open the painful chapter of his life in our family; but that I should profoundly pity any woman who married him.... But I think *you* might now fitly write to the clergyman, and tell him briefly just how Mulholland behaved himself. The poor fool of a girl will probably marry him anyway...."

3. Thomas Gray, "Elegy Written in a Country Churchyard," line 41.

1 FEBRUARY 1887, BOSTON, TO JOHN W. DE FOREST

302 Beacon st.
Boston, Feb. 1, 1887.

My dear De Forest:

May I print from your letter some paragraphs about Tolstoi? Of course I would not give your name, and I suppose they would not be generally traced to you; but if they were you ought to be willing, for they say just what ought to be said, and say it with authority. Please consent, and do it at once.[1]—I was greatly struck by your high estimate of Manzoni. Isn't it strange that most people don't know I Promessi Sposi is one of the very greatest books ever written? Is it because it's always given to beginners in Italian?—I hope you'll like a paper on Manzoni, with many versions from his dramas, which I'm about to print with other essays on the Modern Italian Poets, in a volume.[2]

It touches me, and pleases me immensely that you like my stories, and that you like my praises.[3] I may say at least that both are honest. I'm glad to find that there is a response in print here and there to what I said of you.[4]

Cordially yours
W. D. Howells.

Have ever read any of Valera's novels?—Spanish.[5]

1. De Forest had written to Howells on 24 January 1887 (MH), praising *War and Peace*: "You do right in praising Tolstoi. Something that you wrote a while ago sent me to his *Peace And War*. Up to that time I had regarded *I Promessi Sposi* (with its manifest faults included) as the greatest of novels. Now I put Tolstoi above Manzoni. Perhaps I would not, if I had not been a soldier. Let me tell you, for you can hardly *know* it yourself, that nobody but he has written the full truth about war & battle." De Forest granted Howells permission to print his comments on Tolstoi in a letter of 2 February 1887 (MH). They were subsequently printed in the "Editor's Study," *Harper's Monthly*, May 1887. Howells also elaborated on the Tolstoy-Manzoni comparison, which De Forest had begun, in the May 1889 "Editor's Study": "the Italian's work falls below the Russian's because Manzoni wrote in the infancy of his art and Tolstoi has written in its maturity. The Russian is the more perfect master for that reason, but they are equal and coeval in the inspiration of their work. Both are penetrated with the beauty of Christianity, and both are filled with the same pity for the oppressed, the poor, the lowly, the same abhorrence of violence and pride...."

2. *Modern Italian Poets: Essays and Versions* was published on 1 October 1887 by Harper & Brothers. The chapter on Alessandro Manzoni had appeared as "Modern Italian Poets," *North American Review*, April 1867.

3. See Howells to De Forest, 9 December 1886. De Forest responded to Howells' praise in his letter of 24 January 1887: "It is useless to try to tell you how much I was gratified & flattered by your letter from the West. I consider it the soundest praise that I ever had; that is, it will be the longest to keep in my memory & appreciation." De Forest also praised Howells' novels: "I am glad to have found Tolstoi. I had been reduced, in the matter of novels, to Zola & you; & two men

can't write fast enough for one reader. There are other good story writers, such as James, Cable, Craddock. But they are not to me satisfactory & instructing novelists. I now want somebody from whom I can learn both the *what* & the *how*."

4. See Howells to De Forest, 9 December 1886, n. 3.

5. Juan Valera y Alcala Galiano (1824–1905), a Spanish novelist and critic, met Howells in late 1884 or early 1885. Valera, then Spanish minister to the United States (1884–1886), corresponded with Howells in 1885–1886, commenting favorably on his novels and asking Howells to recommend to the public *Pepita Ximenez* (1874), which Appleton was publishing in an English translation. Howells obliged by praising it and *Doña Luz* (1879) in the "Editor's Study," *Harper's Monthly*, November 1886.

6 FEBRUARY 1887, BOSTON, TO MARIE M. FRÉCHETTE

302 Beacon st.,
Boston, Feb. 6, 1887.

Dear little Vevie:

I got your pretty letter sometime ago, and I was very much pleased that you should think to write to your old Uncle Will. Yesterday, your mother's letter came, and I want you to tell her that I read about Juno at once, and sent the story to St. Nicholas.[1] I wonder who the children were that went to live with Juno? Did I ever see them? I thought the story was beautiful, tell mamma. Tell her, too, that I noticed everything she said about Uncle Sam. He's written to me since I wrote to her; and I shall do what she says.

Now, all the rest is going to be for you. I want to tell you and Mole[2] about John. He is all grown up, and wears a dress-coat at night, when he goes to parties, which he does about three times a week. He makes a great many calls on young ladies, and he *doesn't* carry a dead rat along by the tail to amuse them. He's an awful swell, and has a little moustache. Sunday afternoons he walks with young ladies, and they call him Mr. Howells. Don't you think it's pretty goings-on for a boy?—The river behind our house is all frozen over; and a flock of wild ducks that used to breakfast within stone's throw of the dining-room window, has gone away. Tell Mole that sometimes they have ice boats on the river; they just *zip* along. Sometimes boys walk across from the Cambridge side. Pilla goes to dancing-school every Friday. She's another swell, and there's one besotted boy who walks home with her. Don't you thinks it's perfectly awful.—I'm sorry you're still sick, you poor little maid. We all send our loves to you and Mole and Papa and Mamma.

Your aff'te
Uncle Will.

1. Annie Fréchette's story, "Juno," about W. C. Howells' cow, appeared in *St. Nicholas*, November 1887.

2. Howells Fréchette was Marie Marguerite's younger brother.

9 February 1887, Boston, to Thomas W. Higginson

302 Beacon st.,
Feb. 9, 1887.

My dear Higginson:

I sympathize with your difficulties in getting people to talk, and to talk naturally; but I can't help you out to-morrow night for I was up last night and must be up to-night, and I can't stand three nights hard-running. (What a queer phrase!) I should drop asleep while Bates was turning his romantic poniard round amongst my realistic ribs.[1]

But I thank you all the same.

Yours ever
W. D. Howells.

1. Arlo Bates (1850–1918) was a novelist, poet, and editor of the Boston *Sunday Courier* (1880–1893). Howells had reviewed one of his novels, *A Wheel of Fire* (1885) in the "Editor's Study," *Harper's Monthly*, January 1886, qualifying a generally favorable account of it by stating: "it has its lapses of art, but the lurid theme is kept in the full light of day, and in this sort there is something apparently still to be done with the romantic motive, so apt otherwise to turn allegoric and mechanical on its victim's hand." The March 1887 "Editor's Study" also contains a brief notice of Bates's *Berries of the Brier* (1886), a volume of poetry, for which Howells had faint praise. It seems that Higginson had asked Howells to appear together with Bates at a reading or similar occasion.

14 February 1887, Boston, to Samuel L. Clemens

Boston, Feb. 14, 1887.

My dear Clemens:

That invention of casting brass was to have been applied to wall-paper printing, wasn't it, if the castings could be made free of air-holes?[1] What was the technical phrase for this elimination of air-holes? I want to use this invention in my story.[2]—I've just read your speech to the publishers.[3] Mrs. Howells thought with me that it was delicious, but accused you of inventing that boy's comp.[4] Did you?

Leathers's departure leaves us free to use his name?[5] I will look over that play again.[6]

Yours ever
W. D. Howells.

1. Clemens owned a substantial interest in a patent for "Kaolatype," a process that was meant to supersede the traditional engraving process. Although he invested substantial funds in its development, the enterprise ultimately failed. See *Twain-Howells*, pp. 584–85.

2. In *April Hopes* the Mavering family made its fortune in the wallpaper manufacturing business. At one point in the story, Dan Mavering travels to New York and Washington to investigate the "Lafflin process," a new method of casting "brass patterns without air-holes" that was to revolutionize the manufacture of wallpaper. See *April Hopes*, HE, p. 313.

3. Clemens had addressed a gathering of the New York Stationers' Board of Trade on 10 February, criticizing the stationers for selling textbooks that are used for drumming nonsensical definitions of terms into the heads of schoolchildren. For an account of the banquet, see New York *Herald*, 11 February 1887.

4. Clemens had apparently sent Howells the manuscript of "English as She Is Taught," *Century*, April 1887, in which he expressed his views on the inadequate education provided by the public schools, quoting "the funniest (genuine) boy's composition" he had ever seen. See *Twain-Howells*, p. 585.

5. Jesse M. Leathers was a distant relative of Clemens who claimed to be the rightful heir to an English earldom and wanted Clemens to provide the funds for litigating his claim. On 12 February 1887 (MH) Clemens had written Howells that Leathers, to whom he refers as the "American Claimant," recently died. See *Twain-Howells*, pp. 583, 869–71.

6. *Colonel Sellers as a Scientist,* later called *The American Claimant.*

20 FEBRUARY 1887, BOSTON, TO WILLIAM C. HOWELLS

Boston, Feb'y 20, 1887.

Dear father:

Elinor and I have just got home after a week's absence. We were two days in Lowell,[1] where the sight of the cotton and carpet mills, as humanely managed as such things can be, made us feel that civilization was all wrong in regard to the labor that suffers in them. I felt so helpless about it, too, realizing the misery it must cost to undo such a mistake. But it is slavery.

Last night I had a pleasanter dream of Henry;[2] he forebore to "jounce" me; and I can therefore freely rejoice with you that he's able to be out of bed. But I suspect that he is a greater social ornament there than elsewhere. I'm glad your stove works so well.—I wish Aurelia could write me occasionally.—Here the weather is mild, and I have heard talk of bluebirds, but I haven't seen them yet. The river behind us is quite clear of ice.—Charles Mead & his daughter are in town to day, though not with us.[3]

Winny is better; all the rest are well, and join me in love to you all.

Your aff'te son
Will.

1. The *Critic*, 26 February 1887, reported that "Mr. W. D. Howells, the novelist, has been in Lowell for three days this week, inspecting local manufacturing establishments to obtain material for a new novel." The mills in Lowell were fictionalized in *Annie Kilburn* (1889) as the "Wilmington Stocking-Mills" in chapter 12, even though Howells had written on 26 February 1887 (ViU) to a Mr. Packard at the

Merrimack Mills in Lowell: "I have still to thank you for your kindness in show-ing me through the Merrimac Mills. Will you kindly say to anyone interested that, the newspapers to the contrary notwithstanding, I have not, and never had, any purpose of writing about mill-life in a novel?"

2. Howells had written his father on 13 February 1887 (MH): "I dreamed of Henry last night as I have several times, and he attacked me in that odious way; he does it in all my dreams of him."

3. Charles L. Mead was Elinor Howells' oldest brother. Catherine and Mabel were his daughters, but it is uncertain which one accompanied him on his Boston trip.

27 FEBRUARY 1887, BOSTON, TO GEORGE W. CURTIS

302 Beacon st.,
Boston, Feb. 27, 1887.

Dear Mr. Curtis:

Thank you for the apt words in the last "Chair," which I hope I'm not too fond in thinking just.[1] What really depresses and disheartens me in the outburst against having "commonplace people" in fiction is that the very, very little culture and elegance with which our refined people have overlaid themselves seems to have hardened their hearts against the common people: they seem to despise and hate them. This conviction forces itself upon me, and makes me turn to the barbarous nations with a respect I never expected to feel for them.[2]

Yours gratefully
W. D. Howells.

1. In the "Editor's Easy Chair," *Harper's Monthly*, March 1887, Curtis argued that the modern novelists' use of commonplace characters does not preclude the depiction of heroism. He concluded his remarks as follows: "The novelist is not bent upon the commonplace, nor heedless of heroism. But he describes it as it appears to-day, no longer clad in flowered velvet and wearing a rapier, and he puts us all to the test of our ability to see that the story-teller is doing ... essentially what Scott and Fielding and Cervantes and Homer did, and to recognize in the familiar figures of to-day the qualities that make the plumed and noble figures of yesterday heroic and fascinating."

2. In his reply of 5 March 1887 (MH), Curtis wrote: "I am very glad to get your note, but my words had only the merit of truth! I greatly enjoy watching your fight with the new form of Philisteria, which without the priggishness and awful solemnity of Wordsworth reminds me of his."

27 FEBRUARY 1887, BOSTON, TO WILLIAM C. HOWELLS

302 Beacon st.
Boston, Feb. 27, 1887.

Dear father—

I was amused by the sort of lift there seemed to be in your letter from the loss of your jewel;[1] these things are often blessings in disguise. It must be a great relief for you and Aurelia to be alone, and I congratulate you.

As to the things you see about me in the papers, I hope you'll not let them worry you. They are inevitable, because I'm now something of a "shining mark," and because in fiction I've identified myself with truth and humanity, which you know people always hate. It will pass, and pretty soon I shall be accepted. My ideas are right.[2] I enclose a thing that gave me pleasure, and which I hope may please you.[3]—The letters which Aurelia sent me, are most gratifying. They come too late, apparently, and yet they might have given pain to the poor heart that is still,[4] now; and so perhaps it's just as well.

We are all very well, and join in love to you all.

I enclose a check.

> **Your aff'te son**
> **Will.**

1. W. C. Howells' housekeeper, perhaps Miss Skinner. See Howells to Aurelia Howells, 9 January 1887, n. 1.
2. Howells' father was probably concerned about the criticism Howells was receiving in the press for his advocacy and defense of literary realism. *Lippincott's Magazine*, January 1887, complained that Howells' attention to realistic details makes his books "a little slow" and concluded that "One still reads him, to be sure, with interest, but not so much interest as will make it a real hardship to lay his book aside half finished on some slight interruption." *The Nation*, 10 February 1887, published a stinging review of *The Minister's Charge* and took Howells to task "for downright cruelty and cold-blood in the dissection of the meaner and shabbier part of every man" and for his lack of variety in characterization. See also Cady, *Howells*, II, 28–55; Lynn, *Howells*, pp. 284–88.
3. Howells sent a clipping from *The Beacon*, 26 February 1887, in which he was congratulated on his forthcoming fiftieth birthday and praised for his contribution to American literature.
4. Victoria Howells, who had died in December 1886.

28 FEBRUARY 1887, BOSTON, TO CHARLES E. NORTON

> 302 Beacon st.
> Feb. 28, 1887.

My dear Norton—

Mrs. Howells and I are extremely vexed that we have an engagement for Thursday night. Winny hopes to have the pleasure of coming to you.

—I have been writing about your Carlyle letters to-day for the far-off May "Study."[1] The letters to Miss Welsh were most interesting and important.[2] I hope you'll not dislike my comments.

—I wrote to the Harpers soon after I saw you telling them we could not do the school-reading series. I'm to do them one large volume, as a "Library of Good Reading" for the subscription trade.³ This will be quite out of all imaginable competition.

Yours sincerely
W. D. Howells.

1. Having disliked Carlyle for many years, Howells seems to have approached his review of Norton's edition of the *Early Letters of Thomas Carlyle* (1886) in the "Editor's Study," *Harper's Monthly*, May 1887, with some delicacy. His dislike is quite evident in the review, but he also pointed out that these letters present Carlyle "in a softer light" and reveal an epistolary style that is "clear, straight, and strong." Howells continued, "There is abundant promise of the future Carlyle in them: the independence and the arrogance, the honesty and the bitterness, the true tender sympathy and the strong prejudice, the respect for right, the contempt for most men, the adoration of great power for good, and the inability to abhor great power of any kind—all the strange mixture of qualities which issued in tolerably disrespectful worship of the various military, political, theological, and literary mortals whom he vainly spent his great gifts in painting as heroes."

2. Half of Howells' review is devoted to Carlyle's letters to Jane B. Welsh (1801–1866), whom Carlyle married in 1826.

3. See Howells to Norton, 15 December 1886, n. 3. The project was ultimately abandoned by Howells.

3 APRIL 1887, BOSTON, TO WILLIAM C. HOWELLS

Boston, April 3, 1887.

Dear father—

After a day of storm worthy of January, and a foot of snow, we have the brightest sun and softest air, this morning, and I can fancy you and Aurelia making much of it. You must have bluebirds this morning in Jefferson, and perhaps robins; here we have the warbling of the snow-shovels on the sidewalks.—I wish you could have been here on Thursday to hear the authors at their Reading. I never saw an absolutely full theatre before; but *every* seat was taken, and 500 standing-tickets were sold. As I had read in New York two years ago, I was not much scared, and I at least made myself heard. I gave two little bits from Their Wedding Journey—Isabel's fright of the Three Sisters bridges at Niagara, and the rose of the Hotel Dieu at Quebec.—The Readings netted about $5000 for the Longfellow Memorial Fund.¹—I am glad Henry is well again, and not physically troublesome. As the spring opens, and he can get out more, you will have more relief from him; and also, I hope from your rheumatism. I hope you will be able to find a good girl, to help Aurelia, though I know that it must be a pleasure for you to be alone.

All are well, and join me in love to you all

Your aff'te son
Will.

1. The reading took place at the Boston Museum on the afternoon of 31 March 1887. Besides Howells, James R. Lowell, Edward E. Hale, Oliver W. Holmes, Samuel L. Clemens, Julia W. Howe, George W. Curtis, Thomas B. Aldrich, and Thomas W. Higginson read selections from their works. Charles E. Norton was the master of ceremonies; he introduced Howells with remarks in which he defined the literary realist as "primarily an idealist" and "the deepest of moralists." Norton concluded his introduction by saying, "I present to you the moral writer, the idealist, Howells." See Boston *Transcript*, 1 April 1887. The purpose of the Longfellow Memorial Fund was to landscape the land around the poet's Cambridge home and to erect a statue. See the *Critic*, 9 April 1887.

17 APRIL 1887, BOSTON, TO WILLIAM C. HOWELLS

Boston, April 17, 1887.

Dear father—

Your letter with Aurelia's enclosure came yesterday. Please tell her that I will attend to all her commissions promptly. In regard to the time of my visit I now expect to be with you early in May; but this will depend somewhat on our other plans, which we change almost from day to day. All that now seems certain is that we are to leave this house at the end of the week, and go out to Auburndale for the month of May; I should leave the family there while I paid my visit to you. I will stay as long as possible.

I have not seen the American Magazine, and so have escaped our picture.[1] But I really don't care for those things any longer, and if *I* don't, who does?—We shall be glad to be getting out of town, though May in the country is not particularly amiable here.—I am just reading one of Tolstoi's books[2]—on poverty, and prosperity's responsibility for it,—and I confess it makes me very unhappy. His remedy is to go into the country, and share the labor of his peasants—to forego luxury and superfluity; but I don't exactly see how this helps, except that it makes all poor alike, and saves one's self from remorse. It's a terrible question. How shall it ever be answered? Did you use to be troubled about it? When I think of it, my pleasure in possession is all spoiled.

The family is well, and joins me in love to you all.

Your aff'te son
Will.

1. The magazine in which a picture of the Howells family appeared has not been identified.
2. Tolstoy's *What then Must We Do?* was published in 1886 with the title *Que Faire?* and Howells discussed the book in the "Editor's Study," *Harper's Monthly*, July 1887. He refers to Tolstoy as "the greatest living writer, and incomparably the greatest writer of fiction who has ever lived," and then proceeds to express the unsettling effect the Russian's advocacy of renouncing wealth has on the reader:

"...*Que Faire* is another of those Russian books which have given some people the impression that Russia cannot be an agreeable country to live in. Like the rest of Russian literature, it seems intended to direct the mind to uncomfortable subjects, to awaken harassing thoughts.... After reading it you cannot be quite the same person you were before; you will be better by taking its truth to heart, or worse by hardening your heart against it." See also Howells to Hale, 28 June 1887.

2 MAY 1887, AUBURNDALE, MASSACHUSETTS, TO WHITELAW REID

Lee's Hotel,
Auburndale, May 2, '87.

My dear Reid:

A Mr. Hamlin Garland has called upon me, and has greatly interested and impressed me by his view of literature.[1] He tells me that he has offered you a paper, and the present business is to bespeak your attention, not favor. He is a Westerner, but has come to live—sparely enough, I fancy—in Boston.[2]

Yours ever
W. D. Howells.

1. Garland arrived in Boston during the autumn of 1884, and since that time had been trying to make his way as a teacher, lecturer, and reviewer. Following an enthusiastic notice of *The Minister's Charge* (Boston *Transcript*, 31 January 1887), and emboldened by a letter of introduction from the paper's editor, Edward Clement, young Garland decided to seek out Howells. He made the short railway journey to Auburndale, where the two met and talked about literary matters. Although Howells could hardly approve Garland's ultimate defection from the realist cause, the latter never ceased to look back fondly on their relationship. Recollecting this first meeting forty years afterward, Garland wrote: "How long he talked, or how long I talked, I cannot now recall (the clock stopped for me), but at last, in some deft way, he got me outside, and as we walked down the street toward the station he became still more friendly. He treated me not merely as a literary aspirant, but as a critic in whom he could confide." Of the effect this interview had on the young man's ambitions, Garland said that he "went away like a young squire who had won the accolade. My apprenticeship was over, I had been accepted by America's chief literary man as a fellow, a literary historian." See Garland's *Roadside Meetings* (New York: Macmillan, 1930), pp. 60–61.

2. It is virtually impossible to say whether Reid accepted anything from Garland, since none of the pieces in the *Tribune* are signed, and since Garland himself does not mention the incident.

1 JUNE 1887, AUBURNDALE, MASSACHUSETTS, TO JOHN W. DE FOREST

Auburndale, June 1, 1887.

My dear De Forest—

I enclose a late editorial from the Boston Transcript, in which you will find yourself pleasantly mentioned.[1] Apparently this man knows what he's talking about, as far as yor novel's concerned. But generally the newspaper critic knows little or nothing. I think my paper,[2] which you liked, was true; but I'm afraid it was done more to punish than improve him. Certainly there was rancor towards the Englishry in my soul when I wrote, and I was seeking to revenge myself—in a good cause. Nevertheless the paper was true, and it remains true that it would be difficult to say just what good criticism does. I get awfully sick of the whole literary trade at times; but then I think of the other trades and take heart again.—I'm just home from my old home in Ohio, where I saw a town in full boom from the discovery of natural gas. It was a wonderful spectacle gaseously, materially and morally. I believe I shall try to write a story about it. I saw lots of character, blowing off with almost as much noise as the gas wells themselves.[3]—Don't you read Spanish? Such capital novels the Spaniards write now![4]

Yours ever,
W. D. Howells.

1. The editorial has not been identified.

2. Howells devoted the entire "Editor's Study," *Harper's Monthly*, June 1887, to a discussion of the purpose of literary criticism. He severely condemned the critic who, without working from a clearly defined principle, praises or dismisses works of literature, attempting to dictate to authors what they should or should not write about. This bad habit has developed among American critics because they have modeled themselves on their English counterparts, who belong to a school in which "almost any person of glib and lively expression is competent to write of almost any branch of polite literature...." The chief virtues of the critic, so Howells concluded, are "modesty and candor and impartiality...; for if we should happen to discover a good reason for continuing to exist, these qualities will be of more use to us than any others in examining the work of people who really produce something."

3. Howells had written to Clemens from Findlay, Ohio, on 27 May 1887 (CU; *Twain-Howells*, pp. 593–94) of the forthcoming Natural Gas Jubilee on 8 or 9 June: "The wildest dreams of Col. Sellers are here the commonplaces of everyday experience." Howells later used this experience in writing *A Hazard of New Fortunes* (1890).

4. For Howells' interest in Juan Valera, see Howells to De Forest, 1 February 1887, n. 5; however, the novels of Armando Palacio Valdés (1853–1938) appealed to him even more. He had reviewed *Marta y María* (1883) in the "Editor's Study," *Harper's Monthly*, April 1886, and *Riverita* (1886) and *José* (1885) in November 1886; the "Editor's Study" of January and October 1888, respectively, contains reviews of *Maximina* (1887) and *El Cuarto poder* (1888). For Howells' correspondence with Palacio Valdés, see E. H. Cady, "Armando Palacio Valdes Writes to William Dean Howells," *Symposium* 2 (1948), 19–37.

28 JUNE 1887, LAKE GEORGE, NEW YORK, TO EDWARD E. HALE

Lake George, N Y. June 28, 1887.

My dear Hale:

I got my copy of Tolstoi of Schönhof, but it is now yours, with my regard.[1]

I think Ticknor & Co. would take a translation, and perhaps Cupples,[2] especially if you made it. If you do publish a version, I hope you will write a long introduction or comment. I'll own that this and the other ethical books of Tolstoi—*Que Faire, Ma Religion, La Mort d'Ivan Illitch*—have made me unhappy.[3] They have shown me the utter selfishness and insufficiency of my past life, without convincing me that Tolstoi offers quite the true solution. To work for others, yes; but to work with my hands, I'm not sure, seeing that I'm now fifty, awkward and fat. I worked ten years at a trade—printing—and thirty years I've worked at novelling. Shall I learn still another trade? I doubt; and I'm afraid Tolstoi doesn't value amusement enough in a world that seems to get very wicked without it. I'm afraid also that this fear is a sneaking love of the world anyway in me.

But Tolstoi has freed me in flooring me. Never again can I be a snob; my soul is at least my own henceforth. What a Democrat he is!—But men are so weak that I think much of the good he aims at must be accomplished socially.[4]

Do write about him—preach about him. But first read all his books—read the sketch of him in the June Century.[5]

We are here in Judge Edmonds's cottage, which we've taken for the summer.[6]

Yours ever
W. D. Howells.

1. The particular "copy" of Tolstoy which Howells had bought at Schoenhof's, a Cambridge book dealer, was probably *Ma Religion*. By sending it to Hale, Howells followed up on a conversation he had had with Hale in May 1887 when they fortuitously met in the Albany railroad depot. Howells gave Hale Tolstoy's *Les Confessions* on that occasion, which Hale described in a letter to his wife on 28 May 1887 (see E. E. Hale, Jr., *The Life and Letters of Edward Everett Hale* [Boston: Little, Brown & Co., 1917], II, 327–28); he also alluded to it in a letter to Howells of 17 September 1887 (MH): "I have been, all the summer grateful for the good providence which brought us together that morning. Of course I should have read Tolstoi, had we not met,—but not then nor as I did . . . ." Three years later, Hale suggested that his founding of the Tolstoi Club at Harvard in 1888 was a result of the Albany encounter. See Howells to Hale, 30 August 1888, n. 5, and 6 May 1890, n. 1.

2. Victor W. Cupples (1863–1941) was a London-born publisher who worked for various publishing companies, including Houghton Mifflin and D. Lothrop & Co. In 1902, with Arthur T. Leon, he formed the New York publishing firm of Cupples & Leon.

3. See Howells to W. C. Howells, 17 April 1887, n. 2. Howells had also reviewed Tolstoy's *Ma Religion* (1885) and *La Mort d'Ivan Illitch* (1886) in the "Editor's Study," *Harper's Monthly*, April 1886 and February 1887, respectively.

4. Hale, himself a philanthropist, indicated, in his letter of 17 September, that he was as perplexed as Howells about the implementation of Tolstoy's philosophy. "How the touching [of] elbows is to be done—" he wrote, "is hard to say. In my profession, it comes easier. We are thrown in with all sorts & conditions of men. But for most men,—and for most women, it is very hard to escape the Lady Bountiful position." See also Howells to Hale, 6 May 1890, n. 1.

5. George Kennan, "A Visit to Count Tolstoi," *Century*, June 1887.

6. The Howells family was renting the home of the late John W. Edmonds (1799–1874), judge of the New York First Circuit Court (1845–1847), the New York Supreme Court (1847–1852) and the New York Court of Appeals (1852–1853); he had also been a noted spiritualist. In a letter to his father of 26 June 1887 (MH), Howells described the house and the region: "It is on the West shore of the lake, four miles from from [sic] the Southern end, which they call the head, and it rambles over a considerable space on the hillside, with the water before it, and the spurs of the Adirondacks behind.... The cottage is full of the old Judge's books, and the war clubs, tomahawks and scalping knives that he collected when he was Indian Commissioner; but no ghosts, so far as we know."

28 JUNE 1887, LAKE GEORGE, NEW YORK, TO WILLIAM H. RIDEING

Lake George P. O., N. Y. June 28, 1887.

Dear Mr. Rideing:[1]

Thank you for letting me see the proof.[2] I have struck out some sentences at the beginning because they convey a wrong impression. My whole life except that year in the log-cabin, was passed in towns; I was in *no* wise "a farmer's boy", and my father, I believe, was in his town broad cloth and silk hat on that occasion; we had just come out from Dayton, and he had not lived in the country for twenty-five years.[3] As it stands I'm afraid the story has no significance, and is an unfortunate introduction. If you had a mind to suggest that the simple and homely had always been mixed up with the ideal in my life, or that I was perhaps always apt to dream over its realities till the plain business of it escaped me, you would have some application for the incident, but now there seems none. I suppose that the obvious facts are always giving us vagarians the slip, like our old family cow, unless we follow them up sharply through flood or fire.

Yours sincerely
W. D. Howells.

1. William Henry Rideing (1853–1918) was associate editor of *Youth's Companion* (1881–1918) and managing editor of the *North American Review* (1888–1899).

2. Rideing was seeing through the press his book, *The Boyhood of Living Authors* (1887), and evidently gave the subjects of his biographical sketches an opportunity to make corrections in proof. Howells had recently published "Year in a Log-Cabin, a Bit of Autobiography" in *Youth's Companion*, May 1887, which was later incorporated in Howells' autobiography. See *Years of My Youth*, HE, pp. 300–3.

3. Rideing begins his account of Howells' boyhood with an anecdote from "Year in a Log-Cabin" concerning a literary discussion that took place one afternoon while Howells and his father drove the family cow home. Although he did not delete this story from his book, Rideing makes no reference to "a farmer's boy" and even remarks that the young Howells and his father "were evidently not farmers; both had the appearance of living a city life...."

14 JULY 1887, LAKE GEORGE, NEW YORK, TO CHARLES E. NORTON

Lake George N. Y. July 14, 1887.

Dear friend—

You will not be surprised to find that I am here, for by this time you oughtn't be surprised at any whereabouts of mine. We've taken the old Judge Edmonds cottage for the summer,[1] and Mrs. Howells has re-named it "By George" which she not only considers descriptive, but expressive of the natural feelings of a housekeeper concerning the buffalo-moths in it. But outdoors the cottage is everything we could wish, with hills and waters of the most amiable character all round. The only draw back is the distance from Ashfield, which really seems insuperable. You needn't be told how gladly I would come.[2]

I am proud to send my contribution to the Autograph Quilt—it wont be the first time that people have slept under a work bearing my name.[3]

We are all here together since July 5, when John joined us, after his Harvard exams. He got in with only one condition, which we think is pretty well for a last year's work crowded into two months.—Winny has had one of her lapses—not so bad as last year—and is slowly coming up out of it.—Warner was here, for a day, and told me of your having asked him to the dinner.[4] I wish I could be there. I suppose you will have some ceremony in reference to Mr. Field's gift—what a superb gift![5]—This house is full of old books—old Blackwoods, incomparably dreary and self-satisfied. Lord, what things have been done in the name of Literature—what brutalities, what imbecilities.—I nibble at all sorts of books—V. Hugo's Things Seen (mighty good, in spots) Colvin's new life of Keats; Burke's Sublime and the Beautiful puts me to sleep every day after dinner, but it is good.[6]

The family all join me in love to you and yours. I too wish we might meet oftener—and the time is going.

Yours affectionately
W. D. Howells.

1. See Howells to Hale, 28 June 1887, n. 6.
2. Apparently Norton had issued his annual invitation to the Ashfield Academy dinner.

3. Probably a quilt displaying autographs of notables that Norton may have raffled or sold to raise money for the Ashfield Academy.

4. C. D. Warner had visited Howells on 8 or 9 July at his Lake George cottage.

5. G. W. Curtis reported to Howells on 1 September 1887 (MH), about the festivities at Ashfield: "The dinner was very pleasant. There was a fair, also, and Sally Norton and my daughter with other amateurs have given two charming concerts, all for the Academy. Mrs Field's gift will take the form of a new building for it also, and all goes as merrily as an Academy bell." The gift came from Mrs. John W. Field, in memory of her late husband.

6. Victor Hugo, *Things Seen* (1887); Sidney Colvin, *Keats* (1887), reviewed by Howells in the "Editor's Study," *Harper's Monthly*, October 1887; Edmund Burke, *The Sublime and Beautiful* (1756).

29 JULY 1887, LAKE GEORGE, NEW YORK, TO CHARLES D. WARNER

Lake George, July 29, 1887.

My dear Warner—

I have got both the Christ-Words and the Patton article on Tolstoi.[1] The former makes the book I tho't of unnecessary; it's admirably done, and I'm glad to have it. I'll return the Patton article as soon as Mrs. Howells has had a chance to read it. I think it's a very able, tho' sometimes disingenuous answer to Tolstoi, but it seems written in a cold anger, wh. I don't like. It's strongest point is that against a literalist's refusing to accept Christ literally when He preaches the life to come. But I had already pointed this out in my first review of My Religion.[2]

How delicious, how wise and good your opening essay in the August Drawer is![3] I read it to myself and then to the family with mounting joy in its humor and sense.

What a short time you did stay!

Yours ever
W. D. Howells.

1. During Warner's visit with Howells in early July (see Howells to Norton, 14 July 1887, n. 4) they discussed Tolstoy, and upon his return to Hartford, Warner sent Howells James Barr Walker's *God Revealed in the Process of Creation, and by the Manifestation of Jesus Christ* (1855) and W. W. Patton's article, "Count Tolstoi and the Sermon on the Mount," *New Englander and Yale Review*, February 1887. See Warner to Howells, 9 July (MH) and 25 July 1887 (MH).

2. See Howells to Hale, 28 June 1887, n. 3.

3. Warner, who had become a coeditor of *Harper's Monthly* in 1884, wrote the "Editor's Drawer" department from August 1887 until he took over the "Editor's Study" from Howells in April 1892. In his first "Drawer" he took issue with the universally acknowledged value of keeping a diary, pointing out that diaries indulge in gossip and are unreliable and misleading as historical documents. When Howells wrote his final "Study" for *Harper's Monthly*, March 1892, he paid tribute to Warner's conduct of the "Editor's Drawer," calling the essays "little prodigies, every one, of grace and light; with a playful suffusion, so fine, so elusive, that it often seems flatteringly like the gleam of one's own eye on the page."

18 AUGUST 1887, LAKE GEORGE, NEW YORK, TO GEORGE W. CURTIS

Lake George, Aug. 18, 1887.

Dear Mr. Curtis—

Of course I feel the force of what you say, and that a man strange to the rules of law should have the ground sure under his feet before he questions the decision of two courts of law.[1] In my own case you are mistaken as to a "mastery" of the facts. I have had my original feeling that the trial of the anarchists was hysterical and unjust strengthened by reading a condensed history of it, based upon the original record, and, though printed for the condemned, apparently not garbled or distorted; that is all. This history came to me from some unknown person, and necessarily without knowledge of my feeling on the part of the sender. I now send it to you, and beg you to give an hour or two up to it. I have marked passages to facilitate your reading, and I know you will not think it lost time. Look how the case was worked up beforehand by the press and the police; how the jury was empanelled regardless of the acknowledged prejudices of eight or nine of the jurors; how partial the court's rulings seem to be; how inflammatory the prosecuting attorney's appeals; how purely circumstantial and conjectural the evidence, and how distinctly and squarely met; how that "reasonable doubt" which should have been made to favor the accused was tormented throughout into proof against them.[2]

I feel that these men are doomed to suffer for their opinion's sake; but as my whole life has been given to the study of different questions, I distrust my ability to judge the situation dispassionately. If, on looking at the facts *you* tell me I am wrong, I will know that it is hopeless to attempt anything in behalf of those friendless prisoners. Of course, there is the larger mercy which considers the welfare of the community, and I am not unmindful of that, as I am sure you will not be. But I have spoken with several lawyers about the case, and their belief was that the trial was for socialism and not for murder; that it was necessarily partial.

I need not say anything to arouse your sympathy in behalf of men who seem to have been persecuted rather than prosecuted, and I will spare you any superfluous rhetoric. But I will own that this case has taken a deep hold of me, and that I feel strongly the calamity which error in it must embody. Civilization cannot afford to give martyrs to a bad cause; and if the cause of these men is good, what an awful mistake to put them to death!

Perhaps you will let Norton look at the pamphlet too. I will then be glad to have it back.

Yours sincerely,
W. D. Howells.

1. Howells had written Curtis on 10 August 1887 (MH) about his concern over the Chicago anarchists, who had been sentenced for their role in the Haymarket Riot of 4 May 1886. That letter is the beginning of a large amount of extant correspondence over a six-month period dealing with Howells' efforts to win a pardon for the convicted men; it reads in part: "When I saw you last winter, we spoke in sympathy about the impolicy of hanging the Chicago 'Anarchists.' Within a few week[s] I have read Miss [Niña] Van Zandt's resume of their trial [*August Spies' Autobiography* (n.d.)], which I suppose represents the facts, & I feel more than ever than that [sic] it was not a fair trial, either as to the selection of the jury or the rulings of the judge. The evidence showed that neither Parsons nor Spies was concerned in promoting riot or disorder, and their speeches show them to have been active friends of a peaceful solution of the labor troubles. They are condemned to death upon a principle that would have sent every ardent antislavery man to the gallows." In conclusion, he asked Curtis, "cannot something be done to bring the public to a better mind about them, and to save the American people from allowing an injustice to be done in their name?" Curtis' reply of 12 August 1887 (MH) was cautiously sympathetic: "your name would give gseat [sic] weight to any statement or plea proceeding evidently not from emotion, but from conviction. Why should not you write such a statement and let us all consider whether it would be well to print it in the Weekly? It would have to be very conclusive, undoubtedly, to strike our friends in Franklin Square favorably." See C. and R. Kirk, "Howells, Curtis, and the 'Haymarket Affair,'" *American Literature* 40 (1969), 487–98; Cady, *Howells*, II, 69–80; Lynn, *Howells*, pp. 288–92.

2. Howells sent Curtis *A Concise History of the Great Trial of the Chicago Anarchists in 1886* (1887) by Dyer D. Lum, a Chicago journalist and radical, who stated in his pamphlet that he had been requested by the accused anarchists to officially report their trial. Howells' arguments in this letter are a paraphrase of those presented by Lum, but his appeal for Curtis' support was denied; in a letter to Howells of 23 September 1887 (MH) Curtis concluded that "the men are morally responsible for the crime," and he refused to support Howells' plea. Howells had apparently not received this response when he sent Curtis a letter on 25 September 1887 (MH) for possible publication in *Harper's Weekly* with "a few words of your own in behalf of those friendless men." The following day, 26 September 1887 (MH), he wrote Curtis again, requesting that his letter of the previous day be returned. Howells apparently acted too hastily, for Curtis, in a letter of 27 September (MH), agreed to publish Howells' letter "without comment" if the Harpers approved, although he felt that Howells' bitterly sarcastic tone "would tend to defeat its purpose." In an editorial, "The Anarchists at Chicago," *Harper's Weekly*, 1 October 1887, presumably written by Curtis, the magazine expressed strong sentiment in favor of the Illinois Supreme Court's ruling to uphold the sentencing of the anarchists. See Kirk, *American Literature* 40 (1969), 494–96.

---

2 SEPTEMBER 1887, LAKE GEORGE, NEW YORK, TO JOHN W. DE FOREST

Lake George, Sept. 2, 1887.

My dear De Forest—

I don't know where I shall be, this winter, but when we break up here, about the 20th, we shall go to Dansville,[1] where there's a Sanitorium; I want to see if my oldest girl, who's been suffering from nervous prostration for five or six years can get any help in it.—But why don't you propose taking ten per cent. and letting Ticknor run the risks? I don't know, but I think he would do it.[2]—I hope to spend the winter in

New York, and if Dansville turns out a fraud, perhaps we shall get there in early November. Yet my youngest girl wants to go to Papanti's Saturday Evening Class,[3] and my boy is just entering Harvard; so it may be Boston, after all.—You see, probably, where the soft-heartedness of my hero comes from;[4] but an irresolute man is glad of anything that decides him, even a child's dancing-class. Personally, I feel that there is little or nothing left for me in Boston, and in New York there may be a good-deal.—I was interested by what you say of the national timidity in praise;[5] certainly we're bold enough in censure. Mark Twain (whom you ought to understand and like better than you do) once said that his friends talked mountains of praise, and then went off and printed mole-hills. I dare say it does come somewhat of our fear of what England may say; we're still an awful lot of sneaks; and when we can get one of our own jumped on by that thick-headed bully of a Saturday Review, we are all the rest of us as glad as a pack of nasty, cowardly little boys. A short stay in England is a good remedy for this; you can't be afraid of the Saturday Reviews after meeting the Saturday Reviewers.[6]

I've talked with a good many people about you, and wherever I've met a sound, well-read man, he had read you and liked you. I spoke of Miss Ravenel from my vivid recollection of twenty-one years ago, but I know I'm not mistaken about it.[7] I may be mistaken in thinking that your books in a uniform edition would succeed now; but I do believe the public has been growing towards your kind of work. The novelist is less woman-rid than he once was, and your masculine tone would be better liked; certainly there is a better chance now for your realism. Good Lord! When one thinks of Stevenson and Haggard selling their tens of thousands and you lacking a publisher, it is hard to be patient.[8]

I have made your letter about copyright a text in the Study for October,[9] and have preached a sermon for out and out reciprocity with the English on grounds of abstract morality—actually appealed to the public conscience. But I am not hopeful.—It's not easy to get texts for the Study sermons. And my congregation does an amount of kicking unknown to other sanctuaries. It isn't altogether pleasant to be regularly misunderstood and unfailingly misrepresented, but I keep on with the hope that I may at last let a little light into the general darkness concerning literature and the principles on which it's to be judged.

If I can help you further with Ticknor, eccomi qua![10]

Yours ever,
W. D. Howells.

Excuse the type-writer; my wrist is gone to pieces.

1. The Howells family left Lake George on 15 September and arrived in Dansville, New York, on 21 September.

2. Howells had probably approached Ticknor & Co., the firm that took over the obligations of James R. Osgood & Co. after its failure in 1885, with the proposition to publish De Forest's novels, perhaps in a new, uniform edition. He wrote De Forest on 29 July 1887 (CtY): "You'll see by this letter of Ticknor's that I've been trying to do a stroke of business for you. His offer is a good one .... He is an enterprising publisher, as pubs. go.... I w'd rather make my plates and take 15 per cent. than either let him make them and take 10, or pay all expenses and give him 10." The correspondent was probably Benjamin H. rather than Thomas B. Ticknor.

3. Mildred apparently wanted to attend one of the dancing classes at Papanti's Hall, 23 Tremont Street.

4. Howells is probably referring to Dan Mavering in *April Hopes*, which was then being serialized in *Harper's Monthly*.

5. De Forest's letter containing the remarks to which Howells refers here is not extant, but it may be the same as that from which Howells quoted a passage in the "Editor's Study." See n. 9, below.

6. See Howells to De Forest, 1 June 1887, n. 2.

7. Howells praised De Forest's novel in very high terms in the "Editor's Study," *Harper's Monthly*, September 1887: "As for Tolstoï, he is the incomparable; and no novelist of any time or any tongue can fairly be compared with him .... Nevertheless, if something of this sort is absolutely required, we will instance Mr. J. W. De Forest, in his very inadequately named *Miss Ravenel's Conversion*, as presenting an image of American life during the late rebellion, both North and South, at home and in the field, which does not 'shrink to pitiful dimensions' even when 'put by the side of Tolstoï's' *War and Peace*; it is an admirable novel and spacious enough for the vast drama glimpsed in it."

8. Howells disliked the romantic fiction of Robert Louis Stevenson and H. Rider Haggard. His comments on Haggard in the "Editor's Study," *Harper's Monthly*, July 1887, and the New York *Tribune*, 10 July 1887, are much harsher than his comments on Stevenson in the "Editor's Study," *Harper's Monthly*, May 1886, presumably because of Howells' friendship with Henry James, who was a close friend of Stevenson.

9. Making a case for an English-American copyright agreement in the "Editor's Study," *Harper's Monthly*, October 1887, Howells printed part of a letter from De Forest. It argues that "In our reading we are still colonial; we have never had our war of independence. A host of English novelists fill the minds of our youth with English pictures of life, English ideas and preferences and prejudices. From the age of fifteen the American dude has been revelling by imagination in the aristocratic society of the mother-land, and learning to wish that he could attain to it. It is not to be expected that he should remain fervidly patriotic or democratic in his fancies and manners." Howells added some qualifying remarks and then proceeded to take up the copyright issue. The original of the De Forest letter has not been located.

10. Italian for "Here I am."

7 SEPTEMBER 1887, LAKE GEORGE, NEW YORK, TO EDWARD ABBOTT

Lake George, Sept. 7, 1887.

Dear Mr. Abbott:[1]

I can't help writing to you and thanking you for the very generous words the Literary World has spoken in my behalf in a case where I could not speak for myself. It must be that Mr. Thompson feels very strongly as a literary man about the matter, for he can have no personal feeling against me. In fact, he has some reasons to keep silent, for at every point where I could help him as editor, critic and with publishers, I have invariably rendered him efficient kindness. I own that he has given me pain; but I think that he has done himself harm chiefly. It is no small thing for a man to let his passions carry him so far beyond his documents, as he has done about Tolstoi.[2]

This is for your eye only.

Yours sincerely
W. D. Howells.

1. Edward Abbott (1841–1908), a Congregational clergyman and author, was editor of the *Literary World* (1878–1888, 1895–1903).

2. Howells' initial expression of gratitude refers to an editorial in the *Literary World* of 3 September 1887, entitled "Mr. Maurice Thompson on Mr. Howells." It was the culmination of an attack on Tolstoy and his advocates that Thompson had mounted in an address to the American Association of Writers in Indianapolis, part of which was reprinted in the *Literary World*, 23 July 1887, under the title "Two Opinions of Tolstoy." Thompson's derisive remarks about the "Russian socialistic 'crank'" were juxtaposed with Howells' comments praising Tolstoy's genius that had recently appeared in the introduction to *Sebastopol* (1887). After presenting the two opinions, the editors commented that Howells' interpretation was more "penetrating and sympathetic" and "nearer to the truth" than Thompson's. On 20 August the *Literary World* printed a letter of rebuttal from Thompson, and on 3 September it issued an editorial that sought to lay to rest Thompson's "grossly unfair representation both of Mr. Howells's philosophy of literature in general and of his criticism of Tolstoï in particular."

25 SEPTEMBER 1887, DANSVILLE, NEW YORK, TO ROGER A. PRYOR

The Sanatorium,
Dansville, N. Y. Sept. 25, 1887.

My dear Sir[1]—

I am glad you have taken the case of the Chicago Anarchists, and that you see some hope for them before the Supreme Court, for I have never believed them guilty of murder, or of anything but their opinions, and I do not think they were justly convicted.

I have no warrant in writing to you, except my very strong feeling in this matter,[2] but I am not quite a stranger to you. I had the pleasure of meeting Mrs. Pryor and yourself at Mr. Mead's, in Washington Place, in the spring of '86.[3]

I venture to call myself to her remembrance; and to wish you all success in your effort to save these men.

Yours sincerely
W. D. Howells.

1. Roger Atkinson Pryor (1828–1919), an eminent New York attorney, was defense counsel for the Chicago anarchists in their appeal before the U.S. Supreme Court.

2. Pryor replied to Howells on 27 September 1887 (MH), agreeing that the anarchists had not had a fair trial and thanking Howells for his letter of support, which "is in harmony with the spirit of justice and humanity pervading your writings...." As the appeal progressed, Pryor continued his correspondence with Howells, keeping him abreast of the proceedings (3 October 1887 [MH; *Life in Letters*, I, 394–95]) and enlisting Howells' public support (12 October 1887 [MH]) through the publication of a letter in behalf of the condemned men in the New York *Tribune*. Apparently because he had doubts whether such a step would have the desired effect without jeopardizing his career as a novelist and critic, Howells requested Pryor to withhold the letter, and Pryor agreed in a letter of 1 November 1887 (*Life in Letters*, I, 397–98): "I think, *now*, you did well to suppress the publication; because I am satisfied that, while your chivalry might have somewhat compromised you, it would do no good to the condemned. . . . [¶] Still, I am satisfied that an appeal by you for Executive clemency, would not be ineffectual." However, the Supreme Court decision of 2 November to uphold the convictions caused Howells to take a public stand in defense of the anarchists. See Howells to the editor of the *Tribune*, 4 November 1887.

3. The Howells family was in New York in April 1886 and apparently met the Pryors at the home of Edwin D. Mead, Eleanor Howells' cousin.

1 NOVEMBER 1887, DANSVILLE, NEW YORK, TO JOHN G. WHITTIER

Dansville, N Y. Nov. 1, 1887.

Dear friend—

I enclose a paper on the Anarchists by a very good and very able young minister of Chicago. The conclusions reached there I reached many weeks and even months ago. The fact is, these men were sentenced for murder when they ought to have been indicted for conspiracy.

I believe the mind of the Governor of Illinois is turning towards clemency; several things indicate this.

A letter from you would have great weight with him. I beseech you to write it, and do what one great and blameless man may to avert the cruellest wrong that ever threatened our fame as a nation.[1]

Even if these men had done the crime which our barbarous laws punish with homicide, should a plea for mercy be wanting from *you*?

The press has been atrociously wrong in this matter, and all the more guiltily wrong, because ignorantly so. But here are the facts; Mr. Salter states them as I have long known them; as every one must know them who reads the story of that trial.

Write to the Governor I beg you, and sign your honored and beloved name strong and full to the letter. The time is very short—ten days only.

Yours sincerely
W. D. Howells.

We are here with my daughter—long an invalid.

1. Whittier had written Howells on 21 September 1887 (MH) that although he opposed capital punishment, he had "never interfered with the law as it affects individual cases, and, I can see no reason for making the case of the anarchists an exception." Howells, in an attempt to change Whittier's feelings toward the anarchists, sent him a copy of "What Shall Be Done with the Anarchists" by William Mackintire Salter (1853–1931), a Unitarian minister and lecturer of the Chicago Ethical Society. The paper was first given as a lecture before the Chicago Ethical Society on 23 October 1887 and later published in *Open Court*, October 1887. It is not known whether Salter sent Howells a copy of his lecture or whether Howells read it in *Open Court*. Salter's conclusion was "that the anarchists were tried for murder and are to be hanged for anarchy." Whittier evidently did not alter his original opinion and refused to write a letter or sign a petition for clemency in behalf of the anarchists.

4 NOVEMBER 1887, DANSVILLE, NEW YORK,
TO THE EDITOR OF THE NEW YORK *Tribune*

Sir:[1]

As I have petitioned the Governor of Illinois to commute the death penalty of the Anarchists to imprisonment, and have also personally written him in their behalf, I ask your leave to express here the hope that those who are inclined to do either will not lose faith in themselves because the Supreme Court has denied the condemned a writ of error. That court simply affirmed the legality of the forms under which the Chicago court proceeded; it did not affirm the propriety of trying for murder men fairly indictable for conspiracy alone; and it by no means approved the principle of punishing them because of their frantic opinions, for a crime which they were not shown to have committed. The justice or injustice of their sentence was not before the highest tribunal of our law, and unhappily could not be got there. That question must remain for history, which judges the judgment of courts, to deal with; and I, for one, cannot doubt what the decision of history will be.

But the worst is still for a very few days reparable; the men sentenced to death are still alive, and their lives may be finally saved through the clemency of the Governor, whose prerogative is now the supreme law in their case.[2] I conjure all those who believe that it would be either injustice or impolicy to put them to death, to join in urging him by petition, by letter, through the press, and from the pulpit and the platform, to use his power, in the only direction where power can never be misused, for the mitigation of their punishment.

William Dean Howells.

Dansville, N. Y., Nov. 4, 1887.

1. Howells also sent a cover letter to Whitelaw Reid, 4 November 1887 (DLC), asking him to "kindly print the enclosed letter...." Reid wrote Howells on 8 Novem-

ber 1887 (MH) that he had "printed the letter promptly . . . .[¶] But I don't sympathize one bit with it, & almost want to scold about that, as well as about your quarrel with the critics."

2. Richard J. Oglesby (1824–1899), governor of Illinois, commuted to life imprisonment the sentences of only two of the anarchists, Samuel Fielden and Michael Schwab. They and Oscar E. Neebe, who had been sentenced to fifteen years in prison, were set free by Governor John P. Altgeld in 1893.

11 NOVEMBER 1887, DANSVILLE, NEW YORK, TO FRANCIS F. BROWNE

Dansville, Nov. 11, 1887.

My dear friend:[1]

It is all right. My pride suffered some twinges when I saw my letter in the *Tribune*, with the insulting head-line the night editor had given it;[2] for I perceived that what was written for the eye of a friend was somewhat hysterical in print. But if you and other humane persons believed that it might do good,—even so little where so much was needed—you did right, and I approved and adopt your action.—I don't know yet what the governor has done. While I write that hideous scene may be enacting in your jail yard—the thing forever damnable before God and abominable to civilized men.[3] But while I don't know, I can still hope.

Miserable Lingg! I'm glad he's out of the story; but even with his death,[4] it seems to me that humanity's judgment of the law begins. All over the world people must be asking themselves, What cause is this really, for which men die so gladly, so inexorably? So the evil will grow from violence to violence!

Sometime I hope to meet you and exchange with you the histories of our several experiences in this matter. The last time we met I remember we disagreed about a man named Blaine and a man named Cleveland. How trivial the difference between them seems in this lurid light.

Yours sincerely,
W. D. Howells.

1. Francis Fisher Browne (1843–1913) was a poet and founder and editor of the *Dial* (1880–1913). Browne had sent Howells an undated letter (3 November 1887; MH) and enclosed his poem, "The Message from Judea," which recorded his reaction to that "most terrible day"—the day of the Supreme Court's decision. Howells wrote Browne on 4 November 1887 (Chicago *Tribune*, 8 November 1887) that the "'impending tragedy' . . . blackens my life. [¶] I do not dread the consequences so far as those who believe in anarchy is concerned, but I feel the horror and the shame of the crime which the law is about to commit against justice." See also J. W. Ward, "Another Howells Anarchist Letter," *American Literature* 22 (1951), 489–90.

2. Howells' letter had appeared in the Chicago *Tribune*, 8 November 1887, with the caption "Mr. Howells Is Distressed." Browne explained to Howells in a letter of 8 November 1887 (MH) that when Henry Demarest Lloyd "last evening . . .

asked to print your note to me in this morning's *Tribune*, he suggested that your permission to Mr. Salter to publish a similar note might cover this case also. There was no time to ask your consent . . . ."

3. Albert Parsons, August Spies, George Engel, and Adolph Fischer were hanged in Chicago's Cook County Jail on 11 November 1887.

4. Louis Lingg (1865–1887), one of the anarchists, committed suicide in his cell on the morning of 10 November 1887 by discharging a "fulminating cap" in his mouth.

12 NOVEMBER 1887, DANSVILLE, NEW YORK,
TO THE EDITOR OF THE NEW YORK *Tribune*

To the Editor of The Tribune:[1]

I have borne with what patience I must, during the past fortnight, to be called by the Tribune, day after day imbecile and bad citizen, with the others who desired mercy for the men killed yesterday at Chicago, in conformity with our still barbarous law.[2] I now ask you to have a little patience with me.

It seems, of course, almost a pity to mix a note of regret with the hymn of thanksgiving for blood going up from thousands of newspapers all over the land this morning; but I reflect that though I write amidst this joyful noise, my letter cannot reach the public before Monday[3] at the earliest, and cannot therefore be regarded as an indecent interruption of the *Te Deum*.

By that time journalism will not have ceased, but history will have at least begun. All over the world where civilized men can think and feel, they are even now asking themselves, For what, really, did those four men die so bravely? Why did one other die so inexorably? Next week the journalistic theory that they died so because they were desperate murderers will have grown even more insufficient than it is now for the minds and hearts of dispassionate inquirers, and history will make the answer to which she must adhere for all time, *They died, in the prime of the freest Republic the world has ever known, for their opinions' sake.*

It is useless to deny this truth, to cover it up, to turn our backs upon it, to frown it down, or sneer it down. We have committed an atrocious and irreparable wrong. We have been undergoing one of those spasms of paroxysmal righteousness to which our Anglo-Saxon race is peculiarly subject, and in which, let us hope, we are not more responsible for our actions than the victim of *petit mal*.[4] Otherwise, we could not forgive ourselves; and I say we, because this deed has apparently been done with the approval of the whole nation. The dead men who now accuse us of the suicidal violence in which they perished, would be alive to-day, if one thousandth part of the means employed to compass their death had been used by the people to inquire into the question of their guilt; for, under the forms of law, their trial has not been a trial by justice, but a trial by passion, by terror, by prejudice, by hate, by newspaper.[5]

To the minority who asked mercy for them because they had made this inquiry (but who were hooted at in your columns as ignorant sentimentalists and cowards) the whole business of their conviction, except for the hideous end attained, might seem a colossal piece of that American humor, so much admired by the English for its grotesque surprises in material and proportion. But perhaps the wildest of our humorists could not have conceived of a joke so monstrous as the conviction of seven men for a murderous conspiracy which they carried into effect while one was at home playing cards with his family,[6] another was addressing a meeting five miles away,[7] another was present with his wife and little children,[8] two others had made pacific speeches,[9] and not one, except on the testimony of a single, notoriously untruthful witness,[10] was proven to have had anything to do with throwing the Haymarket bomb, or to have even remotely instigated the act. It remained for a poetic brain to imagine this, and bring its dream yesterday to homicidal realization.

I mean the brain of Mr. State's Attorney Grinnell, who has shown gifts of imagination that would perhaps fit him better for the functions of a romantic novelist than for the duties of official advocate in a free commonwealth.[11]

It was apparently inconceivable to him that it was the civic duty as well as the sacred privilege of such an officer to seek the truth concerning the accused rather than to seek their destruction. He brought into court the blood-curdling banners of the Anarchists, and unfurled them before the eyes of a jury on which eight or nine men had owned themselves prejudiced against Anarchists before the law delivered the lives of these Anarchists into their hands. He appealed to the already heated passions of the jury; he said the seven were no more guilty than a thousand other men in Chicago, but he told them that if they would hang the seven men before them the other nine hundred and ninety-three equally guilty contrivers of bombs would not explode them in the bosom of the impartial jurymen's families and Society would be saved.

If he proved absolutely nothing against the Anarchists worthy of death, it cannot be denied that he at least posed successfully as a Savior of Society—the rôle once filled by the late Emperor of the French, (on the famous 2d December)[12] with great effect against the Socialists of his day. He was, throughout, the expression of the worst passions of the better classes, their fear, their hate, their resentment, which I do not find so much better than the worst passions of the worst classes that I can altogether respect them. He did not show that any of the accused threw the bomb, or had anything to do with throwing it; but he got them convicted of murder all the same. Spies was convicted of murder partly because he conspired against Society with men some of whom he was not on speaking terms with.[13] Among the crimes for which Parsons was convicted of murder was quoting in his paper General Sheridan's belief that a dynamite bomb might kill a regiment of soldiers; and the Supreme Court of Illinois, reviewing the testimony, located him at two points, a block apart, when the bomb was thrown, and found him doubly privy to the act upon this bold topographical conception.[14]

But Mr. Grinnell does not deserve all the honor—if it is an honor—of bringing the Anarchists to their death. He was ably seconded by Judge Gary,[15] whose interpretation of the law against murder, to make it do the work of the law against conspiracy, is a masterpiece of its kind; though perhaps even this is surpassed by his recommendation of Fielden and Schwab to the Governor's mercy because (it is like the logic of a "Bab Ballad")[16] they were pretty-behaved when brought up for sentence. It had indeed been proved, as proof went in that amusingly credulous court, that Fielden was the very man who gave the signal for throwing the bomb; but Judge Gary contributes to the science of jurisprudence the novel principle that if you are pretty-behaved when asked to say why you should not be hung for a crime of which you know your innocence, you ought afterwards to have your sentence commuted. He himself was not always pretty-behaved. When he asked Parsons that comical question, and Parsons entered upon his reasons, he refused to let him pause for a moment's refreshment while delivering his long protest, and thought it good taste and good feeling to sneer at him for reading extracts from the newspapers. Perhaps it was so; or perhaps the judge was tired—the prosecution had been reading whole files of newspapers.

When he said that the seven were no more guilty than a thousand other Anarchists, Mr. Grinnell was counting for Chicago alone; but he could doubtless have figured up ten thousand men equally guilty, upon the same medieval principle, if he took in the whole country. Seven is rather a small percentage, though seven is a mystical number, and he may have thought it had peculiar properties for that reason; but it always struck me as much too few, or wholly too many, according as the men accused did or did not do murder. With his love of poetic justice, (I will call it melodramatic justice if the word poetic seems too strong) I rather wonder that Mr. Grinnell did not at least want the men's families hanged; but since he did not ask this, I do not see why he could not have satisfied himself with having the seven Anarchists hanged in effigy. Possibly if Parsons, believing that he could suffer no wrong in an American court, had not come back and voluntarily given himself up after having made good his escape,[17] Mr. Grinnell would have demanded that sort of expiation for him.

But this is mere conjecture, and I have wished to deal with facts. One of these is that we had a political execution in Chicago yesterday. The sooner we realize this, the better for us. By such a perversion of law as brought the Anarchists to their doom, William Lloyd Garrison who published a paper denouncing the constitution as a compact with hell and a covenant with death, and every week stirred up the blacks and their friends throughout the country to abhor the social system of the South, could have been sent to the gallows if a slave had killed his masters.[18] Emerson, Parker, and Howe, Giddings and Wade, Sumner and Greeley,[19] and all who encouraged the war against slavery in Kansas, and the New England philanthropists[20] who supplied the Free State men with Sharp's rifles could have been held "morally responsible," and made to pay with their persons, when John Brown took seven Missourians out of their beds and shot them.[21] Wendell Phillips, and Thoreau, and the other literary men whose sympathy inflamed Brown to homicidal insurrection at Harper's Ferry, could have been put to death with the same justice that consigned the Anarchists to the gallows in Chicago. The American law yesterday was made to do a deed beside which the treatment of William O'Brien by British law for the like offence, is caressing tenderness.[22]

But the men are dead. They are with God, as the simple, devout old phrase goes; or if the scientific spirit of the age does not consent to this idea, I will say that they are at least not with the newspapers. They are where, as men your words cannot hurt, nor mine help them more. But as memories, they are not beyond the reach of either, and I protest against any farther attempt to defame them. They were no vulgar or selfish murderers. However they came by their craze against society it was not through hate of the rich so much as love of the poor. Let both rich and poor remember this, and do them this piece of justice at least.

I dread the Anarchy of the Courts, but I have never been afraid of the prevalence of the dead Anarchists' doctrine, because that must always remain to plain common sense, unthinkable; and I am not afraid of any acts of revenge from their fellow conspirators because I believe they never were part of any conspiracy. I have no doubt that Judge Gary will live long to enjoy the reward upon which he has already entered in his re-election. I have no question either as to the safety of Mr. State's Attorney Grinnell, and I hope he has not suffered too keenly from the failure to realize his poetical ideal in the number of the Anarchists finally hanged. He himself helped to reduce it to four; perhaps he will yet wish that none had died.

Dansville, Nov. 12, 1887.   W. D. Howells.

1. Although it is possible that Whitelaw Reid refused to print this letter, Howells probably never sent it.

2. The *Tribune* attacked Howells by name and by implication for his public defense of the Chicago anarchists in the following issues: 22 October, 6, 8, and 11 November 1887. See also Howells to Browne, 11 November 1887, n. 3.

3. The next day was Monday, 13 November.

4. A medical term for a form of epilepsy.

5. Among the many editorial expressions of opinion in favor of executing the anarchists, perhaps the most vulgar example was a cartoon in *Life* depicting seven hooded figures hanging from a gallows; the caption read: "Seven Up. A Game that will be Played in Chicago Next Month." For this and other examples of the pervasive atmosphere of lyncherism, see Cady, *Howells*, II, 71–73.

6. George Engel, editor of *The Anarchist*, wrote in his "Autobiography" (1887): "On the evening of May 4 I was at home playing cards. . . ." See Lucy E. Parsons, ed., *Life of Albert R. Parsons with Brief History of the Labor Movement in America also Sketches of the Lives of A. Spies, Geo. Engel, A. Fischer and Louis Lingg* (Chicago: L. E. Parsons, 1889), p. 281.

7. Michael Schwab was addressing a group about the "eight hour movement" on the far northwest side of Chicago.

8. Presumably Oscar E. Neebe; the State's case against him was the weakest.

9. Actually three of the anarchists—Spies, Parsons, and Fielden—spoke to the crowd at Haymarket Square.

10. Harry L. Gilmer, a painter, testified that Spies provided the match to light the bomb's fuse. For an account of the inconsistencies in Gilmer's testimony, see Henry David, *The History of the Haymarket Affair* (New York: Farrar & Rinehart, 1936), pp. 264–68.

11. For an account of the courtroom tactics of Julius S. Grinnell, see David, pp. 253ff.

12. Louis Napoleon Bonaparte (1803–1873) retained his presidency of France by ordering the army to seize power on 2 December 1851.

13. Spies was editor of *Arbeiter-Zeitung*, an anarchist newspaper which advocated the overthrow of the capitalist state and the destruction of private property by force. The paper published articles dealing with the manufacture and use of explosives.

14. Parsons was editor of the anarchist paper *Alarm*, and in his presentencing address to the court he quoted General Philip H. Sheridan's comment on the efficacy of dynamite. See *Life of Albert R. Parsons*, p. 154. He had spoken at the Haymarket meeting but left when it began to rain and before the bomb detonated.

15. Joseph E. Gary (1821–1906), a member of the Cook County Superior Court (1863–1888), wrote "The Chicago Anarchists of 1886: the Crime, the Trial, and the Punishment," *Century*, April 1893. He defended the jury's sentencing of the anarchists and, by implication, his own part in it, by arguing that the membership of all the defendants in the International Association of Workingmen constituted prima facie evidence of their complicity in a conspiracy, the aim of which was to incite such violent acts as led to the death of officer Mathias J. Degan. "And if by the law of the State of Illinois, preëxisting and known," Judge Gary maintained, "the anarchists residing in Illinois were guilty of murder by engaging in a conspiracy the natural and probable result of which could be anticipated, and that result murder, it is childish whimpering for their adherents to complain that the law defied by the anarchists was upon their defeat enforced against them."

16. A nonsensical song by William S. Gilbert.

17. Parsons had fled to Geneva, Wisconsin, after the Haymarket bomb exploded, and he later went to Waukesha, Wisconsin, hiding out in disguise. His wife and the defense counsel, William P. Black, urged him to give himself up, and he did so on 21 June 1886.

18. The radical abolitionist William Lloyd Garrison (1805–1879) argued in *The*

Liberator that because the U.S. Constitution sanctioned slavery the Federal Union should be dissolved.

19. Of all these well-known antislavery advocates only Samuel G. Howe (1801–1876) has not hitherto been identified in these volumes. He and his wife, Julia Ward Howe, edited the Boston antislavery paper, *Commonwealth* (1851–1853), and were engaged in philanthropic work.

20. The "Secret Six," a group of New Englanders who supported militant abolitionists (including John Brown), consisted of Samuel G. Howe, Theodore Parker, Gerrit Smith, George L. Stearns, Thomas W. Higginson, and Franklin B. Sanborn.

21. In the so-called Pottawatomie Massacre, 24–26 May 1856, John Brown and his guerrilla troops killed five men.

22. William O'Brien, the editor of *United Ireland*, was convicted of using seditious language at a meeting of the National League in Mitchellstown, Ireland, and sentenced to three months in jail. His appeal against the sentence was refused.

13 NOVEMBER 1887, DANSVILLE, NEW YORK, TO WILLIAM C. HOWELLS

Dansville, Nov. 13, 1887.

Dear father—

We expect to go to Buffalo tomorrow or Tuesday, and leave Winny here. Her care must be moral quite as much as physical, and the doctors, after carefully studying her case, prefer us to be away from her. We shall go to the Hotel Niagara, and you can hereafter address me there.

I've had no letter from you this week, but I suppose you got my last. I sent you the Tribune with my unavailing word for the Anarchists.[1] All is over now, except the judgment that begins at once for every unjust and evil deed, and goes on forever. The historical perspective is that this free Republic has killed five men for their opinions.—I have had many letters thanking me for my words. The Pres't of the American Press Association, (which supplies Joe with his stereotype plates?) says, "Your stand in regard to the Anarchists meets with my most cordial approval. Society will commit a great blunder—a great crime would be the better term—if the Anarchists are hung."[2] Harriet Prescott Spofford writes, "Great as your work is, you never wrote more immortal words than those in behalf of these men who are dying for free speech."[3] So it goes. Of course I get abuse in print; but that doesn't matter.

With love to all

Your aff'te son
Will.

1. See Howells to Editor of *Tribune*, 4 November 1887.
2. O. J. Smith to Howells, 11 November 1887 (MH).
3. Spofford to Howells, 8 November 1887 (MH). Howells also received letters of support for his statement in the New York *Tribune* from Frank W. Bellew, 6 November 1887; James V. Blake, 8 November 1887; Edmund Noble, 8 November 1887; Edwin D. Mead, 8 November 1887; Charles Allen, 14 November 1887; William A. Hovey, 20 November 1887; Dr. S. J. Bumstead, 27 November 1887 (all at MH).

18 November 1887, Buffalo, to Anne H. Fréchette

> Hotel Niagara,
> Buffalo, Nov. 18, 1887.

My dear Annie:

It's a very, very long time since I've heard from you, and it's my own fault, for I'm afraid I've neglected your letters. I hope you are all well, and that your lovely and interesting children are getting into the winter without too much trouble of mind or body. I know that Mole must have a great deal to preoccupy him; but I hope he hasn't forgotten his Uncle Will; and the manful struggle we made together in the cause of ameliorative table-manners when we last met. And dear little Vevie, how much I'd like to see her, and take up our common interests with her. What does she study? What does she read? *Can* she be as cunning as ever? Do tell me about yourself, and Achille, whom I think it one of the misfortunes that I can't see every day. He and father seem to me two perfect gentlemen, always.

I want to tell you how charming we all thought your story in *St. Nicholas* was.[1] Pilla, especially, was delighted. I wish you could write more.

I suppose you wouldn't be much surprised at getting a letter from me in the moon; but I ought to try to explain why we're in Buffalo. For the last two months we've been at the Sanatorium in Dansville, where we took Winny when we left Lake George. I think she'll get well there if anywhere, and the doctors have judged it best that we should be away from her. So, we've come to this wonderful new hotel, the most exquisite place of the sort that I ever was in. I daresay Aurelia has told you about it. She it really was who found it, for she read me the advertisement when she came on with Pil and me in October, and she passed a day here with us. We've now been here three days, and we expect to stay till into February, if we can stand the climate, and all goes well with Winny. There's a good Art School,[2] where Pil can study, and she can get French and dancing. To-night she's gone with a party of young girls to the Dickens' reading.[3] I think I shall have time for work, and it is pleasant to be so near dear old father. (Isn't it nice, Willy naming his boy for him?)[4] I hope to have him here, and go to see him more than once during our stay. The only objection we have to the place is a queer one, and I'm afraid you won't think it's sincere. Elinor and I both no longer care for the world's life, and would like to be settled somewhere very humbly and simply, where we could be socially identified with the principles of progress and sympathy for the struggling mass. I can only excuse our present movement as temporary. The last two months have been full of heartache and horror for me, on account of the civic murder committed last Friday at Chicago. You may have seen in the papers that I had taken part in petitioning for clemency for the Anarchists,[5] whom I thought unfairly tried, and most unjustly condemned. Annie, it's all been an atrocious piece of frenzy and cruelty, for which we must stand ashamed forever before history. But it's no use. I can't write about it. Some day I hope to do justice to these irreparably wronged men.

I'm busy with another story, which will deal rather with humanity than with love. I think I shall call it *The Upper and the Nether Millstone*,[6] and the hero to be a minister who preaches the life rather than the doctrine of Christ. Have you read Tolstoi's heart-searching books? They're worth all the other novels ever written.

Elinor is well, and joins me in love to you all. I'm well, too, except for turning my ankle, the other day. That has kept me indoors since. Very best love to Achille, the children, and yourself.

> Your affectionate brother,
> Will.

1. See Howells to Marie M. Fréchette, 6 February 1887, n. 1.
2. The Buffalo Academy of Fine Arts.
3. Dickens' son, Charles Dickens, read selections from *Dr. Marigold* and *The Pickwick Papers* at Concert Hall.
4. William Cooper Howells II (1887–1940) was the son of William Dean Howells II, Howells' nephew, and Alice Pierce Howells. He was born on 16 November, the first great-grandchild of W. C. Howells.
5. See Howells to Editor of *Tribune*, 4 November 1887.
6. Later renamed *Annie Kilburn*.

20 NOVEMBER 1887, BUFFALO, TO WILLIAM M. SALTER

> The Niagara,
> Buffalo, Nov. 20, 1887.

Dear Mr. Salter—

I'm greatly your debtor for all those papers, which I read with the helpless grief and rage which seems to be my part in this business. But now that the worst has happened, can't we do something to begin the work of history concerning those men? I have suggested to Mr. Browne of the Dial, the publication of a book embodying expressions of sympathy and protest from those who made them, and a narrative of the efforts of the clemency committees.[1] A very clear and unimpassioned statement of the facts of the trial, execution and burial should be included. I will gladly contribute a letter, which is the only thing not covered by my present contracts. What do you think of the plan? The profits of the book sh'd go to the dead men's families.

Dr. Leffingwell[2] went on from Dansville to Chicago to attend the funeral.[3] I gave him a card to you, but he couldn't find your house. He reported of the funeral just what your wife and sister said.—It was he who drew up the petition which was telegraphed abroad from Springfield as the first in due form to reach the governor. I signed it first, but the credit belongs to him. He wrote a year ago to Oglesby asking commutation.

Yours hastily,
W. D. Howells.

1. In his reply to this letter, dated 27 November 1887 (MH), Salter reported: "Mr. Browne writes that the plan of a book is impracticable—I fear McClure & Co. would not publish it & perhaps would not allow him to edit it. I mean to go on to see him."

2. Albert Leffingwell (1845–1916) was a proprietor of the Dansville Sanatorium, where Winny was being treated. He wrote Howells on 3 December 1887 (MH): "Could not Mr Salter take up that *Memorial?* I wd give $50.— toward expense of publication, if you will write something for it."

3. The public funeral for the executed anarchists was held on 13 November 1887. See H. David, *The History of the Haymarket Affair* (New York: Farrar & Rinehart, 1936), pp. 464–65.

1 DECEMBER 1887, BUFFALO, TO WILLIAM M. SALTER

The Niagara,
Buffalo, Dec. 1, 1887.

My dear friend—

I found your letter here yesterday when I came home from New York, and I don't know how to thank you enough for the gift of poor Spies's note.[1] I value it most highly: it seemed to be the touch of a dying man on my hand. I suppose that you and I have the same reservations in regard to him; but we must both allow that he was a noble, unselfish and heroic soul. We ought not to leave his memory and that of the others to infamy; but I can well understand why Mr. Browne cannot undertake the memorial.[2] I cannot because my Harper engagement covers all my work; but can't you? I will contribute a letter—the only form not cut off by my contract—and I will help you in any way I can. Wouldn't Mr. Lloyd associate himself with you in the work? I read and will read again Mr. L.'s address to the Governor.[3] How could that man resist such facts?—In New York, I met Mr. O. J. Smith of the American Press Association, who said he knew the bailiff who "fixed" the jury: a perfectly unmoral creature.—Gen. Pryor, with whom I had been in correspondence since he took up the Anarchists' case, asked me to dinner, and there I met half a dozen men of our thinking.[4] He told me that *after* their case was lost with the U.S. Supreme Court, the Anarchists paid him and the others up in full. Spies wrote to thank him the day he was murdered. Can you get me a copy of the Illinois Supreme Court opinion? And there is a law journal in Chicago which reviewed that opinion, about Oct. 1st; can you get that?[5] The large scroll of pictures came. Many thanks. I send a small check, for it's a shame to let you lose a cent in these kindnesses.

Don't you think Most's conviction a great injustice? He was tried for his speech of Nov. 12, and condemned for his book of four years ago![6] This can't last. Sometime the conscience of the people will be stirred.

Yours sincerely
W. D. Howells.

1. Salter had enclosed with his letter to Howells of 27 November 1887 (MH) a note from August Spies (not located) written on the morning of his execution. See H. A. Wilson, *Illinois State Historical Society Journal* 56 (1963), 16.

2. See Howells to Salter, 20 November 1887, n. 1.

3. Henry Demarest Lloyd had written Governor Oglesby on 9 November to appeal for justice and mercy toward the Chicago anarchists; the letter was published in the Chicago *Tribune*, 10 November 1887. Lloyd had earlier given Salter money for the anarchists' cause.

4. Howells had gone to New York to participate in the International Copyright Readings on 29 November. There he met with O. J. Smith, who told him about Henry L. Ryce's alleged attempt to fix the jury, and he had dinner with Roger A. Pryor, who, on 21 November (MH), had invited Howells and a "few friends of your craft...."

5. A review of the decision by the Illinois State Supreme Court was written by Judge Benjamin D. Magruder, "The Judgment Against the Anarchists Affirmed," *Chicago Legal News*, 17 September 1887.

6. Johann Most (1846–1906), a famous anarchist, was arrested on 12 November 1887 for giving an inflammatory speech about the execution of the Chicago anarchists. His book *Revolutionäre Kriegswissenschaft* (1885?) gives instructions for making bombs, weapons, dynamite, and other explosives; excerpts from it were published in *Alarm* and *Arbeiter-Zeitung*. In the well known "Editor's Study," *Harper's Monthly*, September 1886, in which Howells writes about "the more smiling aspects of life," he also mentions Most: "Whatever their deserts, very few American novelists have been led out to be shot, or finally exiled to the rigors of a winter at Duluth; one might make Herr Most the hero of a labor-question romance with perfect impunity...." See H. David, *The History of the Haymarket Affair* (New York: Farrar & Rinehart, 1936), pp. 530–31.

1 DECEMBER 1887, BUFFALO, TO BENJAMIN H. TICKNOR

The Niagara,
Buffalo, Dec. 1, 1887.

My dear Ticknor—

The American Press Association, which supplies stereotype plates to country papers, has proposed to me to give *Silas Lapham* serially in that way.[1] If you see no great objection to the plan I am inclined to favor it. The story would be printed "By arrangement with Messrs. Ticknor & Co.," and you w'd be furnished with a list of the papers publishing the story, so that you could place the cheap edition accordingly.

Please let me hear from you.

Yours ever
W. D. Howells.

1. O. J. Smith wrote Howells, 11 November 1887 (MH), that he "would prefer to withhold a definite proposition for the use of 'Silas Lapham' in stereotype plates" until he could discuss the matter with Howells personally in New York. Ticknor's reply to this letter has not been found, but Smith's plan was never realized.

7 DECEMBER 1887, BUFFALO, TO COURTLANDT PALMER

Hotel Niagara,
Buffalo, Dec. 7, 1887

Dear Mr. Palmer:[1]

I send you my only copy of The Tribune letter,[2] but yours much more nearly expresses my mind. I didn't know you had written anything, but I wished when I read what you said at that Union Square meeting to send you a *stretta di mano*.[3] What courage and nobleness of heart you showed in writing that letter in the midst of the base terrorism that weighed upon the minds and souls of men in those forever infamous days. The nation remains dishonored till the memory of the victims of civic murder at Chicago is rehabilitated. I'm trying to get some one there to put together a record of the Clemency movement, and your letter should be in it.—What a terrible mistake to put *more* hate into the hearts of the poor! Don't people know that a change is impending, in which the last shall be first? It seems as if some madness possessed us to go on doing more and more wrong.

What a burlesque of justice the trial of that wretched Most was! Tried for his speech and convicted for his book![4] The Chicago business over again. What worse Anarchy could there be?

I thank you for what you suggest about your club. If I come to New York, I'll gladly think of it.

Kindly return my Tribune letter.

Yours sincerely
W. D. Howells.

1. Courtlandt Palmer (1843–1888), a wealthy New Yorker and advocate of liberal ideas, became president of the Nineteenth Century Club in 1880. He spoke at a meeting at Cooper Union on 28 November 1887, which was dedicated to the memory of the four Chicago anarchists who had been executed.
2. See Howells to Editor of *Tribune*, 4 November 1887.
3. Italian for "handshake."
4. See Howells to Salter, 1 December 1887, n. 6.

25 DECEMBER 1887, BUFFALO, TO WILLIAM M. SALTER

Buffalo, Dec. 25, 1887.

Dear Mr. Salter—

I've no doubt you and Mr. Lloyd are right about the time for making a studied and historical expression in regard that Infamy, which the fact of Magruder's residence in Chicago helps to make intelligible.[1] Some one wrote me from Decatur, Ills., that probably Gov. Oglesby was influenced against the men by his ambition to be nominated for the Vice Presidency.[2] Facts will accumulate from which a fresh light can be thrown on the whole affair.—The press continues as atrocious as ever, but I believe that it never fairly represented the whole sentiment of any community. Every now and then I hear of some good man who loathed that injustice as we did. Several such I know of in Buffalo, where the papers were prompt to class me with Train and Niña Van Zandt[3] (I say nothing against her) when my letter appeared.[4]—I have read the last matter you sent me, as I have always read about the subject, with an indignation inexpressible. I don't wonder the friends and followers of the dead are furious. How hard it is, when a great wrong has been done, not to say and then to think that its victims were wholly right! That is the devil of it; the train of evil seems to warp and twist all things awry as it goes on, when once its infernal impetus is given.—I was greatly disappointed in Parsons' face: it seems almost foolish or insane. His speech gave me an expectation of something much higher; there were very striking things in it.—If you think a course of the Alarm will profit me by all means subscribe for me.[5] Hitherto I must own I haven't found Anarchy very thinkable, as a political system, though yesterday it suggested itself as something of general consent, like etiquette or social usage—something that is to prevail through reason and convenience. Is that what they mean?—Do you know about the case of Rev. J. C. Kimball of Hartford, who preached a clemency sermon, and met with persecution in his community?[6] I will send you his pamphlet.

Yours sincerely
W. D. Howells.

1. Benjamin D. Magruder, a judge of the Illinois Supreme Court, read the verdict on 14 September that upheld that of the lower court.
2. Dr. S. J. Bumstead to Howells, 27 November 1887 (MH).
3. The eccentric liberal Charles Francis Train, lecturing around the country on behalf of the anarchists, suggested that if the public wanted seven men to hang, the seven judges of the Illinois Supreme Court would be better choices than the anarchists. Niña Van Zandt, the daughter of a wealthy family, fell in love with Spies during the trial and married him by proxy while he was in jail.
4. See Howells to Editor of *Tribune*, 4 November 1887.

5. The *Alarm* was an anarchist paper originally edited by Albert Parsons. In contrast to Howells' reaction to Parsons' photograph, his response to Spies's face was that it seemed "intelligent, earnest, *good....*" See Howells to Salter, 11 December 1887 (IGK).

6. According to Kenneth R. Andrews, *Nook Farm: Mark Twain's Hartford Circle* (Cambridge, Mass.: Harvard University Press, 1950), p. 54, "...John C. Kimball declared from the Unitarian platform that the hanging of the Haymarket Anarchists was comparable to the crucifixion of Christ." Kimball was pastor of the First Unitarian Congregational Society of Hartford.

8 JANUARY 1888, BUFFALO, TO GEORGE BAINTON

The Niagara,
Buffalo, N.Y. Jan. 8, 1888.

My dear Sir[1]—

I wish I might say something useful in reply to your very kind letter.[2] I began to write by imitating the authors I admired, and I worked hard to get a smooth, rich classic style. The passion that I afterwards formed for Heine's prose freed me from this slavery, and taught me to aim at naturalness. I seek now to get back to the utmost simplicity of expression, to disuse the *literosity* I tried so hard to acquire—to get the gait of compact, clear talk, if possible, informal and direct. It is very difficult. I should advise any beginner to study the raciest, strongest, best *spoken speech*, and let the *printed speech* alone: that is, try to write straight from the thought, without bothering about the manner, except to conform to the spirit or genius of the language. I once thought Latinized diction was to be avoided; I now think Latinized syntax is to be guarded against.

Yours sincerely
W. D. Howells.

1. George Bainton, an English clergyman, compiled and edited *The Art of Authorship, Literary Reminiscences, Methods of Work, and Advice to Young Beginners, Personally Contributed by Leading Authors of the Day* (1890). He introduced the section on Howells with a brief headnote, in which he asserts that the author's "ideal is to paint life as it is, simply to hold up the mirror to nature."

2. Bainton's letter to Howells is not extant, but it evidently was a form letter requesting authors to discuss their craft and careers. *The Art of Authorship* contains most of the comments Howells makes in this letter about the development of his style, although several misquotations considerably alter their meaning.

14 JANUARY 1888, BUFFALO, TO JAMES PARTON

The Niagara
Buffalo, Jan. 14, 1888.

My dear Parton—

Thank you for both kind, friendly letters. I think I now understand the Newburyport situation, and I will wait till the frost is out of the ground before buying or hiring.[1] We expect to start East, Feb. 3, and to bring up either in Boston or New York. If the former, I shall run up to see you before the spring throes begin.

My first thought in connection with Newburyport was that you and yours were there, and so we should not be alone. You may add as many more nice people to the prospectus as you like, but you would be enough.

Mrs. Howells's family came on the Noyes side from your town, and a Reverend of that name (long since with God—perhaps) was bitter against the witches.[2] But my wife bears them no malice, if you still have them.

With cordial regards from us all to your family,

Yours ever
W. D. Howells.

1. Because of the strenuous social life and a longing "for a roof of my own" (Howells to C. E. Norton, 5 January 1888 [MH]), Howells made plans to leave Buffalo. He had written to Parton on 3 January announcing that he was considering Newburyport, Massachusetts, as a possible new residence, and asking Parton's help in finding lodgings. Parton's replies of 8 January and 13 January 1888 (both at MH) contained information about houses that were for rent or for sale. When Howells raised some questions about the healthfulness and sanitary conditions of the town (Howells to Parton, 25 January 1888 [OOxM]) Parton replied that lung disease was common in that area (Parton to Howells, 28 January 1888 [MH]). Despite Howells' move to New York in February, he expressed continued interest in Newburyport and wrote Parton on 24 February 1888 (Arms) that he would visit there "later in the spring." Parton, still anticipating Howells' relocation to Newburyport, continued to write him about the housing market (3 March [OFH], 8 March [MH], and 23 March [MH]), but Howells never did move to Newburyport.

2. The Reverend James Noyes (1608–1656) was born in Wiltshire, England, and came to New England in 1634. His second son, James (1640–1719), also a minister, settled in Stonington, Connecticut, in 1654, where he lived for the remainder of his life. Howells' comment about the Reverend Mr. Noyes being a persecutor of witches in Newburyport is apparently legend rather than fact, since such persecutions did not begin there until the 1690s.

15 JANUARY 1888, BUFFALO, TO HAMLIN GARLAND

The Niagara,
Buffalo, N. Y. January 15, 1888.

Dear Mr. Garland:

I am glad to have your letter and to know what you are doing and intending.[1] Your time must come for recognition, but you are already a power, and that is more than a name, which is sometimes a hindrance to full use of one's strength.

I'm interested by what you say of the drama and if you can fit your character play to some character actor, you'll succeed.[2] But I'm still more interested by what I will call your appeal to me. You'll easily believe that I did not bring myself to the point of openly befriending those men who were civically murdered in Chicago for their opinions without thinking and feeling much, and my horizons have been indefinitely widened by the process.[3] Your land tenure idea is one of the good things which we must hope for and strive for by all the good means at our hands.[4] But I don't know that it's the first step to be taken; and I can't yet bring myself to look upon confiscation in any direction as a good thing. The new commonwealth must be founded in justice even to the unjust, in generosity to the unjust rather than anything less than justice. Besides, the land idea arrays against progress the vast farmer class who might favor national control of telegraphs, railways, and mines, postal savings-bank-and-life-insurance, a national labor bureau for bringing work and workmen together without cost to the workman, and other schemes by which it is hoped to lessen the sum of wrong in the world, and insure to every man the food and shelter which the gift of life implies the right to. Understand, I don't argue against you; I don't know yet what is best; but I am reading and thinking about questions that carry me beyond myself and my miserable literary idolatries of the past; perhaps you'll find that I've been writing about them.[5] I am still the slave of selfishness, but I no longer am content to be so. That's as far as I can honestly say I've got.

You ought to get acquainted with Robertson James (a brother of the novelist) who lives at Concord, and is an ardent Georgeite.

We shall be leaving Buffalo in about a fortnight, for either New York or Boston; but my address is always with the Harpers.

Yours cordially,
W. D. Howells.

1. Garland's letter has not been located.

2. Probably Garland's first play, "Under the Wheel," which was published in the *Arena*, July 1890. See also Howells to Garland, 27 August 1890.

3. For Howells' attitude toward the Chicago anarchists see letters dated from 18 August to 25 December 1887.

4. Garland's interest in Henry George's single-tax theory began in 1884, after he read *Progress and Poverty* (1879), but he did not become an active single-taxer until he returned to Boston in 1887. Garland sent Howells single-tax literature and talked with him about George's ideas. See Howells to Garland, 21 October 1888 (CLSU). Later Howells reported to his father that he and Garland were to spend an evening with Henry George. See Howells to W. C. Howells, 22 January 1893 (MH; *Life in Letters*, II, 31–32). For a discussion of Garland's single-tax activities see Donald Pizer, *Hamlin Garland's Early Work and Career* (Berkeley: University of California Press, 1960), pp. 45ff.

5. Howells is here alluding to his writing of *Annie Kilburn*, which had been in progress ever since his visit to the Lowell textile mills in February 1887. Although the novel, which began in serial in *Harper's Monthly*, June 1888, does not directly endorse George's single-tax scheme, one of the characters, the lawyer Putney, advocates it.

22 JANUARY 1888, BUFFALO, TO WILLIAM C. HOWELLS

Buffalo, Jan. 22, 1888.

Dear father—

I shall so soon be with you again for a few days that it's hard to put together the usual letter.—I am to give a public reading here on the 2d, for the benefit of a charity, and I hope to go to Jefferson the next day.[1] This morning I went to see guard-mounting and inspection at the U. S. military post near by, and was impressed, as I always am, with the sort of perfection which military discipline gives. It made me think how in a true civilization, such a training could be made to serve peace and humanity. I've been reading a work on Socialism,[2] and I incline greatly to think our safety and happiness are in that direction; though as yet the Socialists offer us nothing definite or practical to take hold of. They mostly show us a general theory, with no immediate steps leading to it.

I shall have a bit more of my story to read you.[3]—Glad to hear that you're all mending. With love to all,

Your aff'te son
Will.

1. Howells read selections from *The Minister's Charge*, *Italian Journeys*, and *Their Wedding Journey* at the Chapter House for the benefit of the Fitch Creche charity on 2 February.

2. Probably Laurence Gronlund's *Co-operative Commonwealth* (1884), which Howells reviewed in the "Editor's Study," *Harper's Monthly*, April 1888. "His co-operative commonwealth," Howells wrote, "is the reconciliation of interests which now antagonize one another, the substitution of the ideal of duties for the ideal of rights, of equality for liberty. In his state we should have fewer laws but more law, less force but more justice, more self-sacrifice and less suffering. . . . One may read his books without risk of offence to one's patriotism or humanity, whatever one concludes as to the wisdom or practicality of his teachings, and with great advantage to one's knowledge of a palpitant question." Gronlund (1846–1899) was a Danish-American social theorist who became a member of the Socialist Labor party in 1888. In 1898 Howells was quoted as saying: "It was ten years ago . . . that I first became interested in the creed of Socialism. I was in Buffalo when Laurence Gronlund lectured there before the Fortnightly Club. Through this address I was led to read his book, 'The Co-operative Commonwealth,' . . . ." See U. Halfmann, ed., *Interviews with William Dean Howells* (Arlington: University of Texas, 1973), p. 52; also C. Wright, "The Sources of Mr. Howells's Socialism," *Science and Society* 2 (1938), 514–17, and G. Arms, "Further Inquiry into Howells's Socialism," *ibid.*, 3 (1939), 245–48.

3. *Annie Kilburn*.

4 FEBRUARY 1888, JEFFERSON, TO EDMUND C. STEDMAN

Jefferson, Ashtabula co., Ohio, Feb. 4, '88.

My dear Stedman—

How kind of you to write me that long, friendly letter![1] It dropt into a moment of my life when it seemed as if I were a literary Ishmael, and it made me feel at once like the legitimate seed of Abraham,—after a good bargain. I was so glad of it, that I can't yet be sorry I almost extorted it from your overworked hand and brain. I'm obliged to you also for Mrs. Cavazza's review. People take me so viciously awry, and think (or say) that I have no serious meaning when my whole trouble has been to sugar-coat my medicinal properties; and she not only feels all my meaning, but puts it with greater distinctness and aptness than I could myself if I tried to phrase it. And how extremely clever her little parting sting was![2]

We have had a very interesting winter in Buffalo (every inch of this America is interesting) and Thursday my wife and daughter went East to Boston, and Friday I came here to visit my dear father, now eighty, but young as ever in his concern about human affairs and his whole intellectual life.—I wish I could meet you some time, and have a long talk about literature, and about the economic phases which now seem to me so important. I fancy we might find ourselves on common ground, where we now appear to differ. At any rate you would not find me wanting in honor for the hand that has kept the Lamp alight and aloft above all the dust and din of commerce these many years. I send you the poem you wanted—the one I now like best of mine.[3]

Yours ever
W. D. Howells.

1. Stedman had written Howells on 1 February 1888 (OFH), thanking him for his "beautiful & scholarly volume—*Minor Italian Poets* [sic]. Beautiful, except the portraits.... The Lord sends good (& bad) poets, & the Devil sends wood-engravers." Most of the essays in *Modern Italian Poets* (1887) had been previously printed, some as early as 1867. See Gibson-Arms, *Bibliography*, p. 34.
2. Elisabeth J. Cavazza (pseudonym for Elisabeth Jones Pullen, author of *Don Finimondone; Calabrian Sketches* [1892] and *Mr. Whitman; a Story of the Brigands* [1902]), according to Stedman's 1 February letter, was "a very bright & dear little woman, & the best female Italian scholar I know of." Her review of *April Hopes* in the Portland, Maine, *Press* of 28 January 1888 praises Howells' subtle and accurate treatment of character, especially in Alice Pasmer, who "is a singularly exact study of a young girl swayed by inconsequent and foolish impulses under the domination of a morbidly alert and ingeniously mistaken conscience...." The reviewer then points out that Howells' novel "is in some sort a plea upon the other side of the cause superbly argued by George Eliot in Romola.... Of course Alice is as much less of an angel than Romola as Dan is more of a man than Tito; for she is selfish, hysterical and vehement as unsteady; and he would have been incapable of going far in the direction of his amiable shiftiness. Yet there is a

certain grotesque resemblance of the situation." Finally, Mrs. Cavazza gently chides Howells' realism for lacking incident, passion, and drama; and she suggests that the amateur photographer in the novel, who can only take pictures of unmoving subjects, works under the same limitations as the realistic novelist. The extent to which Howells had become the subject of public discussion is suggested in another passage in Stedman's letter: "I see by the papers, that you are after the hardlings again, but haven't yet read the Feby. *Harper.* However good or bad your notions may be, you certainly are *written about* more than any American who ever lived & wasn't a general or President."

3. Howells sent Stedman an autograph copy of "The Song the Oriole Sings," which Stedman intended to bind into his own copy of his *Poets of America* (1885). See *Life in Letters*, I, 409.

26 FEBRUARY 1888, NEW YORK, TO WILLIAM C. HOWELLS

46 West 9th st.
New York, Feb. 26, 1888.

Dear father—

I received your letter about the house-trade with Willy, and shall be interested to know what you finally decide upon. I think that if Willy feels himself able to meet the interest regularly, it will be the best disposition of the old place, and the pleasantest that you can make.[1]

Elinor and Pilla joined me on Wednesday, and we are now settled, I suppose, till May. It's a great comfort after our wanderings to have even this image of a home. The place is very convenient, and I think we shall get on well. Of course, with John at college, and Winny under treatment,[2] the financial drain is pretty strong; if we were together our present arrangement would be cheap enough. Fortunately, we hear good news from Winny, at last, and with many pull-backs, she seems really getting better.—As yet we've seen very few people, and we have the promise of a quiet time—perhaps the deceitful promise. I wish I could look in on you this pleasant Sunday morning, and see for myself how you're getting on. I hope Henry will continue his good winter life through the year.[3]—I return Annie's charming letter. With love from all to each of you

Your aff'te son
Will.

1. W. C. Howells was considering the sale of a rental property to his grandson, William D. Howells II. In a letter to his father, 14 February 1888 (MH), Howells warned against the problems that might result from selling to a relative. If Willy could not pay the house note, "we could not press him for it, as if he were a stranger." The sale was eventually abandoned, and a house trade was negotiated instead, a development that pleased Howells. He wrote his sister Aurelia on 11 March 1888 (MH) that "father's trade with Willy...seems to me a very good thing on both sides. I hope that the papers will be clearly understood, and carefully

drawn, so that there may be no trouble between kindred from them.... The thing oughtn't to be managed in any sentimental way at all."

2. John was at Harvard and Winifred at Dansville, New York.

3. Henry's good behavior was apparently short-lived. In his 11 March letter to Aurelia, Howells wrote: "I'm sorry Henry's moral improvement doesn't keep pace with his material gain, and that you are having more trouble with the poor fellow." Henry's violence caused bodily harm to his father later that month, according to Howells' letter to his father, 19 March 1888 (MH): "I'm distressed beyond measure at your hurt. How many times have I had a vision of just such an accident to you at Henry's hands! I think that unless you and Aurelia realize that from this time forth there is *no* safety for you but in keeping him *closely confined,—locked up—* he will cause your death."

3 MARCH 1888, NEW YORK, TO GEORGE W. CURTIS

46 West 9th st.,
March 3, 1888.

My dear Curtis—

Your kind note enclosing Pellew's article has come back to me from Buffalo. I thank you for both, though as I told you I had seen the article.[1]

I've known Pellew for three years, and I've never seen him in the state in which too many others seem to have met him. He was in and out of my house familiarly, and was the delight of us all, for from youngest to oldest, we felt his rare quality and his admirable ability and learning, which were almost without alloy of egotism. He has had a hard time since he left college, and discouragement has been, I'm sure, a large element in any temptation to which he has yielded. I don't think he's earned any money except by helping Mr. Jo. Quincy,[2] and at times he has been quite shabby—slovenly he would be in purple; he would get a leg in one sleeve and an arm in another, and rest in absent-minded content. He often came with a single overshoe; I dare say his stockings were as heedlessly put on. But he was always full of high discourse, to which one could not listen without profound respect for his extraordinary mind. Some time ago I tried to find him a niche in the house of our good Brothers,[3] and I didn't conceal what I'd heard to his disadvantage. Perhaps some day you can speak a favoring word for him.—His Woman Suffrage pamphlet is masterly.[4] I must hereafter count myself a believer in the reason as well as the right of women's voting, and I must own that he has persuaded me.

Yours cordially
W. D. Howells.

1. George Pellew (1859–1892), poet and literary critic, wrote "A Word for Mr. Howells" in the Boston *Post*, 27 February 1888. It was a response to an anonymous

letter to the editor, "A Word on Mr. Howells," Boston *Post*, 24 February 1888, in which Howells was criticized for accepting Zola's latest novel, *La Terre*, and for revealing, in his own novels, an insufficient understanding of the New England personality. Pellew defended Howells for "adopting a theory of literary criticism that is closer in agreement with the scientific method than the personal criticism that reflects chiefly the likes and dislikes of the critics."

2. According to Howells' brief biographical sketch "George Pellew," *Cosmopolitan*, September 1892 (reprinted in the "Introduction" to *The Poems of George Pellew* [1893]), after graduation from Harvard in 1880, Pellew spent five years "in quite futile attempts to establish himself in the practice of law." He then went to Ireland and wrote *In Castle and Cabin; or, Talks in Ireland in 1887* (1888), which was read "more in England than here." Pellew had probably been the legal assistant to Josiah Quincy (1859–1919), a Democratic member of the Massachusetts General Court and later a reform-minded legislator who, like Pellew, favored woman suffrage.

3. Harper & Brothers.

4. *Woman and the Commonwealth: or A Question of Expediency* (1888). In the preface to this pamphlet Pellew gave a special word of thanks "to my friend, Mr. Josiah Quincy, of Quincy, who reported the municipal suffrage bill in the last General Court...." Pellew believed that the Municipal Woman Suffrage Bill must be enacted so that the question of woman suffrage could be practically tested.

11 MARCH 1888, NEW YORK, TO HAMLIN GARLAND

> 46 West 9th st.,
> N. Y., March 11, 1888.

Dear Mr. Garland—

I read your criticisms with great interest and respect.[1] I supposed that the social intent of the book—the teaching that *love is not enough in love affairs*, but that there must be parity of ideal, training and disposition, in order to ensure happiness—was only too obvious. I meant to show that an engagement made from mere passion had better be broken, if it does not bear the strain of temperament; every such broken engagement I consider a blessing and an escape.—To infuse, or to declare, more of my personality in a story, would be a mistake, to my thinking: it should rather be the novelist's business to keep out of the way. My work must take its chance with readers. It is written from a sincere sense of the equality of men, and a real trust in them. I can't do more.

I wish I had seen your papers in the *American*—one extract in a newspaper greatly pleased me.[2] "Zury" slipped thro' my fingers—I hardly know how; but sometime I shall get round to it.[3]

> Yours sincerely
> W. D. Howells.

I'm glad of the success of your lectures, as the papers report it.[4]

1. In his review of *April Hopes*, Boston *Evening Transcript*, 1 March 1888, Garland praised Howells' humor and style, but raised the more fundamental question

about the novel's basic intent and purpose. Garland assumed that Howells had written a social satire about the "useless, amiable and purposeless life certain wealthy Americans lead ...." But he complained about the absence of a direct attack on the evils of society: "He takes it for granted that preaching about life is absolutely unnecessary and bad art, and that making a transcript of real life is enough .... Those who know Mr. Howells feel a loss in a book like 'April Hopes,' because he does not allow his strong, fine and tender personality to appear in overt fashion ...." See also *April Hopes*, HE, pp. xxiv–xxv.

2. "Boy Life on the Prairie," *American*, January, March, April, June, July, October 1888.

3. The early chapters of Joseph Kirkland's *Zury, the Meanest Man in Spring County* (1885) describe the poor farm conditions in the Midwest. Howells reviewed this novel in the "Editor's Study," *Harper's Monthly*, June 1888, praising Kirkland for making "it his business to realize for us the character of a man whom early hardship nerved to the acquistion of wealth, and who gave his whole life, up to a certain point, to getting value together ... not because he loved money as the miser does, but because he enjoyed its chase as men do the pursuit of any ambition. This is the modern type, the American type, and Mr. Kirkland has the credit of first putting it in fiction, as far as we know."

4. Garland spoke about the single tax before the Boston Anti-Poverty Society on 22 February 1888. The *Standard*, a single-tax weekly edited by Henry George, noted on 31 March that Garland, vice-president of the society, would speak "to any person or organization who will arrange for meetings."

1 APRIL 1888, NEW YORK, TO WILLIAM C. HOWELLS

46 West 9th st.
N. Y. April 1, 1888.

Dear Father—

I've had your various notes and postals, and am glad you are relieved about Henry and are getting better yourself.[1] I hope it will not be a great while before I shall see you both, for we now intend to take Winny away from Dansville, and I shall be going out after her, and shall then run on to see you.[2] It now seems probable that we shall get the house at Auburndale, and settle ourselves in it, but there's still a hitch.[3] We all like New York a great deal, and I suppose our plans will include 3 or 4 months of the winter here, after this. But we are very fickle, and Winny's a sad problem, which we wish to solve in some way best for her.—Tell Aurelia that I'm within a few chapters of the end of my story;[4] when I come out, I'll bring the MS. to read to you.—We go out very little in N. Y., but a great many people come to see us, and Pilla has a lively, pleasant time. She works faithfully at her drawing, and is greatly interested in it. She and her mother join me in love to you all.

Your aff'te son
Will.

1. See Howells to W. C. Howells, 26 February 1888, n. 3.
2. Howells had written his father on 25 March 1888 (MH): "Winny seems to be much the same. If we can settle ourselves suitably at Auburndale, we shall bring

her home, where we can care for her, and have her with us." Instead, Winifred joined the family in their New York home in early April, and for a brief time Howells was guardedly optimistic. On 15 April (MH) he wrote to his father that "Winny has been very poorly since she came; but yesterday her new doctor seemed to have made a start with her in the right direction. She suffers a good deal of pain always after eating; but her mind exaggerates all her experiences. We hope now for good results."

3. In the letter of 25 March to W. C. Howells, Howells reported that "we can have the stone house at Auburndale, if we like, and . . . I'm having an architect look it over, to see what condition it is." Howells did not buy the Auburndale house, but rented a house in Little Nahant, near Boston, with the hope of restoring Winny's health with the sea air. See Howells to W. C. Howells, 27 May 1888 (MH).

4. *Annie Kilburn.*

5 APRIL 1888, NEW YORK, TO SAMUEL L. CLEMENS

46 West 9th st.,
N. Y. April 5, 1888.

My dear Clemens—

I have read your two essays with thrills almost amounting to yells of satisfaction.[1] It is about the best thing yet said on the subject; but it is strange that you can't get a single newspaper to face the facts of the situation. Here the fools are now all shouting because the Knights of Labor have revenged themselves on the Engineers, and the C. B. & Q. strike is a failure. No one notices how labor has educated itself; no one perceives that *next* time there wont be any revenge or any failure! If ever a public was betrayed by its press, it's ours.[2] No man could safely make himself heard in behalf of the strikers any more than for the anarchists.

By the way have you seen Rev. Kimball yet?[3] When you do, give him my regards.

Yours ever
W. D. Howells.

1. Together with his letter of 31 March 1888 (MH), Clemens sent Howells two papers, "The Knights of Labor—The New Dynasty" and, probably, "Machine Culture." The subject of these papers is summarized in Clemens' cover letter: "The thing which has made Labor great & powerful is Labor-saving machinery—& nothing else in the world could have done it. It has been Labor's savior, benefactor; but Labor doesn't know it, & would ignorantly crucify it. But that is human, & natural. Every great invention takes a livelihood away from 50,000 men—& within ten years *creates* a livelihood for *half a million.* But you can't make Labor appreciate that: he is laboring for *himself*, not the breadless half million that are issuing from his loins." For further details see *Twain-Howells*, pp. 597–99.

2. The firemen and engineers of the Chicago, Burlington, & Quincy Railroad went on strike in March 1888. However, engineers and firemen from Eastern railroads (especially the Reading, whose strike in December 1887 was unsuccessful because of the strike-breaking efforts of the Brotherhood of Locomotive Engineers, the

bargaining agent for the C. B. & Q. strikers) filled the abandoned jobs, not engineers belonging to the Knights of Labor as the newspapers reported, and the strike was ended on 4 April. Howells, a stockholder in the C. B. & Q., wrote an open letter, "Was There Nothing to Arbitrate?" in *Harper's Weekly*, 21 April 1888, advocating arbitration rather than violence in settling the dispute and placing the burden of arriving at a successful resolution on the management of the company.

3. See Howells to W. M. Salter, 25 December 1887, n. 6.

14 APRIL 1888, NEW YORK, TO THOMAS S. PERRY

46 West 9th st.,
New York, April 14, 1888.

Dear Perry:

It's a long time that I've had you on my conscience, and now you're both a duty and a privilege, of which I was freshly reminded, the other day, by getting these *Figaros* from the good Father Fay.[1] I read with some mystification about the decadents; how could I read myself easiest into some knowledge of them? Are they possibly the Next?

We have been two months in New York, in this flat (where you must not address me, but continue to direct c/o Harper's) and I have been trying to catch on to the bigger life of the place. It's immensely interesting, but I don't know whether I shall manage it; I'm now fifty-one, you know. There are lots of interesting young painting and writing fellows, and the place is lordly free, with foreign touches of all kinds all thro' its abounding Americanism: Boston seems of another planet.

I enclose my letter about the Anarchists, which I wrote just before their civic murder.[2] I came to that mind about it through reading their trial, in which they proved themselves absolutely guiltless of the murder charged upon them; but it was predetermined to kill them. They died with unsurpassable courage. Of course I had nothing to do with their opinions, though some of the papers abused me as heartily as if I had proclaimed myself a dynamiter. I wish I could go fully into the subject.

You'll be glad to know that the Adventure book is about printed,[3] and that they will begin taking subscriptions in May. The subscription man is full of hope and energy.

Lowell talked here last night to the Independents,[4] but I couldn't—or didn't—go. I care little for either party. Sometimes I think that if there were a labor party, embodying any practical ideas I would vote with it; but there's none. Very soon, I'm afraid, we shall have trouble with that element, and partly thro' the fault of those who won't deal fairly with it. The C. B. & Q. strike has been badly managed by the road; though you won't hear a hint of this in the press. It is through the forbearance of the Engineers that the road isn't ruined, for they could refuse its cars on every other line.[5]

There isn't much in literature that's new. Pellew's going to have a paper in the *Forum* on fiction.[6] He did a most generous thing by me in a letter to the Boston *Post*,[7] and I think has really turned the tide of contumely, in several places. I'm treated quite decently now.

To-night I go to dine at an Italian place with W. H. Bishop, Boyesen and "Sidney Luska"—a delightful fellow, and a most ardent convert to realism.[8]

I've had two charming letters from Fay, with word from you, and I read with great interest what you said of Tolstoi's play.[9] How I wish I could have seen it!

I hope Mrs. Perry keeps well in the midst of her happiness and usefulness, and that you, dear fellow, are gorging whole libraries without a pang of indigestion.

You'll see James's extraordinary *tour de force* about Stevenson in the *Century* for April.[10] It is really the most remarkable piece of shinning round the question I ever saw. I fancy it was something he was asked to do.

My wrist is played out—not my love.

Yours ever,
W. D. Howells.

1. Mildred Howells notes that the Reverend Hercules Warren Fay was a mutual friend of Howells and Perry. See *Life in Letters*, I, 412. He contributed book reviews and notes, mostly dealing with French literature and theology, to the *Nation*. Fay's "Figaros" may have been back issues of *Figaro: A Political, Literary, and Critical Journal*, which was published in London.

2. See Howells to the Editor of the New York *Tribune*, 4 November 1887.

3. *Library of Universal Adventure by Sea and Land Including Original Narratives and Authentic Stories of Personal Prowess and Peril in All the Waters and Regions of the Globe* was published by Harper & Brothers on 17 May 1888. Howells and Perry compiled and edited the volume.

4. James R. Lowell spoke at Steinway Hall in New York on 13 April to the Reform Club. For a transcription of his speech see the New York *Times*, 14 April 1888.

5. See Howells to Clemens, 5 April 1888, n. 2.

6. George Pellew, "The New Battle of the Books," *Forum*, July 1888. The article, while taking the side of the realists, sought to establish a common bond between the realists and the romanticists, arguing that their aims "when intelligently understood and pursued are identical," although the two schools do "indicate slightly different points of view."

7. Probably "A Word for Mr. Howells." See Howells to Curtis, 3 March 1888, n. 1.

8. "Sidney Luska" was the pseudonym of Henry Harland (1861–1905), a New York editor and novelist. The dinner probably took place at Moretti's, on East 14th Street, which was popular with literary and theatrical people. The restaurant appears as "Maroni's" in *A Hazard of New Fortunes*. See *Twain-Howells*, p. 602.

9. Fay's letters have not been located, but they probably contained a summary of Perry's opinion of Tolstoy's *The Power of Darkness* (1886), which had been banned but was nevertheless produced by the Théâtre Antoine in Paris in 1888.

10. Henry James, "Robert Louis Stevenson," *Century*, April 1888. James praised Stevenson for his "portrayal of the strange, the improbable, the heroic...."

29 APRIL 1888, NEW YORK, TO WILLIAM C. HOWELLS

The Chelsea, 222 W. 23d st
N. Y., April 29, 1888.

Dear father—

We had to leave our apartment in 9th street, which we could only get for two months, and we are here now till we settle ourselves in the country. We want Winny to get all the benefit she can from her present treatment, and we may be in New York the greater part of May. But nothing is settled yet.

This is one of the vast caravanseries which are becoming so common in New York,—ten stories high, and housing six hundred people. We take an apartment of four rooms, and eat in the restaurant. Probably we shall do something of the kind next winter, though there are a great variety of ways of living in N.Y., and all expensive.

I hope you'll be able to replace Martin satisfactorially.[1] Perhaps a good, strong woman would be best; but I've really nothing to suggest. As soon as I can I'll come to see you, but at present I can't fix any time.

All join me in love to you all.

Your aff'te son
Will

1. Martin was probably Henry Howells' attendant and a domestic helper employed by W. C. Howells to protect him against such outbursts of violence on Henry's part as Howells occasionally mentions in his letters. See Howells to W. C. Howells, 26 February 1888, n. 3.

27 MAY 1888, BOSTON, TO MADISON J. CAWEIN

Revere House,
Boston, May 27, 1888.

My dear Mr. Cawein[1]—

Your lovely little book has followed me here from New York with your letter, and I hardly know how to thank you for the gratifying inscription of the volume.[2] My family have been reading it with the delight that your other poems gave, and I expect soon to share their pleasure.

I was greatly touched and interested by what you told me of yourself. Of course I understand your uneasiness in your present situation, and I can't think any relation to a "betting-house" fortunate.[3] But your conscience is in your own keeping, and so long as that is unspotted, you have nothing that ought really to make you unhappy. You have youth, and you have already shown mastery in verse. A life of success is before you, and it is for you to make it beautiful and beneficent or not.

I expect to be near Boston all summer, and I shall always be glad to see you. My address is in care of Harper & Bros., N. Y.

With cordial regard,

Yours sincerely
W. D. Howells.

1. Madison J. Cawein (1865–1914), a Kentucky poet, had been praised by Howells privately in a letter to Cawein, 25 February 1888 (KyLF), and publicly in the "Editor's Study," *Harper's Monthly*, May 1888, for his first volume of poetry, *Blooms of the Berry* (1887). In his review Howells called him a "Western poet" and felt that "there is much that is expressive of the new land as well as of the young life in his richly sensuous, boldly achieved pieces of color." Howells' only qualification was that Cawein's poems are sometimes "enveloped in flavors too cloying for the critical palate...."

2. *The Triumph of Music, and Other Lyrics* (1888), which Howells later reviewed in the "Editor's Study," *Harper's Monthly*, September 1888, again pointing out the similarity between Cawein's poetry and Keats's, and noting "the ripening of qualities felt in his first volume." Cawein had written Howells on 19 May 1888 (MH) that he was sending a copy of his volume of verse, which he dedicated to Howells.

3. In his letter of 19 May, Cawein lamented: "Working as I do—an assistant cashier in a large betting establishment here in Louisville, in other words, in a gambling house, you can imagine what encouragement in associates and surroundings is mine to the encouragement & inspiration of poesy." He longed for a change from his job because he was only able to write poetry "in 'between races' and on 'off days.'"

8 JULY 1888, LITTLE NAHANT, MASSACHUSETTS, TO WILLIAM C. HOWELLS

Little Nahant, July 8, 1888

Dear father—

It's very comforting to hear of your having that useful Mrs. Scott and her boy to help you with Henry, now that he's so bad.[1] No doubt there are drawbacks, but from this distance the arrangement seems ideal. I hope you'll be able to continue it as long as you like. I had Winny out driving today for an hour and a half. We have got her to eating fairly well, but she's still addicted to keeping indoors, and this we have to fight. At the Sanatorium she seems to have been allowed to form every bad habit of invalidism, and now we must break them up by force; it's an awful job, I assure you, and has it's ludicrous as well as sorrowful side.[2]—The rest of the family are well and enjoying themselves greatly in this beautiful place of which the surprise doesn't seem to wear off. I must try to get it sketched by John to show you.—I am satisfied with the Republican ticket,[3] and shall gladly vote it, though I might not, if there were any candidate embodying my hopes of nationalizing the industries, resources and distributions of the country.[4]—I was interested to see that you were president of a Harrison club; I can just remember you in a hunting-shirt in the other Harrison campaign.[5] What shadows we seem when one thinks of such a thing!—All join me in love to you all.

> Your aff'te son
> Will.

1. See Howells to W. C. Howells, 29 April 1888, n. 1.
2. Since Winifred's return to her family from the sanatorium at Dansville, Howells had periodically reported to his father on her gradual improvement. On 17 June (MH) he said that "Winny" is getting slowly, very slowly better; she now sometimes eats without being forced to do so." His letter of 1 July (MH) was even more optimistic: "I have to report a very decided change for the better in Winny's case. Yesterday was the best day she's had; she was up most of the time, and out on the bay for an hour." Winny's condition, however, showed no continued improvement, causing Howells to limit his activities and travel for fear of leaving her alone.
3. Benjamin Harrison (1833–1901), the victor in the 1888 presidential election, was the Republican nominee for president, and Levi P. Morton (1824–1920) was his vice-presidential running mate.
4. At this time Howells was becoming increasingly disenchanted with the traditional political parties. Edward Bellamy wrote him on 17 June 1888 (MH): "What you say about 'nationalist' having occurred to yourself also as a good designation for a party aiming at a national control of industry with the resulting social changes, strongly corroborates my belief that the name is a good one and will take." After Howells moved back to Boston in 1889, he attended meetings of Bellamy's Nationalist Club, whose members, like Howells, believed in the need for a redistribution of the country's wealth. See also Howells to W. C. Howells, 9 November 1890, for Howells' attitude toward political parties.
5. William Henry Harrison (1773–1841) was elected the ninth president of the U.S. in the so-called "log cabin campaign" of 1840.

9 AUGUST 1888, LITTLE NAHANT, MASSACHUSETTS,
TO THOMAS W. HIGGINSON

> Box 311 Lynn, Mass.
> Little Nahant, Aug. 9, 1888.

My dear Higginson:

It's very kind of you to write to me about my story.[1] My wife also blamed it for its grimness, and I have felt a want of texture in it. Of course, one doesn't offer such a thing as completely representative, and the cheerful aspects are not purposely left out; they simply don't come into the scheme so much as the others.

I was wrong to let a New Englander use "fool" adjectively,[2] but I couldn't resist the color it promised to give; it's a tint of my native Southern Ohio parlance.

I have heard cat-birds break out singing at midnight, as if they were singing in their sleep.[3] It didn't seem a completed strain, but a snatch, a fragment. I ought to have given a notion of this.

I've heard my wife talk a thousand times of Dorr Bradley,[4] whom she declares much nicer than Putney. But she says she sees the resemblance. I really had in mind a brilliant man, long dead of drink, whom I knew on the Western Reserve, when a boy: he lent me Macaulay's essays and used to talk literature with me; he was most vividly profane and pyro-technically witty.[5] I wish now I'd reproduced him more perfectly; but I've been sensible, all through this story, of not quite *clicking*. We can't always judge; and I am most sincerely grateful for your good word.

It has been a hard year for my wife and me, wandering about in the health-search for Winny. At last she seems better, but O what a heaviness of the heart still at times!

Why Holden? Where? What?[6]

Yours cordially
W. D. Howells.

1. Higginson commented on the chapters of *Annie Kilburn* in the August *Harper's Monthly*, in a letter to Howells of 7 August 1888 (MH): "Let me say first that the scenes & characters in these chapters seems [sic] to me done in your very best touch. The previous chapters have seemed to me a little less firm in touch & too predominantly *grim*. Here in our little Holden [Massachusetts] there are people of different ages, farming people, whose houses are full of living homely sunshine & who are contented with life, although perhaps poor & even invalids. I wish I could anchor you beside some such people, until you had sketched their life."

2. In the same letter Higginson wrote: "You make Putney use *fool* as an adjective. This is a (vivid) phrase introduced within a few years by the Southern novelists, beginning I think with Miss Murfree, but it seems to me that so essentially local a type as Putney would never have used it." Higginson referred to Putney's mention of the "fool boycottings" in *Annie Kilburn* (1889), p. 120.

3. Higginson also objected to the cat-bird's "wild song" at night in *Annie Kilburn*, p. 143, pointing out that only the night hawk and chirping sparrow occasionally sing at night.

4. Higginson asked Howells in the letter of 7 August: "I wonder if you ever saw Dorr Bradley at Brattleborough—he was not intemperate—but his unceasing fire of wasted brilliancy was like Putney's, & he was in the second generation of brilliant lawyers." Bradley has not been further identified.

5. This companion of Howells' youth has not been identified, but a passage in *Years of My Youth*, HE, p. 77, recalls in general terms the spirited literary talk that took place in the Jefferson printing office.

6. Holden, Massachusetts; see n. 1, above.

30 AUGUST 1888, LITTLE NAHANT, MASSACHUSETTS, TO EDWARD E. HALE

Little Nahant, Aug. 30, 1888.

Dear friend—

It was very, very kind of you to think of writing me about my story, and I needn't tell you I'm glad of your praise.[1] But if you read it to the end you'll see that I solve nothing, except what was solved eighteen centuries ago. The most that I can do is perhaps to set a few people thinking; for as yet I haven't got to *doing* anything, myself. But at present it seems to me that our competitive civilization is a state of warfare and a game of chance, in which each man fights and bets against fearful odds.[2]—Eddy Mead has sent me your paper on Wealth in Common,[3] which I shall read, and I'm anxious to see your books.[4] John will gladly join your Tolstoi club.[5] He's read a great deal of Tolstoi, and has had him much talked into him. Of course, I should like to join, though I suppose I shall be in N. Y. in the winter. I hope to get intimately at that vast mass of life.

We came here on my daughter's account, and after tormenting her all summer upon a theory of treatment, find it probably all a cruel blunder, and are now hoping to get Dr. Mitchell to take her.[6]

Yours cordially,
W. D. Howells.

Box 311 Lynn, Mass.

1. Hale had written Howells on 28 August 1888 (MH): "I write to thank you, from the bottom of my heart for Annie Kilburn: first that you are willing to attack such problems,—and second that the attack is so nice,—so kind,—so direct,—and as I think so successful. Of course I have been interested from the beginning. But now you are fairly at the work [?] we shall all be helped and I think all encouraged— It is a pulpit indeed—to write such a book for a million readers—"

2. Howells' deep concern over the "fearful odds" in the economic game of chance was soon to become the major theme in *A Hazard of New Fortunes* (1890) and *The World of Chance* (1892).

3. "Wealth in Common," *Lend a Hand*, June 1888. In 1889 Edwin D. Mead and Hale coedited the *New England Magazine*; Hale retired from editing the magazine in 1890, but Mead continued as editor until 1901.

4. See Howells to Hale, 28 October 1888, n. 1.

5. See Howells to Hale, 28 June 1887, n. 1. Hale described the Tolstoi Club to Howells in his letter of 28 August: "...I propose to form [the Club] of 15 undergraduates,—15 young men of Boston not in college—and such as they may join:— to choose from time to time new members—always with the view of touching elbows more with the line—and the officers—as men march."

6. Before sending Winifred Howells to Dr. S. Weir Mitchell for treatment in Philadelphia, Howells consulted two doctors in New York in September, but they were probably unable to help. See Howells to W. C. Howells, 18 November 1888.

28 SEPTEMBER 1888, LITTLE NAHANT, MASSACHUSETTS,
TO THOMAS W. HIGGINSON

Little Nahant, Sept. 28, 1888.

My dear Higginson:

Why Tolstoi at second hand when you have him at first?[1] But if you must, nobody could speak better for him than E. E. Hale. As for me, even if I were not suffering *peine forte et dure*[2] with my work, still I would not undertake a task I'm so wholly unfit for. Tolstoi tells us simply to live as Christ bade us, socially and politically, severally and collectively. There's no more of it, but Heaven knows that's enough, and hard enough.

It's very kind of you, and I am

Yours cordially
W. D. Howells.

1. Higginson may have wanted Howells to speak on Tolstoy at a meeting of the Reform Club in Boston.
2. French for "strong and severe pain."

29 SEPTEMBER 1888, LITTLE NAHANT, MASSACHUSETTS,
TO WILLIAM C. HOWELLS

Little Nahant, Sept. 29, 1888.

Dear father—

I sent you a line yesterday, which I suppose is just about reaching you. Elinor and I were six days in New York, and looked at nearly a hundred flats and houses. We had to come off without getting one of either positively; but we're now in treaty for a house, which I suppose we shall get. Every thing that would suit our complicated family was frightfully dear, and we shall not now place ourselves permanently; but the house is large and very sunny.[1]

We expect to be here through October, but if the weather gets much sharper we shall flit sooner.

How I wish I could see you again! Such a brief glimpse![2] I'll do my best to get out again before many months, or perhaps you could come to New York. That wouldn't be so hard as coming to Boston.

My next year's story will go into Harper's Weekly.[3] We've given up the plan of short stories,[4] and I have a scheme for one that I greatly like. I'll tell you of it soon.—I send a lot more English papers.

Love to all from all.

Your aff'te son
Will.

1. The house-hunting was not finished until Howells' next visit to New York, 6–10 October. Before he decided on an apartment at 330 East 17th Street, he wrote to his father on 7 October 1888 (MH): "It's wearing, sickening business; and I watch my money flow as a stuck pig its life-stream. It's horrible to me to spend so much, but I seem bound to it hand and foot. How I envy your simple, quiet righteous life! Someday I should like to write the tragedy of a man trying to escape from his circumstances. It would be funny."

2. Howells had made a brief visit to Jefferson in connection with his trip to the Columbus centennial celebration, 1–10 September.

3. *A Hazard of New Fortunes* appeared serially in *Harper's Weekly*, 23 March– 16 November 1889. The idea for the novel had been germinating for almost a year. See Howells to De Forest, 1 June 1887.

4. Henry M. Alden wrote Howells on 14 September 1888 (MH) that the Harpers were eager to have Howells write a series of New York sketches. Alden quoted from a letter he had received from Joseph W. Harper, Jr.: " 'I[']m quite sure that we could enlist Howells's sympathy, his altruism—in other words, his warm democratic heart in the preparation of a *feuilleton* for the *Weekly* which would be a powerful presentation of the life of our great metropolis, social, educational, economical, political . . . . [¶] Possibly lessons might be drawn from these observations, showing the real assimilation of interests in these diverse classes & occupations of the community, with suggestions for the improvement of society, with the conclusion that one man is as good as another & "a good deal better, too." But I should not make this the avowed object of the series—for the avowal would deter readers.' " The plan for the sketches was abandoned in favor of *A Hazard of New Fortunes*.

10 OCTOBER 1888, LITTLE NAHANT, MASSACHUSETTS, TO HENRY JAMES

Little Nahant, Oct. 10, 1888.

My dear James—

I found your letter here when I came home this morning from a house-hunt in New York. I write at once, or I shall never write, to say that it gave me great joy to know from you that I had given you pleasure. These things needed to be said, and I was glad to say them;[1] I wish I could have said them more at length; and I want to tell you now that I think your Partial Portraits wonderfully good work.[2] It makes all my critical work seem clumsy and uncouth. Surely you were born with the right word in your mouth; you never say the wrong one, any way.— Of course the bestialità will keep being said; but I think there is distinctly a tendency to a better sense of you here, if you really care for the fact. I'm not in a very good humor with "America" myself. It seems to me the most grotesquely illogical thing under the sun; and I suppose I love it less because it wont let me love it more. I should hardly like to trust pen and ink with all the audacity of my social ideas; but after fifty years of optimistic content with "civilization" and its ability to come out all right in the end, I now abhor it, and feel that it is coming out all wrong in the end, unless it bases itself anew on a real equality. Meantime, I wear a fur-lined overcoat, and live in all the luxury my money can buy. This now-ended summer it brought us the use of a wide-verandahed villa on forty acres of seclusion where poor Winny might get a little better possibly. The experiment isn't wholly a failure; but helplessness and anguish still remain for her; and this winter she will go to New York with us, for such doctoring as we can get there. I've found an apartment in two floors, in a huge old house overlooking

Livingstone Place, where we shall dwell in some rooms of rather a European effect. (I have mainly in mind a metal-framed mirror.) I fancy the place would please Gosse, whom kindly tell with my love of our whereabouts. I'm glad he's half one of us, and rather sorry he denies us a great poet; he's a great American poet himself on his mother's side, it seems.[3]

Pillà draws in a life class in New York, and that is one of the larger reasons why we go there. But at the bottom of our wicked hearts we all like New York, and I hope to use some of its vast, gay, shapeless life in my fiction. I suppose our home—such as it is—will be there hereafter in the winter, though we expect always to drift back to this good Boston region for the summer.

Mrs. Howells charges me to say that her heart was in all those words of mine that pleased you; and that she reads no one else with half so much pleasure. Pilla follows you with as much ardor as her mother.—John is a sophomore, weighty and learned, but not literary, and poor Winny hasn't read a book in years.

We all join in love to you.

Yours cordially
W. D. Howells.

1. Howells had bestowed high praise on James's recent short fiction in the "Editor's Study," *Harper's Monthly*, October 1888. "It is in a way discreditable to our time [he wrote] that a writer of such quality should ever have grudging welcome; the fact impeaches not only our intelligence, but our sense of the artistic. It will certainly amaze a future day that such things as his could be done in ours and meet only a feeble and conditioned acceptance from the 'best' criticism, with something little short of ribald insult from the common cry of literary paragraphers." Commenting on "A London Life" and "The Liar," Howells concluded: "There are depths under depths in the subtle penetrations of this story, the surprise of which should not be suffered to cheapen the more superficial but not less brilliant performance in 'The Liar'; for there too is astonishing divination, and a clutch upon the unconscious motives which are scarcely more than impulses, instincts." In a letter of 29 September 1888 (MH) James thanked Howells for his perceptive remarks: "It's really a strange, startling, reviving sensation to be *understood*—I had so completely got used to doing without it.... You have washed me down deliciously with the tepid sponge of your intelligence."

2. James's *Partial Portraits* (1888) was published by Macmillan & Co., London.

3. James had written of Gosse in his letter of 29 September: "He is very intelligent, but *manque de fonds*, & has lately lost his unspeakable father, inherited a little money & discovered the pedigree of his mother—an American, to his extreme surprise, by parentage, & of old Massachusetts *Hancockic* stock: whereat he is much excited." The allusion to Gosse's denying America a great poet refers to his article, "Has America Produced a Poet?" *Forum*, October 1888, which argues that there were no American poets who had attained the stature of the "twelve worthies" of English poetry. Howells responded in the "Editor's Study," *Harper's Monthly*, February 1889, to what he felt was an unconvincing argument.

28 OCTOBER 1888, LITTLE NAHANT, MASSACHUSETTS,
TO EDWARD E. HALE

Little Nahant, Oct. 28, 1888.

My dear Hale—

I am afraid that I am going away to New York for the winter without seeing you, for which I am truly sorry. The summer has been one of worrying work; and of harassing cares for my wife and me with our sick daughter; then there has come with the little leisure much fatigue. I needn't bother you, though, with excuses for what is my own loss; only, don't think me insensible of it.—I read the "Vacations" going out to Ohio, and I take the "Boss" with me.[1] I value all you do in that direction, and admire the charm you give the evident intention. It is work that no one else can do, and it teaches me patience with conditions that I believe wrong, but that must be borne, with all the possible alleviations, till they can be very gradually changed. I do not think there is any final hope of justice under them, but then I know from myself—my own prejudices, passions, follies—that they cannot be bettered except through the unselfishness you enjoin, the immediate altruism dealing with what now is. I know this, while I am persuaded also that the best that is in men, most men, cannot come out till they all have a fair chance. I used to think America gave this; now I don't.—I am neither an example nor an incentive, meanwhile, in my own way of living; I am a creature of the past; only I do believe that I see the light of the future, and that it is this which shows me my ugliness and fatuity and feebleness.—Words, words, words! How to make them things, deeds,—you have the secret of that; with me they only breed more words. At present they are running into another novel,[2] in which I'm going to deal with some mere actualities; but on new ground—New York, namely; though I take some of my characters on from Boston with me. I hardly dare ask you to look me up in any spare moment you may have there; but I am to be found at 330 East 17th st.

Yours sincerely
W. D. Howells.

1. Hale's *Mr. Tangier's Vacations* (1888) is the story of a philanthropic businessman who undertakes the improvement of the social and economic life of a rural village by bringing all of its inhabitants into closer social intercourse. *My Friend the Boss* (1888) documents the rise of John Fisher, a successful manufacturer who has risen through the ranks, and contributes much of his time and money to the improvement of his community.
2. *A Hazard of New Fortunes.*

330 East 17th st.,
New York, Nov. 6, 1888.

Dear Mr. Garland:

I feel a good deal like the clergyman who had preached a sermon against Atheism and was complimented on it by a parishioner, who added, "But, parson; I do believe there *is* a God."

Annie Kilburn is from first to last a cry for *justice*, not *alms*; in Peck's failure and death, even, it is that; and you and the Standard coolly ask me why I do not insist upon justice instead of alms.[1] Really, I hope you will read the story in justice, if not alms to the friendless author. Read Mr. Peck's sermon.[2] It could hardly have been expected that he should preach the single tax; but short of that what more could you have?

Yours sincerely,
W. D. Howells.

1. Garland's comments on *Annie Kilburn* may have been in a letter to Howells, now lost; but the author of the column "Current Thought" in the *Standard*, 3 November 1888, wrote: "What Mr. Howells apparently does not see at all, and what the great Russian [Tolstoy] whom he follows sees but dimly is this: That the problem fronting humanity is, not how to do *good* to the poor, but how to do justice to them, and give them a chance to do good to themselves. The poor suffer because society robs them. What the men who would reform society have to do is simply to put a stop to the robbery. And for this end the rich man can work as efficiently as the poor man if he only will." Garland apparently took Howells' advice that he reconsider his interpretation of *Annie Kilburn*. In a review for the Boston *Transcript*, 27 December 1888, he pointedly counters the charge made by the *Standard* reviewer, citing, as Howells did, the portrayal of Peck's failed Tolstoy-like idealism. Garland singles out Dr. Morrell's pragmatic appraisal of the "dreamer" Peck, concluding that "This shrewd comment upon the doctrine Tolstoï has made famous is commended to those who think Mr. Howells capable of being a blind follower of any man."

2. In *Annie Kilburn*, chapter 22, the Reverend Mr. Peck preaches social justice to his congregation: "the instinct of righteous shame which . . . stirs in every honest man's heart when his superfluity is confronted with another's destitution, and which is destined to increase in power till it becomes the social as well as the individual conscience. Then, in the truly Christian state, there shall be no more asking and no more giving, no more gratitude and no more merit, no more charity, but only and evermore justice; all shall share alike, and want and luxury and killing toil and heartless indolence shall all cease together."

18 November 1888, New York, to William C. Howells

330 East 17th st.,
Nov. 18, 1888.

Dear father:

We are about to send Winny to Dr. Weir Mitchell, who had offered to take her three years ago. I go on with her to Philadelphia tomorrow; and I feel that we are making a last effort for her cure, for if he cannot help her, I don't know who can. Of course, we have come to this only thro' the entire failure of our experiment. She has fairly baffled us, and has almost worn her mother out. There are some proofs that she suffers little or no pain, but she manages to work upon our sympathy so that we are powerless to carry out our plans for her good.—It will be a fearfully costly experiment,—perhaps $2000 in all—but we *must* make it, or else let her slide into dementia and death. Of course we are glad that Mitchell will even try to do anything for her, but we are not very hopeful.[1]

To-day I met Hinton on Broadway, and had a moment's chat with him. His beard is white, and he is poor, but he had the old sweetness, and I liked him for his affectionate inquiries about you.[2] He had not heard of Victoria's death and was deeply touched by it. He wanted me to tell you so.—His wife was with him—not the one I saw last.

I'm glad you enjoy the books, and you can give Willy[3] some, if you choose. But they were primarily for you. I remember his asking me for books when I saw him last.

All join me in love to you all.

Your aff'te son
Will.

1. Howells reaffirmed his faith in Mitchell and described his treatment of Winny in a letter to W. C. Howells of 25 November 1888 (MH): "Rest, utter and profound, without the torturing stress to any sort of exertion or responsibility, is what she needs, and what she will be given. If you could once see Dr. Mitchell, you would see how he differed from all other specialists, and would not have a doubt but she was in the best and wisest and kindest hands in the world. He did not conceal from me that he thought it a very difficult case; her hypochondriacal illusions and obstinacy in her physiological theories complicate it badly; but everything that can be done will be done...." In another letter to his father, dated 2 December 1888 (MH), Howells reported on Winifred's progress, of which he had been informed during a luncheon meeting with Mitchell in New York on 30 November: "He told me that his hope was in Winny's condition being hysterical, and destined to change when her body and brain were nourished. His feeding is for this end, and he will of course keep it up, whether she consents or not. It has already come to a tussle of wills, and he believes that as soon as she finds that he is absolutely unyielding, she will give in."

2. Richard J. Hinton, whom Howells first met in 1861, was associated with several newspapers in New York, Washington, D. C., and San Francisco. Howells

published Hinton's essay "Organization of Labor: Its Aggressive Phases" in the *Atlantic*, May 1871, while he was editor of that magazine. For an account of Hinton's relationship with the Howells family, see Clara and Rudolf Kirk, " 'The Howells Family' by Richard J. Hinton," *Journal of the Rutgers University Library* 14 (1950), 14–23.

3. William D. Howells II.

23 NOVEMBER 1888, NEW YORK,
TO THE EDITOR OF THE NEW YORK *Sun*

I.

Sir:[1]

I have been of course interested in the two articles which you have printed this week on my "socialism", supposed or actual.[2] But that question does not seem to me of prime importance, and I am moved now to write you chiefly because I wish respectfully to dissent from a position in your second article which I think not only untenable but very regrettable in a director of public opinion. I mean that passage in which you say that the courts having dealt with the case of the Anarchists, all legitimate discussion of it ceased.

Since when were courts infallible? I am old enough to remember a decision of even the Supreme Court of the United States (in the case of Dred Scott)[3] which provoked the dissent of a good half, at least, of the American people; and I recall with still greater distinctness the discussion of the John Brown case after the court had dealt with it. Was this discussion legitimate, or not?

It must be evident to you upon reflection that nothing is final in human affairs; and that as soon as any legal decision is rendered, the question of its righteousness begins. In this very case of the Anarchists it began in all the newspapers; and it seems to me that I had the same right to declare it unjust that the newspapers used to declare it just. The laws are made not only for judges to expound, but for every common man like me to understand for himself; or else they are a cruel mockery. Above the Courts is Justice as Christ is above the Churches, and both speak directly to something God put in us to make us know them, and enable us to judge the Courts and the Churches. I honor the Courts and the Churches; but when I must surrender my reason to a Judge, I will give my conscience to a Priest.

II.

Will you excuse me if I venture to dissent from another position of yours? You say that I was among the "sentimentalists" who petitioned the Governor of Illinois for mercy to the condemned Anarchists. I own with joy that I was of those who did so ask mercy; but I cannot consent to be called a sentimentalist for that reason. Ex-Senator Lyman Trumbull of Illinois and the eminent journalist Henry D. Lloyd were of them, too, as well as attorneys like Ingolf Boyesen, and three or four judges of Chicago Courts.[4] Do you call such men sentimentalists; and if you do, why? Did they ask mercy because they were sentimentalists, or did they become sentimentalists by virtue of that act?

If neither, then from which of my books do you infer that *I* am a sentimentalist? You are so good as to say that you hold me in affection and esteem; you add even stronger expressions of regard: at the same time you call me a novelist of the watering-place piazza, and you say that I hold sentimentally the theories you attribute to me. You must see that all this is a little confusing. I am used by this time to being called hard names by those who hate my way of writing novels; but if *you* like me and respect me, why do you treat me with contempt?

III

I must refuse to believe that I am a sentimentalist because I am a novelist. That might have been true of the novelist in times past; but it is not true of any modern-minded novelist; it is not true even of me, I think, for if my trade has taught me anything it has taught me to abhor sentimentality: the sentimentality which lusts for blood, and cries out for an "example", as well as the other kinds.

V.

When it comes to my "socialism" are you quite sure of your facts? Are you sure of any facts beyond my well-known admiration for Tolstoi as a man and an artist, and of my respectful attitude towards the books of Laurence Gronland? I might easily have abused them; but I had not the conscience to do so, for they seemed to me the work of an honest man who wished well and not ill to other men.

Socialism, as I understand it, is not a positive but a comparative thing; it is a question of more or less in what we have already, and not a question of absolute difference. Every citizen of a civilized State is a socialist. You are yourself a socialist, if you believe that the postal department, the public schools, the insane asylums, the almshouses are good things; and that when a railroad management has muddled away in hopeless ruin the money of all who trusted it, a Railroad Receiver is a good thing. If I believe that the postal savings-banks as they have them in England; and national life-insurance as they have it in Germany, are good things, I differ from you in degree, not in kind; and even the socialist who wishes to see the whole of commerce and production in the hands of the State, (with us, the people) differs from you in degree and not in kind. The Treasury Department now does its own printing. If the War Department did its own tailoring, and employed poor women to make army uniforms at a living wage instead of giving the job for contractors, to fatten on, it would be exactly the same thing in kind; and why should you think it so very bad?

VI.

I will close this little appeal to your sense of justice, with a story. It is a true story, and as we realists say, palpitant.

Yesterday afternoon, I went out to walk on the Avenue—not Fifth, but Third,—and I saw a decently dressed man stoop and pick up from the pavement a dirty bit of cake or biscuit, which he crammed into his mouth and greedily devoured. Then I saw this man go along the curb-stone, and search the garbage of the gutters like a famished dog for something more to eat. Being a sentimentalist, a promoter of bloody riot, a watering place piazza novelist and what else you like, the sight made me sick, sick at heart; and after I had got by a little I went back, and made shift between the poverty of the man's English and my French, to know his need, and gave him some money. It was not much, it was very little; but he caught my hand between his work-hardened palms, and clung to it, and broke down, and cried there on the street in the most indecent manner. For me, I went away sorrowful, not because there were not places enough for that hapless wretch to go to, for charity if he could find them, but because the conditions in which he came to such a strait seemed to me Christless, after eighteen hundred years of Christ.

I thought how in a truly Christian community there would have been a bureau of labor to which he could have gone for *work*,—not alms—and by which, if there were no work here, he would have been sent to any point in our borders where there was work.[5]

This was a piece of my "socialism," I suppose. Even then I had read your first article, and I knew that there must be some occult connection between my "sentimentality" and the throwing of dynamite bombs; and that I, who deplore all violence and think that every drop of human blood shed in a good cause helps to make a bad one, must somehow be playing into the hands of the most murderous minded criminals. But for your reasoning on the subject I should have supposed that the whole tenor of my literature and my life was counter to disorder of all kinds, and especially to disorder that in a free country applies the theories and methods of those who struggle against a despotism. I hope there will be some who will think it superfluous for me to have said this even in reply to your reasoning.

W. D. Howells.

1. The many internal revisions, the inconsistency of the sectional numbering, and the fact that the manuscript is among the Howells papers at Harvard suggest that this is the draft of a letter that was never sent.

2. The articles have not been located.

3. Dred Scott, an escaped slave, was denied his freedom by the Supreme Court in its decision of 6 March 1857, in *Scott vs. Sanford*, a decision that declared the Missouri Compromise to be unconstitutional.

4. Lyman Trumbull (1813–1896) was a U.S. senator from Illinois (1855–1873); Ingolf R. Boyesen, younger brother of Hjalmar H. Boyesen, was a prominent Chicago attorney; Judges Tuley, Moran, Booth, McAlister, and Baker signed a petition for the commutation of the anarchists' sentences.

5. Howells expanded on his charitable experiences with indigents, deadbeats, and others, his ambivalent attitude toward the practice of giving, and some of the problems which confronted him in his philanthropy in "Tribulations of a Cheerful Giver," in *Impressions and Experiences* (1896).

7 DECEMBER 1888, NEW YORK, TO THEODORA SEDGWICK

330 East 17th st.,
N. Y. Dec. 7, 1888.

Dear Miss Theodora:[1]

Your kind note touched Mrs. Howells and myself in a tender place by its reference to old days in Cambridge—young days, and very happy ones for us. I suppose it's because we can't go back to all of that Cambridge that we do not go back to any of it. What a circle it was: Longfellow, Lowell, the Jameses, Mr. Norton, Agassiz, Dana, Prof. Child—centuries may not bring its like again. That time is particularly associated in my mind with your Aunts Ashburner,[2] and all the lovely hospitalities of their house. I was so sorry to see none of you when I called. Will you give them our love? And tell them that no kindness of those they ever showed us has been forgotten.

You know perhaps that we've sent poor Winny to Dr. Weir Mitchell at last, as we ought to have done at first. He thinks she is doing well, and gaining strength, but he could not tell me the case was an easy one.

Pillà is well, and much absorbed in her drawing with Abbott Thayer.[3] He praises her work, and that makes us as happy as people of fifty have any right to be.—I'm at work on a new story,[4] into which I'm loosely weaving the thoughts that New York makes me think. There's always pleasure in work, but sometimes I feel that it's gone on a good while.

Mrs. Howells and Pillà join me in best regards.

Yours sincerely
W. D. Howells.

1. Theodora Sedgwick was C. E. Norton's sister-in-law; her "note" to Howells, which this letter answers, has not been located.

2. Anne and Grace Ashburner.

3. Abbott Thayer (1849–1921) was an American painter of portraits and ideal figures.

4. *A Hazard of New Fortunes.*

16 DECEMBER 1888, NEW YORK, TO JOHN G. WHITTIER

330 East 17th st.,
New York, Dec. 16, 1888.

Dear Mr. Whittier:

A letter from Boston printed in the Tribune of this morning represents you as saying to an interviewer that I asked you to join me in "protesting" against the execution of the Anarchists at Chicago, and that you supposed my admiration of Tolstoi caused me "to take an interest in those creatures."[1]

I am sure that you would not wish me to rest under the injustice which I feel this does me, without bringing my sense of it to your knowledge. What I asked you to do was to join me in petitioning the governor to commute the mens' sentence, and in urging you to this I gave as my reason that I did not think they had been fairly tried. You thought they had, and you refused, in terms of the greatest kindness to myself. In making our correspondence the subject of comment, I can only regret now that you should not have remembered the real nature of my appeal to you and the ground for it.[2]

Yours sincerely
W. D. Howells.

1. In an article entitled "Mr. Whittier's Opinions," New York *Tribune*, 16 December 1888, Whittier was quoted as having remarked that Howells had asked him to protest the execution of the Chicago anarchists in 1887, but he refused. Whittier's reasons for refusing quoted in the *Tribune* are almost verbatim those stated in Whittier's letter to Howells, 21 September 1887 (MH). See Howells to Whittier, 1 November 1887, n. 1.

2. Whittier responded somewhat apologetically to Howells in a letter of 19 December 1888 (MH; John B. Pickard, ed., *Letters of John Greenleaf Whittier* [Cambridge, Mass.: Harvard University Press, Belknap Press, 1975), III, 735–36), stating the facts surrounding Howells' plea for Whittier's intercession on behalf of the anarchists as he recalled them and elaborating on his session with the reporters: "In conversing with the writer of the [*Tribune*] letter, I think I said that I supposed thee thought that the extreme penalty of death might cause the victims to be regarded as martyrs; and I mentioned that thy interest in Count Tolstoi's nonresistance views, with which I have much sympathy myself, may have influenced thee in this case. [¶] The writer of the Tribune letter is a truthful and honorable gentleman, and if his version of the matter is incorrect it is doubtless owing to a lack of explicitness on my part in a desultory conversation. [¶] Our relations as authors and friends have been too intimate and pleasant to allow

me to even unintentionally misrepresent thee. I would be the last person to believe that the crime charged upon the accused persons is less deetestable [sic] and awful to thee than to myself."

23 DECEMBER 1888, NEW YORK, TO WILLIAM C. HOWELLS

330 East 17th st.,
Dec. 23, 1888.

Dear father:

We have John with us again,—for the day only. To-morrow he goes to Philadelphia, and so on round the circle to Chicago and back to Boston. I enclose the programme of the concert his fellows gave last night; the audience was immense, and very fashionable.[1] John bore himself finely, and played well. He is such a dear boy, and so loving to us; there was a swell reception for the clubs after the concert, but he did not care to go; he came and spent the evening with us.—I will see if he can stop off to see you, but I'm afraid it can't be managed.

I don't wonder you ask how far I could carry a sequel to Their Wedding Journey, but that is not really the plan of the new story. Basil March simply comes to New York in charge of a literary enter- prise, and the fortunes of this periodical form the plot, such as there is.[2] I've written 500 pp., and hope to have 800 done before I begin printing. It will be my longest story, I think.

—John has just come in, and says he doesn't know which way they're coming from Chicago. If it's by the L. S. & M. S.[3] he may be able to stop, and will gladly do so, if he can. But don't expect him.—Dr. Mitchell lunched with us Thursday. He says Winny has gained ten pounds, but she still very obstinate in her delusions though she doesn't fight the feeding, now. On the whole he is very hopeful. We unite in love to you all.

Your aff'te son,
Will.

1. John Howells was most likely on tour with the Harvard Glee and Banjo Clubs. The clubs gave a concert in Cambridge on 21 December, in New York at Chickering Hall on 22 December, in Philadelphia on 24 December, and in Chicago on 29 December.
2. March, in *A Hazard of New Fortunes,* moved from Boston to New York to edit *Every Other Week* magazine.
3. The Lake Shore & Michigan South Railroad.

10 JANUARY 1889, NEW YORK, TO THOMAS B. ALDRICH

330 East 17th st.,
N. Y. Jan. 10, 1889.

My dear Aldrich:

Don't you want to order a little paper or something about something or other from W. H. Bishop, who is now in Paris?[1] Art, I fancy, might be his best hold. I happen indirectly to know that an increase of family has brought him a disproportionate decrease of fortune—the decrease is as triplets to twins. Of course, this is necessarily very confidential, and I write only in the hope that you may be really wanting something from Bishop, but had n't thought of it. *If* you should, and will send me the money I'll forward it to him.

Yours ever
W. D. Howells.

P. S. Of course you ought to be free even of my knowledge whether you act on my suggestion or not. So I open this, to say that Bishop's address is 38 Duquesne Avenue, Paris, and if you have anything to say you can write him directly.

1. William Henry Bishop lived in France until 1893, when he returned to America to accept an instructorship of modern languages at Yale. While in Paris, Bishop's wife gave birth to their older son, Duquesne. Aldrich published Bishop's "A Paris Exhibition in Dishabille," *Atlantic*, May 1889.

13 JANUARY 1889, NEW YORK, TO WILLIAM C. HOWELLS

New York, Jan. 13, 1889.

Dear father—

I wrote to Aurelia[1] in reply to her letter about the box of clothes, which I think she distributed very wisely and generously. I am sorry she had to be troubled about them.—I have not much news. President Hayes has been in town, and spent two evenings with us.[2] He talked of Harrison whose ability he rated very high. He laughed at the rumor that he was going into the cabinet.[3]—Friday night I went to a Socialist meeting, of the American Section. It was as quiet and orderly as a Sunday School, and people whom the reporters represent as violent conspirators were poorly dressed, well behaved listeners to a lecture which dealt patiently with hard facts. The lecturer told them that the way to national control of business was already opened by the great "trusts." One gets life in curious slices in N. Y. Friday afternoon I went to two fashionable teas, as a preparation for this Socialist meeting. One very rich young fellow, whose family has a house at Newport, is a member of this "Section."

We hear good news from Winny.[4]

With love to all from all,

> Your aff'te son
> Will.

1. Howells to Aurelia Howells, 7 January 1889 (MH).

2. According to Hayes's diary entry of 6 January 1889, he visited Howells that evening, but the date of his second visit to Howells is unknown. See Charles R. Williams, ed., *Diary and Letters of Rutherford Birchard Hayes* (Columbus: Ohio State Archaeological and Historical Society, 1925), IV, 434.

3. While Hayes sought no position in Benjamin Harrison's administration, some observers may have felt that he was being considered for one because of his frequent correspondence with Harrison. In fact, however, Hayes only acted as counsel to Harrison in helping him select his cabinet officers.

4. Howells had written his father on 6 January 1889 (MH): "Dr. Mitchell was here yesterday, and spoke very hopefully of Winny. From 58 she has gone up to 71 lbs., and she gains every day. When she has 10 or 12 lbs. more he will get her out of bed, and perhaps send her to the seaside. She is still very stubborn, and has to be forced along the path to health with a very firm hand, which fortunately he has. There is none of the Dansville sentimentality in the business; she would instantly take advantage of that."

27 JANUARY 1889, NEW YORK, TO RICHARD H. NEWTON

> 330 East 17th St.
> Jan'y 27, 1889

Dear Mr. Newton[1]—

I heard you today with unspeakable satisfaction, and with such unflagging interest as I have never before bro't to any public discourse. Surely such words as yours must have weight at last with those that heard you; I found myself wishing to know how many they put to shame (as they did me) for the comfort we dare to take while there is a hopeless want in the world. I thank you for my share of the humiliation. Some time I should like to "tell my experience"—my religious, my economic experience; for it is that, rather. It seems a strange thing that I should once have been wholly deaf and blind to such truth as you preached today, such gospel.

I wish I might come next Sunday to hear you; but I shall not be able to do so. I hope your sermons on the Incarnation will be printed, and then I can read them; but I must not let you infer that my interest is that of one inside of any creed. (I've a dread of not always being outright about this.) What you said in the pulpit and in your note has given the great subject fresh attraction for me. Of course, in a loose and stumbling way I've thought about it, and from my early instruction in Swedenborgianism—I've had some doctrine concerning it.

—I sent the "Italian Poets" to the church, not knowing your home address. I don't feel that the point in Arnaldo da Brescia is important;[2] it surely struck me as curious.

Yours sincerely
W. D. Howells.

1. Richard Heber Newton (1840–1914), pastor of All Souls' Episcopal Church in New York (1869–1902), was considered the foremost liberal preacher in his denomination and was most interested in civic and labor questions as well as spiritualism, psychic research, and evolutionary science. His sermon topic on 27 January was "Is Poverty Providential or Perpetual?" Newton claimed that poverty could be reduced by man's working with God: "Back of every human effort to discover truth, to mitigate the evils of life, to reform the wrongs of society, to help individual men to a truer manhood, the world to a truer social order... is the Infinite and Eternal Energy, God Himself." See New York *Times*, 28 January 1889.

2. In the chapter on Giambattista Niccolina in *Modern Italian Poets* Howells discusses *Arnaldo de Brescia* (1843), Niccolina's tragedy in which the social ideas of the Roman Catholic Church are criticized.

15 FEBRUARY 1889, NEW YORK, TO HAMLIN GARLAND

330 East 17th st.,
Feb'y 15, 1889.

My dear Garland:

I shall be very glad to submit to the Harpers anything you get ready, and I'm sure they will give your work attention.[1]

—I'm afraid I never wrote to say what an excellent notion your N. E. Conservatory professorship seemed.[2] I'm working very hard on my story—"A Hazard of New Fortunes"—and I forget some things: perhaps I *did* write to you; it was strongly in my mind at the time your letter came. I haven't met any of your George friends,[3] personally yet. Do you know George De Forest Brush, the painter?[4] He's a burning Georgian, and has a George Sunday school, where he preaches the doctrine. He's a wonderfully good painter, too.

Yours sincerely
W. D. Howells.

1. *Harper's Weekly* published two stories by Garland in 1889, "Under the Lion's Paw" (7 September) and "Old Sid's Christmas" (28 December).

2. From 1885 to 1891 Garland lectured intermittently at both the Boston School of Oratory and at the home of Mrs. J. Wentworth Payson. He possibly envisioned establishing a professorship at the New England Conservatory of Music, which would enable him to speak on both literary and social topics.

3. See Howells to Garland, 15 January 1888, n. 4.

4. George De Forest Brush (1855–1941) was an American artist, who won the first Hallgarten Prize in 1888. Howells may have met him on 3 January 1887, at the organizational dinner of a new social club, whose members were to represent literature, art, music, science, medicine, architecture, and law. Brush was a member of this club. See Augustus Saint-Gaudens to Howells, 30 December 1886 (MH). There is one extant letter from Brush to Howells, bearing only a 4 March date but no year (MH), in which Brush invited Howells to his studio in New York.

24 FEBRUARY 1889, NEW YORK, TO EDMUND W. GOSSE

330 East 17th st.,
N. Y. Feb'y 24, 1889.

My dear Gosse:

I was perfectly delighted to get your lovely note,[1] and I immediately went to the expense of the February Fortnightly—pirated edition—so as to see what you had said of me. It was richly worth the money; and I am very proud and thankful. I have to take my humility in both hands in order to keep a place so far above the salt. I'm especially obliged to you for writing about Ibsen just now, and for being what Mrs. Howells calls so informatory, for we've just been reading his wonderful plays, and wanted to know all about him. Perry tells me (from Paris) that there's a regular Ibsen boom in Germany. No, black care has not left so much laugh in me as there used to be, but I don't abide your being less gay so patiently. Our poor Winny is a wreck of health and youth—sick for years yet to come, I'm afraid. John is in Harvard, a Sophomore, and Pillà is here with us studying art. She was lately at Boston, where she almost danced herself dead, and has been slowly resuscitating since she came home. She is nearly seventeen and I nearer fifty-two. Doesn't it seem absurd for a contemporary to have got past the half century in that way? I never can make it seem right. They celebrated Lowell's 70th birthday at the Tavern Club on the 22d.[2]—When we lived in Cambridge, an old gentleman came 80, and a lady sent him 80 English violets. These graceful acts console us for the loss of youth.

Our principle is against going out, and Mrs. Howells really doesn't, but she drives me forth, and acquires merit with her own conscience while she stores up a just contempt for my inconsistency. In this way I see a good deal of society. Every body has an evening, and as there are about 1,500,000 people in New York, you can imagine how many evenings there are in a week. For instance this is Stedman's evening, and so is it Huttons.[3] I ought to go both, but I shall not. Which would *you* go to?—I suppose if I were not old and sore and sad I should like life here. It's very simple and irresponsible, and hell seems farther than at Boston, because people agree not to think about it.—I wonder if you'll care to read my N. Y. story that's coming out in Harpers Weekly soon?[4]

The family join me in love to both you. Farewell. Drop a giggle now and then to the thought of

Your faithful
W. D. Howells.

1. Gosse wrote Howells on 30 January 1889 (MH; *Transatlantic Dialogue*, p. 212): "I take your good, gracious and kindly words in February's *Harper* as a personal greeting. Oddly enough in January's *Fortnightly* I permitted myself a little friendly word about you." For Howells' comments on Gosse in the February "Editor's Study," see Howells to James, 10 October 1888, n. 3. Gosse's essay, "Ibsen's Social Dramas," *Fortnightly Review*, January 1889, contains only a brief mention of Howells.

2. The banquet was held in Boston at the Carrolton Hotel.

3. Edmund C. Stedman and Laurence Hutton.

4. *A Hazard of New Fortunes.*

4 MARCH 1889, NEW YORK, TO WILLIAM C. HOWELLS

New York, March 4, 1889.

Dear father—

I telegraphed you yesterday that our poor suffering girl had ceased to suffer.[1] It was Saturday evening, at Merchantville, near Philadelphia, from a sudden failure of the heart. The funeral will be from Dr. Mackenzie's church in Cambridge,[2] to-morrow at 2 o'clock.

Sometime I will try to tell you more. "Her Angel doth always behold the Face of our father."[3]

With love to all from our broken hearts,

Your aff'te son,
Will.

She loved you dearly, and Aurelia

1. Winifred Howells died on 2 March. Howells asked Horace E. Scudder in a letter of 3 March 1889 (MH) to have the sexton at Dr. McKenzie's church receive Winny's remains upon arrival in Boston and to select her burial plot in the Cambridge Cemetery.

2. Alexander McKenzie (1830–1914) was pastor of the First Church of Cambridge (1867–1910). During this period he also lectured at Harvard and became secretary of the Harvard Alumni. While Howells was editor of the *Atlantic*, he published McKenzie's article "Washington in Cambridge," July 1875.

3. The source of this quotation has not been identified.

7 MARCH 1889, BOSTON, TO S. WEIR MITCHELL

Boston, March 7, 1889.

Dear Dr. Mitchell:

I must not let your kind letter and that of your son go unanswered longer.[1] They brought us the sad satisfaction of knowing that the end which came so suddenly must have come soon at the best, and we are almost happy to be assured that it was not through any error or want of skill; though this was what we believed from the first. The torment that remains is that perhaps the poor child's pain was all along as great as she fancied, if she was so diseased, as apparently she was;[2] and that homesickness was added when she had to leave you.

When we see you, as we hope to do the next time you come to New York, perhaps you can reassure us on these points.

You may like to know that our dear girl's funeral was attended in Cambridge by those who had loved her in her innocent and joyous childhood, and that Lowell followed her dust to where it shall return to the dust of the common death, the common life.

All now is over, and my wife and I are united in recognizing the devoted efforts you made, in your great science, to give her back strong and well. Her death does not change our sense of this.

With my regards to your son,

Yours sincerely
W. D. Howells.

1. Neither letter has been located. Mitchell's older son was named John Kearsley Mitchell.
2. Evidently Mitchell's autopsy of Winifred revealed an organic malady. See also Cady, *Howells*, II, 98, and Lynn, *Howells*, p. 298.

10 MARCH 1889, BOSTON, TO WILLIAM C. HOWELLS

Boston, March 10, 1889.

Dear father—

Winny's funeral was on Tuesday afternoon, in the chapel of the church in Cambridge, where she used to come to Sunday School. All her old friends and ours were there: Lowell, Norton and his children, Aldrich, Scudder, the Shalers, Mrs. Child, the Allyns;[1] and the rest. The coffin was covered with flowers, and under these lay the sweetest and frailest flower of all, broken away forever from our earthly life and love. Our dear child looked very noble and beautiful in death, very calm and resigned; but we all felt that it was only an image of her. Sometime, I will tell you all; I can't, now.—Elinor went back to New York yesterday with John and Pilla; and I have staid to see the sweet image of our Winny laid in the ground.

> "Lie gently on her bosom, mother Earth!
> Her little foot was ever light on thee."[2]

I feel as if she were a child again; and since our loss we have learned that in some things she was indeed never otherwise. Only the exquisite Mind, strong and clear, so that what she said and wrote, astonished me by its perfection, found its development in the delicate framework of her earthly being.

With dearest love to you all,

Your affectionate son,
Will.

1. The Allyns have not been identified.
2. The source of this quotation has not been identified.

22 MARCH 1889, NEW YORK, TO WILLIAM C. HOWELLS

New York, March 22, 1889.

Dear father—

I hardly know how to begin my letter, and I can confess without wounding you that I find it a sore burden to write. You know there can be but one thing in my mind. Elinor and I talk it over continually, and when I am alone I recall and reclaim all I did, and reconstruct the past from this point or that, and dramatize a different course of events in which our dearest one still lives. It is anguish, anguish that rends the heart and brain; but you can understand how inevitable it is. It must go on, I suppose, till the futile impulse wears itself out. Elinor and I now feel, as we never did before, the comfort you must have in having still kept your afflicted child with you. Of course, we believed we were sending ours to get well; her death was a thought that never occurred to us, and apparently never occurred to others.[1]

I am going on tonight to try to find a house near Boston; but I expect to be home Wednesday morning. I have written somewhat during the past week; but my head feels very weak.

I wonder if Joe ever got the letter I wrote him care of the Wolters'?[2] In his last he does not speak as if he intended to come here at all. I don't quite understand. Of course I would be most glad to see him, and so would Elinor. All join me in love to you all.

Your aff'te son,
Will.

1. Elinor Howells apparently had to be persuaded by her husband to send Winifred to S. Weir Mitchell for treatment. In a letter to W. C. Howells, 17 March 1889 (MH), Howells said: "...I must tell you how bravely Elinor has borne it [Winny's death], with always a first thought for me in her own anguish. This is the more generous in her because she yielded to me in all the details of this last attempt to restore Winny to health. It is forever too late, now, to undo any part of it, and I can only console myself by thinking of the absolute confidence I had in what was known to me as the highest skill and greatest experience."

2. In a letter to Aurelia, 25 November 1900 (MH), Howells mentioned a "Cousin Mary Wolter" and her husband; but who they were and whether they are the Wolters (or Walters) mentioned here is not known.

5 APRIL 1889, NEW YORK, TO EDWARD E. HALE

330 East 17th st.,
April 5, 1889.

My dear friend:

I cannot quite tell you how very sweet and good I find it you to have written me, and to have tried to see me. God knows how humbly grateful I should have been for the help that I think I might have got from meeting you. Truly, I feel quite beaten into the dust, from which I do not know how to lift myself. The blow came with terrible suddenness,[1] when we were hoping so much and fearing nothing less than what happened. The most that I can say to myself is that she could not have died out of her time, unless all that exists is a shabby mockery unworthy even humanity. I account for the fact upon this ground, and I am trying, as I can, to imagine her well and happy somewhere. I wish to think of her as not only freed from her long pain, but emancipated from what is clumsy and cruel and uncouth in all earthly conditions. But at the end, I come back sore from head and to foot and grovel in the mere sense of loss. Never to hear, never to see, never to touch, till time shall be no more! How can I bear that? And that is what I must bear. It makes one mass of anguished egotism of me, and shuts me up from all the things outside of myself in which I have been lately interested, so that I do not know how to acknowledge fitly the fact you tell me about the Tolstoi club. But some day I shall be glad of it; and I suppose ashamed of these groans and cries. What you said of your children, those you have and those you have lost, went to my heart.

Yours sincerely
W. D. Howells.

1. Winifred Howells' death on 2 March 1889.

7 APRIL 1889, NEW YORK, TO MONCURE D. CONWAY

330 East 17th st.,
April 7, 1889.

My dear Conway:

I went to see you this afternoon, but when I heard the cheerful voices in your rooms, I had not the courage to go in. I merely wanted to thank you for your loving letter, in which your sorrow touched hands with ours, and helped us through a moment of that which we must bear while we live.[1] It is heavy—crushing—and it does not avail to remember that all must not only die, but must writhe in the anguish of bereavement till the law of death is fulfilled in the last of our poor, bewildered race, for which truly there seems no reason. All the feet that dance must drag bleeding over the way that we are now going. It is a part of Nature; the child of whom you and I talked before she was born[2] could come into the world upon no other condition. Her gentleness, her divine intelligence, the loveliness of her most angelic character, and the beauty of her patient wisdom could not save her from the law. So I suppose the law is not evil. But I do not in the least pretend to more than this, and nothing explains it to me further. If some great being fashioned us to bear what the common lot involves, and tempered us to this hideous strain, how great he must be, merely to have imagined creatures like the mortals he made. I can a little imagine him from them; and as I can conceive of no hate that could have framed a law so dreadful as the law of death, I must believe that Love did it.

Yours ever
W. D. Howells.

1. Conway's letter of condolence has not been located.
2. Conway visited Howells in Venice six months before Winifred's birth. See Howells to Hale, 13 June 1863.

26 APRIL 1889, NEW YORK, TO ALICE JAMES

330 East 17th st.,
N. Y. April 26, 1889.

Dear Miss Alice:[1]

I have not yet had the strength to reply to your brother **Harry's** beautiful letter about Winny;[2] but I must try to send you some word of thanks for yours. It is strange, and not strange, either, that the greatest help and kindness in this bewildering grief of ours, should have come from your father's children; for your brother William said something that more than anything else enabled our hearts to lay hold on faith again, and supplemented with a hint of hope those perfect terms in which Harry had expressed our loss.[3] And now your message, with its memory of another world, completely past, is an intimation that we may somewhere else survive that of today, too, and of all earthly morrows.[4] I cannot tell you with what tenderness I recurred to those Sundays, when you mentioned them, and with what vividness your dear father and mother's presence was with me again.[5] I was greatly privileged to know such a man as he, and things that he said have enriched my life with a meaning that did not all appear in the moment. It consoles and encourages me that such a mind as his held fast to such a belief as his.

Our dear girl is gone—we begin to realize it, to yield, almost to consent. But whether we consent or not, we are helpless. I conjure her back in gleams and glimpses of her old childish self, presently obscured by the sad phantom of the long suffering before the close. It is useless; we shall go to her, but she shall not return to us. This fact has changed the whole import of death and life; they seem at times almost convertible.—I wish I could say something fit about her. I cannot. Only this I say, that she now seems not only the best and gentlest, but one of the wisest souls that ever lived. It is hard to explain; but she was *wise*, and of such a truth that I wonder she could have been my child. Pillà and her mother are well. We shall go to the vicinity of Boston for the summer, to have John with us as long as possible. You know he is now a Harvard Sophomore.

The family join me in love, and in the warmest wishes for your welfare.

Yours sincerely
W. D. Howells.

1. Alice James (1848–1892), the sister of Henry James.
2. In a letter to Howells of 20 March 1889 (MH), Henry James had written: "I *can't* talk of death without seeming to say too much—I think so kindly of it as compared with life—the only thing we *can* compare it to. I remember your grave & tender little Winnie in ... far years of Sacramento St. & small childhood undreaming of later woes. The later woes I have never ventured to speak to you of—they were *un*talkable—& I know they were for you a perpetual fountain of pain. When a man loses a loved child everything that is most tender in him must be infinitely lacerated: yet I hope there is a sort of joy for both of you in the complete extinction of so much suffering—to be young & gentle & do no harm, & only to pay for it as if it were a crime—I *do* thank heaven, my dear Howells, both for your wife & yourself, that *that is* over."
3. William James wrote Howells on 11 March 1889 (MH): "she's saved no doubt from many a harrowing year of invalidism here below, and her form is somewhere permanent."
4. The letter of condolence from Alice James has not been located.

5. During the early years of Howells' friendship with Henry James and his family, the two young authors would take Sunday walks to Fresh Pond and discuss their work, their pasts, and their futures. Howells was frequently entertained in the home of Henry James, Sr., and his wife, Mary Walsh James. For a discussion of the early years of the Howells-James relationship, see Leon Edel, *The Untried Years* (Philadelphia: Lippincott, 1953), pp. 268–76, and Howells' own brief reminiscences in his letter to James, 7 June 1889.

26 MAY 1889, CAMBRIDGE, TO WILLIAM C. HOWELLS

> Mt Auburn Station,
> Cambridge, May 26, 1889.

Dear father:

You see by the address given that we have got back to our old haunts. I think this house is in some ways more beautiful even than that at Little Nahant.[1] It is a vast old place, the country seat of the Brooks-Winthrop family,[2] and it is sub-let to me for a very low rent till December. We can then stay on if we like, but we shall probably go into Boston or on to New York for the winter.—We overlook Fresh Pond from the southward, and are only twenty minutes from Harvard Square by horse car, yet we are in the midst of fields and market gardens. It is a great relief to be settled again, and I see the way to a summer of peaceful work, if nothing happens. Pilla is in raptures with the place; and when I first saw it I thought with that mechanical action of customary ideation, "How Winny will like it." With our quieting down our sorrow, gentle and uninsistent like her, has come back, and her poor mother and I have gone all over the past again, and tried to retrieve the irrevocable. This must go on while we live, I suppose; but with less and less poignancy, I imagine.—We have a chill, easterly storm, this morning, full of old association.

All join me in love to you all,

> Your aff'te son
> **Will.**

Don't be depressed by my letter. I must write from a mood, but we have many brighter moods.

1. The Howells family spent the summer and early fall of 1888 in Little Nahant, Massachusetts.
2. An estate of twenty acres, named after Peter C. Brooks and bordering on School and Belmont Streets in Belmont. The John P. Cushing place (see Howells to James, 7 June 1889) was immediately west of it. Howells used the Mt. Auburn station, Cambridge, address for his mail, but Belmont for telegrams.

7 JUNE 1889, CAMBRIDGE, TO HENRY JAMES

Mt. Auburn Station,
Cambridge, June 7, 1889.

My dear James:

I shall never be able to thank you rightly for that letter you wrote me about Winny.[1] My wife and I both felt that you had given words to the mute despair and wonder we were in, and had lightened our burden by speaking out its very form and essence for us. My phrase offends me now by its coldness, but indeed none could impart the tender, fond gratitude we felt toward you. I thought I would write you at once, but I could not, for I wished to make you the intimate of our sorrow, and I found that in the letters which I did write I was breaking my heavy heart into mere rhetoric. In every way the expression of our bereavement escapes me; and I suppose we do not yet realize what has happened. For twenty-five years she was ours, and for three months we have lost her, after such long defeated hopes of having her back strong & well. You know perhaps the poor child was not with us when she died; she died home-sick and wondering at her separation, in the care of the doctors who fancied they were curing her. "All happiness is alike, but every sorrow has its own physiognomy,"[2] and every trait of anguish is in this experience. I wonder we live; it seems monstrous. But the fact is real only in the little stabs it gives us through every beautiful or joyous thing that she does not share with us. When I came out to see this lovely old place, which we've taken for the summer I thought, "How Winny will like it!" No bird sings, no flower blows but to the effect of some such pang.—It's no use; I might as well stop. For a time I felt like a wretched worm that had been trodden on; I could only writhe.—About the future we profess to know nothing. If I could believe I was to meet her again I should be the lightest hearted man alive.—I hope some time to write you a letter worthier your friendship, but I want to tell you now how much you are present with us all in the story you are writing.[3] Each number of the Tragic Muse we say we will read aloud; then we find each has read it. I am glad that as *I* read it I can own its superiority without a pang. No work equals it, for its subtle penetrations; it's incomparable in language and in clear sense of things. I wish it would never end; it satisfies me inexpressibly. I wish you could see how fully not only Mrs. Howells, but our young Pillà appreciates your work in it.

—We are in the Brooks Place, next the Cushing Place,[4] which you must remember of old. We look across meadows and market gardens to Fresh Pond, on whose shores I have wandered with you—on whose waters, I rowing, you told me the plot of Roderick Hudson.[5]

All join me in love.

> Yours affectionately
> W. D. Howells.

1. See Howells to Alice James, 26 April 1889, n. 2.

2. Howells used the same phrase in a letter to Edwin L. Godkin, 29 March 1889 (MH), where he identified it as being Tolstoy's.

3. *The Tragic Muse* (1890) was serialized in the *Atlantic*, January–December 1889. Howells reviewed it in the "Editor's Study," *Harper's Monthly*, September 1890. where he especially praised the moral ambivalence James maintains throughout his novel: "Vice is disposed of with a gay shrug, virtue is rewarded by innuendo. All this leaves us pleasantly thinking of all that has happened before....In the nineteenth century, especially now toward the close of it, one is never quite sure about vice and virtue: they fade wonderfully into and out of each other; they mix and they seem to stay mixed, at least around the edges." Howells also had praise for James's style, calling it "a sweetness on the tongue, a music in the ear."

4. See Howells to W. C. Howells, 26 May 1889, n. 2; also R. B. Betts, *The Streets of Belmont* (Belmont, Mass.: Belmont Historical Society, 1974).

5. See Howells to Alice James, 26 April 1889, n. 5.

15 JUNE 1889, CAMBRIDGE, TO JOHN M. HOWELLS

> Brooks Place,
> June 15, 1889.

Dear John:

Last night I felt so anxious about myself I resolved if able to make a minute of what I could now leave the family.

My life is insured, with four policies in the Mutual Life Ins. Co., of New York: One paid-up policy for $3000, now worth with dividends nearer $5000 than $4000; one endowment for $2000, worth now about $2150; one semi-endowment for $10,000 worth $10,500; one semi-endowment for $10,000 worth $10,200—in all $28,450. Sam. Wells[1] would see these paid up.

I own free of all incumbrance and insured till June 21, 1894, the house on Concord Ave., Cambridge,[2] which rents for $800 and brings in $600 clear of taxes and repairs. We may therefore call it practically worth $12,000—cost $15,000 at least.

I have $11,000 to my credit in the New England Trust Co.

I have $10,000 stocks in C. B. & Q.[3] and Atchison, Topeka and Santa Fé. That is, I paid that money for it; but at current rate the stock is worth about $6000.

All this makes $57,450. which at 5 per cent. should give an income of nearly three thousand. But out of this I always wish father paid $300 while he lives, and yr. Aunt Aurelia that sum afterwards while yr. Uncle Henry lives.

My books are now all in the hands of Houghton, Mifflin & Co., and Harper & Bros. and should yield at least $1,500 a year. Refer all my contracts to S. Wells.

> Your affectionate father
> W. D. Howells.

P. S. Wells has my R. R. stocks. Policies in my strong box, with contracts.

1. Howells' attorney.
2. The house at 37 Concord Ave., built in 1872–1873.
3. Chicago, Burlington, & Quincy Railroad.

23 JUNE 1889, CAMBRIDGE, TO ARTHUR G. STEDMAN

> Mt. Auburn Station,
> Cambridge, June 23, 1889.

Dear Mr. Stedman:[1]

Our dear girl's poems were printed in the Century, April '86; Dec. '83; Oct. '87, and other places I can't now indicate.[2] But I'm going to collect her verses in a little book, with a sketch of her sweet, short life, for private distribution,[3] and if you will give me your friend's name and address, I will gladly send him a copy.

My wife and daughter join me in kindest regards to you and your father and mother. It is consoling to know you miss us; I hope to spend some part of next winter near you.

> Yours cordially,
> W. D. Howells.

1. Arthur Griffin Stedman (1859–1908), the son of Edmund C. Stedman, graduated from Yale in 1881 and spent the rest of his life in New York City, where he worked as an editor, reviewer, and magazine writer.
2. The three poems by Winifred that Howells remembered as having been published in the *Century* are "Love's Chase. After Reading Herrick" (December 1883), "Past" (April 1886), and "The Missing Glove" (October 1887).
3. One hundred copies of *Winifred Howells* (1891) were privately printed. Howells commented to W. C. Howells in a letter of 17 November 1889 (MH): "I have just finished my memoir of Winny, which I am going to print. It does not please, for when I match it with the truth in her, it has a false ring. But it seems the best I could do; and it will only be one more blunder for her wisdom and goodness to forgive. That will be easy for her."

14 July 1889, Cambridge, to William C. Howells

July 14, 1889.

Dear father:

I enclose a letter from Mr. Douglas,[1] which makes a gratifying reference to you and Joe. Who is your friend in Edinboro'?

I am feeling anxious about Aurelia, for if her condition is neglected she may get some deep-seated and disabling complaint. I hope you will have her case promptly looked to.[2] The going up and down stairs is one great cause of her trouble, and that can be stopped by bringing Henry down and giving him the rooms either on the north or south side. I suppose you would have to bar the windows, but this w'd be better than having Aurelia an invalid for life. No doubt you have thought of some such plan.

I have finished Taylor's book, which I found interesting to the end, and now I will send it you. Notice what he says of the nature of the Deity, and how he shows that the Universe is necessarily the full expression of his power, while of his co-ordinate attributes—his wisdom, goodness, and justice—we have only glimpses. There is a great deal of suggestion, a great deal of comfort, in it all.[3]

—Pilla has Lucia Fairchild[4] visiting her, but the summer is passing rather quietly for us all.

I send a small check, for Sam, which you can give him as you think he needs it. How gladly I would help him out of all his troubles. But that can't be done.[5]

> Your affectionate son,
> Will.

1. David Douglas, Howells' publisher in Edinburgh.

2. Howells had written his father on 11 June 1889 (MH) that he hoped Aurelia would see a physician, if necessary "the best woman doctor in Cleveland," and that he would pay her expenses. The nature of the illness is not known.

3. Only a few days later, Howells expressed a similar reaction to Isaac Taylor's *Physical Theory of Another Life* (1858). In a letter to Samuel L. Clemens of 17 July 1889 (CU; *Twain-Howells*, pp. 605–6) he wrote: "I read something in a strange book . . . that consoled a little, namely: we saw and felt the Power of Deity in such fulness that we ought to infer the infinite Justice and Goodness which we did not see or feel."

4. The daughter of Howells' friend and former neighbor at Belmont, Charles Fairchild.

5. Samuel Howells had probably lost his job in Buffalo. Howells wrote his father on 28 July 1889 (MH): "I had a letter from Sam this week. He says his steady work has given out; and I sent him a letter to one of the editors. I am none the less sorry for Sam because I think the fault must be largely in himself: he gets out of more work than any other ten men."

4 AUGUST 1889, CAMBRIDGE, TO FRANCIS W. CROWNINSHIELD

> Mt. Auburn Station,
> Cambridge, Aug. 4, 1889.

My dear Frank:[1]

Between Appletons and Harpers, I think I should choose Appletons. My own experience of the Harpers is an ideally friendly and cordial one; I have the greatest regard for them; and I merely fancy, without knowing why, that the chances of promotion would be greater with another house. For another reason, I should prefer Putnams to Appletons, Holt to Putnams, and Stokes to Holt;[2] and that is, a younger house, with a less fixed tradition, will be apt to do a more various business and give you the range of the trade quicker. You ought to look forward to an interest, and with a small house you could do this more hopefully than with a large one, where you would have more competitors. There's no secret of the business that isn't known to all the publishers alike. In a small house you would meet authors and artists more, and be thrown with the young fellows destined to do the work you would some day publish. An old house is more apt to publish old established authors. When you've made up your mind, I'll be glad to give you a "character".

With the family regards to you all,

> Your friend
> W. D. Howells.

1. Francis Welch Crowninshield (1872–1947), son of Howells' friend Frederic Crowninshield (see Howells to Aurelia Howells, 30 March 1902, n. 1), began his career in one of the bookshops of George H. Putnam in 1890. From 1895 to 1900 he was editor of the *Bookman*. He later became a member of the editorial staff of the *Metropolitan* (1900–1902), *Munsey's* (1902–1907), the *Century* (1910–1914), *Vanity Fair* (1914–1936), and *Vogue* (1936–1947).

2. The publishers Howells named are Harper & Brothers, G. P. Putnam's Sons, D. Appleton & Co., Henry Holt and Co., and Frederick A. Stokes Co.

26 AUGUST 1889, CAMBRIDGE, TO BURT G. WILDER

> Mt. Auburn Station,
> Cambridge, Aug. 26, 1889.

Dear Prof. Wilder:[1]

I neither smoke, nor invent heroes, nor instruct my illustrators. Besides the nefarious cigar, the artist in question[2] introduced two dogs, without a health-certificate from M. Pasteur, into his picture; and I had mentioned none. But really, if I had occasion to describe a smoking company, I should lavish pipes and cigars upon them without scruple, and should enjoy a perfectly good conscience. It is not well to confound the aesthetical and the ethical.

Yours sincerely
W. D. Howells.

It is the business of a novelist to recognize the facts of life, and with regard to such a middle species as smoking, he is bound to no moralization. Even with vices and crimes, he should not be *directly* moralistic.[3]

1. Burt Green Wilder (1841–1925), a professor of physiology, comparative anatomy, and zoology at Cornell, wrote at the head of a typed copy of Howells' letter: "Correspondence with Mr. W. D. Howells as to Smoking in Fiction. In [Harriet E. Monroe, "Statesman and Novelist: A Talk Between Senator Ingalls and Mr. Howells,"] *Lippincott's Magazine*, Jan., 1887, p. [132], it is said that he does not smoke himself; in Harpers' [sic] Magazine, Dec. 1888, p. [27], an illustration of his Farce [*A Likely Story*], represents a man smoking a cigar; when the farce was performed at Siasconset, Mass., that character smoked; I asked Mr. Howells, Aug. 22, 1889, whether he authorized the feature in the illustration. His reply was:" Then follows the text of the letter.

2. The artist's signature is illegible, and his name is not listed in the table of contents.

3. Wilder replied to Howells on 26 August 1889 (typed copy at NIC): "I trust your letter does not imply that the novelist must not only avoid offending the smokers by uttering no objectionable sentiments, but must even court their approbation by introducing, or condoning the introduction of, a direct example of what many reasonable persons regard as undesirable; the better the farce, too, the worse the example."

23 SEPTEMBER 1889, CAMBRIDGE, TO HARPER & BROTHERS

Mt. Auburn Station,
Cambridge, Sept. 23, 1889.

Gentlemen:

In view of the proposed change in our agreement talked over with Mr. J. Henry Harper,[1] I have to suggest two plans:

I

I will write you the *Study* and a farce *each* year, and *every other* year, a novel to run through twelve numbers of the magazine, and to make not less than one hundred and fifty magazine pages; for this work you shall pay me $10,000 a year; and for anything more, you shall pay me extra, taking all I write, or allowing me to sell it elsewhere. Or,

II

For $13,000 a year I will write you the Study, the Farce and the Novel, as before stated, and will give you all I can do besides.

I should prefer this last arrangement, for it would enable me to work with a mind absolutely free, and in the year when I was not writing the novel, I believe I could give you more value for less money than if I sold my product to you piecemeal.

I propose the longer novel not only to make up quantity, but because I have found, in the *Century*, that my stories running through the year, like A Modern Instance and Silas Lapham have had better success than the short novels. As the interest develops slowly, if at all, in my work, I think the protracted publication better for it.

During the off-year, or when I was not writing the novel (which would be nearly as great in quantity as the two I now give you) I believe I could write plays, sketches, children's stories, etc., such as you could use in all your different periodicals, and I think that the whole quantity I could give you in two years would be greater than at present, when I have to contrive the scheme of a story each year.

I shall be glad to hear from you as soon as possible, in regard to these propositions.[2]

Yours sincerely
W. D. Howells.

1. Harper & Brothers had written to Howells on 17 September 1889 (MH): "In pursuance of the intimations given you in our recent conversations with you, . . . we hereby give you formal notice of our desire to terminate the arrangement at present existing between us, on the 1st of January 1891. We hope in the meantime to make a new arrangement with you, more advantageous both to you & to us, whereby we shall continue to have the exclusive use of your literary work; and, with this in view, we would like to have from you, at your convenience, your own views & suggestions as to a new agreement. . . ."

2. Howells' publisher was not willing to accept his alternative propositions, and informed him in a letter of 27 September 1889 (MH) that "we have concluded to defer making further arrangements until the expiration of our present agreement. . . ." Howells apparently replied on 28 September that he wanted some definite arrangement, and on 2 October 1889 (MH) Harper & Brothers made a counterproposal: "After talking the matter over, we thought that it might on the whole be better both for you & for us that some rate per thousand words be settled upon for the first consideration of anything which you might write, after the expiration of the present agreement. In such event you would be free to offer elsewhere anything which we might find that we could not use. Naturally, we should wish to use as much as we could find place for. [¶] We would be pleased to have you conduct the *Study* during 1891, at the present rate; and if the *Young People* story [*A Boy's Town*], to which you referred in our last interview, does not come under the existing agreement, we would like to be advised of your terms for it, for use in the *Young People* during 1891 & subsequently in book form." For the conditions of Howells' new agreement, see Howells to Harper & Brothers, 17 October 1889.

17 OCTOBER 1889, CAMBRIDGE, TO SAMUEL L. CLEMENS

> Mt Auburn Station
> Cambridge, Oct. 17, 1889

My dear Clemens:

This last batch, about the king's and Boss's adventures, is all good; and it's every kind of a delightful book.[1] Passages in it do my whole soul good.—I suppose the Church will get after you; and I think it's a pity that you don't let us see how whenever Christ himself could get a chance, all possible good was done. I don't mean the fetish, the fable Christ, but that great, wise, serious, most sufficing man. Read Brace's *Gesta Christi*, and you'll get at it all.[2]

How soon shall I have the whole book? Must begin the Study by the 25th.[3]

> Yours ever
> **W. D. Howells.**

1. Howells was reading the revised proofs of *A Connecticut Yankee in King Arthur's Court* (1889) because, as Clemens put it in his letter to Howells of 5 August 1889 (MH; *Twain-Howells*, pp. 608–9): "If Mrs. Clemens could have sat down & read the book herself, I could have got you off, maybe, but she has not had an hour's use of her eyes for reading since she had the pink-eye six months ago. So she is afraid I have left coarsenesses which ought to be rooted out, & blasts of opinion which are so strongly worded as to repel instead of persuade. I hardly think so. I dug out many darlings of these sorts, & throttled them, with grief; then Steadman [sic] went through the book & marked for the grave all that *he* could find, & I sacrificed them, every one." Howells wrote, agreeing to review the proofs, on 10 August (CU; *Twain-Howells*, pp. 609–10), but because of his visit to his father in Jefferson from about 6 September to 18 September, he did not begin reading immediately. On 19 September (CU; *Twain-Howells*, p. 612) Howells gave Clemens his initial reaction to *A Connecticut Yankee*: "Last night I started on your book, and it sank naturally into my dreams. It's charming, original, wonderful—good in fancy, and sound to the core in morals. So far I find nothing but a word or two even to question."

2. Howells mentioned Charles L. Brace's *Gesta Christi, or A History of Humane Progress Under Christianity* (1880) in his review of *A Connecticut Yankee* in the "Editor's Study," *Harper's Monthly*, January 1890; he considered the book a good supplement to Clemens' view of Arthurian monastic life. See *Twain-Howells*, p. 614.

3. Clemens had hoped to have a notice of *A Connecticut Yankee* appear in the December 1889 "Editor's Study," but because of delays in the publication of the book, Howells' review had to be postponed.

17 OCTOBER 1889, CAMBRIDGE, TO HARPER & BROTHERS

> Mt. Auburn Station,
> Oct. 17, 1889.

Gentlemen:

I have your letter of the 16th,[1] and I now accept your offer of $5000 for a farce, and for the Editor's Study during 1891, upon the condition that I offer all that I may write during that year, at $50 a 1000 words for the Monthly and $30 for the Weeklies; with the understanding that each piece of work is to be accepted only by the periodical to which it is offered and if rejected, the right to offer it elsewhere becomes mine.

> Yours truly,
> W. D. Howells.

Messrs. Harper & Brothers.

1. Harper & Brothers had written to Howells on 8 October 1889 (MH), agreeing to the conditions Howells had outlined in a letter the previous day. The Harpers' letter of 16 October (MH) clarified some matters in regard to English magazine publication of Howells' work. The present letter simply repeats the conditions proposed earlier.

30 OCTOBER 1889, CAMBRIDGE, TO CHARLES D. WARNER

> Mt Auburn Station,
> Cambridge, Oct. 30, 1889.

My dear Warner:

I hoped to be in Hartford a week ago,[1] and make verbal answer to your note. Even now, when I don't see the hour of meeting you, I feel like asking you to postpone the Thackeray difference to that future, for it's a vast subject.[2] But I want to thank you for the Bishop's message.[3] I'm so glad I pleased the clever girl and her people; I never thought she could be naughty, though she was appallingly brave, and I hated to see her jumped on by those newspaper brutes who could only take her courage grossly. Still I hope her future floriculture wont produce any more Roses of Flame.

I've not read the Master of Ballantrae, and don't expect to read it. Why should one bother with improbabilities at my age? Probabilities are bad enough. As for the English critics, they are mostly unauthorized to speak of any work of art.[4]—I hope soon to get your novel.[5]

> Yours ever
> W. D. Howells.

1. Howells and his wife had been invited to visit the Clemenses in Hartford, but because of Elinor Howells' poor health and their search for a house in Boston, Howells postponed the trip until 3 November. See Howells to Clemens, 22 and 27 October 1889 (both at CU; *Twain-Howells*, pp. 616–17).

2. Warner had written Howells on 20 October 1889 (MH) that while he liked much of the "Editor's Study," *Harper's Monthly*, November 1889, he disagreed with Howells' statements regarding Thackeray, who is referred to as a "caricaturist" and presented as an example of the decline of English fiction since Jane Austen.

3. Bishop Thomas Underwood Dudley (1837–1904), the second Episcopal bishop of the diocese of Kentucky, had met Warner in New York and asked him to thank Howells for his notice of *The Rose of Flame and Other Poems of Love* (1889) by Anne Reeve Aldrich in the "Editor's Study," *Harper's Monthly*, September 1889. The volume of poetry had caused somewhat of a scandal in the author's family, which included the bishop's wife; and Howells agreed as to the indelicacy of certain poems. "We are not inclined to draw the line [of propriety] very fast," he wrote, "or draw it very close; but we suggest that there are risks in not drawing it at all. Yet this said we are bound to recognize the truth, the power, of Miss Aldrich's verse at its best . . . ."

4. Robert Louis Stevenson, *The Master of Ballantrae: A Winter's Tale* (1889). Warner had asked Howells' opinion of the novel in his letter of 20 October and added: "I like many things in it—tho' it never approaches probability, but I cannot comprehend what the English critics say—as if it were the one perfect novel of this generation."

5. *A Little Journey in the World* (1889).

24 NOVEMBER 1889, CAMBRIDGE, TO WILLIAM C. HOWELLS

Mt. Auburn Station,
Nov. 24, 1889.

Dear father:

Elinor and I are alone this morning: John, I suppose, is oversleeping himself after being at the great Harvard Foot Ball game at Springfield;[1] and Pilla has been passing the night at the Scudders in Cambridge. We are getting ready to go into our flat,[2] and it brings real pangs, with its associations of other preparations for housekeeping. We are past middle life, now, and it seems a cruel burlesque of our youthful beginnings. We should like to stay where we are in the country; but it would be hard for Pilla who needs some life outside to help her react against the sadness of ours. I find myself in the strange mood of wishing to live only from moment to moment: to write, to read, to eat, above all to sleep and forget. I have no longer any objects in the world, any incentives beyond these. The finality seems forever gone out of earthly things. It may come back, but I doubt it.—I hope you are getting on without much rheumatism, and that all your heating arrangements are working well. Does Henry show any of the strange symptoms that alarmed you last winter, or is he merely weak? What do you hear of Sam and his family? Annie wrote me that Georgy[3] had a very good offer of marriage which she refused; this is probably well for the young man, but a pity for Sam, poor, weak creature. To be the natural consequence of one's self is terrible, but quite inevitable, though perhaps somewhere Mercy stays the end.—I'm writing a queer thing that I call The Shadow of a Dream.[4] It begins in the March Harper.—The Hazard of New Fortunes is published on Tuesday.[5]

Our love to all.

Your aff'te son,
Will.

1. The Harvard-Yale football game was played on 23 November.
2. Howells and his family moved to 184 Commonwealth Avenue, Boston.
3. Probably the daughter of Samuel Howells.
4. *The Shadow of a Dream* was serialized in *Harper's Monthly*, March–May 1890. Howells wrote W. C. Howells on 15 December 1889 (MH): "I've pretty nearly finished my novelette, *The Shadow of a Dream*, which I think you'll fancy. The motive is rather romantic, but the treatment very realistic."
5. See Howells to W. C. Howells, 1 December 1889, n. 2.

1 DECEMBER 1889, CAMBRIDGE, TO WILLIAM C. HOWELLS

Mt. Auburn Station,
Dec. 1st, 1889.

Dear father:

We are scratching our things together for the move into Boston on Tuesday,[1] and there are phalanxes of trunks every where. Our apartment promises to be comfortable, and I suppose we shall be glad of the change when once it's made; but I hate to leave the country. Life has narrowed itself so closely to the walls of home that if it were not for the children, I think Elinor and I would be glad to see nothing more of "society." But we must keep doing it for their sake, with the aching conviction at heart that our tenderness for them in this yielding is not for their real good.

I send you a copy of the cheap edition of my book which is just out.[2] You haven't told me what you thought of the latter part of it. I wish you would.—I do not suppose it will succeed. Sometimes I think the public is thoroughly tired of me; heaven knows I'm tired of the public. If I could live without writing I don't believe I should write any more. My notion of bliss is a big greenhouse for raising English violets, and a poultry yard attachment. But I dare say I shall never realize it.

John came out, and we had a pleasant Thanksgiving.

With our love to all,

Your aff'te son,
Will.

1. The move to 184 Commonwealth Avenue was delayed from 3 December to 9 December 1889.

2. *A Hazard of New Fortunes* was first published in a paperbound edition on either 26 or 27 November; the earlier date is indicated at the end of Howells' letter to his father of 24 November, and the later one is given in Gibson-Arms, *Bibliography*, p. 37. The clothbound edition was issued two months later.

22 DECEMBER 1889, BOSTON, TO WILLIAM C. HOWELLS

184 Commonwealth Ave.,
Dec. 22, 1889.

Dear father:

I have been at the colored Methodist Church this morning,[1] in a bath of primitive Christianity. Boston gives its stamp of decorum to most things, but it doesn't get through the black skin. On the whole I felt softened and humbled among those lowly and kindly people.— John is going up to Ottawa to spend part of Christmas week with Annie, and we shall be very quiet here. Annie writes that you fear rheumatic fever for Henry. I hope it wont come to that.—The 17th was our dear girl's first birthday in heaven.[2] It was a heavy day for us on earth.—I don't know of anything to write. The weather is very mild, but we have a rain that may bring us cold.—The influenza that is making all Europe sneeze is said to have reached us, and John says several students have it. But as yet we all keep well.—I'm going this afternoon to the service in the First Spiritual Temple, on the next corner—one of the finest buildings in the city.[3] I haven't the least notion what the worship will be, but I thought I'd like to see.—We had a glorious Nationalist (socialist) meeting in Tremont Temple this last week: a full house of nice people, and most enthusiastic.[4]

All join me in love to each of you.

Your aff'te son,
Will.

1. Howells used this experience two years later in chapter 8 of *An Imperative Duty*, HE, pp. 62–66.

2. Winifred Howells would have been 26 years old on 17 December.

3. The First Spiritual Temple, now the Exeter Street Theatre at 26 Exeter Street, was built in 1885.

4. The meeting of the Nationalists (organizations inspired by Bellamy's *Looking Backward*) was on 19 December. Although Howells attended and S. L. Clemens had been invited to speak, neither is listed among the speakers in the Boston *Transcript*, 20 December 1889. See also Howells to Wood, 31 December 1889, and C. and R. Kirk, "Howells and the Church of the Carpenter," *New England Quarterly* 32 (1959), 185–206.

25 December 1889, Boston, to Charles E. Norton

Boston, Dec. 25, 1889.

Dear friend:

Your Fitzgerald came yesterday, and I am reading it with solid joy.[1] It is a book wholly to my mind, and most refreshing in its purely literary interest amid the "dusty ways to death" in which I mostly walk. I'm so glad to find many of the letters to you.[2] How high and beautiful you have kept your life, and wreathed with what graces of immortal friendships!

Pillà is quite overcome by the honor of your gift to her. I have great hopes that your Vita Nuova[3] will inspire her to some finer work than she has lately attempted. She and I wanted to send you her Dobson,[4] but her mother would not let us; said it was trivial, however pretty, and so not worth your having.

Was ever a man so sweetly and generously praised as I by Curtis?[5] I could not write him fitly about it; but all the same I felt it every word; and I was simply amazed at the magnanimity with which he attributed merit to my work at the cost of old favorites. There is a man of a wholly different make from me: he does good because he loves; I because I hate.

Dunque, a Domenica![6]

Yours affectionately,
W. D. Howells.

A letter has just come from Wm. Gray (Earl of Stamford) with some love for you in it.[7]

1. Norton probably sent Howells *Letters and Literary Remains of Edward FitzGerald*, ed. William Aldis Wright, 3 vols. (1889).

2. The first volume contains thirty-four letters from FitzGerald to Norton.

3. Norton's *The New Life of Dante, An Essay with Translation* (1859).

4. Probably Mildred Howells' copy of a work by the English painter William Dobson (1610–1646).

5. George W. Curtis praised *A Hazard of New Fortunes* in the "Editor's Easy Chair," *Harper's Monthly*, January 1890, stating: "It is what has long been desired and often attempted, but never before achieved, a novel of New York life in the larger sense....a piece of realism as holds the mirror up to nature, and at once illustrates and vindicates every principle which the [Editor's] Study has maintained and applied in its judgments of contemporary story....It is a story of real life in the truest sense, a microcosm of America, a tale which, like all works of the imagination, reveals another world beneath itself."

6. Italian for "So, until Sunday."

7. William Gray (1850–1910), ninth earl of Stamford, a mutual friend of Howells and Norton, visited America in 1890.

29 DECEMBER 1889, BOSTON, TO SAMUEL L. CLEMENS

184 Commonwealth Avenue.
Boston, Dec. 29, 1889.

My dear Clemens:

I have just heated myself up with your righteous wrath about our indifference to the Brazilian Republic.[1] But it seems to me that you ignore the real reason for it which is that there is no longer an American Republic, but an aristocracy-loving oligarchy in place of it. Why should our Money-bags rejoice in the explosion of a Wind-bag? They know at the bottom of the hole where their souls ought to be that if such an event finally means anything it means *their* ruin next; and so they *don't* rejoice; and as *they* mostly inspire the people's voice, the press, the press is dumb.

—I wish I could go to West Point with you,[2] but I can't, or rather I wont; for I hate to shiver round in the shadow of your big fame, and I guess I hate the sight of a military-factory too, though I'm not sure; I suppose we must have 'em a while yet.

As for the Hartford end of your invitation, any and every time! We're all glad you're coming here.[3]

Yours ever
W. D. Howells.

1. On 15 November 1889 Emperor Dom Pedro II of Brazil was overthrown and a republican form of government was formed. Clemens responded enthusiastically to this event, especially since the proclamation of the Brazilian republic coincided with the publication of *A Connecticut Yankee*. "These are immense days!" he wrote Howells on 22 November (MH; *Twain-Howells*, pp. 621–22). "Republics & rumors of republics, from everywhere in the earth....I want to print some extracts from the Yankee that have in them this new breath of republics." Clemens' expression of wrath about official American indifference to these political developments may have appeared somewhere in print, but it has not been located.

2. Clemens was to give a reading from *A Connecticut Yankee* at the U.S. Military Academy on 11 January and had invited Howells to join him. "I am to be the guest of the Superintendent, but if you will go I will shake him & we will go to the hotel" (23 December 1889; NN; *Twain-Howells*, pp. 624–25).

3. In the letter of 23 December Clemens invited Howells to visit him in late January so that Howells could see the Paige typesetter in operation and read to the Clemenses more of *The Shadow of a Dream*, which he had begun to read during his Hartford visit on 2–3 November. Clemens also promised "to run up & stay over night with you as soon as I get a chance."

30 DECEMBER 1889, BOSTON, TO HJALMAR H. BOYESEN

184 Commonwealth Avenue.
Boston, Dec. 30, 1889.

You dear Boy!

I would give more than I can afford to be sitting down with you to a good long evening's talk; and I want to tell you, once for all, that I learned last winter to know that of the few pleasant things life has left me, your friendship is one of the sweetest. Your sending me Björnson's words adds value to them.[1] Can I say better than that?

We are back here in this town where I thought never to live again. But it was inevitable we should come; for John is in Harvard, and Pilla wished it. Please heaven we shall be in New York again finally. Not that I haven't many good friends here; but the place seems lonely, and there is one dear ghost—Pazienza![2]—I wish I could go and live in some place where I never was before.—How is Dr. Rainsford?[3] Is he well again? And tell me something about your boys, and how your wife is fighting the social battle, this winter.—We have pulled all our old belongings out of storage, and got them about us again—horrible to look at—and life is jogging on. I've just finished a novelette, three numbers, to begin in an early Harper, which I hope you'll like—The Shadow of a Dream; almost romantic in motive.

We all join in love to the Boyesens.

Yours affectionately
W. D. Howells.

1. Boyesen may have sent Howells a copy of the English translation of Bjornstjerne Bjornson's novel *In God's Way* (1890), or perhaps he sent Howells greetings from their mutual friend.
2. Italian for "patience."
3. William Stephen Rainsford (1850–1933) was rector of St. George's Church in New York (1882–1906).

31 DECEMBER 1889, BOSTON, TO JOHN S. WOOD

184 Commonwealth Avenue.
Boston, Dec. 31, 1889.

Dear Mr. Wood:[1]

I was very glad indeed to get your letter, with its at least not discouraging news about Mrs. Wood.[2] Will you give our cordil regards and good wishes to her and to Mr. and Mrs. Harris?[3]

I would like immensely to see you again, and to have a long talk with you, at the Aldine, or elsewhere. (We never did have that Welsh Rarebit at the University!) We are settled in an apartment here till our boy is out of Harvard; then ho, for New York! In the meantime, I hope often to be there, and to report to you the first visit.

You ought to have been at the Nationalist Anniversary, here. Tremont Temple *filled* at fifty cents a head, and an enthusiasm of the warmest kind. There cannot be any doubt of the spread of the doctrine, and amongst the most intelligent class. Bellamy spoke most valuably, and Edward Everett Hale magnificently.[4]

> Yours sincerely,
> W. D. Howells.

1. Possibly John Seymour Wood (1853–1934), a New York author and lawyer. His letter, to which Howells is here replying, has not been located.
2. Mary Harris Wood.
3. The Harrises have not been identified.
4. See Howells to W. C. Howells, 22 December 1889, n. 4.

3 JANUARY 1890, BOSTON, TO JAMES PARTON

> *184 Commonwealth Avenue.*
> Boston, Jan. 3, 1890.

My dear Parton:

I've been trying to get my breath ever since that glorious blast of yours came and took it away.[1] Ah, that was something *like* praise! And I accept it just as joyfully as if it belonged to me. In a way it did. Whatever they may say against me, they cannot deny that here and there I do get a little life into literature, and that when I don't, at least I have tried.

I think we both have at heart more than literature the humanity that is above literature, and that we honor its service. Except for that service, the calling seems so beggarly; and I look back with wonder at the darkened mind in which I thought the business of turning phrases sufficient in itself.

I note your counsel about writing undermuch rather than overmuch, and I will heed it all I can. But there are ten novels that I should like to write, yet; and I should like to write them now.

New York interested me immensely, and after John is out of Harvard, I expect to go there part of every winter. But I love the country too much to be willing to live in any city as an open and acknowledged thing. I look forward to an old age occupied with poultry and English violets, perhaps varied with a pig or two.

Do you ever come to Boston? What a pleasure it would be to house you in our flat, if you would come to us! I assure you that Mrs. Howells exulted in your letter as much as I did, and has as grateful a heart for it. Since you saw us under your own roof at Newburyport, we have lost our dear, sick girl, and with her most of the meaning and all the dignity of life.[2] And where is she, and shall I ever see her again? The world has largely resolved itself into this question, for me. Almost thou persuadest me to be a Pagan, when I think what a lovely nature, and what a true, good, unselfish life you have always been; but how can I give up that hope, that prayer? Well, each one to his own dark riddle.

I should try this winter to interest myself in some of the charity work here; but while I see the necessity of it, I see the futility so clearly that I have not much heart for it.[3] If it were possible to write and read sixteen hours and sleep eight it would be very simple.

With love from us all to the whole Parton household,

Yours cordially,
W. D. Howells.

I work the type-writer myself; so I don't apologize for it.

1. Parton had praised *A Hazard of New Fortunes* as "one of the greatest and purest pleasures...ever enjoyed" in a letter to Howells of 30 December 1889 (MH). He also claimed that Howells' works "are the highest and soundest moral influence now active in the United States."

2. See Howells to W. C. Howells, 4 March 1889.

3. Howells probably considered becoming an active member of the Church of the Carpenter, a mission of the Episcopal Church which had developed from the Society of Christian Socialists in Boston. Though Howells occasionally attended services and meetings of this group, he did not formally join. See C. and R. Kirk, "Howells and the Church of the Carpenter," *New England Quarterly* 32 (1959), 185–206. For Howells' attitudes on doing charitable work, see also 2 February 1890 to W. C. Howells and 4 February 1890 to Mrs. Fields.

5 JANUARY 1890, BOSTON, TO AURELIA H. HOWELLS

184 Commonwealth Avenue.
Boston, Jan. 5, 1890.

Dear Aurelia:

I want to tell you how pleased we all are with your New-Year's Gifts. John is going to write you, about his; he found it just the thing for the wall of his college-room; and Elinor thought hers particularly nice, and is going to use them every day. I fancy from the signature among the golden-rod that Mary[1] painted mine in that tasteful way; but did you embroider the initials on the back? Pilla will speak of hers when she can get her breath from the whirl of society. It's amusing to see her go it.

She is with us very little, only putting in for repairs from time to time. For instance, she went out to lunch yesterday at President Eliot's in Cambridge, and from there to a dinner and an evening party; to-day I join her and she lunches at the Norton's; then she comes in, and has a girl friend to dinner here, & I suppose some student will drop in. As she is a sensible girl, I want her to get her surfeit of society early, so that she will know it means nothing and can come to nothing. Of course there is a complete lapse of her drawing, and as her heart is really in that, I hope she will soon begin to hanker for it. In New York she was rather lonely, and we want these two winters in Boston to be as full of gayety as she desires, for when we go back to New York her work must begin. John has already sobered down into a grave and reverend junior; at the Saturday evening dances he makes it his business to look after the plain and neglected girls, and see that they have a good time.

I enclose a letter from James Parton, the historian and biographer, which I thought you and father would like to see.[2] You must send it back when you've read it. I haven't any notion as to how the book's selling; but I fancy it must be doing better than usual.

Tell father that the spiritual service I attended the other Sunday consisted of some solo-singing, and "speaking by guides" or inspiration, and very little inspiration. Women did the whole thing.

I've begun writing A Boy's Town,[3] and I think I shall get a grip of it by and by, though the start is not easy.

I dream of Winny a good deal, but grotesquely for the most part. Last night I was to be hanged for something, and I had a chance to escape; but I reflected, "No, I am tired of living; and it's only a momentary wrench, and then I shall be with *her.*" It was coherent and more logical than most dreams.

All join me in love to each of you.

>Your aff'te bro.,
>Will.

1. Mary Elizabeth Howells.
2. See Howells to Parton, 3 January 1890, n. 1.
3. Howells had discussed this project with Harper & Brothers in September 1889; it was published serially in *Harper's Young People*, 8 April–26 August 1890, and in book form on 11 October 1890.

17 JANUARY 1890, BOSTON, TO CHARLES D. WARNER

184 Commonwealth Avenue.
Boston, Jan. 17, 1890.

My dear Warner:

My father, who will be 83 years old in May, writes me from Ohio: "I have been reading Warner's story of A Little Journey in the World.[1] I am very glad to see him take so just a view of the plutocracy that is fastening its grasp upon the country. I am glad so many good writers are waking up to see and expose the abomination—which is terrible to contemplate. If only the literary power of the country can be kept in this direction, it may help to save it, and the sooner it comes to the rescue the easier the conquest will be. We have just disgraced the State of Ohio by the election of a Golden Calf to the U. S. Senate.[2] That calf will soon be a brazen bull, that will return to gore and trample down the little humanity remaining with us."

Yours ever,
W. D. Howells.

1. Warner's novel, published in 1889, was the first part of a trilogy dealing with a theme that was of particular interest to Howells at this time—the acquisition of a great financial fortune.
2. Calvin Stewart Brice (1845–1898), a Democratic member of the U.S. Senate (1891–1897), was born in Ashtabula County.

2 FEBRUARY 1890, BOSTON, TO WILLIAM C. HOWELLS

184 Commonwealth Avenue.
Boston, Feb. 2, 1890.

Dear father:

I am sorry you had any sort of anxiety because I failed to write you last Sunday. I had been at New York, and I stopped to see Mark Twain at Hartford,[1] and we talked so much all day, that the letter-writing went out of my head. He and his wife and Elinor and I are all of accord in our way of thinking: that is, we are theoretical socialists, and practical aristocrats. But it is a comfort to be right theoretically, and to be ashamed of one's self practically. I went to New York to be at a dinner the Harpers made for E. A. Abbey,[2] the artist, and there I met, among many other artists, the one whose card I enclose. He is from Ohio, and he came up to tell me that he was the chum of a boy named Howells at School in Cleveland. I thought it must be Willy, but it proved to be our dear Johnny[3]— "the sweetest fellow I ever knew," he said, and he told me that he tied

Johnny's cravat for him the last day he went down stairs; perhaps then he was feeling sick and weak.—I thought you might like to hear about it. This artist is very talented and valued by the Harpers. He is just going or gone to Japan for them. I have seldom met any one I liked more on short notice.[4]

The family are all well here, and I hope this will find you better, and out of bed. I don't like your pains and aches, and I wish I could abate them.

With our united love to each,

Your aff'te son,
Will.

1. Howells left Hartford on 26 January.
2. J. Henry Harper gave a dinner for Edwin Austin Abbey (1852–1911) at the Union League Club in New York on 23 January 1889. Abbey, a painter and illustrator, worked as a staff illustrator for Harper & Brothers at intervals throughout his career. In 1885 he moved to England, sharing a house with Howells' friends, Francis D. Millett and his wife. On 23 April 1890 Abbey married Mary Gertrude Mead, the daughter of Frederick Mead (1848–1890), Elinor Howells' youngest brother.
3. Howells' brother John, who died in 1864 while attending school in Cleveland.
4. Most likely H. Humphrey Moore, the illustrator of Pierre Loti's "Japanese Women," *Harper's Monthly*, December 1890.

4 FEBRUARY 1890, BOSTON, TO ANNIE A. FIELDS

184 Commonwealth Avenue.
Boston, Feb. 4, 1890

Dear Mrs. Fields:
I went to the Charity Building this afternoon,[1] meaning to go in and offer myself up on the handiest altar of good deeds I could find; but after hanging round in the halls awhile, came away like a bashful boy without having the courage to go in anywhere. How could I be of use in the organization? I have so many afternoons that I merely spend in cursing the day I was born.

Yours sincerely
W. D. Howells.

Think of Imovili's[2] upping and writing me again the other day! I wish Miss Jewett would go on writing Teaby things till the crack of doom.[3] Though when you come to think of it, why should doom crack, anyway?

1. Probably the Associated Charities of Boston. Apparently Howells did gather sufficient courage finally to go in, since on 21 February 1890 he wrote a letter to

"Gentlemen" (PU; Clara M. Kirk, *W. D. Howells, Traveler from Altruria 1889–1894* [New Brunswick, N. J.: Rutgers University Press, 1962], p. 26) seeking employment for Adam Kaylan, who had been out of work since Christmas 1889. Kaylan's case had been referred to Howells by the Associated Charities.

2. Possibly James R. Lowell.

3. Sarah Orne Jewett's short story, "The Quest for Mr. Teaby," was published in *Strangers and Wayfarers* (1890). For Howells' brief notice of the volume see the "Editor's Study," *Harper's Monthly*, April 1891, comparing Jewett's stories favorably to those of Maupassant and praising them for "the perfect artistic restraint, the truly Greek temperance...." See also Howells to Jewett, 1 February 1891.

7 FEBRUARY 1890, BOSTON, TO SAMUEL L. CLEMENS

184 Commonwealth Avenue.
Boston, Feb. 7, 1890.

Dear Clemens:

Herne is immensely pleased with main points of play—fire extinguisher, phonograph, telephone scene, drunken scene; but we both think the materialization must all come out, and Sellers kept sane, and broadened, deepened, softened—made everything Raymond could do and all he couldn't do. If you can get the play back from Burbank, I'll sketch a new plot keeping all the good that's now in it, and involving your notion of rich international marriage. Then Herne will be sure whether he wants it. I like him better and better. He was wonderfully intelligent about the piece, and could edit it splendidly, and play it to break your heart with joy.[1]

Yours ever
W. D. Howells.

1. Howells had written to Clemens on 28 January 1890 (CU; *Twain-Howells*, p. 628) explaining that he was negotiating with James A. Herne (1839–1901), a popular American playwright and actor, in an attempt to revive the play (*Colonel Sellers as a Scientist*, later called *The American Claimant*) that he and Clemens had written collaboratively some years earlier. The play, which had never proved very successful, was based upon Clemens' character Colonel Mulberry Sellers from *The Gilded Age* and was a sequel to an earlier play by Clemens (*Colonel Sellers*) which had been acted quite successfully by John T. Raymond (1836–1887). Accordingly, Clemens and Howells first discussed the production of *Colonel Sellers as a Scientist* with Raymond in 1883–1884. After initially agreeing to produce it, Raymond later decided not to act the play, objecting, among other things, to Sellers' materialization of dead bodies and the plot elements having to do with the English earldom. Clemens wrote to Howells on 15 September 1884 (MH; *Twain-Howells*, pp. 506–7) informing him of Raymond's decision. Following Raymond's refusal of the play, Clemens and Howells discussed production schemes with various other actors and managers. An agreement was ultimately reached in May 1886 whereby the elocutionist A. P. Burbank (1846–1894) would put on the play at Daniel Frohman's Lyceum Theatre in New York. At this point, however, Howells lost faith in the venture and wrote to Clemens on 11 May 1886 (CU; *Twain-Howells*, p. 558) instructing him to withdraw the play from production. A year later, when Bur-

bank reopened negotiations, a second agreement was reached, under the terms of which he finally brought the play to the stage in New Brunswick, New Jersey, on 10 September 1887. Burbank then toured briefly, although not very successfully, with the play. Nevertheless, he retained the rights to production and had to be consulted before Howells could enter into any new agreement with Herne. Clemens wrote to Howells on 31 January 1890 (MH; *Twain-Howells*, pp. 628–29) outlining a tentative deal whereby Burbank would relinquish his rights to the play in return for Clemens' securing him the part of Hank Morgan in an upcoming dramatization of *A Connecticut Yankee*. This deal, however, was apparently never realized.

9 FEBRUARY 1890, BOSTON, TO WILLIAM C. HOWELLS

184 Commonwealth Avenue.
Boston, Feb. 9, 1890.

Dear father:

I need not tell you how glad I should be to visit you this winter, but unless you are sick, or have some special urgency for seeing me, I think I had better wait till spring. The journey is long, and the risks of cold, and so on, are considerable. As so much depends on my keeping well and in good working condition I do not feel it quite selfish to look carefully after myself, and on the other hand I know it is a real sacrifice not to be with you oftener. That is the greatest happiness, after being with my own here, that I now have left in life; and I am sure that if there were any direct occasion for my presence, in your circumstances or health, you would tell me. I expect to have two or three months of leisure this year, and I hope to spend a good deal of the month of June with you, which is not so very far off, as times goes.[1] Then I shall have finished the boy's book I'm now writing[2] and shall not have begun any other, and so can fold my hands with you a while. But if you need me, or greatly desire me, sooner, I will of course come sooner.

I am surprised, in delving in my childish past as I do in the Boy's Town, to find how much I can remember, and how clearly. It makes me think that my strongest faculty, after all, may have been an art of seeing and hearing everything. I am sure I c'd not invent half as many things, thoughts, ideas, as I can remember. Pretty soon I shall have proofs of my stuff, and then I will send it to you for your revision.

Have you seen a book of Lawrence Oliphant's called Scientific Religion?[3] Bald Swedenborgianism much of it, but with bits of his own inspiration. Upon the atomic theory he builds the notion of pain-atoms and joy-atoms, each one of which shall be a compensation for each one of the others.

I am going out to Norton's to-day with Pilla, to see Lowell. We have been there several Sundays this winter, and it is a kindly renewal of old relations that is very pleasant. Lowell greatly admires Pilla. The last time when she was there, he jumped up after she had left the room, and said, "Why she's an angel!"—Louis Dyer is here with his English wife,[4] rather a quiet, reserved person; they lunched with us, and on the stairs Mrs. Dyer said, "Mr. Howells, I want to tell you that your daughter is the most beautiful creature I ever saw." I told Pil, and asked her if she was not surprised. "No," she said, in her slow, tranquil way, "I could see it gradually taking effect on her"—meaning her beauty. She's delightful, and absolutely simple.

John is tugging away at his mid-year exams, and we see little of him. With dearest love to each from all,

> Your affectionate son,
> Will.

1. Howells visited his father in May 1890.
2. *A Boy's Town.*
3. Laurence Oliphant's *Scientific Religion, or Higher Possibilities of Life and Practice Through the Operation of Natural Forces* (1888) was influenced by Thomas Lake Harris, the founder of the Brocton, New York, and Santa Rosa, California, settlements, which were established to realize the principles of Christian Socialism.
4. Dyer, who now lived in Oxford, England, returned to Boston in December 1889 to deliver eight lectures at the Lowell Institute, which were later published as *Studies of the Gods in Greece at Certain Sanctuaries Recently Excavated* (1891). His wife was the former Anne Macmillan, daughter of the publisher Alexander Macmillan.

18 FEBRUARY 1890, BOSTON, TO JAMES R. LOWELL

> *184 Commonwealth Avenue.*
> Boston, Feb. 18, 1890.

Dear Mr. Lowell:

It cost me as sore a pang as you suffered when I came to that place in your note where you said you must stop;[1] for then I realized that I had put a burden upon you in telling you how much I wished your letter.

Your praise is as sweet to me to-day, after thirty years, as when it first put heart into me; but more than your praise I value your love, and it is that I now thank you and bless heaven for.

> Your affectionate
> W. D. Howells.

1. Lowell had written Howells on 17 February 1890 (MH; M. A. D. Howe, *New Letters of James Russell Lowell* [New York: Harper & Brothers, 1932], pp. 335–36) that he had to stop writing because of a pain in his back. The letter praised *A Hazard of New Fortunes*: "I was really delighted with it. The characters are excellently varied, discriminated & antithesized. There is also a deep moral in the book,

for which I like it all the more, since it isn't rammed down my throat. Old Dreyfoos [sic] is as tragically pathetic as Père Goriot & in a more human way. But what shall I say of Fulkerson? He is my darling. Whenever you let him make his exit, I think you a selfish & stingy old hunks who want him all to yourself. I can't part with him, & shall break through the hedge of my thorniest convictions to *interview* him from time to time."

5 MARCH 1890, BOSTON, TO MONCURE D. CONWAY

184 Commonwealth Avenue.
Boston, March 5, 1890.

Dear Constant, Faithful Friend:

Say anything you like about me in your Hawthorne.[1] But it was just *before* the War I saw him: in '60, with one of those loveliest letters, that Lowell alone can write. Hawthorne kept it, and his wife gave it me back. Hawthorne took me up on the hill behind Wayside, and we had a silence of half an hour together. He said he never saw a perfectly beautiful woman; askt much about the West, and wisht he could find some part of America "where the cursed shadow of Europe hadn't fallen."

How like you and dear Mrs. Conway still to like my poor old Italian Journeys![2] Bless you both. We are just off to New York for a week. My wife is not very athletic.—I wish I *could* see your "G. W. and Mt V.", but I never did.[3]

Yours sincerely
W. D. Howells.

Kiss Venice for me!

1. Conway had written Howells from Italy on 17 February 1890 (MH) that he was "hard at work" on his biography of Hawthorne. He quoted a paragraph from his manuscript on the meeting between Howells and Hawthorne, asking whether Howells would like to have it suppressed or corrected. The passage indicates that the meeting took place during the Civil War and that Howells, upon his departure, was given a card of introduction to Emerson, with the message "I find him worthy." Conway retained the passage in print but added as a footnote lines 7–10 of the present letter. See *Life of Nathaniel Hawthorne* (1890), p. 202, and *Literary Friends and Acquaintance*, HE, pp. 47–51, where Hawthorne's message reads "I find this young man worthy," and he speaks of the "damned shadow" of Europe.

2. Conway and his wife, according to the letter of 17 February, were rereading Howells' *Italian Journeys*, and they liked it better than ever. "Since I read this beloved book in Italy I have concluded that I never read it before—though I thought I had. The former impression is 'wan as the moon by the sun descried.' "

3. Conway edited and wrote the introduction to *George Washington and Mount Vernon; a Collection of Washington's Unpublished Agricultural and Personal Letters* (1889), and he hinted broadly that he would be pleased if Howells were to notice it in *Harper's Monthly*. "It cost months of labor," he wrote in his letter of 17 February, "costly visits to Va., & no end of pains, but no paper seems to know of it."

27 MARCH 1890, BOSTON, TO HORACE E. SCUDDER

184 Commonwealth Avenue.
Boston, March 27, 1890.

My dear Scudder:

I should be a very unworthy and ungrateful person if I failed to thank you for the kind things in your review of my novel.[1] They were very, very kind indeed, and often altogether satisfying. Sometimes, I felt as if the review had been written by a person who had known me when I was a very little boy, and not a very good little boy, either; but I saw that this was a condition of the reviewer's art, and that I could not possibly be regarded by the most tolerant criticism as I regard myself: an intellectual and moral colossus, with one foot on Scylla and the other on Charybdis, and the navies of the world sailing between my legs. In other respects I feel hopeful of you, and I expect you yet to join me in defiling the tomb of Scott and plucking all the fathers of romance by the beard.

> Yours cordially,
> **W. D. Howells.**

1. "New York in Recent Fiction," *Atlantic*, April 1890. Scudder gave special praise to Howells' characterizations in *A Hazard of New Fortunes* and concluded that Howells' earlier books about New England life would have had a "deeper truthfulness" if he "had applied his present method and used his present power in the portraiture of life in New England."

1 APRIL 1890, BOSTON, TO ELIZABETH S. PHELPS WARD

184 Commonwealth Avenue.
Boston, April 1, 1890

Dear Mrs. Ward:

I am sorry, but I cannot. I am not fit to read in public, and I do not wish to espouse that cause merely because I love it.[1]

Mrs Howells has gone nowhere this winter, and I'm afraid lunch is beyond us both, but some day I hope to run out and see yourself and Mr. Ward. Thank you for that kind word whispered on the scrap enclosed in your letter.[2] Beautiful she was indeed. But I have almost learned not to speak of her, so much has her loss passed all speech, all thought.

With my wife's love, and my best regards,

> Yours sincerely
> **W. D. Howells.**

1. In her letter to Howells of 31 March 1890 (MH), Mrs. Ward had asked Howells to "read at the Suffrage affair on April 9*th*. . . . [¶] I should feel a hundred per cent happier over it, if you would be there, and the 'Cause' would rejoice thereat."

2. A sympathy note on the death of Winifred Howells.

6 APRIL 1890, BOSTON, TO WILLIAM C. HOWELLS

> *184 Commonwealth Avenue.*
> Boston, April 6, 1890

Dear father:

I have yours sending my letter back.[1] I was sure the dream would interest you.

I hope poor Aurelia is feeling no effects still from her fall, but is all right again. She and I are pretty well cushioned; nevertheless it is better not to fall.

Will you please tell Joe that it is always the same old type-writer; but I change the plate of type at pleasure. I suggested the script-font I now use, and it is called after me—the "W. D. Howells Special." It's the only writing-font in use on any machine.—I think I can help Joe to a type-writer when he really wants one.

You askt me once if the old German revolutionist who dyed your watch yellow in Columbus, were not the origin of Lindau. Yes, he suggested him, but Limbeck and others helped materialize him.[2]—I don't really know where Dryfoos came from, but I suppose I could think him back to somebody.

The next time Annie makes Sam's fortune I wish she would lend him the money to enjoy it on. It has cost me $125 to move him to Washington, and I doubt very much whether he can get on any better there with his $20 a week than he did with his $12 in Buffalo. He is always the same Sam, and what is worse, his family is the same.

I enclose an article from the new London literary paper that may interest you.[3]

With our love to each,

> Your aff'te son
> Will.

1. Neither letter has been located.

2. Howells mentions the German watchmaker and jeweler, though not by name, in *Years of My Youth*, HE, p. 117; for Limbeck, see Howells to Dune Dean, 9–11 September 1857, n. 2. Lindau is, of course, a character in *A Hazard of New Fortunes*, as is Dryfoos, mentioned in the following sentence.

3. The article has not been identified.

19 APRIL 1890, BOSTON, TO HARPER & BROTHERS

184 Commonwealth Avenue.
Boston, April 19, 1890.

Gentlemen:

I confess that I was puzzled and hurt by the terms of your earlier letter, but your latest has certainly made all perfectly and heartily right between us.[1]

The occasion of my writing to you was an offer for a novel from me, made by the Mc Clure Syndicate on behalf of the New York Sun.[2] I explained my obligations for the year 1891, and when the offer was repeated for 1892, I told Mr. Mc Clure that I felt bound by the kindness you had always shown me to ask what if you had any wish regarding my work beyond 1891. I could not be as explicit in writing you then as I am now without seeming to bring some sort of pressure upon you; but I kept his offer waiting till I heard from you. Then I accepted it.

No arrangements that I have made affect the *Study*; but I should like to talk definitely with you about it and I hope to see you early in May.[3]

1. Howells had asked Harper & Brothers in a letter of 9 April 1890 (draft at MH; the actual letter appears to have been dated 10 April) "whether you have any wish or intention in regard to my work beyond the year 1891." He requested an "early and explicit reply." Harpers replied on 14 April (MH) that they were "not prepared at present to make any engagement beyond the year 1891, as kindly proposed by you, further than we have already made." Howells sharply replied to them on 15 April (draft at MH) that he "did not ... 'propose' any prolongation of our relations beyond 1891. In view of some matters offering for the future, I wished to consider any possible plans of yours; for I thought this your due. Your letter of yesterday leaves me free to act; but I am not willing to have you suppose that I was seeking a further engagement, which I should have felt it unbecoming and unwise to do." Harpers responded with a conciliatory letter to Howells on 18 April (MH), admitting their letter of 14 April was "careless & ungracious" and expressing their mortification "at the Dryfoos-*père* aspect of our letter...." They asked Howells, "Would it be proper for us to inquire, in strict confidence, as to the nature of the engagements you have in contemplation for '92, & whether or not they would be likely to interfere with the continuance of the *Study* for that year?"
2. Samuel Sidney McClure (1857–1949) had founded the McClure Syndicate in 1884. He had apparently approached Howells on two issues: first, to write a novel for syndication; second, to edit "an illustrated monthly magazine or miscellany of the highest literary character" which would begin publication in December 1891 (unsigned contract, McClure to Howells, n.d. [MH]). Howells wrote McClure on 6 April (ViU): "I think it will be better to let the matter of the story rest till we see [each] other again, and the other matter too. I don't see how we could manage both very well; the first would kill off the chances of the second." Though Howells never did edit McClure's proposed magazine, he wrote the syndicated novel, *The Quality of Mercy, a Story of Contemporary American Life*, published in the New York *Sun*, 4 October 1891–3 January 1892. For the financial details of McClure's offer of magazine editorship see Cady, *Howells*, II, 163–64.
3. The signature is missing from the draft of this letter, which is its only extant form.

27 April 1890, Boston, to William C. Howells

184 Commonwealth Avenue.
Boston, April 27, 1890.

Dear father:

I don't remember ever to have heard the thrushes in Jefferson; but in New Hampshire they sing divinely, and they made the summer evenings glorious at Lake George. It will be a part of my welcome if I can find them in your woods.

It's really a great help and pleasure to find that you like the Boy's Town so well. Of course, now it's done, it must take it's chance; but I'm very willing to be persuaded the chance is good. The page is uniform with that of all my 12 mo. books, and the B. T. will be included in the sets, finally, but will first be issued as a holiday book next Christmas.— The *Dawn* is edited by the pastor of the Church of the Carpenter.[1] The Christian Socialists are more to my mind than the Nationalists;[2] but I doubt if I shall openly act with either for the present. The C. S. have loaded up with the creed of the church, the very terms of which revolt me, and the N. seem pinned in faith to Bellamy's dream. But the salvation of the world will not be worked out that way. I liked that bill of Stanford's in the Senate to lend farmers money from the Treasury surplus on their mortgages[3]—I should like to see the government lending to any one on good security at interest so low that industry might live and usury perish. By and by labor will be so pinched that the politicians will have to put a socialistic plank into a platform, and then the party that stands on it will win.—With love from each to each.

Your aff'te son
Will.

1. *The Dawn*, the official publication of the Society of Christian Socialists, was edited by the Reverend William Dwight Porter Bliss (1856–1926), an Episcopal rector of Grace Church in South Boston and later pastor of the Church of the Carpenter. Bliss and the Reverend Francis Bellamy, Edward Bellamy's cousin, organized the Christian Socialists in 1889; on 13 April 1890 the Church of the Carpenter held its first service. Howells' letter to his father of 20 April 1890 (MH) noted that he had attended the inaugural service: "It was like seeing the old faith renewed in the life. All sorts of people were there. Robert Treat Paine, one of the rich old Boston swells, and great grandson of the Signer of the Dec. of Ind., took a prominent part. The world does move." C. and R. Kirk, "Howells and the Church of the Carpenter," *New England Quarterly* 32 (1959), 196–98.

2. See Howells to W. C. Howells, 8 July 1888, n. 4.

3. Republican Senator Leland Stanford (1824–1893) of California proposed a bill to provide for loans on lands to be administered by the Treasury Department. According to the bill, any U.S. citizen or anyone declaring his intention to become one who owned unincumbered agricultural land could apply to the land loan bureau for a loan from these certificates, to be secured by lien on the land, the loan not to exceed half the assessed value of the land. The measure was defeated by Congress as being economically unsound.

6 MAY 1890, BOSTON, TO EDWARD E. HALE

184 Commonwealth Avenue.
May 6, 1890

My dear Hale:

Your letter finds me on the eve of another of those mystical N. Y. C. R. R. episodes.[1] I am starting Westward tonight, to see my dear old father in Ohio, and so you see I can't come to the Ladies' Night.[2] Please tell those nice boys why.

I always have a heavy heart in leaving home, but your words have shed a cheering ray over my four-track path.[3] Praise *is* sweet, and I feel as if I might have been the man to deserve it, though I know I'm not. I am all the time stumbling to my feet from the dirt of such falls through vanity and evil will, and hate, that I can hardly believe in that self that seems to write books which help people. But if any one can stay himself by such a scuffed and bemired creature as I, he is welcome, though I take leave to think what is true of his support, all the same.

Yours cordially
W. D. Howells.

1. For the "mystical" railroad episode, see Howells to Hale, 28 June 1887, n. 1. Howells' reply is to a letter from Hale dated "Between Syracuse & Rochester / Monday Morning" (MH; most likely 5 May 1890), which contains this passage: "It was at Albany that you gave me Tolstoi's *Confessions*—on which I have talked so much to others— and which gave the name to our Tolstoi club[.]"

2. Hale had invited Howells, Elinor, and Mildred to "Ladies' Night" at the Tolstoi Club on Monday, 13 May, indicating that "Jack" (John Howells), being a club member, would also be there.

3. Hale's letter contains glowing praise of Howells' latest novel: "The Hazard of New Fortunes is more than masterly. It is good. It is good in all ways—chiefly because it will make people better. It will make them think and it will make them think right. In other words it is going to do—what before you began it, you swore by the Living God it should do."

6 MAY 1890, BOSTON, TO MADISON J. CAWEIN

184 Commonwealth Avenue.
May 6, 1890.

Dear Mr. Cawein:

I have not read your last book yet, but I hope to do so soon.[1] In the meantime, don't be troubled by the critics. Even when they mean well, they don't know much, and are not worth minding. The only question for you is, Have I satisfied my conscience as a man and a man of letters? The rest you can safely leave.

Yours sincerely,
W. D. Howells.

1. Probably *Lyrics and Idyls* (1890). Cawein wrote Howells on 25 July 1890 (MH) that the remarks on critics in the "Editor's Study," *Harper's Monthly*, August 1890, helped him to understand the hostility of critics: "Heretofore, I do not hesitate to say, the newspaper and other reviews have worried me not a little, but with time have gradually grown hardened to them. I often wondered why certain papers seemed especially hostil [sic] to works of mine; and why they incessantly persisted in lugging your name . . . into a notice of a vol. which you had not even dreamed existed much less seen; all this because you were audacious enough to speak well of some previous book of mine. Thanks to the kindness of the 'Study' I now understand. The pleasure to them, it appears, lies in the bald fact that not being able to control & dominate the ideas & the true literary acumen of a far higher authority, they still possess the power to disagree openly with that authority, making that difference public & of weight through the columns of some large city daily."

15 JUNE 1890, BOSTON, TO WILLIAM C. HOWELLS

184 Commonwealth Avenue.
June 15, 1890.

Dear father:

I sent you a check on Friday,[1] which I hope reached you last night; and I write this morning just to give you a letter to open at the usual time.— I woke with a severe headache, which a cup of coffee has washed away; but while the anguish lasted I had some sharp tho'ts; and I confess I look forward with terror to the pain that must come probably before my life is let out of this gross bulk of mine, when it is time. I suppose it is right, so, and no doubt I shall be helped to bear it. But think what mother suffered! And Johnny, and Sissy and Winny![2] And why?—That Why is so much in my mind that I wonder it doesn't show phosphorescently on my forehead, and still more on my bulging stomach. I feel about equal to a half hour with Jerry,[3] this morning, whose whistle I should like to hear. Poor bird, and poor boy overhead: I hope he's getting on a little more peaceably with his tormenting demon.

My sympathies are much more than I can say with you and Aurelia, whose hard lot I truly pity. I hope you may soon have pleasant, settled weather, and get some joy of the abundant out-doors you have round you. How is the strawberry-bed doing? How does the meat-cutter work? All details of your life are important to me.

The family are not up yet, so I send my love alone.

Your aff'te son
Will.

1. Howells' check for fifty dollars, mailed with a brief note on 13 June (MH), was to pay for a caretaker for Henry Howells, who at this time appears to have been an especially heavy burden on W. C. Howells and Aurelia. On 11 June 1890 (MH) Howells had reported to his father that he read a letter "in which Aurelia expresses a great desire to have you try to get another man from Dr. Richardson, who shall

have had experience, as an attendant for Henry. She tells how terribly you have been broken up, both of of [sic] you, and how you have suffered from Henry's late bad spell."

2. Howells' brother John, his sister Victoria, and his daughter Winifred.

3. W. C. Howells' pet bluejay.

15 JUNE 1890, BOSTON, TO JOHN W. DE FOREST

184 Commonwealth Avenue.
June 15, 1890.

My dear De Forest:

Your letter followed me to Ohio, where my absence from my wonted environment operated a kind of moral disability in me that has lasted ever since. I remember your article very well, and I share your pleasure in the corroboration your theories have received.[1] I will write to Scribners, and ask them for the book of Dr. Taylor. It is curious how willingly we adopt any hypothesis proposed by authority; but I have a kind of personal comfort in having it afterwards refuted. A friend and I have just been talking to-day about the want of evidence in creation that the Creator is especially interested in man. We have always supposed he is; but why?

In my pleasure that you like my work in fiction[2] I grieve that we get no more from you. By the way, why not offer your MSS. to the J. W. Lovell Co.?[3] He (L.) is a reformed pirate, but so is the best of the rest, and he is now trying to publish good books. Suppose you send him a novel? If you have your Atlantic article by you, could you lend it me?

Yours ever
W. D. Howells

1. De Forest wrote Howells on 5 May 1890 (MH), referring to his (De Forest's) article, "The Cradle of the Human Race," *Atlantic,* February 1878. He mentioned that Howells "spoke lightly of [it] at the time," but that the theory it advanced on the autochthonous origin of the European race had now been confirmed by Isaac Taylor's *The Origin of the Aryans* (1890). Howells reviewed Taylor's book in the "Editor's Study," *Harper's Monthly,* November 1890, partly at De Forest's request, and apparently sent him a draft for correction. See De Forest to Howells, 17 June and 11 September 1890 (both at MH).

2. In the same letter De Forest commented: "I have read all your later books, & have admired every one of them to the final line, although I have not written you about them. I should say that your New York story [*A Hazard of New Fortunes*] is your broadest & strongest yet, although it is difficult to point out any work for special distinction where all are marked by such a singular uniformity of excellence. You have now, as I honestly & firmly judge, put yourself ahead of Jane Austen. You have equal truth in perception & painting of human nature; & you have greater variety of classes & personages,—in short a larger view of society."

3. Although noting that "My mind is drying up, & I do almost nothing but read," De Forest mentioned in his letter of 5 May that he had "three ms volumes

on hand." Evidently without De Forest's prior approval, Howells wrote to J. W. Lovell on 15 June (CtY): "It is I who have urged Mr. De Forest to offer you a novel. While I was the editor of The Atlantic I published *Kate Beaumont*, by him; and I think it one of the best American novels ever written, as was his *Miss Ravenel* and his *Playing the Mischief*. I believe the time has come when an edition of all his novels would pay." Lovell (1852–1932), was the former president of the John W. Lovell Co., a New York publishing firm that issued many cheap pirated editions of British writers. From 1889 to 1893 Lovell's interests were consolidated into the United States Book Company, which he served as vice-president and president until its financial failure in the panic of 1893. Neither Lovell nor the United States Book Company published any of De Forest's works.

19 JUNE 1890, BOSTON, TO JAMES R. LOWELL

184 Commonwealth Avenue.
June 19, 1890.

Dear Mr. Lowell:

By this letter of Lawrence Barrett's you will see that he wishes to do a play of Tennyson's, and that he asks me to ask you for a letter that will introduce him favorably to Tennyson's notice or knowledge.[1] I have long thought Barrett the most intellectual actor on our stage—much the make of Irving in most ways.[2] He is a generous, impulsive, faithful Irishman, true and good, and a lover of what is fine and high. I am sure that if Tennyson let him do his play—and I don't see why he should make a difficulty—Barrett will produce it superbly as to the staging, and sympathetically as to the acting: he will approach the work with reverence, and the most ardent purpose of rendering it justice in every respect. If you care to favor him with a word to send to Tennyson, you may safely say that he is an actor of the few who put both mind and soul at the service of their art. He is a good fellow, in fine, whom I wish luck.

Yours sincerely
W. D. Howells.

1. Barrett wanted to produce Tennyson's *Becket*, and approached Howells to request Lowell to secure the poet's "blessing" and his help in making some changes for the stage. Lowell complied with this request. See Barrett to Howells, 18 June 1890, and Lowell to Howells, 19 June 1890 (both at MH).
2. Henry Irving, the British actor.

6 JULY 1890, WILLSBOROUGH POINT, NEW YORK, TO WILLIAM C. HOWELLS

Green Mt. View House,
Willsboro' Point, N.Y., July 6, 1890.

Dear Father:

I feel like saying, with the easy going Quaker, "Just as thee damn please," about which house you deed to me. You may have some feeling, which w'd be natural, about living in your own house, and so w'd rather give me the Cleveland than the Warren house;[1] and I wish you to consult any sentiment you have. *My* sentiment is for the old home-house, where I was once so ambitious and unhappy, where dear mother died, and Winny took her first steps on this path of pain. I think, too, that it would be better now, to make the effort to break the will regarding that house than it will be later. All the brothers and sisters can give their consent, and I suppose, the Court will readily give the order. Joe says the expense will be considerable, but he does not say how much, and I wish he could give me an approximate sum. Please ask him to do this, before we take any steps about either of the other houses.

I wish, how much I wish! you were here this heavenly Sunday morning. There is no describing this weather, with the lake so fresh before, and the mountains so blue on either side; you must feel it, to realize it. I don't know just how long we shall stay here;[2] there is no companionship for the children, for we are only two families in the house; and besides, now that we're at the gates of the Adirondacks, we feel like pushing in. But I'll give you due notice of our move.—The history of this house is a tragedy. The owner of the beautiful farm where it stands, an old soldier, began taking boarders, made money, became ambitious, built the hotel, and mortgaged everything to pay for it. Last year it was sold at auction; and the poor old fellow is living with his old wife in a second floor tenement in Rutland, picking up what jobs he can get.—With love to all,

> Your aff'te son,
> Will.

1. For W. C. Howells' acquisition of the "Warren house," see Howells to W. C. Howells, 23 July 1886.
2. Howells and his family arrived in Willsborough on 30 June and left on 14 July. It is located on Lake Champlain, just across from Vermont.

11 JULY 1890, WILLSBOROUGH POINT, NEW YORK,
TO SYLVESTER BAXTER

> Willsboro' Point, N. Y., July 11, 1890.

My dear Baxter:

I should like to read Morriña;[1] but I must wait awhile before I can ask you to send it me, for I am uncertain how long we shall be here, or anywhere. Perhaps we shall settle in the Adirondacks; perhaps go back to the seashore. I wish, meantime, you were here with me beside Lake Champlain, not only for the loveliness but for the whole life. Sometime

I will tell you the economic tragedy of this Point; but I can tell you now that Bellamy's book[2] and the doctrine it preaches have penetrated much farther into the interior than I had imagined. Our landlord, a shrewd old ex-cavalryman accepts it all, and he says the Adirondack people are discussing such things in public and private. Meanwhile, the old political mechanism works on; but it is all undermined, and some day it will drop in with a "sickening thud" and a puff of dust and that will be the end of the two parties and a new third party will win: so this thinking landlord's boarder thinks.—Have you read Harold Frederic's novels?[3] Very good central New York country life, done with roughness but force, and full of an indirect groping toward the new economic as well as artistic truth.—Thanks for hints about Lloyd's book.[4]—The family join me in regards.

> Yours ever
> W. D. Howells.

1. *Morriña* (1889) by Emilia Pardo Bazán. Howells wrote Baxter on 22 October 1890 (CSmH) that *"Morriña* . . . is one of the most lovely, and natural, and pathetic stories I've ever read." He reviewed this novel in the "Editor's Study," *Harper's Monthly,* April 1891, where he compared the Spanish author with Sarah Orne Jewett, praising especially her characterizations: "characters are expressed in colors of conduct and in shades of behavior, always distinct, but nowhere insisted upon; you know them as if you had lived with them."

2. *Looking Backward.*

3. Howells reviewed three of Frederic's novels in the "Editor's Study," *Harper's Monthly,* October 1890. *In the Valley* he dismissed rather scornfully as a historical romance with pretty staging and wooden characters. But he had praise for *The Lawton Girl* and *Seth's Brother's Wife* (1887); about the latter he wrote that "what seem to us the newest and best things . . . are his dramatic studies of local politics and politicians. . . . The Boss of Jay County, with his simple instinct of ruling and his invulnerability to bribes, is an example of Mr. Frederic's fidelity to conditions not much understood by people out of politics, which are managed by ambition rather than by money, as a general thing. Next to this in value is the truth, almost as novel, with which farm life, inside and out, is painted: it is so true that as you read you can almost smell the earthy scent of the shut-up country parlors; and the sordid dulness of those joyless existences lies heavy on the heart." See also Howells to Roosevelt, 26 October 1890.

4. Possibly Henry Demarest Lloyd's *A Strike of Millionaires Against Miners; or, The Story of Spring Valley* (1890), dealing with the strike and lockout of the miners of Spring Valley, Illinois, in 1889.

17 JULY 1890, LAKE PLACID, NEW YORK, TO LAURENCE HUTTON

> *Stevens House,* . . . .
> *Lake Placid, N. Y.* July 17, *1890*

My dear Hutton:

We are here, after two weeks on Lake Champlain, and now, having exploited the Adirondacks, we "some think" of using up the Catskills.

Did you mean business by wishing we would come to Onteora?[1] If you did, tell us how to get there, and what the Fox and Bear would ask for eating us by the week: say 3 persons in 3 rooms, and after mid August a 4th in 1 other room; all grown-ups, and troublesome, fastidious people. Also, kindly set forth the social attractions of your rugged community; we are from Boston, Mass., and very particular. Are you artistic, or intellectual, or simply Beautiful? We prefer all three.

You had bettter write quickly, if you wish to secure us, as we change our minds from moment to moment.

Best regards to Mrs. Hutton, Mrs. Dodge, the Wheelers, etc.[2]

Yours sincerely
W. D. Howells.

The alluring Mc Clure,[3] or the mccluring Allure said something about fully furnished cottages, which the Bear and Fox bestowed upon their friends.

1. Laurence Hutton had written Howells on 24 June 1890 (MH) that "the Colony" (i.e., the Onteora Club at the Bear and Fox Inn, near Tannersville, New York) was "wailing" for Howells' presence. Mark Twain and his family spent the summer of 1890 with the Onteora Club, a group of congenial people gathered there by Mrs. Candace Wheeler. See A. B. Paine, *Mark Twain* (New York: Harper & Brothers, 1912), II, 899–901. Howells wrote to Mrs. Wheeler on 24 July 1890 (NjP), expressing his regret at not being able to make definite plans and his hope that he and his family might come in September: "Everything you and Mr. Hutton the True and Kind have told me about Onteora is most tempting; and the terms for the cottage and board are, like Law, 'the perfection of Reason.'"

2. Mary Mapes Dodge (1831–1905) was the editor of *St. Nicholas Magazine* (1873–1905); Dunham Wheeler was the secretary of the Onteora Club, and his daughter Dora was an artist who painted the portraits of many contemporary English and American literary figures.

3. S. S. McClure.

17 AUGUST 1890, SARATOGA, NEW YORK, TO ANNE WHITNEY

Saratoga, Aug. 17, 1890

Dear Miss Whitney:[1]

Your letter gave me a great relief as well as a great pleasure,[2] for I was able to say to myself, "Now she understands why I wished to remain on the critical ground, and help fight the battle in my own way, without ranging myself under a banner."

—Pride, yes; but peace comes from loving,[3] and I am afraid that I hate the wrong more than I love the right.

I am glad of every word of your letter.

Yours sincerely
W. D. Howells.

1. Anne Whitney (1821–1915) was a sculptor who lived in Boston.

2. Miss Whitney wrote Howells on 28 July 1890 (MH) that she had finished reading *A Hazard of New Fortunes,* which she considered a "gift ... to me & to the world." She especially praised the deep "art-interest the work has for me,—Its dramatic completeness—the perfect drawing of each character—& the just proportions maintained in the group & that balance of character always suggested & honestly kept in view which on the whole—on any given plane of life—is likely to underlie the tyranny of circumstance—so that whether the individual shall go this way or that way is an even chance."

3. In her letter, Miss Whitney expressed her opinion that Howells' novel would "do a great enlightening work—a work that should make both for your pride & peace."

24 AUGUST 1890, SARATOGA, NEW YORK, TO WILLIAM C. HOWELLS

Saratoga, Aug. 24, 1890.

Dear father:

Tell Annie that we are all sorry she and Achille couldn't see their way to that little visit; but it will keep for some other summer. I don't know how long we shall stay in Saratoga yet; we may go Wednesday to Lake Luzerne; but it isn't settled.[1] The strike seems to be impending all round, and we may yet have to get back to Boston on foot. I think there's a general change of feeling in favor of the men, tho' most of the newspapers keep shouting for the road. The Central officials have shown themselves liars from the beginning; and it was they who really began the strike by discharging the men who wanted the weekly payments bill passed. A very notable fact is that both the great Albany papers, Republican & Democratic, censure the road severely, and the strike is at its worst in Albany. If it extends, it will cause great suffering, and the arrogance of the road will be the cause. Already the strikers are agitating for the nationalization of the roads.[2]

John is at Mt. Desert,[3] but we expect him by the end of the week. We are all well, and enjoying Saratoga hugely. The place is endlessly interesting.—I am glad you are getting on so well again, and that poor Henry is quiet. I should like to be with you, to help in the housekeeping, and enjoy some of the unmolested talks with the Annie-folks. You must give my love her and Achille, and both the children. In fact we all join in love to all of you.

Your aff'te son
Will.

1. Howells and his family went to Lake Luzerne, New York, on 2 September rather than 28 August as he suggests.

2. On 6 August the New York Central Railroad discharged some of its employees allegedly because they were not needed during the slack season and had

been shiftless and disobedient. The fired men claimed that they were being punished for their union activities in the Knights of Labor. The strike began on 9 August and ended on 18 September, but the strikers were not rehired by the railroad. Howells' friend, Gen. Roger A. Pryor, a defense lawyer for the Haymarket anarchists in 1887, was the attorney representing the Knights of Labor in the arbitration talks with the New York Central.

3. Mount Desert Island, off Bangor, Maine.

27 AUGUST 1890, SARATOGA, NEW YORK, TO HAMLIN GARLAND

Saratoga, Aug. 27, 1890.

My dear Garland:

I don't think it would be well for me to introduce or indorse your play.[1] It has good legs of its own, and can stand on them without any sort of bolstering. I know the suggestion comes from your generous willingness to do anything and everything for your friends, and I love you for it; but I don't believe in it.

I shall be glad to see your new play;[2] but wait now till I can send you a settled address. We go from Saratoga next Tuesday, and I'm not sure where, yet.

I've had a bad summer for work, but I've kept at *An Imperative Duty* as well as I could, and I hope it's coming out right. It's not far from finished—will be longer than the *Shadow of a Dream*.

The family join me in cordial regards.

Yours ever
W. D. Howells.

1. *Under the Wheel* (originally titled "Jason Edwards"), first published in the *Arena*, July 1890, was a single-tax drama. Howells had written Garland on 6 June 1890 (CLSU) that "The play mounts to a powerful effect that thrills, and it reaches an end that leaves me thinking most earnestly. It is *good*, and though I shall have some minor reproaches to make it when we meet, I wish now only to praise it." For an account of the composition and publication of the play see Donald Pizer, *Hamlin Garland's Early Work and Career* (Berkeley: University of California Press, 1960), pp. 79–83.

2. "A Member of the Third House: An American Play of To-Day," which Garland had begun in June 1890 and finished in August. Howells wrote Sylvester Baxter, 22 October 1890 (CSmH): "Hamlin Garland has written a very strong play dealing with the monopolistic corruption of legislation, such as the Nationalists have set themselves against. He calls it The Member of the Third House, and he proposes to read it in public some time next week, hoping to find a manager for it. Could you get a paragraph into the [Boston] Herald embodying these facts—all but that about his hope? I think such a play might do great good." Garland's reading of the play took place at Chickering Hall in Boston on 30 October 1890.

9 SEPTEMBER 1890, LAKE LUZERNE, NEW YORK, TO THOMAS S. PERRY

Lake Luzerne, N. Y. Sept. 9, 1890.

My dear Perry:

I hope now to see you again before long, but I wish even at this tardy date to acknowledge the letter I got from you early in July.[1] We have been blown about by all the winds of fortune for the last two months: 14 days at Willsborough Point; 14 at Lake Placid, 12 at Plattsburgh; 21 at Saratoga, 8 here—this is the mathematical anatomy of our illiad. But thank goodness, it's nearly ended. In the meantime, I've seen great numbers of my species, including curious varieties from Troy Town and Albany. Some persons of old family from New York who semi-scorned me for my newness, have gone far to convince me that the snob was not wholly evolved in Boston.

—I got my copyright rec't in August, and the Hazard[2] had then sold well on to eighteen thousand; the Shadow,[3] near eight. Our Adventures[4] had sold in the year past 1100 copies; and I feel that we shall yet be able to retire on that book.

—I have been working my way fitfully toward the end of my story—I call it An Imperative Duty—and I've nearly reached it. Perhaps it will please, but I don't know. The girl in it is coming out perversely—like a girl.[5]

—This village is not a misspelling of the Swiss concern, but was named after one of Louis XVI's ministers in the revolution.[6]

Yours ever
W. D. Howells.

1. Perry's letter has not been located.
2. *A Hazard of New Fortunes.*
3. *The Shadow of a Dream.*
4. *Library of Universal Adventure.*
5. Rhoda Aldgate, the girl who unexpectedly learns that she is partly black.
6. Chevalier de la Luzerne, the French minister who negotiated the peace with the United States in 1781.

17 SEPTEMBER 1890, LYNN, MASSACHUSETTS, TO WILLIAM ARCHER

Prescott House,
Lynn, Mass., Sept. 17, 1890.

My dear Sir:[1]

I should feel myself as graceless as some people seem to think me if I failed to thank you for the kind expressions concerning myself in your paper in the New York Dramatic Mirror of September 13th.[2] But the personal matter is of little importance compared with the aesthetic question, and I thank you even more for the expressions not concerning me. I read a paper of yours in the New Review last year,[3] which I was tempted to make a joyful noise over in the "Study," but somehow refrained, and so spared you the infamy of my praise in public. But you shall not escape it in private. A few more such papers as that, and the light which everyone else sees will begin to pierce the skulls of even Anglo-Saxon dramatic critics. The poor fellows are not to blame for their stupidity; God made them stupid, but unless He has been greatly misunderstood He did not make them proud of their stupidity. What I am trying to teach them in this country, where the theatres are to the dramas as the religions are to the gravies—a hundred to one—is that if we are ever to have American plays they must come out of American life, and they cannot naturally appear with a Parisian trousseau. This appears to vex them, and so they call names. I expected something of the sort. Of course, the things here that I have praised with many reservations are "poor things, but our own." They are poor in trying to be like the old stage-plays, but the worst of them have astonishing gleams of truth in them, and so I try to make people believe that so far as they *are* our own they are good. It is "hard sledding." Still, there is some little response. The public and the managers are more intelligent, I think than the critics.

Yours very truly
W. D. Howells.

Wm. Archer, Esq.

1. William Archer (1856–1924) was a Scottish critic and dramatist. He began his career as a dramatic critic for the London *Figaro* (1879–1881) and later was a critic for the *World* (1884–1905), the *Nation*, the New York *Tribune*, and the *Manchester Guardian*. His translations of Ibsen's plays were widely read and used, and they contributed significantly to the growth of Ibsen's popularity among the English public.
2. Archer's article "The Old Criticism and the New," New York *Dramatic Mirror*, 13 September 1890, praised Howells as being the "champion of the new school" which focuses primarily on character development instead of action as the essential element in drama. He also defended *A Hazard of New Fortunes* against the "sneers" of Edward Fuller, a Boston critic who championed the "old school" of criticism.
3. "The Dying Drama," *New Review*, September 1889.

25 SEPTEMBER 1890, LYNN, MASSACHUSETTS, TO HENRY JAMES

Prescott House,
Lynn, Sept. 25, 1890.

My dear James:

The vain wish to write you something worthy in answer to that magnificent letter of yours about my book has kept me from writing to you at all.[1] Now I come meekly, guiltily, and own that I never could have fitly acknowledged it, and that I ought to have known I couldn't. I don't even know how to thank you. Your praise is princely; when I read your letter I felt as if I had been created a peer, or something. Then, Balestier[2] comes along six months later, and full of the memory of your kindness for me, uses me as if I were really a titled person. That youth made a gay time for us while he stayed with us in Saratoga, and we had ever so much talk of you. He will have told you of our plan of getting you to come and live there, in a house with a bronze boot-black for a fountain on its lawn, and amusing you with a toboggan-slide, to the perpetual music of McGinty and Annie Rooney.[3] We said, "Saratoga is the place for James. It's the *only* place that would reconcile him to America." I suppose we thought no other place could be so bad, even in America, and the whole country would profit by the contrast. We spent three weeks there, Mrs Howells and I with great amusement, and Pilla with rebellion and abhorrence.—But I wont speak of our goings and comings, or of our stayings, for Balestier will tell you all. Now we're back near Boston, waiting to get into our flat, if we can't exchange it for a furnished house.—I've just finished another novelette (An Imperative Duty) which completes my work for the year, and I have three months of distracting leisure before me. I'm in despair how to employ it unless I give it to writing letters to you, and trying to retrieve myself.—I'm glad to say that The Tragic Muse is almost the tutelary deity of our reading public, as I hope the publishers' returns will persuade you to believe.[4] It's a pity they don't publish fifty cent editions of your books, as I now have the Harper's do simultaneously with the bound editions of mine. You ought to be got into the hands of the people.—My wife wants me to thank you for your good will towards her sister; I hope Mrs. Shepard may yet see you.[5]—I gave Osgood's young partner a note to you; McIlvaine is an admirable fellow.[6]—Scudder, the new *Atlantic* editor told me with great pleasure of the letter you had written him. He will make a good editor, and I think your relations with him will be very agreeable—he's so intelligent and jolly.[7]—I wish you could see a bit of this American weather today—so bright and thin and keen, you can almost hear it rattle. But I wish more I could meet you in London, which I don't know now that I shall ever do. I look forward to the winter in Boston with a feeling of satiety towards the place. I can only console myself by reflecting that it is much too good for me. I have that consolation in regard to everything, but I don't find it makes me less exacting.

Since we got back we've seen no one. I heard from Perry (whom I *did* see, however) that Lowell is still poorly, and is low spirited.[8] Your brother Wm. I had a glimpse of the other day at Lynn station, when he waggled his hand to me from the car window—I suppose he was going home from the mountains.

Balestier told me of the play you've been writing, and of the processes of selfsacrifice you've been through for it.[9] I hope with all my heart they'll avail. From time to time I yearn towards the stage, but I don't suppose I shall ever do anything for it. The novel is such a *free* fight, you don't want ever afterwards to be tied up to any Queensbury rules.[10] We've just been visited by a young poet, from Louisville, Kentucky,[11] a young man of great promise and some beautiful performance, whom we had the pleasure of seeing look upon the ocean for the first time. He's a most gentle, refined creature, whose hard fate it is to be an accountant in a betting-house, the head of which has killed his man, and never goes out at night without an armed guard. He's killed *two* men, but one was black, and he doesn't count *him*. Just now a judge is holding court in one of the vendetta districts of Ky., with a regiment of soldiers. I mentioned this to Cawein, and he said, "Oh, they *always* have to have troops where there are feuds."—My wife and daughter join me in love.

Yours ever
W. D. Howells
(c/o Harpers.)

1. James wrote Howells on 17 May (MH; printed with omissions in Percy Lubbock, ed., *The Letters of Henry James* [1920; reprint ed., New York: Octagon Books, 1970] I, 163–66), praising *A Hazard of New Fortunes*: "you have never yet done anything so roundly & totally good.... The life, the truth, the light, the heat, the breadth & depth & thickness of the Hazard, are absolutely admirable." In other parts of this long letter James explained his sense of Howells' strengths and limitations as a novelist, essentially making the point that his scope is narrow but that his treatment of his chosen material is very fine. "The novelist is a particular *window*," James wrote in general terms, "absolutely—& of worth in so far as he is one; & it's because you open so well & are hung so close over the street that *I* could hang out of it all day long. Your very value is that you choose your own street— heaven forbid I should have to choose it for you. If I should say I mortally dislike the people who pass in it, I should seem to be taking on myself that intolerable responsibility of selection which it is exactly such a luxury to be relieved of."

2. Charles Wolcott Balestier (1861–1891), an author and publisher who had sent stories and essays to the *Atlantic* during Howells' editorship, was the representative of John W. Lovell, for whom he secured original manuscripts for publication. While in England he joined in partnership with William Heinemann to form Heinemann & Balestier, which published English and American books on the Continent; he also became an especially good friend of James and Edmund Gosse. Balestier wrote

Howells on 12 July 1890 (MH) that he was coming to America for a week in September, at which time he tried to negotiate a contract with Howells for the publication of Howells' books by Lovell.

3. Two popular songs, "Down Went McGinty to the Bottom of the Sea" by Joseph Flynn and "Little Annie Roonie" by Michael Nolan.

4. James's *The Tragic Muse* was published in America by Houghton Mifflin & Co. and in England by Macmillan. Unfortunately, Howells' hopes for a promising sale were not realized: no more than 1,500 copies appear to have been sold. See Roger Gard, ed., *Henry James: The Critical Heritage* (New York: Barnes & Noble, 1968), p. 553.

5. Howells had requested that James be of assistance to Joanna Mead Shepard when she reached Italy. But James notified Howells on 27 July 1890 (MH) that he had to decline, being "far away & almost beyond the radius of her charm."

6. Clarence W. McIlvaine (1865–1912), a former employee of Harper & Brothers, joined in partnership with James R. Osgood to form the London publishing company of Osgood, McIlvaine & Co. It was the English representative of the Harpers, and when Osgood died in 1892, Harpers absorbed the firm and McIlvaine became a vice-president in charge of their London office.

7. Horace E. Scudder edited the *Atlantic* from 1890 to 1898.

8. T. S. Perry wrote Howells, 7 September 1890 (MH): "I have seen J. R. L. who appears rather dejected, tho' making a good fight against the inevitable fate of mortals...." Lowell died 12 August 1891.

9. Balestier was probably referring to James's dramatization of *The American*, which he worked on throughout 1890. The task was finally completed, though, and the play opened on 3 January 1891 at the Winter Gardens Theatre in Southport, near Liverpool. See L. Edel, *Henry James: The Middle Years, 1882–1895* (Philadelphia: Lippincott, 1962), pp. 280–88.

10. John Sholto Douglas Queensberry (1844–1900) was the originator of the rules that govern the modern sport of boxing. The rules were drafted in 1865 and by 1889 were standardized and widely used in the United States.

11. Madison J. Cawein.

26 OCTOBER 1890, BOSTON, TO THEODORE ROOSEVELT

> 184 Commonwealth Ave.,
> Boston, Oct. 26, 1890.

Dear Mr. Roosevelt—

John Hay once said one of those things to me about the ways and tricks of politicians which illumined my life-long knowledge of them, as one knows them in the country, and so I was able to recognize the truth of Frederick's picture when I saw it. I'm surprised—or I should be surprised if I were younger—that it's importance was not more felt. Didn't you think the whole book, except the mugwumping, very good?[1]

I hardly hope to be in Washington, this winter, and I don't yet see the hour of New York; but I would like so much to meet you again, questions or no questions.[2]

> Yours cordially,
> W. D. Howells.

1. Roosevelt, then a member of the United States Civil Service Commission, wrote Howells on 20 October 1890 (MH) in response to the October "Editor's Study": "Politics being rather my hobby I was much pleased to see you mention appreciatively the political portions of 'Seth's Brother's Wife', by Harold Frederick. I have always esteemed them particularly good, for they are curiously true to life—except the entirely unnatural touch which makes the 'boss' turn semimugwump on the last page of the book, apparently simply to make an ending of conventional virtue. [¶] Our average educated man is singularly ignorant of the real motives and methods of the politicians, especially the country politicians; and I always draw a breath of relief when I read something by somebody who *does* understand them." See Howells to Baxter, 11 July 1890, n. 3.

2. Howells had probably met Roosevelt in New York some time after the latter returned to the East from the Dakota Territory in 1886. Roosevelt wrote Howells in his letter of 20 October that he had "been treasuring up some questions I wished to ask you—they are rather too involved to write them."

28 OCTOBER 1890, BOSTON, TO MABEL LOOMIS TODD

184 Commonwealth Ave.,
Boston, Oct. 28, 1890.

Dear Mrs. Loomis:[1]

When you showed me Miss Dickinson's poems, I did not half know how good they were. Will you kindly look over this review,[2] and tell me whether I have misreported the things you told me of her life, or whether I have any right to report them at all. I'm very anxious not to intrude upon personal grounds. Please let me have the proof back at once. I'm afraid I shall have to cut it down somewhat.

—I liked extremely the "temperament," as the critic's slang now is, of that little story you sent me.[3] Nothing could have been better treated, but story, there is none there that I hadn't known the likes of before. I wish you would do sketches, studies, without bothering about a story.—My wife, sick, and my daughter, well, join me in duty to you and love to the dear little girl.[4]

Yours sincerely
W. D. Howells.

1. Mabel Loomis Todd (1856–1932) was a lecturer, author of popular science books, and poet. With Thomas W. Higginson she edited two series of *Poems by Emily Dickinson* (1890–1891) and a third series by herself (1896); she also edited *Letters of Emily Dickinson* (1894).

2. Howells reviewed *Poems by Emily Dickinson* in the "Editor's Study," *Harper's Monthly*, January 1891. In his detailed and perceptive discussion, after commenting briefly on Dickinson's life, Howells stresses her poems on death, which "have a fascination above any others in the book...." He finds many of them "terribly unsparing...but true as the grave and certain as mortality" and considers their "rough" poetic form a distinctive characteristic: "the artist meant just this harsh exterior to remain, and...no grace of smoothness could have imparted her intention as it does."

3. Perhaps "The Witch of Winnacunnett," *New England Magazine*, January 1891. Todd had published a few articles—mostly on her travels and on astronomy—prior to her attempt at fiction.

4. Mabel Todd's daughter, Millicent Todd Bingham (1880–1968), later became a noted geographer and conservationist.

9 NOVEMBER 1890, BOSTON, TO WILLIAM C. HOWELLS

Boston, Nov. 9, 1890.

Dear father:

You will be glad to know that Elinor is very much better, and is in a fair way to be as well as ever very soon; though she still has to lie down a great part of each day.[1]

You mustn't be too much cast down by the elections.[2] I look forward to the decay of both the old parties, and the growth of a new one that will mean true equality and real freedom, and not the images we have been mocked with hitherto. The poor Negroes whom we laughed at for expecting the government to give them each "forty acres and a mule," have a truer ideal of a civilized state than the manufacturers who want more and more tariff but won't raise their workmen's wages a cent. Whatever we confess to the enemy, we must confess to ourselves, that in the matter the Republicans have been humbugging, and that in putting forward such men as Quay,[3] who corrupted the Pennsylvanians with one hand while he defeated the Lodge elections bill with the other,[4] they have been false to the good in them. At the same time I have not the least faith in the Democrats. But my faith in the grand and absolute change, sooner or later, is so great that I don't grieve over their success. They are sure to abuse their victory, and then they will be out of power again, and I hope that a party "of the people, for the people" will rise up in their place, and make this a country where no man who will work need want.

All send love to each of you.

Your aff'te son,
Will.

1. Howells had written his father on 19 October 1890 (MH) that his family was well "except Elinor who is at the period of afflictions, and has been worn down into bed by the worry of settling for the winter."

2. Howells' staunchly Republican father must have been disconcerted about the November elections, in which the Democrats won a sizable majority in the House of Representatives (253 to 88); in the U.S. Senate, however, Republicans continued to outnumber Democrats (47 to 39).

3. Matthew Stanley Quay (1833–1904) was an influential and allegedly corrupt Pennsylvania politician who served in state government (1865–1887) and as U.S.

senator (1887–1904). He was chairman of the Republican National Committee in 1888 and managed Benjamin Harrison's presidential campaign.

4. The Federal Elections or "Force" Bill originated in the House of Representatives in 1890. It called for the supervision of congressional elections by federal officers in any district where such supervision was requested by five hundred voters. The intention of the bill was to prevent fraud or the intimidation of voters, especially Southern Negroes, in any part of the country. Henry Cabot Lodge (1850–1924), a Republican representative from Massachusetts (1887–1893) and chairman of the House Committee on Elections, strongly supported the measure, but when the bill went to the Senate, Quay organized the opposition, and it did not pass.

16 November 1890, Boston, to William C. Howells

184 Commonwealth Avenue.
Boston, Nov. 16, 1890.

Dear father:

We have had a nice long letter from Eliza giving an account of the wedding which seems to have been very successful.[1] I am glad of the pleasure which she and Joe feel in Mary's marriage, and I shall always be sorry that I had to disappoint them by not coming to the ceremony. Elinor seems quite well, and in a little time—right after Thanksgiving—I hope to be with you.

There is a great deal of excitement here about the failure of Baring Bros.,[2] and people are asking where the calamity will end. In any case it will begin again, sooner or later, for that is in the constitution of things, as they now are. But I hope the Nationalists will not fail to point the moral in this case, and show that it is not the Barings that have failed but our whole economic system. The worst for me is that the Barings were the chief backers of the Atchison & Topeka road, and that my $6000 of stock, which I bought at $1.13 is now worth 24 cents.[3] It was honest money, that I had earned, not made; but perhaps I had no right to have money in stocks. It looks now as if Jay Gould might gobble the whole concern.[4] But no one really knows what rascality is plotting in the darkness, and things must of course go from bad to very much worse before any radical reform comes.

This is another of the beautiful days we have been having nearly the whole month. I think we have not been nearly so rain-soaked as you. I hope we may have pleasant weather for my visit, and be able to get outdoors a little together.

With our united love to you all,

Your aff'te son
Will.

1. Mary Elizabeth Howells, the oldest daughter of Joe and Eliza Howells, married Willis Shumway in early November. Howells wrote his father on 19 October (MH) that he planned to attend the wedding; but he was unable to go, probably because of Elinor's health.

2. The century-old London banking house, Baring Brothers & Co., and their American representatives, Kidder, Peabody & Co., controlled Atchison, Topeka & Santa Fe stock. On 14 November the stock began to drop sharply, and as a result of the decline all other railroad stocks fell. The reason for the trouble was a rumor that because the Barings needed to raise cash to protect some of their other foreign investments in Africa and South America, they would sell their stock in Atchison, Topeka & Santa Fe. However, with loans from the Bank of England and the Rothschilds, the Barings did not have to sell their holdings.

3. See Howells to John M. Howells, 15 June 1889.

4. Jay Gould (1864–1923), the robber-baron owner of the Missouri Pacific Railroad, was rumored to be trying to take control of the Atchison, Topeka & Santa Fe so that he could fulfill his desire to own a complete transcontinental railway line.

25 NOVEMBER 1890, BOSTON, TO MABEL LOOMIS TODD

> *184 Commonwealth Avenue.*
> Boston, Nov. 25, 1890.

Dear Mrs Todd:

Your story is on the general level of so many American stories.[1] It is in nowise so good as that printed sketch you sent me. Did you ever know anything like it in life? *I* never did. People don't perpetrate that sort of revolting and criminal self-sacrifice. If it were life, your Dorothy and Doctor would have got married, & let the others go, as they ought.

The manner is not simple and direct like that of your sketch. Why don't you read Tourguenief, Björnson, Tolstoï, the great masters of simplicity? You can do good work, *but* this story is not good. I'm sorry to be so unfavorable.

> Yours sincerely
> **W. D. Howells.**

1. The story Mrs. Todd had submitted to Howells has not been identified. See also Howells to Todd, 28 October 1890.

22 DECEMBER 1890, BOSTON, TO HOWARD PYLE

> 184 Commonwealth Avenue,
> Boston, Dec. 22, 1890.

My dear friend:[1]

Your story is most powerful and irresistibly true. It thrilled me deeply as I read it, and though I now call it true, because it is consonant with the most reasonable conjecture of the life hereafter, yet I felt a certain sympathy with Colonel Singleton, as I have always felt with the brother of the Prodigal. I know we must be swept clean of ourselves before the Lord can enter in—I have been taught so—but it seems hard. But this is beside the real matter. You have written a romance which I think will vividly impress every reader. It is most real to me from beginning to end, and it interests me all the more because I have had it in mind myself to write a story of the future life, on an extended scale, using Swedenborg for my *entourage*. I venture to suggest that you leave out the explicit references to Swedenborg and the New Church, because I'm afraid they will circumscribe your audience. The romance ought to be printed in *Harper's* or the *Century*, not in any sectarian periodical. I congratulate you heartily on a fine and noble piece of work, whose implications are infinitely more than artistic.

My reading dream-wards, so far as Du Prol was concerned,[2] ended in an argument for metempsychosis, or paleogenesis! I was deeply disappointed —as deeply as you with your astronomers. I was grievously vexed, as well as disappointed; but I will enclose a dream of my own, which I think will interest you. Kindly return it, when you have read it.[3]

I wish we could meet, and talk again. Letters are not my natural expression, though literature is; I feel that I don't get myself out in them; my phrases hide me. You are a man I would like to be sincere with: that is, appear no better than I am; and I tell you honestly that for the greater part of the time I believe in nothing, though I am afraid of everything. I do not always feel sure that I shall live again, but when I wake at night the room seems dense with spirits. Since this dream which I wrote out for my father I have had others about my daughter, fantastic and hideous, as if to punish me for my unbelief.

Yours faithfully,
W. D. Howells.

1. Howard Pyle (1853–1911), an author, illustrator, and fellow Swedenborgian, had sent Howells on 21 December (MH) a draft of his story "In Tenebras," which was later published in *Harper's Monthly*, February 1894.

2. Karl Freiherr von Prel (1839–1899), a German scholar of mysticism and the occult, became well known for his work on the psychology of dreams, *Oneirokritikon* (1865); his *The Philosophy of Mysticism* appeared in English translation in 1889. Pyle had written in his letter of 21 December: "I wish I knew what has been the result of your last summer's reading upon the subjects of dreams. I myself mistrust all such philosophical speculations most heartily."

3. The enclosure has not been identified.

9 January 1891, Boston, to Henry M. Alden

> *184 Commonwealth Avenue.*
> Jan'y 9, 1891.

My dear Alden:

I never was an abolitionist strictly speaking.[1] My father was an anti-slavery Whig, a Freesoiler and a Republican, and I followed him. But I know that in the last years before the war, no man was free to think or to speak against slavery in the South; so men thought falsely and spoke hollowly. The same state of intellectual decay came about from slavery that came from Jesuitism: literature turned to cheap rhetoric, logic to sophistry. The good work in the South now comes from Freedom, the source of all good.—I had no preoccupations against McClellan; but I have read some of his letters; they settled the question with me. I think Hay and Nicolay treated him, upon his own showing, very mercifully.[2]

I am always glad not to have said the extreme things, but if that question between us had led to nothing but the letter you have just written me, I should feel rewarded for having yielded to you. I do most cordially respect and trust you.—In the same sort, I am now content not to have said my say about Lang's rubbish;[3] I see how it would have embarrassed you, and I know how many strings you have to keep straight. But do you think—quite apart from all this—that it is best to regard the Study as speaking editorially? My name goes with it, and I know that I differ from you and Curtis and Warner on many literary points.[4] If there is ever question of its positions, would n't it be easy to say they are *my* positions?

I will think over your suggestions for future numbers. I have always my great anxieties to make it good, and I will gladly make it as attractive as I can.[5]

My love, all our loves, to you and yours—particularly Mrs. Alden. I will send you the little monograph about Winny.[6]

> Yours ever
> W. D. Howells.

Howard Pyle has done a *great* story, which he's let me see. I hope he'll let you see it.[7]

1. In the "Editor's Study" for February 1891, which was then in print though not yet published, Howells had written about the state of prewar Southern literature that "for the most part the pro-slavery men wrote worse and spoke worse, in the artistic sense, than the antislavery men; perhaps the habit of declaring wrong right, in defiance of reason, resulted in an intellectual decay which inevitably expressed itself in bombast and swagger." Alden objected to this judgment in his letter to

Howells of 8 January 1891 (MH): "I cannot *now* feel that the Southern people or their representatives were essentially on a lower ethical plane than were we of the North. Indeed, we abolished the only slavery existing that had any virtue in it. Our economic slaveries (though scientifically better managed) were, for all that they implied in our spiritual character, far more deplorable than negro-slavery." Seeking a cause for the severity of Howells' remarks, Alden speculated that "This sort of judgment struck me as not at all characteristic of you; & I could only account for it on the ground of some strong individual feeling persisting from some former period." It was probably this latter comment that prompted Howells' response.

2. One of the books reviewed by Howells in the February "Study" was the ten-volume biography by John Hay and John Nicolay, *Abraham Lincoln: A History* (1890). Alden apparently canceled some of Howells' remarks concerning Lincoln's uneasy relationship with General George B. McClellan (1826–1885). "...I thought it was better that certain passages should not stand," he wrote to Howells on 8 January, "& that...only those things should be said which would be pertinent to the revelation of Lincoln's character...." For the Hay and Nicolay discussion of McClellan, see in particular IV, 180–93.

3. Andrew Lang (1844–1912), English man of letters, apparently took issue in print with Howells' appreciation of Emily Dickinson (in the "Editor's Study" for January 1891), although the source of Lang's "rubbish" has not been located. "After all," Alden consoled Howells in the same letter, "what you said of Emily Dickinson stands & will stand." Alden's conciliatory tone probably derived, at least in part, from his decision not to print Howells' uncomplimentary review of *The World's Desire*, coauthored by Lang and H. Rider Haggard. Lang was, as Alden put it, "so good a friend of the Magazine in England," that adverse criticism of his work might have proved awkward for the Harpers, particularly since they not only became the American publisher of his romance, but for a time considered running it as a serial in *Harper's Monthly*, which occasioned a letter of "cordial appreciation" from Alden to Lang. As Alden confided to Howells, "He [Lang] might have made the matter embarrassing to the house by quoting from our letter in print; & unfortunately I cannot plead my case with him as I can with you. I can beg any thing of you."

4. G. W. Curtis and C. D. Warner served in editorial capacities for *Harper's Monthly* under Alden's editorship.

5. Alden had suggested that Howells might divert his attention for a time in the "Study" with "literary reminiscences" or a discussion of "the *literary movement in the West*," suggestions that Howells never took up. Alden's seeming lack of confidence in Howells' judgment, together with the apparent reluctance of *Harper's* to involve itself in critical dispute, may have led to Howells' decision, reached some time in January of 1891, to stop writing the "Editor's Study" once his current contractual agreement was fulfilled. Howells' last "Study" appeared in the March 1892 *Harper's Monthly*.

6. In his letter, Alden had requested a copy of the privately printed untitled little biographical volume on Winifred Howells (1891). See Gibson-Arms, *Bibliography*, p. 38.

7. See Howells to Pyle, 22 December 1890, n. 1.

11 JANUARY 1891, BOSTON, TO WILLIAM C. HOWELLS

184 Commonwealth Avenue.
Boston, Jan'y 11, 1891.

Dear father:

I am glad you could write me that short note and postal, but they show your thoughtful love more than your strength, and I shall be

anxious, of course, till I hear that you are quite well again. Is there anything I can do to make your house warmer or more weatherproof? How
did you get your cold? I do hope you will be as careful as human nature
will allow. Of course I shouldn't want you deprived of the right of taking
cold, if it were not for the possible pneumonia.—The Russian Stepniak
has been with us again.[1] After his lecture on Sibereian Exiles, yesterday,
he came home to dinner with me. We stopped on the way at an engine
house (the one I once took you to) and saw them hitch up for an alarm.
Stepniak was delighted, and slid down the brass pole himself as the
firemen do, from the dormitory to the engine room. He is a big man in
a black ulster, and he looked like a bear on a pole. At dinner, he cares
nothing for what he eats, but eats a lot.—His lecture was amazing in the
facts of cruelty and oppression it gave. It seems incredible that those
things should be going on now, every day.[2]—Pilla is still doing society on
a large scale. Last week she went to three balls, and was everywhere admired and courted. She takes it all very simply and coolly, and I think
will be no sorrier than we when it's all over.—I've made what seems a
very good beginning on my new story and have got 112 pages of it done.[3]
I wish Aurelia could jot me down some of the more characteristic aspects
of life at Quebec in the winter—the look of the streets, sleighs, etc.; things
that would most strike and concern a stranger. I want my defaulter to
arrive in mid-winter. How about the river and railroads?

We are all well and join in love to you all.

Your aff'te son,
Will.

1. Sergei Mikhailovich Kravchinski (1852–1895), a Russian revolutionary and
author who used the pseudonym "Stepniak," had probably met Howells in late
December 1890. Edward R. Pease, general secretary of the Fabian Society in London,
had written Howells on 12 December 1890 (MH) to introduce him to Stepniak. On
4 January 1891 (MH) Howells wrote his father: "We have the great Russian
Nihilist, Stepniak, here. He is a most interesting and important man; one of
those wonderful clear heads that seem to belong to other races than ours. He
went to a club dinner with me, and talked for an hour or two about conditions in
Russia, with a moderation and lucidity that enchanted everybody.—He is a great
reader of my books, and he told me that his chief wish in coming to America
was to meet me. He said he found the same qualities in my work that he found
in the Russian novelists; when we came away from the dinner he said that he
recognized my types in the men he had met." Stepniak was on a lecture tour in
America in order to enlist the support of influential Americans for his fight against
political repression in Russia, and to raise money for the Russian Free Press Fund,
an organization dedicated to propagandizing on behalf of various Russian opposition groups. See also Howells to Garrison, 19 April 1891, n. 1.

2. Stepniak had documented the misery of Russian life in his book *The Russian Peasantry* (1888), which Howells reviewed in the "Editor's Study," *Harper's
Monthly,* October 1888. For a complete account of Stepniak's American tour, see
Charles A. Moser, "A Nihilist's Career: S. M. Stepniak-Kravchinski," *American Slavic
and East European Review* 20 (1961), 65–71.

3. *The Quality of Mercy.*

29 JANUARY 1891, BOSTON, TO CHARLES A. DANA

184 Commonwealth Avenue.
January 29, 1891.

Dear Mr. Dana:[1]

I have twice had some talk with Stepniak the Russian Nihilist about a plan he has for promoting the liberal cause in Russia by constantly reporting to the world outside the facts of oppression occurring there. I told him that I thought the only way to raise money for the work was to convince some great journal that it could find its account in these reports as (exclusive) news; and I said I would propose the matter for him to The Sun. He had thought of another journal, but at my instance he made the enclosed synopsis of his scheme, which is now first submitted to you.[2] I think a glance at it will suggest the interest and importance of the matter he could furnish, and it would be in good newspaper form, after passing through his hands, for he is a practiced journalist. I myself have no doubt he will do all he says; but the business aspect is for your sole consideration, especially as I understand from Stepniak that he will want some advance of money to make a beginning.

If the affair strikes you favorably, he will call on you in New York, four or five weeks from this; and I wish you would ask him to do this, for I think you could not fail to feel the uncommon quality of the man.

I should be glad to serve him with you, for I like him, and I believe that I should be serving you at the same time. But that is a point for you to decide.

Yours sincerely
W. D. Howells.

P. S. If you do not care to make affairs with him, kindly return me his letter.

1. Charles Anderson Dana (1819–1897), formerly connected with the New York *Tribune* (1847–1862), was an assistant secretary of war (1864–1865). He played a major part in founding the New York *Sun*, becoming its managing editor and part owner in 1868, a position he used to make the *Sun* into one of the most successful and respected journalistic enterprises of its time. In October 1891 the *Sun* began the serialization of Howells' *The Quality of Mercy*.

2. Besides describing the Russian plight in the monthly newspaper *Free Russia*, Stepniak wanted to organize an American Society of Friends of Russian Freedom—a group Howells refused to join (see Howells to Garrison, 19 April 1891)—in order to mobilize public opinion for his cause. He also wanted to have his views disseminated in the American press. He published three articles on the Jewish problem in Russia in Dana's New York *Sun*. Besides helping him in this latter venture, Howells wrote James Burton Pond (1838–1903), a New York lecture manager, on 27 January 1891 (typed copy at WHi) to help Stepniak organize his midwestern lecture tour. Howells suggested that Henry D. Lloyd help Stepniak in Chicago, and com-

mented on Stepniak's lecture on Tolstoy, characterizing it as "one of the most important things I ever heard, and its intellectual grasp was wonderful. I didn't agree with it all. It was unsympathetic and it had the revolutionist's grudge for the non-resistant in it; even the literary strictures were some of them not to my thinking just; but these defects did not disable the thing as a whole. Simply as a study it was large, bold and massive to [an] extraordinary degree."

30 JANUARY 1891, BOSTON, TO THOMAS W. HIGGINSON

184 Commonwealth Avenue.
Jan'y 30, 1891.

My dear Higginson:

I am exceedingly obliged to you for your printed paragraph, and still more for your letter. The "Hazard" has sold 20,000 in a year, and *you* have praised it. I am content with much more than most of the saints ever had.[1]

But you are quite right in your criticism of the opening passages; long stretches of carpentery, where I arrived at little or nothing of the real edifice. I may tell you that they were done when we were losing, when we lost, our Winny, and that I was writing in that stress because I *must.* Afterwards I could not change them. Cosa fatta capo ha.[2]

It was very sweet and good of you to favor me against the odds you met, and I thank you with all my heart. I was curious to know just what you said, and it is better than I hoped.

There is very much in your letter that goes with what I have been thinking of late.

Yours sincerely,
W. D. Howells.

1. Howells wrote Higginson on 29 January 1891 (NN; G. S. Hellman, "The Letters of Howells to Higginson," *Twenty-Seventh Annual Report of the Bibliophile Society* [Cedar Rapids, Iowa: Torch Press, 1929], p. 48): "I am long past the time of hunting down compliments; but a Higginson does not praise a Howells every day; and the latter H. would like really to know what the former H. said of him at the Nineteenth Century Club. If you have any report of your remarks will you kindly lend it me? Otherwise do not bother about me, farther. I caught some echoes in the Transcript, and felt proud and glad—till I remembered that I should not survive the second glacial epoch, anyway." The topic of Higginson's speech was "Americanism in Literature; or the New World and the New Book," and he praised Howells in particular for his portrayal of character, especially in *A Hazard of New Fortunes.* For a complete transcription of the speech see Higginson's *The New World and the New Book: An Address Delivered Before the Nineteenth Century Club of New York City, Jan. 15, 1891 with Kindred Essays* (1892), pp. 1–18. In his reply to Howells of 30 January (MH) Higginson continued his remarks on *A Hazard of New Fortunes* and commented on Howells' criticism and critical reputation. Higginson claimed that because the novel had been issued in weekly installments, Howells did not have as large an audience as Howells claimed. "I also said that I often could not agree with

your criticism, thought it too polemic & that your reasons...were not so good as your opinions." He further noted that "it was not the fashion in N. Y. to admire you," though it was fashionable to do so in Boston, and concluded: "If I could write fiction as you do, I would leave Criticism to those who cannot create."

2. Italian for "I have accepted the accomplished fact."

1 FEBRUARY 1891, BOSTON, TO SARAH ORNE JEWETT

184 Commonwealth Avenue.
Feb'y 1, 1891.

Dear Miss Jewett:

I had written about your book for some far forthcoming Study,[1] and when I took it up just now to read something over again in it, I thought I had thanked you for it. Thank you now, and always.—I opened and read The White Rose Road, which I had left because I always want to read Mr. Teaby and Going to Shrewsbury whenever I come in eyeshot of them. But the W. R. R. is beautiful, and it made the tears come into my eyes out of the everlasting ache in my heart for all that is poor, and fair and pitiful.

You have a precious gift, and you must know it, and can be none the worse for your knowledge. We all have a tender pleasure in your work, which there is no name for but love. I think *no* one has shown finer art in a way, than you, and that something which is so much better than art, besides. Your voice is like a thrush's in the din of all the literary noises that stun us so.

I hope your mother is better, and that we shall see you before long in Boston. Give my love to your nephew, and our united affection to all your house.

Yours sincerely,
W. D. Howells.

1. For Howells' notice of Jewett's *Strangers and Wayfarers,* see Howells to Fields, 4 February 1890, n. 3. The three stories included in the volume were all originally published in the *Atlantic:* "The White Rose Road" (September 1889), "The Quest of Mr. Teaby" (January 1890), and "Going to Shrewsbury" (July 1889).

8 FEBRUARY 1891, BOSTON, TO WILLIAM C. HOWELLS

184 Commonwealth Avenue.
Boston, Feb. 8, 1891.

Dear father:

I hope you received last night the bed-shirts I sent you by express on Friday. The woollen one was an experiment which I wanted you to try.

If you find it comfortable, I can send you another. The two larger shirts are for Henry. I could not find any pijamahs, except Woollen ones at the store where I bought the shirts, and they were rather expensive— $3.00—and I was afraid the stuff might be too hot. I will look further during the week. . . . We are having the usual Sunday snow-storm, this morning, and it looks as if it might keep on and be a Monday one before it got through. The winter has been rather trying, but so far we have escaped colds, and I don't propose to complain of a season that has used me well. I am able to drub away at my story,[1] so far, without the loss of a day; and that is saying a good deal. The copy has grown rapidly under my hands, but I find it more and more difficult to satisfy myself with my work; I seem to be always experimenting, always exploring a new field. But I suppose this is a condition of interest in the matter. . . I must tell you much I felt for you in the death of old Charley.[2] The poor creature had a character of his own, which even I, a comparative stranger, was sensible of, and which you must have felt very intimately. Besides, these dumb witnesses of our lives become centres of association, and we cannot lose them without losing great part of ourselves. Johnny, mother, Victoria, Winny, were all the affectionate friends of the poor beast who is gone, and he was something to remember them each by. I am glad that he passed away so peacefully; no man could make a quieter or more dignified end . . . Pilla has been having a great week of balls, having been at four of them; but now Lent comes in and puts a stop to her folly and ours. I don't feel quite easy at letting her go through it all; but I confess I have a want of fixed principles in regard to such matters, and so let things drift. I fail to see the good of simply denying her the pleasures in her reach with no object in view beyond the denial. Life is a very complex thing, and I am glad I have got so far through it without having done any worse than I have, though heaven knows I have done badly enough. Everyone has great need of forbearance, and I have great hesitation about taking any hard and fast course with the children. They cannot see with my old eyes till they are as old as I, and then I need-not bother about them. I have tried to give them right ideas, generous and kindly ones, and I must leave conduct to these, and trust to luck a good deal.

I am anxious to hear that you are wholly yourself again. Don't be very impatient to get out; you must have good deal of weather indoors, in spite of your double windows, which, by the way, you've never told me about yet. With united love to all,

Your aff'te son
Will.

1. *The Quality of Mercy.*

2. Charley was W. C. Howells' horse. According to Howells' letter to his father of 18 January 1891 (MH), "He came into the family about the time I left it...."

---

15 FEBRUARY 1891, BOSTON, TO WILLIAM C. HOWELLS

184 Commonwealth Avenue.
Boston, Feb. 15, 1891.

Dear father:

I just send a line to save you from the disappointment of getting no letter. I went up to Concord last evening, and spent the night with Robert James, who took me to see a farmer's family, who are mediums. We had a seance of an hour, and the most wonderful things happened. The floor and walls were shaken, and the table lifted and banged with blows as from a hammer, and tappings galore. Most of the things were done in the dark, but some of the blows were given in the full lamp-light. I don't know what it was, and it all sounds absurd when you tell it; but I was badly rattled at the time, and I don't want to see any more of the performance.[1]

The family are all well, and I hope you are getting round again. I am glad the night gowns suited.

With love to all,

Your aff'te son
Will.

1. Howells wrote Robertson James, a brother of Henry James, on 10 February 1891 (OFH) that he would arrive in Cambridge on 14 February and spend the night at James's house "after the spooking." Apparently Howells' interest in spiritualism revived at this time, for on 22 February (MH) he reported to his father about his having been present at "a talk of some members of the Psychical Research Society.... It was a sort of ghost-story swap. It had the final futility of all those things; but I told the story of the phantasm seen by Joe's friends, the Moreys, at Deer Isle, and the Secretary would like to have him write it out. He will remember it was the face of the father which the family at home saw looking in at the window while the sun was dying in Chaleur Bay."

---

25 FEBRUARY 1891, BOSTON, TO SYLVESTER BAXTER

184 Commonwealth Avenue.
Boston, Feb. 25, 1891.

My dear Baxter:

I wish you would talk with some skilled reporter, and find how they "get onto" things. Do they ever stand in with detectives, and learn before hand of cases likely to be made public, such as defalcations?

I'm not satisfied with the way I've got my reporter on the track of the defalcation I'm working out, and which he begins to work up on some hints he gets of it before the company confesses it. How, for instance, would a reporter begin to suspect that all was not right with the treasurer of some fat company? Is there any sort of gossip-exchange where such things are talked up? Do expert-examiners ever *leak* to reporters? Is there anyone who could give a fellow he liked a straight tip concerning a case like that?[1]

Do come to my rescue, like a good boy!

Yours ever
W. D. Howells.

1. Howells was gathering information to use in sketching the actions of Pinney, the reporter-detective in *The Quality of Mercy.* As a newspaper man of long and varied experience, Baxter could give authoritative advice, but his reply to Howells' inquiry has not been located. See also Howells to W. C. Howells, 1 March 1891, n. 2.

1 MARCH 1891, BOSTON, TO WILLIAM C. HOWELLS

184 Commonwealth Avenue.
Boston, March 1, 1891.

Dear father:

You will be thinking that I was born today fifty four years ago, and I might as well own it. But let us say as little about it as possible. It will be two years tomorrow since Winny died. I must pass from my birthday into this shadow as long as I live. I am sorry to hear that you are still so weak and poorly; but I hope the weather will soon be kinder to you and let you out of doors, and then you will gain strength. It is grievous to me that I see no hope of being with you during Annie's visit. A visit later from me will help tide you over a vacant space after she's gone.—Three days ago I was in despair about my story; I had gone off on a false tack, and I shall have to throw away two hundred pages, but now I'm all straight again, and shall start fair tomorrow.[1] I went yesterday to see the chief of the detective agency here,[2] and laid my scheme before him. He praised it highly for its entire probability, and was delighted that I was not going to take a melodramatic view of the detective's work. I found him a most intelligent and even cultivated man; he knew my name, and had read several of my books. He entered most sympathetically into my business and gave me exactly the points I wanted. It was a curious experience for me, and last night I had another one, still more curious. This was a dinner at the Chinese restaurant, with a party of literary people. Of course the whole thing was very outlandish, from the bird's nest soup onwards, but the ten or twelve dishes were very good, and they gave me no trouble during the night—not even the boned duck that was served with it's bill on. I enclose the bill of fare, which Mole[3] may amuse him in finding out the right way of reading. This was put up in the form and shell of a cannon-cracker. We had our choice of chopsticks and knives and forks; I took the latter to eat with. The wines, or brandies rather, which we drank out of china cups holding about two spoonfuls were distilled from rice, roses and apricots, and were all very hot and heady; one had to be very sparing, for the "dlunk" which we were warned of seemed to lurk in every drop. I will send you a newspaper account of the dinner and perhaps I can get one of the flashlight fotos for you.

Joe seemed to think I had not done right to refuse Georgy's request to help her about getting a place;[4] I asked him if he had written to the commissioner for her, so that I should know how to act, but he has n't answered me. I wish you would punch him up about it. I also asked him whether he had got the order of court yet for selling the home-house.[5] I should be glad if he could give me an account of the Morey phantasm soon.[6]

I don't know that there's anything to piece out this letter with, except lots of love to you all and to the Annie folks. You can tell her that we had Mrs. Macoun Kingman and her husband to dinner the other day.[7] Elinor has taken a great fancy to her.

Your aff'te son,
Will.

1. Howells' progress on *The Quality of Mercy* began to improve after this false start. On 22 March 1891 (MH) he wrote W. C. Howells: "I'm getting on well, now, with my story, but it's a queer thing, and I have written 600 such pages as this without getting over a week in time. Of course I had to lay out the ground carefully, and I expect to put up the rest of the edifice rapidly. But I never had material behave so before. The thing is about a third done, as I now see it." After a week of slow progress on the novel, Howells resumed his rapid pace, so that he could report to his father on 9 April 1891 (MH): "I've been booming on my story this week, and seem really to have got my grip on it after a long season of despair. If I have luck I can easily finish it by July—the time I had fixed in my mind." But even though the writing progressed well, Howells expressed a general feeling of despair to his father on 12 April (MH): "It's an awful trade and when I think all the others are worse, I am not very gay. Still, one lives." At this time Howells also complained with increasing frequency about physical fatigue and pains in his legs and feet.

2. O. M. Hanscom of the Pinkerton Detective Agency. Howells asked Houghton, Mifflin & Co. on 2 March 1891 (MH) to send Hanscom paperbound copies of his novels. See also Howells to Baxter, 25 February 1891. Howells also appealed to John Codman Ropes (1836–1899), a Boston lawyer and military historian, on 25 March 1891 (ViU) for help on his story: "It concerns a defaulter who has defrauded the company he is treasurer of, in the usual way, without at first meaning to do it. As usual, he is given a a [sic] little time to make up his shortage, and he starts for Canada. There is question whether he is not killed in a railroad wreck on the

way; some think yes and some no. His real estate—a fancy farm and country seat in the interim—have been long before deeded to his two daughters, when he was an honest man and had a right to give the property. After the lapse of five or six months, a detective finds him living in Canada, and persuades him to come home and risk his trial. On the way, he dies suddenly in the detective's charge. An eminent detective has told me that this is all probable and well imagined, as far as his profession is concerned. But I am in doubt about the legal steps; and some words you dropped, the other night, made me think you could guide my feet aright from your experience as well as learning."

3. Howells Fréchette.

4. Sam Howells' daughter was trying to get a job in the office of the Commissioner of Agriculture. On 5 April 1891 (MH) Howells wrote his father that he would help Georgy in getting a job, asking for the commissioner's first name, native state, and "previous condition of servitude...."

5. See Howells to W. C. Howells, 6 July 1890.

6. See Howells to W. C. Howells, 15 February 1891, n. 1.

7. Minnie Macoun Kingman was the wife of Rufus Anderson Kingman, a Boston physician.

3 MARCH 1891, BOSTON, TO SAMUEL L. CLEMENS

Boston, March 3, 1891.

My dear Clemens:

I talked your letter into a fonograf in my usual tone, at my usual gait of speech. Then the fonograf man talked his answer in at his wonted swing and swell. Then we took the cylinder to a type-writer in the next room, and she put the hooks into her ears, and wrote the whole out. I send you the result. There is a mistake of one word. I think that if you have the cheek to dictate the story into the fonograf, all the rest is perfectly easy.[1] It wouldn't fatigue me to talk for an hour as I did.—They wont lease a machine for less than a year, but you see that the whole expense, cylinders and all, is only $115.

It is a mighty good notion to write Sellers out in that way, and I am curious to see what you've done. My wife has Mrs. Clemens's letter, and will shortly fix a date for our appearance in Hartford. She is pretty poorly, and we shall go to New York first for a radical change, and then work back by Hartford.[2] It's very sweet of you both to let us come, and we join in love to you both.—This machine is a Hammond; I wish it was a fonograf.[3]

Yours ever,
W. D. Howells.

1. Clemens, in a letter to Howells of 28 February 1891 (NN; *Twain-Howells*, p. 637), requested that Howells test a phonograph for its clarity at the New England Phonograph Company in Boston. Clemens said that he was suffering from rheumatism in his right arm, which hindered his writing his new novel, *The American Claimant* (1892), a narrative version of the Howells-Clemens play. He wished to

rent a phonograph so that he could dictate his book into it at the rate of 4,000 words per day.

2. The Howellses visited New York 9–11 March, stopping in Hartford on the return trip; they probably stayed with the Clemenses until 13 March.

3. Howells' typed letter contains many hand corrections, indicating the difficulties he had with the typewriter.

19 APRIL 1891, BOSTON, TO WENDELL P. GARRISON

Boston, April 19, 1891.

My dear Mr. Garrison:

I have thought the matter of the Russophile Society over again, and I have returned to my first feeling about it. I doubt its usefulness, and I am sure that I ought not to let my name be used to influence others where I have not a distinct conviction, and intend to take no part in the work always to be done. So I shall not be able to sign any public appeal.[1]

Yours sincerely,
W. D. Howells.

1. Sergei Stepniak had been trying to organize an American Society of Friends of Russian Freedom, and he wanted Howells to join and to sign a petition of sympathy with the Russian revolutionary cause. Other prominent Americans, literary figures, including Clemens, Higginson, Julia Ward Howe, and others, had signed but Howells refused. On 18 April 1891 (MH) Stepniak had written Howells to enlist his support, assuring him that he would not be expected to participate actively in the cause and that his signature would be all that was expected of him: "Yours is one of the few American names which have an authority not only in America but in England, France and Russia as well: *all* your novels are translated into Russian and your name is familiar as well as your individuality to many thousands of Russians." See also Howells to W. C. Howells, 11 January 1891, n. 1.

20 APRIL 1891, BOSTON, TO ROBERT U. JOHNSON

Boston, April 20, 1891.

My dear Mr. Johnson:[1]

I pity you with all my heart, and I wish your family well back in your keeping again.

As to Hauer,[2] I am afraid he is deceived: he does not want a Home, but a living. That is, I think he is really poor, but he has no real desire to retire from the world. I gave him $10 in Boston in '86 to help take him to the Hampton Soldier's Home; $5 and a suit of clothes at Nahant in

'88 to get home to Germany. In New York, '89, he wanted the R. R. fare between Bremen and his native village. I gave him $1, and told him when he brought me his steamer ticket, I would give the rest. He never brought it; but three weeks later the clerk of a 25 cent lodging house in the Bowery told me Hauer was still there. Now I perceive that he never meant to go to Germany anymore than to the Soldier's Homes. If I were he, I should not go, and probably I should tell lies to keep from going.

You must of course act on your own principles and theories. If Hauer came to me again, and I believed him in need, I should not inquire into his desert.

Yours sincerely
W D Howells.

1. Robert U. Johnson (1853–1937), a minor poet, was associate editor of the *Century*, and succeeded Richard Watson Gilder as editor in 1909.

2. Hauer has not been identified.

30 MAY 1891, BOSTON, TO WILLIAM C. HOWELLS

Boston, May 30, 1891.

Dear father:

I haven't heard from you the whole week, and I'm afraid you've been too anxiously considering the question of the operation on Henry.[1] I don't think you should let it worry you. I suppose he is not in pain, and you could, with a good conscience postpone the whole affair, since it is not certain that the trephining would cure him. If you wish me to take any decided ground about it, or if I can relieve you by doing so, I will.

I write to you tonight, because I want to work on my "Study" tomorrow. I am going to New York for a couple of days, and I must make up for lost time. Pilla and John went this morning; Nelly Shepard[2] is to be married Monday, and Pil is to be one of the brides' maids. Elinor is not going to the wedding; she's better than she was, but she dreads excitement.

I've got well forward on my story,[3] and really have a clear light on it at last. It will be very different from all my other novels, and will succeed for different reasons, if it succeeds at all. I think I have some good points in it.

I suppose that you know I've offered Willy[4] a good chance to get possession of the old house. As you and I once thought it might be well to do, I've proposed to let him have the house and half the land.

Elinor joins me in love to all.

Your aff'te son
Will.

1. W. C. Howells was contemplating surgery—probably brain surgery—for his son Henry. Throughout the ordeal of deciding, Howells provided counsel to his father. He wrote to him on 9 May 1891 (MH): "If the operation succeeds he will no longer be the burden and danger he now is, and must be with each year of your age; but if it fails, I do not know what [we] are to look for.... We are all the more sacredly bound by Henry's helplessness to care for his life, because he cannot take any part of the risk himself." Besides offering advice and payment of medical expenses, Howells consulted Boston surgeons for their opinions of his brother's chances for a successful operation.

2. The daughter of Augustus D. Shepard.

3. After proclaiming good progress on *The Quality of Mercy* in April, Howells encountered some difficulties. On 17 May 1891 (MH) he had written W. C. Howells: "I am on another rough place in my story, which has given me no end of trouble, either because the subject is difficult, or because I'm less facile than I was. I think perhaps the plot was too strong. I get on better with something of slighter texture, that needs to be made much of." Two days later, 19 May (CU; *Twain-Howells*, pp. 643–44), Howells wrote S. L. Clemens: "I have been worrying away on my story till it is [sic] seems the most fool and futile thing ever attempted. Really I feel sometimes like simply running away from it."

4. William Dean Howells II. See also Howells to W. C. Howells, 6 July 1890.

11 JUNE 1891, BOSTON, TO HENRY M. ALDEN

Boston, June 11, 1891.

Dear Mr. Alden:

At the time Messrs. Harper & Brothers consented to let me write the *Sun* story first,[1] they had already terminated our contract for the 12½ per cent. payment by their own act, and if they had remembered this they could not have expected me to take that rate for the book; especially, as they had agreed shortly before to pay me 20 per cent. for *The World of Chance*.[2]

My proposal to write The *Sun* story first was made in their interest, of which I have always been as observant as of my own; for I foresaw that otherwise the two serials would be running simultaneously. I cannot regard that consent as a favor to me; for I told you, when I last spoke of it with you that I was myself indifferent about it.

I think that in view of all the circumstances they should pay me 20 per cent. on all copies, cloth and paper alike, of the *Sun* story, I making the plates; and if they are of the same mind, we will consider the matter closed.[3]

Yours sincerely
W. D. Howells.

1. *The Quality of Mercy.* See Howells to Harper & Brothers, 19 April 1890, n. 1 and n. 2.

2. Serialized in *Harper's Monthly*, March–November 1892, and published in book form by Harper & Brothers in 1893.

3. Alden's letter to Howells, 10 June 1891 (MH), indicated that the Harpers

would "cheerfully offer" him a royalty of twenty percent of the retail price of the clothbound copies of *The Quality of Mercy* and ten percent of the retail price of the paperbound copies. Harper & Brothers, in a letter to Howells of 17 June 1891 (MH), agreed to Howells' terms.

14 JUNE 1891, BOSTON, TO WILLIAM C. HOWELLS

Boston, June 14, 1891.

Dear father:

I am glad you can leave me so free about the time of my visit to you. The heat *does* try me, terribly, and exposure to it seems to bring distressing pain in the head. But our plans for the summer are not fixed, yet, and you may be sure that if I can arrange to go to you in July better than in September, the earlier time will be my preference.—I am so glad the chair has come, and is a comfort to you.[1] I got the style that Aurelia indicated, and I feel pretty sure that it is better than anything I could find here. I expect to take "turn about" in it with you when I go out.—This is John's last week in Harvard, Class Day coming the 19th. So far as I know he is the first college bred man of our name, and it will be interesting to see whether he is an improvement on the rest of us. I am not satisfied with this part of my doing, any more than the rest. The whole of life seems unreal and unfair; but what I try to teach the children is to be ready for the change that *must* come in favor of truth and justice, and not to oppose it. Of course the world still looks beautiful to them; they cannot see it as I do; but I hope they can see the right. In the meantime Elinor and I live along like our neighbors; only, we have a bad conscience. Sometimes, however, the whole affair goes to pieces in my apprehension, and I feel as if I had no more authority to judge myself or to try to do this or that, than any other expression of the Infinite Life,—say a tree, or a field of wheat, or a horse. The only proof I have that I ought to do right is that I suffer for my selfishness; and perhaps this is enough. I dare say God can take care of all the rest. I wish I could once leave it to him.[2] With our love to all,

Your aff'te son
Will.

1. Howells had bought his father an easy chair.
2. Howells had written his father on 7 June 1891 (MH) on a mutual acquaintance who had been treated unjustly in Howells' estimate: "Do you remember old Senter, the pressman at the State Journal office? He turned up, the other day, white-haired, rheumatic, a business failure many times over, and wanted me to help him look up some means of living. He has finally taken a book agency, and a letter of mine commending his book. Isn't it sad, isn't it wicked, that we live in an economic world where a man after hard work of a life time, must still be troubled about his livelihood? Such a state of things is blasphemous, insulting to God; and yet we call it the mysterious order of Providence!"

23 JUNE 1891, BOSTON, TO RICHARD W. GILDER

184 Commonwealth Avenue
Boston, June 23, 1891

Dear Mr. Gilder:

I have your kind letter of yesterday.[1]

As soon as we can quiet down from tearing out of our house and storing our furniture, I will write you fully my idea of *Business is Business*. This I understand to be the drift of your wishes, and it is entirely right and fair. I should not like myself to be otherwise dealt with in your place. The misgiving I had before was that you had perhaps lost faith in me to some degree and that, I knew, would affect my faith in myself so that I could not even set my proposed story before you in the light I wanted you to see it in. But your letter has changed all that.[2]

I may say now that my story will be a symphony of many voices concerning Business, business methods, business morals, business aims, business men. It *ought* to interest Americans more than any other novel of American life. It would appeal to *men*, as S. Lapham did, and even more; but I expect the gods to send me a love story for the heart of it. I shall build it very solidly up from the ground; but I hope to have some skylights in. It is a great subject; it has been a good while in my mind. The scene would be New York, which I found so lucky for the Hazard of N. Fortunes.

As to prices, we can talk them after you say you like my synopsis. My daughter is going to visit Mrs.[3]   in August, and I may perhaps see you in Marion.

Yours sincerely
W. D. Howells

1. Gilder's letter has not been located.

2. The project for a novel about American businessmen and methods never appears to have been realized. At this time Howells was still under contract with Harper & Brothers to furnish them a novel for 1892; this turned out to be *The World of Chance*, which Howells began to write in early August. See Howells to W. C. Howells, 2 August 1891 (MH) and Howells to Sylvester Baxter, 5 August 1891 (CSmH). Apparently the idea of writing about matters of business was not entirely abandoned; Howells' essay, "The Man of Letters as a Man of Business," appeared in *Scribner's*, October 1893.

3. The person who copied the holograph was unable to decipher the name and suggested a number of possible readings: "Inches" or "Lucloes"; another person who saw the original suggests "Tuckes," "Tuches," or "Tucker."

17 JULY 1891, INTERVALE, NEW HAMPSHIRE,
TO AURELIA H. HOWELLS

Intervale, July 17, 1891.

Dear Aurelia:

I ought to have told you before that the rug we sent out has been in John's room at Harvard. Elinor and I bought it for him in New York, and he was glad to send it to his grandfather when he broke up his college housekeeping. I thought it would be pleasant for father to know this. The children have both gone off tonight on a straw-ride, with 10 or 12 other young people to a hotel further up in the mountains where they will dance. A long wagon body, well bedded with straw, and drawn by six horses formed the conveyance. It was a gay sight to see them start. Pilla is having a great time. There are lots of girls, and nice young fellows, and she is a favorite, as everywhere. It is right for her to have this harmless pleasure, but I think of Winny and her pain. Now, that we've made up our mind about buying a horse, I want you to do it soon, so you can have some good of it in the hot weather.[1]

How nice it is about your heifer. I'm so glad she's turned out so well.

I'm pushing through the proof of The Sun story, and perhaps I can bring it with me when I come. It's called *The Quality of Mercy.*—The *Imperative Duty* has waked an Irish howl against me,[2] and is likely to make noise enough. They can't see that it is not I who felt and said what Olney did.

All join in love to you all.

Your affte'ly
Will.

1. See Howells to W. C. Howells, 8 February 1891, n. 2.

2. In the opening chapter of *An Imperative Duty*, which appeared in *Harper's Monthly*, July 1891, Howells describes working-class women gathered in the Boston Common as seen by Olney, the protagonist: "The old women were strong, ugly old peasant women, often with the simian cast of features which affords the caricaturist such an unmistakable Irish physiognomy; but the young women were thin and crooked, with pale, pasty complexions, and an effect of physical delicacy which might later be physical refinement."

25 JULY 1891, INTERVALE, NEW HAMPSHIRE, TO SAMUEL S. McCLURE

Intervale House,
Intervale, N. H. July 25, 1891.

My dear Mc Clure:

I am stereotyping the *Sun* story,[1] and have got about half of it in type, but until I have made formal delivery of it to Mr. Laffan,[2] and have his approval of your wish to have some account of it for your circular, I do not feel quite free to furnish it. Even then I do not think it would be well to give away the idea of it, and I could only supply you generalities. It would be for him to say whether I could let you have an advance copy much as I should like, to do so.

You are making a splendid showing, and I congratulate you. I wish I could do it in person. Perhaps I shall see you in New York, if I pass through on my way to Ohio about mid-August.—I am just going to begin my story for Harpers.[3]

Yours cordially,
W. D. Howells.

1. *The Quality of Mercy*, which was syndicated by S. S. McClure.
2. William M. Laffan.
3. *The World of Chance* was the new novel for the Harpers, but before it began serialization early in 1892, *The Quality of Mercy* turned out to be quite successful. According to McClure's letter to Howells of 9 October 1891 (MH): "Your novel is taking splendidly. This is somewhat of a surprise to me, inasmuch as I had supposed that your work would not attract the million audience. Mr. Nixon, of the Chicago Inter Ocean was here yesterday, and he told me casually that they had to print on Monday a second edition of the Sunday which contained the first instalment of the novel. I could have sold the novel much more widely if it had commenced a little later in the season. As it is, the novel will appear in the Philadelphia Inquirer, Chicago Inter Ocean, Cincinnati Commercial Gazette, Toronto Globe, as well as the Boston Herald."

9 AUGUST 1891, INTERVALE, NEW HAMPSHIRE, TO WILLIAM C. HOWELLS

Intervale, Aug. 9, 1891.

Dear father:

I supposed, from Aurelia's letter, that you had decided to buy the percheron colt, but you know best what to do. I hope my cautions about the colt's age and temper did not limit you against your judgment. All that I want is for you to have a suitable horse, and to have it while you can drive before the fall rains begin.[1]

It is very nice of them to ask me for the Centennial poem at Hamilton, but it's quite impossible for me to write it.[2] My experience of the State Centennial in 1888 was that such occasions have no real use for poems, and that if I wrote one it would not be listened to. So I am taking my sorrow comfortably.

I hope before a very great while, now, to see you, but I can't yet say just when. You may be sure it wont be later than I can help.—Dr Worcester,[3] the Swedenborgian, has a cottage here, and has called on me. He is a very good man, but affects my unregeneracy like one who had been conscientious to consciousness, and had kept himself so much in hand that he had nothing else there. But this is a first judgment. The other world oughtn't, perhaps, to have too much say in this? I prefer a good man after your make—if we must *have* good men.—I seem to have stirred up the Englishmen, now, by my little book on Criticism and Fiction—made up from the *Study*—and they are gnashing their teeth at a great rate.[4] I think I shall live through it, probably. The worst of it is the way the American sneaks accept them as authority; but even that is not mortally bad.

The family join me in love to all.

Your aff'te son
Will.

1. See Howells to W. C. Howells, 8 February 1891, n. 2.

2. The celebration in Hamilton began on 17 September and ended on 19 September 1891.

3. John Worcester (1834–1891) was a clergyman who became pastor of the New Church Society of Newtonville, Massachusetts, in 1869; in 1878 he became an instructor of theology at the New Church theological school in Boston, and in 1881 he was appointed president of the school.

4. Howells' comments on English authors and critics brought on a storm of angry reviews of *Criticism and Fiction* (1891), a collection of pieces previously published in the "Editor's Study." While not all British reviews took sharp issue with Howells, some of the more belligerent ones appeared in the *Literary World* (14 August 1891), the *National Observer* (5 September 1891), and *Saturday Review* (25 July 1891). See J. A. Dowling, "W. D. Howells' Literary Reputation in England," *Dalhousie Review* 45 (1965), 281–82. Howells himself later referred to the volume as a bottle of that "gall and wormwood" he had administered to the public in the "Editor's Study" over several years. Its content, he continued, had been "received with wry faces and retchings, and among the inhabitants of the British Isles has produced truly deplorable consequences." See "Editor's Study," *Harper's Monthly*, March 1892.

4 SEPTEMBER 1891, INTERVALE, NEW HAMPSHIRE,
TO ROBERT U. JOHNSON

Intervale, N. H., Sept. 4, 1891.

Dear Mr. Johnson:

I have been extremely interested in that story of Miss Crim's which you have kindly sent me, and in the very extraordinary coincidence of parts of it with my own story of *An Imperative Duty*. You tell me that *Was it an exceptional Case* was written in 1889; my story was imagined many years ago, and actually written last year, after being first cast in quite a different form. So I cannot account for the resemblance upon the principle of telepathy; but must fall back upon mere, blind chance, which frequently sends the same invention in duplicate and triplicate to the Patent Office.

I am glad you have given me the opportunity to testify to the fact that Miss Crim's story was in no possible wise suggested by mine: I do not even think that mine was stolen from hers.

You are very welcome to print this letter if you believe it will preclude the question that might arise with some.[1]

Yours sincerely,
W. D. Howells.

1. Matt (Martha Jane) Crim's short story "Was It an Exceptional Case?" was first published in the *Century*, October 1891, and later included in her collection of stories, *Beaver Cove and Elsewhere* (1892). A notice of the literary coincidence was printed in "The Lounger" column of *The Critic*, 3 October 1891: "In each story the heroine is a girl of mixed blood, adopted, educated and brought up in refined society, and kept in ignorance of her parentage until she arrived at womanhood. In each case a lover is relinquished upon the revelation of the truth of the heroine's origin. There is also a similarity between the two stories in that each girl is adopted by an aunt, and the fact that these women both confess the deception which has been practiced—one to a physician and the other to a priest, the penitent in each case dying soon after the confession has been made." With it appeared the first paragraph of Howells' letter to Johnson.

6 SEPTEMBER 1891, INTERVALE, NEW HAMPSHIRE, TO AURELIA H. HOWELLS

Intervale, Sept. 6, 1891.

My dear Aurelia:

I hope you are getting on pleasantly, although you have not me to provide for. I missed you greatly in Buffalo, where I had the loveliest kind of Sunday a week ago. I stopped at the Niagara, and had a gorgeous parlor, bed room and bath, which turned out to be the "compliments" of Mr. Lewis, the proprietor. After seeing Dr. Wilcox,[1] I called on a young literary friend (Hibbard)[2] and he two-horse couped me round all day. His mother made me stay to dinner, and they sent me off to the train in the evening full of champagne and truffles. I wish you could have been with me.

In New York, Mr. Laffan of the Sun would not hear of my submitting my story to him, but drew his check for it at once, though I told him I left him perfectly free to reject it, if he did not like it when he had read it.[3] I still have great misgivings about it. I know it has distinct faults, but I hope they wont be found out.

I think often of my visit to you:[4] of the long, pleasant drives, of the evenings round the lamp, of our pleasant meals. The more I see of men, the more I prize father's society. It is the "best" society in the world, and you ought to be every moment proud of it, and glad of it.

As if to exasperate me the hotel lawn has covered itself with mush-rooms since last night's rain! Is n't it trying?

All are well, and join me in love to each of you. Speak of me to poor Henry.

> Your aff'te bro.
> Will.

1. Howells consulted Dr. Wilcox, a Buffalo surgeon, on 30 August 1891 about the possibility of the success of an operation on Henry Howells. He wrote to his father on 30 August 1891 (MH) of the doctor's optimism about a cure for Henry's fits, and he expressed his trust in Wilcox as "a capable and reliable man." See Howells to W. C. Howells, 30 May 1891, n. 1.

2. George Hibbard (1858–1928), an artist and author of such volumes as *Induna, and Other Stories* (1891) and *The Governor, and Other Stories* (1892).

3. *The Quality of Mercy* began to appear in the New York *Sun* in October.

4. Howells had visited his family in Jefferson during the last week of August.

20 SEPTEMBER 1891, INTERVALE, NEW HAMPSHIRE, TO WILLIAM C. HOWELLS

> Intervale, Sept. 20, 1891.

Dear father:

I send you a line this morning to let you know that apparently I am entirely well again. My attack was not severe, and it was only my proper share of a very popular disorder here, this fall. I hope that you are escaping it. I have had letters from Aurelia, Joe, and Willy,[1] the past week, and this must serve as a sort of round-robin to all.—Tell Joe I thought his reply to Captain Reeve in the Sentinel, masterly, and Reeve's letter very disingenuous.[2] I hope there is no danger of the man's election, but the party of the perverse sometimes effects astonishing results.—The editors of the Hamilton Democrat telegraphed me to send them a sentiment for their centennial issue, and I did so. I hope this is the last of the centennials for the present. I shudder at the notion of a Martinsville centennial. Do you suppose they will have one? I have lived in so many places that I am identified with much more than my share of centennials.[3] The only centennial I now care to celebrate is yours, so that when people come up to me and ask, "You don't say you're his father!" I can answer, "Oh, no; only his elder brother." There would be some fun in that. But we needn't hurry. I'm getting along, pretty well, on my new story, The World of Chance; and when I come out next, I hope to have a lot to read to you and Aurelia. I'm glad to hear that Henry is so quiet, and that your pleasant drives continue. With love to all from all of us,

> Your aff'te son,
> Will.

1. William Dean Howells II.

2. The dispute between Joseph A. Howells and Captain Leander C. Reeve, the representative for Ashtabula County in the Ohio General Assembly, grew out of an attempt by real estate "boomers" in the village of Ashtabula to have the county seat moved there from Jefferson. In a personal letter to Reeve, Joe suggested that the captain introduce the necessary legislative proposal on behalf of his constituents, but being opposed to the measure himself, that he allow the bill to die in committee. Reeve apparently succumbed to the influence of the "boomers," however, and actively sponsored the move, justifying his change of mind with the claim that Joe had urged a duplicitous course of action upon him. Joe then replied publicly to this charge in the *Sentinel*, 17 September 1891, inserting also in that edition a special section, which contained Reeve's somewhat specious attempt at self-vindication. It is to these latter two items, then, that Howells' letter refers. In the end, nothing much came of the whole affair: the legislation failed to pass before the election recess of the Assembly; and Captain Reeve, despite his failure to win the Republican nomination, retained his seat by running as an independent.

3. See Howells to W. C. Howells, 9 August 1891, n. 2.

18 OCTOBER 1891, BOSTON, TO WILLIAM C. HOWELLS

Boston, Oct. 18, 1891.

Dear father:

I send you back Annie's and Vevie's[1] delightful letters. I hope Vevie will have many rides on Katy-back,[2] and I wish I could be by to see her enjoying them. In fact I should like to be round with Katy all the time.— I am getting the better of the cold that I caught two weeks ago, and I think there has been nothing of the grip in it. But I am not very strong, somehow, and I get very tired very easily. I look forward to a winter in New York with loathing; I would so much rather be in the country; but it will be well for the work I am trying to do, and it seems the only thing for the children. We have had several letters from John during the week, and he seems to be getting on well.[3] I'm glad he has written to you. We hope to be with him before this time Sunday after next. Between the two cities I prefer New York; it is less "dour," and there is more for me to see and learn there.—My story, The Quality of Mercy, seems to be taking well, here; and in Chicago the Inter-Ocean had to print a second edition of the first number.[4] I'm getting on in The World of Chance, though I haven't a strong grip on it yet. That will come with patience and work, though.

Elinor and Pilla are very well, and join me in love to all.

Your aff'te son
Will.

1. Marie Marguerite Fréchette.

2. W. C. Howells' new horse. See Howells to W. C. Howells, 8 February 1891, n. 2.

3. Howells wrote his father on 27 September 1891 (MH) of John's itinerary: "John

left us on Friday for a day or two at the seaside and in Boston. Tuesday evening he expects to start West, and to be with you Wednesday afternoon."

4. See Howells to McClure, 25 July 1891, n. 3.

21 OCTOBER 1891, BOSTON, TO JAMES R. OSGOOD

Boston, Oct. 21, 1891.

My dear Osgood:

Mr. Douglas has written to me saying that he will bring out An Imperative Duty in the shilling edition, and sending me a check for it. His letter closes with this statement: "No one can foresee what may be the effect of the new copyright act on the literature of both countries, and I wish to tell you, in case you have application from your old publisher Mr. Osgood, or any other English firm offering you terms by which you can make money that you are to consider yourself quite free to enter into them for any editions in England to be published at a price not less than 5/. I mention this in case you should be applied to, and I should not wish to stand dog in the manger."[1]

I understand from this that he will hereafter probably publish only a cheap edition of my books. If it appears to you desirable to come to any agreement with him, of a general nature, you know I should prefer you to any other publisher for such editions as he does not want to issue. The thing may look too complicated to you, or I may not be worth while as an author; you are to decide; I merely put you in possession of the facts.[2]

Yours ever
W. D. Howells.

I hear of English schoolboys liking A Boy's Town; but there is no English edition, and they see only borrowed American copies.

1. David Douglas, Howells' publisher in Edinburgh, wrote on 2 October 1891 (MH) that because of the new copyright act he had canceled the octavo pages of *An Imperative Duty*; he also praised Howells for his "powerfully told" story. Douglas prefaced his concluding remarks (quoted in this letter to Osgood) with the statement that he was "disappointed at the non popularity of your books among British readers . . . and at the comparative failure of my efforts to make them a big success yet I am proud of having introduced them here and grateful to you for your appreciation of what I have been able to do."

2. Osgood, McIlvaine & Co., the English agents for Harper & Brothers, did not publish any of Howells' works.

22 OCTOBER 1891, BOSTON, TO BRANDER MATTHEWS

Hotel Berkeley,
Boston, Oct. 22, 1891

My dear Mr. Matthews:[1]

I have sometime had it in mind and heart to tell you what very fine work I thought you were doing in criticism for the *Cosmopolitan*: I trust you wont think me the less disinterested in my liking because in your last number you have treated me not quite like the Pariah those English and their apes affect to consider me.[2] I told Mr. Alden, the last time I saw him (in August) what I tell you now: that your work is better than that of any other critic of your generation among us. I had to make exception of your elders of course. I like your fighting in the open; I like your spirit, and I like your manner. Some day when we meet I will set myself right with you about Thackeray, and show you why I think him a caricaturist both in the serious and the comic sort.[3] Long before most other critics were "toiling over the problems in college classrooms"[4] which I have approached in my dotage, I had read every line of Thackeray, and most of him a dozen times; I know him *au fond*, and whether I speak rightly or not, I speak of what I know. Trollope is incomparably the finer and truer artist, and will be so held in the final accounting. He was to me a thoroughly hateful person, at the same time.

I have always felt my limitations in criticism, but I still hoped I might hide my ignorance from others. When we meet you must tell me just where you found me most unlettered. In the meantime I thank you cordially for the kind things you found it in you to say of "C and F." It isn't so pleasant or so mild a book as it will seem ten years hence when you've all gone beyond it!

Yours sincerely
W. D. Howells.

1. James Brander Matthews (1852–1929), who soon became a good personal friend of Howells, wrote a literary column for *Cosmopolitan* and taught English literature at Columbia University (1891–1924).

2. "Recent Essays in Criticism," *Cosmopolitan*, November 1891, was mostly favorable toward Howells' *Criticism and Fiction*. See Cady, *Howells*, II, 51–52.

3. Matthews felt that Howells was unfair in his appraisal of Thackeray. In his essay he said: "to speak of him [Thackeray] as a caricaturist merely, is to use language carelessly; and to praise Trollope at Thackeray's expense is an abuse even of the privilege of polemical criticism." See Howells to Warner, 30 October 1889, n. 2.

4. Howells is quoting inaccurately from Matthews' essay: "it is true . . . that Mr. Howells has brought the zest of discovery to his new appreciation of certain of the classics which other critics toiled over in college classrooms."

24 OCTOBER 1891, BOSTON, TO "MY DEAR SIR"

Boston, Oct. 24, 1891.

My dear Sir:[1]

I am glad to have you or any one say a good word for labor: I have been, with hands and head, a laborer all my life, and I like sympathy. But perhaps if you will look a little more closely at my paper in the Study you will not find the obvious meaning the only meaning, or even the chief meaning.[2] At any rate I hope you will revise your impressions of it.

Yours sincerely
W. D. Howells.

1. The recipient of this letter has not been identified.
2. In the "Editor's Study," *Harper's Monthly*, November 1891, Howells took issue with English critics, such as Arthur Quiller-Couch, who presumed to define what was or should be the characteristics of an American national literature. He especially argued against the proposition that literature about the working class was a proper goal for American authors to pursue, concluding with the following observations: "The life of toil will do very well for nations which do not honor toil, to read about; but there is something in the very reverence we have for it that renders the notion of it repulsive to us. This is very curious; and we do not attempt to explain it.... The life of toil! It is a little too personal to people who are trying to be ladies and gentlemen of elegant leisure as fast as they can. If we have had to dig, or if we are many of us still digging, that is reason enough why we do not want the spade brought into the parlor."

25 OCTOBER 1891, BOSTON, TO WILLIAM C. HOWELLS

Boston, Oct. 25, 1891.

Dear father:

I am glad you have made a peaceful arrangement with your rascally tenant at Cleveland. A quarrel, or a contention of any kind, is horrible; it's hell; and injustice is much easier to bear, though I don't like injustice.—The events in this family seem to be all literary, and our last and greatest is the appearance of Pillá's poem in the first place of the new volume of St. Nicholas.[1] I send you the magazine, that you may see what a very perfect little thing the poem is. There are certain notes and turns in it that remind me of Winny's writing.—Yesterday I went out to look over the Cambridge house,[2] which is vacant, and which I shall be glad to have a tenant in, if only to banish the ghosts of our own past. It is awful to pass through a place which we had such hopes of passing our whole life in, and I'm so glad for your sake that you are not living in the old home-house. By the way, if you and Aurelia will look it over, and have any "reparations" made that you think best, I shall think it a good thing.—Last night I went to a Club dinner, where a lot of fat comfortable people sat gorged with good cheer, and listened to speeches about the tenement house horrors, and how to abate them. It was comical. The attitude of a rich man towards the poor is that of a thief who parts with a little of his booty that he may be allowed to keep the rest. It is hard for him to understand that the system which suffers riches or poverty is without remedy for the wrongs it involves.—We hear good news from John.

With love to all,

Your affect'te son
Will

1. "Romance," *St. Nicholas*, November 1891.
2. The house at 37 Concord Avenue, where the Howellses lived 1873–1878.

5 NOVEMBER 1891, BOSTON, TO THOMAS W. HIGGINSON

Hotel Berkeley,
Nov. 5, 1891.

My dear Higginson:

Those things are not matters of taste only, but of reason too; and if they were defects you may be sure I should not have so consciously indulged them. I believe and feel it to be the genius of the English language to put the preposition at the end of the sentence; it makes a lighter and pleasanter movement in the prose, and it is more conformable to good colloquial usage, to do so. I have studied much upon it, and the effect is not the effect of haste with me.[1]

I wish you had sent me your praises. I would much rather have my sins left with God; though this is asking a good deal of one's friends, perhaps, and I am sure you are one of mine. But boldly and proudly as I refuse your blame, I am not proof against your kind words about my story. If there were any gratitude in fiction it *ought* to be good; it cost me so much trouble!

We are here, perching for our plunge into the boiling pitch of N— Y— life.[2]

Yours sincerely
W. D. Howells.

1. Apparently Higginson had criticized what he considered Howells' ungrammatical usage in *The Quality of Mercy*, which was then running in a number of newspapers, including the New York *Sun*. Higginson's desire for orthodox grammar—

as well as punctuation and capitalization—was most notably demonstrated in his edition of *Poems by Emily Dickinson*. See Higginson's *The New World and the New Book* (1892), pp. 198–205; also R. W. Franklin, *The Editing of Emily Dickinson: A Reconsideration* (Madison: University of Wisconsin Press, 1967), pp. 22–26.

2. The Howells family moved to New York on 8 November.

22 NOVEMBER 1891, NEW YORK, TO WILLIAM C. HOWELLS

> Hotel Albert,
> New York, Nov. 22, 1891.

Dear father:

I hope your snow is all gone by this time, for after a little shiver of cold we have got our summer weather back again, today.

Yesterday I went up to Springfield with the children to see the great foot ball match between Yale and Harvard. It is always a splendid and stirring sight, and I like to get such things in my note book. To our great grief the luck was against Yale, though for a whole hour at one time the fellows fought over about fifty feet of ground with no apparent advantage to either side. It was mostly pushing, being pulled down by the legs and fallen upon a dozen deep. 20,000 people looked on, and special trains brought them in from every direction.

I am getting on pretty well with my story,[1] though my grip has not quite tightened on it yet. New York is a prodigious field of material for me, though an excitement gets into my nerves that is not favorable for working it up. I suppose that will pass.

This afternoon I am to have a call from an American socialist, who writes to tell me that he has "an independence", and so I suppose doesn't wish to borrow. His name is Wilshire—that of the good merchant, you know, who ransomed Capt. Riley.[2]—All join me in love to all.

> Your aff'te son,
> Will.

1. *The World of Chance.*

2. Henry Gaylord Wilshire (1861–1927), a Los Angeles publisher and business executive, became a member of the Nationalist movement in 1888 and in 1890 was the Nationalist candidate for the U.S. House of Representatives. In 1900 Wilshire established a socialist newspaper, *The Challenge*, but in 1901 he moved it to New York, and it became the monthly *Wilshire's Magazine*. Howells here recalls an incident from a book he probably read as a boy, *An Authentic Narrative of the Loss of the American Brig Commerce* ... (1817) by Captain James Riley. Riley was shipwrecked on the west coast of Africa in August 1815, taken prisoner by Arabs, and sold into slavery together with other survivors from his ship. He finally succeeded in buying back his freedom and that of his men with a loan advanced to him by William Willshire of Mogador, Morocco. See also Howells to W. C. Howells family, 21 April 1860.

12 DECEMBER 1891, NEW YORK, TO CHARLES E. NORTON

The Cosmopolitan Magazine, ...
New York, Dec. 12, 1891.

Dear friend:

I fancy that it must have been with something like a shock you learned of the last step I have taken, in becoming editor of this magazine.[1] Nothing was farther from my thoughts when I saw you a few weeks ago. The offer came unexpectedly about the beginning of this month, and in such form that I could not well refuse it, when I had thought it over. It promised me freedom from the anxiety of placing my stories and chaffering about prices, and relief from the necessity of making quantity, as well as full control of the time of publishing them, so that hereafter I can hope to finish each before I begin to print. These were my selfish reasons for accepting the offer, and they were first. Then, the magazine is in such a state that I can hope to do something for humanity as well as the humanities with it. If I cannot, I can give it up, but the outlook is cheerful; and I wish to begin by asking you for that poem of Lowell's about Grant, if you are free to let me have it.[2] The pay will be as good as the best, and I am sure you will not be ashamed to see it where I shall put it in the May number, which will be my first. If you could let me have my choice of some others among the poems we looked over together, I should be glad.

I mean to conduct the magazine so that you will be willing to print something of your own in it. I am to be associated with the owner, Mr. John Brisben Walker, a man of generous ideals, who will leave me absolute control in literature, and whom I think with in many other matters.—When we meet, I can speak more fully of the whole affair. We have found a house at last, after a month's misery in looking, and the fatigue is slowly dropping from me. How I wish I could see you! Write to me at 241 East 17th st., and accept for you and yours our united love.

Yours ever
W. D. Howells.

1. John Brisben Walker (1847–1931), editor (1886–1905), owner, and publisher (1889–1894) of *Cosmopolitan*, had originally asked Howells to consider writing a series of essays for his magazine when Howells' contract with Harper & Brothers terminated (Walker to Howells, 18 November 1891 [MH]). After Howells refused, he and Walker began negotiating the terms on which Howells would assume the editorship of *Cosmopolitan*. On 4 December 1891 (MH), Walker wrote Howells: "In order that you may hold in writing the terms of our arrangement with reference to your editorship of the Cosmopolitan, I send you this. Your letter to me reads as follows: 'I accept your offer to edit the Cosmopolitan, conjointly with you, on the terms and conditions we have agreed upon, for the sum of ten thousand

($10.000–) dollars a year. In case we should not wish to continue our relations beyond the year, each shall be free to give the other six months notice and end there. I shall be ready to begin my work on the 1st day of January 1892....' [¶] As the result of a subsequent conversation it was determined that you should receive from the Cosmopolitan the sum of Five thousand ($5.000–) dollars, in addition to the ten thousand mentioned in your letter—making fifteen thousand per annum in all—in consideration of which sum, your entire time should be devoted to the interests of the Cosmopolitan and you should furnish during the year some short stories or one long story of sixty thousand words as shall be deemed best and that except the novels now being published or which have been already announced, no work of yours shall appear in any publication except the Cosmopolitan—this not to interfere however with the production of any play of yours upon the stage." Howells signed this letter on 8 December 1891, and he wrote W. C. Howells on 7 December 1891 (MH): "I have a good arrangement money wise, and work that promises to be pleasant and useful. His offer to me was a great surprise, and I had to do some quick thinking."

2. Lowell's poem "On a Bust of General Grant" was published in *Scribner's*, March 1892. Howells published Lowell's "The Nobler Lover" in *Cosmopolitan*, May 1892, instead; later that year he published Lowell's "For a Birthday" (June) and "Love and Thought" (July). Norton was Lowell's literary executor.

13 DECEMBER 1891, NEW YORK, TO WILLIAM C. HOWELLS

> 241 East 17th st.,
> New York, Dec. 13, 1891.

Dear father:

There is not much more to tell you of my magazine engagement than I told in my last. I am to get out the May number for my first, and I am to have sole charge practically; each may end the engagement by six months' notice. The owner, John Brisben Walker, was born in western Pa., brought up on newspapers, went to West Point, and settled in Colorado, where he had ranches and mines. He is a millionaire and a catholic, but he has very strong socialistic tendencies, and he got himself well scalded by the catholic press for his address at Washington, preaching human equality and the duties of men to men.[1] So far, so good. Of course the affair between us is an experiment, and it may not work, but I shall do my best while it lasts. The money basis is good.[2]

We are here in a very pleasant furnished house, which we have taken till June.[3] We shall meanwhile look up a flat, and bring on our own things from Boston towards spring.

I am so sorry you have had such a bad time with Henry, but glad it's over for a while. Poor boy! I wish something could be done for him. You must speak to him for me, and tell him I should like to see him. The children will write soon. All join me in love to each of you.

> Your aff'te son,
> Will.

1. The content and occasion of Walker's address have not been further identified.

2. Howells further elaborated the reasons for his accepting the editorship of *Cosmopolitan* in a letter to W. C. Howells, 20 December 1891 (MH; *Life in Letters*, II, 20): "I suppose that the lifelong habit of being on a salary had something to do with it. Then, though I could sell my stories well, I should have to bargain about each one of them, and I should have to write a great many. Now, the magazine work will allow me to write a short one each year, and it will give me change of work, and put me in the current of events. If it doesn't kill me, it will rejuvenate me, and I don't think it will kill me. The best thing about it is Mr. Walker's infatuation with his bargain; yet it is terrible, in a way, to have a man so satisfied with you. He couldn't be more so; he might be less."

3. Howells' next move in New York was in the fall of 1892 to 40 West 59th Street.

20 DECEMBER 1891, NEW YORK, TO HAMLIN GARLAND

The Cosmopolitan Magazine, ...
Dec. 20, 1891.

My dear Garland:

It is no use to talk serial to me at present: I want a short story; or, I should like to consider something like a vivid study of the *personnel* of the farmers' alliancers as you met them lately in the West: their griefs and hopes, their minds and manners; something very realistic. Perhaps, a brief sketch of some young fellow who comes to the convention, with his history and character in the form of fiction?[1] Or, old fellow.

Yours ever
W. D. Howells.

1. Garland may have submitted his novel *A Spoil of Office* (1892), which was published serially in the *Arena*, January–June 1892, or his novella "Ol' Pap's Flaxen" (1892; published in book form as *A Little Norsk*), which was published serially in the *Century*, March–May 1892. Instead Howells published Garland's short story "At the Brewery" (later entitled "Saturday Night on the Farm" in *Prairie Folks* [1893]) in the *Cosmopolitan*, May 1892. Howells had written Garland on 16 December 1891 (CLSU) that he wanted him to submit "within the next six weeks something as good as The Return of the Private, or Up the Coulé...."

TEXTUAL APPARATUS

Introduction

THE letters selected for inclusion in these volumes of Howells correspondence are printed in clear text in the form reproducing as nearly as possible their finished state. The record of the alterations which took place during composition and which are evidenced on the pages of the manuscripts is presented in the textual apparatus which follows, in combination with the record of editorial emendations. The letters have been editorially corrected only in specific details and only when the original texts would make no conceivable sense to the reader. Thus Howells' few eccentricities of spelling and punctuation and his occasional mistakes and oversights have generally been retained. However, inadvertent repetitions of letters, syllables, or words—usually a result of moving the pen from the end of one line to the beginning of the next—have been emended and recorded in the apparatus. In cases where the actual manuscripts are not available and transcriptions or printed versions of letters have served as the basis for printing here, errors in those materials have also been retained, since the actual source of the error—Howells, the transcriber, or the printer—cannot be identified.

Except where extraordinary conditions have made it impossible, the following procedures have been followed step-by-step in the preparation for publication of the text of each letter, whether the extant form of it is the original document or an unpublished or published transcription. First a clean, typed transcription of the final form of the extant material is prepared from a facsimile of it. Then duplicate copies of this prepared transcription are read and corrected against the facsimile by the editor of the volume and by one of the editors of the letters series. At the same time drafts of the apparatus material are prepared, recording all cancellations, insertions, revisions, and illegible words or letters in the text, as well as possible compounds, end-line hyphenated, which must be resolved as hypenated or unhypenated forms. These drafts of the apparatus also include questions about proper interpretation of textual details. The corrected and edited transcriptions and accompanying apparatus are conflated at the Howells Center and any discrepancies identified and corrected. At this stage transcriptions and textual apparatus are completely reread against the facsimile of the original. The resultant material is next checked by a different editor against the original holograph, copy, or printing; he verifies all details, answers insofar as possible all remaining questions, and indicates matter in the original which has not been reproduced in the working facsimile. This completes the process of preparing printer's copy.

At this point the texts of the letters—though not the corresponding apparatus—are set in type. The typeset texts are proofread once against the facsimiles of the original documents and once more against the prepared printer's copy; necessary corrections are made in both typeset text and apparatus, and the apparatus is keyed to the line numbering of the typeset texts. After correction by the printer of the typeset text and the setting in type of the textual apparatus, these materials are proofread in full once more against the printer's copy, and the apparatus is proofread again separately. At every point at which revises are returned by the printer they are verified against the marked proofs.

This procedure—involving as many different people as possible from among the editors of the volumes, the series, and the Howells Edition staff—has been adopted to guarantee that the printed texts are as accurate as the combined energy and attention of a group of trained and experienced editors can make them. It will, we hope, warrant our statement that the errors, oversights, and possibly unidiomatic readings of the texts are those of the original documents and not of the editors. Further, since even the detailed textual record presented in this apparatus cannot fully indicate the physical condition of the letters, the editorial materials prepared during the assembly of these volumes are all being preserved, and can be consulted by anyone who wishes to see them—at the Howells Center at Indiana University as long as it is in operation for preparation of texts for "A Selected Edition of W. D. Howells" and in a suitable public depository thereafter.

The editorial considerations and procedures outlined above underlie the actual presentation of the letters printed in these volumes. Each letter is introduced by an editorial heading identifying the date and place of composition and the name of the correspondent to whom it is directed. The date and location identified in this heading may be different from those provided by the letter itself, since the content of the letter or other pertinent evidence can indicate that those details are inaccurate. When such cases arise, they are discussed in appropriate footnotes.

The translation of the ranges of handwritten and typewritten material and printed stationery into the stricter confines of the printed page obviously demands the adoption of certain formal and stylistic conventions. Regardless of their arrangement or placement on the original page, inside addresses are presented in one or more lines above the single line containing the place of origin and date provided in the letter. This format is followed regardless of the placement of the dateline at the beginning or at the end of a letter. When handwritten or printed letterheads provide more elaborate information than basic identification of place or origin and date, the additional information is omitted and its absence signaled by the appropriate placement of ellipses. The use of capitals or a combination of capitals and small capitals in printed letter-head forms has been reduced here to capitals and lowercase letters. In the printing of letters and datelines in the present text, italic type is used to indicate matter which occurs in the original as part of printed sta-tionery, and roman to indicate portions supplied by Howells himself. The distinction between print and handwritten or typed portions of heading information can be significant in that a printed letterhead in particular does not necessarily indicate that the letter itself was written in that place. If Howells supplied location information different from that of a printed letterhead, the printed letterhead is considered simply a mark on the paper and has been ignored in the presentation of the text.

The beginning of the body of the letter after the salutation has been consistently set off by a paragraph even if Howells continued on the same line or used any other unconventional spacing. Similarly, the positions of the complimentary close (e.g., "Yours ever") and the signature in relation to the body of the letter have been standardized without regard to Howells' widely varying usage. The relative spacing of the indentations of paragraphs has been normalized to conform to the typography of these volumes; this principle has been applied also to unindented paragraph breaks which occur in the originals. The interruptive or appositive dash within sentences and the transitional dash between sentences (the latter almost the equivalent in sense of the paragraph break) have been set in standard typographical form, and relative length not indicated. The long *s* of Howells' youthful hand has been set consistently in the ordinary typographical form. Underlined words have been set in italics without regard to the position or relative length of the underlining; when the form of the underlining indicates, however, that Howells clearly in-tended to emphasize only part of a word (e.g., *every*one), then only that part has been italicized.

When texts are derived from machine-printed rather than handwritten telegrams, the full capitalization used there has been reduced to capitals and lowercase letters, with an appropriate note in the textual apparatus. The same procedure has been followed for letters typed on typewriters using only capital letters. Where texts are derived from copies of now-missing letters rather than from manuscripts, any typographical peculi-arities of those forms—indentation, employment of capitals and small capitals in proper names, and so on—have been altered to conform to the format of the present edition. But only this strictly typographical altera-tion has been enforced; the errors in spelling and punctuation and the revisions and cancellations within these materials have all been considered textually significant and a potentially accurate record of the originals upon which they are based.

Postscripts which follow upon the signatures in the original letters are placed in this same position in the printed text, but marginal notes and postscripts placed eccentrically are printed where they seem to belong within or after the body of the letter, and their original locations indicated by editorial notes in the apparatus to the letter. The presence or absence of page and leaf numbering or the location of such numbering on the original pages has not been recorded.

In the preparation of the texts and apparatus, those marks, and those marks alone, in the text of the letter which could be interpreted as slips of the pen have been ignored. All other marks, including wiped-out words or letters, erased material, incomplete words either canceled or uncanceled, and random letters have been recorded. Illegible words or letters are identified in the apparatus by the abbreviation *"illeg."*

The presentation of this information in the apparatus demands the use of certain symbols and abbrevations to conserve space. The record for each letter is introduced by the same editorial heading that introduces the item in the text proper. Then follows a note on the number of pages (i.e., sides of individual sheets or of segments of sheets created by folding which have been written on). Next is provided an abbreviated indication of the kind of text and the presence or absence of authorial signature (A.l. = Autograph letter; A.l.s. = Autograph letter signed; T.l. = Typescript letter; T.l.s. = Typescript letter signed; A.n. = Autograph note; A.n.s. = Autograph note signed; T.n. = Typescript note; T.n.s. = Typescript note signed). If the authorial text is of a kind not represented by these eight abbreviations, it is described fully (e.g., "Mostly in autograph of Elinor M. Howells"; "Telegraph form written in Howells' hand"; "Typed telegram"). If the text is based on a transcribed copy, that fact is noted together with information about the source of the transcription, if known; if the transcription is a published text, the author, title, and other bibliographical information are provided —in the cases of both published and unpublished transcriptions the number of pages of text is ignored as textually irrelevant. This information is followed in turn by the standard abbreviation for the library in which the original document or extant transcription is located,[1] or by the short-form designation for a private collection.

Following this heading appears the record of the internal revisions and cancellations in the letter document and any emendations made by the editors. All such revisions, even in typed letters, may be assumed to be

---

1. The system of abbreviations used in this edition is that described in *Symbols of American Libraries*, 10th ed. (Washington: Library of Congress, 1969).

by Howells, unless otherwise noted in the apparatus. Each entry in this record begins with the citation of the number or numbers of the lines in the text of the printed letter in which the cited material occurs. This numbering is based on the count of full or partial lines of type, and begins with the first line of the document, whether that be inside address, date, or salutation; it does not include the formal editorial heading which precedes each letter.

Sentences, phrases, words, or parts of words inserted into the running text of the document are indicated in the record by placement within vertical arrows, ellipses being used to abbreviate passages of four or more words. Thus:

↑evade↓   with↑out↓   ↑directly . . . exchange.↓

No distinction is made between words inserted above the line and those inserted below it or manuscript revisions fitted into typescript lines, and the color of ink or the medium (pencil, pen, typewriter) used for corrections or additions is not described. The presence or absence of a caret or other conventional symbol for the insertion of the material is not recorded. When a word has been written over some other word or part of a word, that fact is indicated by the use of the abbreviation "*w.o.*" (for "written over") following the final reading and preceding the original. Thus:

parties *w.o.* party   people *w.o.* ple

Words canceled in the original are indicated by placement in pointed brackets in the context of citation of sufficient words from the text of the letter (either before or after the canceled words or phrase) as printed in this edition to identify its location. Thus:

went ⟨to⟩   ⟨we went⟩ I walked

An italic question mark within brackets following a word indicates a degree of uncertainty about the interpretation provided. The combinations of these various symbols and abbreviations should be self-explanatory: e.g., ↑⟨this⟩↓ indicates that the interlined word "this" has been canceled.

All editorial revisions are signaled in the apparatus by a left-opening bracket (]) : preceding it appears the reading of the text as printed in this edition, and following it the reading of the original. When the editorial revision involves only the emendation of punctuation, each curved dash (∼) following the bracket stands for a word preceding the bracket. When it has been necessary to supply words, letters, or marks of punctuation missing in the original not because of oversight or error in composition but because of the present physical condition of the document—badly faded ink; deteriorated or torn paper, blots, or water-spots—the reconstructed portions are signaled by being placed between vertical lines: Thus:

af|te|r |the| commit|tee| met

Virgules (slashes) are used to indicate the end of a line of writing in the original document. All other editorial comments, including description of the placement of postscripts and marginal notes or the presence in a document of notes or comments in another hand believed to be contemporary with the composition or receipt of the letter, as well as information about specific textual details not covered by the basic system of symbols and abbreviations outlined here, are provided in italic type within brackets.

In addition to the textual record which follows, this edition of letters contains a section headed "Word-Division," consisting of two separate lists: one, List A, indicates the resolution of possible compounds occurring as end-line hyphenations in the original documents, and the other, List B, the form to be given to possible compounds which occur at the end of the line in the present text. A description of the keying system employed in these lists and the process by which editorial decisions about the resolution of such end-lines were reached are provided in the headnote to that section.

C. K. L.
D. J. N.

Textual Record

2 January 1882, Cambridge, to Charles Fairchild. 5 pp. A.l.s. MH.

   10 and *w.o.* is   12 makes ⟨me⟩   17 to⟨cha⟩   17 place. *w.o.* ∼,
23 ⟨I⟩ we   23 live] have   27 that ⟨we⟩ I   27 that do *w.o.* to do
30 ↑ever↓   30 only] only/only   33 you ⟨can⟩   35 was *w.o.* is

19 January 1882, Boston, to James R. Osgood. 2 pp. A.l.s. MH.

   9 anything,⟨⟩

19 February 1882, Boston, to William C. Howells. 3 pp. A.l.s. MH.

   1 19 *w.o.* 17   17 sad *w.o. illeg.*   28–31 -as about . . . . Will.]
[*in margin and across salutation and dateline, first page*]

2 March 1882, Boston, to Alfred A. Reade. 1 p. A.l.s. CSmH.

2 March 1882, Boston, to William C. Howells. 2 pp. A.l.s. MH.

7 March 1882, Boston, to George W. Cable. 2 pp. A.l.s. LNHT.

   6 And ⟨yet⟩

18 March 1882, Boston, to John Hay. Location of MS. unknown.
Life in Letters, I, 310–12.

26 March 1882, Boston, to William C. Howells. 4 pp. A.l.s. MH.

   7 ⟨clo⟩ conclude   18 ⟨En⟩ Edinburgh   21 awful] [*Howells accidentally wrote* awfut, *then canceled the crossing of the* t]

2 April 1882, Boston, to Charles D. Warner. 6 pp. A.l.s. CtHT.

   14 sail *w.o.* sh   22 collapse.] [*Howells canceled part of a semicolon
to make a period*]   22 We *w.o.* we   27 ↑a↓   28 are] are are
29 and ⟨fel⟩   33 ⟨tells⟩ told

8 April 1882, Boston, to Thomas W. Higginson. 2 pp. A.l.s. NN.

6 books at all that] [*Howells had written* books at that, *then corrected at* to all *and added at* in margin]   11 advice *w.o.* co

18 April 1882, Boston, to Samuel L. Clemens. 4 pp. A.l.s. CU.

9 did *w.o.* do   15 ↑used to↓ tremble⟨d⟩   28 Mrs. . . . letter.] [*in margin, first page*]

21 May 1882, Lexington, Massachusetts, to Victoria M. Howells. 3 pp. A.l.s. MH.

9 ↑each↓ other⟨s⟩   13 ⟨time⟩ ↑season↓

12 July 1882, Toronto, to James R. Osgood. 4 pp. A.l.s. NN.

5 ordinary *w.o.* nor   8 wish *w.o.* wife   8 nascent *w.o.* ris
12 ↑and noble↓   13 that the *w.o.* that that   14 ↑as well as romantic↓
14 romantic.] ∼   18 though *w.o.* al   18 ⟨kn⟩ now   19 [*at the beginning of the paragraph Howells sketched a pointing hand*]
23 ⟨with⟩ ↑from↓   23 ↑"serial↓   26 ↑you↓ here

21 July 1882, Quebec, to Victoria M. Howells. 6 pp. A.l.s. MH.

3 accept *w.o.* ask   28 —without ⟨of⟩   28 be *w.o.* me
30 Father] He ↑Father↓   36 ↑are↓   37 though⟨t⟩   38 on *w.o.* or
38 at *w.o.* as

31 July 1882, London, to William C. Howells, 4 pp. A.l.s. MH.

20 ⟨head⟩ hay   36 ⟨at⟩ perhaps   39 ⟨j⟩ children

1 August 1882, London, to Edmund W. Gosse. 2 pp. A.l.s. British Library.

5 August 1882, London, to James R. Osgood. 4 pp. A.l.s. MH.

5 ↑or↓   6 ↑M. D.↓   8 he *w.o.* his   11 as ↑to↓   24 ⟨g⟩ Conway
26 working *w.o.* illeg.   31–34 He's . . . . Howells.] [*across salutation, first page*]

26 August 1882, London, to Edmund W. Gosse. 2 pp. A.l.s. British Library.

7 30 *w.o.* illeg.

1 September 1882, London, to Samuel L. Clemens. 3 pp. A.l.s. CU.

12 ⟨we⟩ it   18 $50 *w.o.* $52   23 these *w.o.* them   23 ↑people↓
25 a wonderful] a a wonderful   31 Mallory⟨'⟩s

2 September 1882, London, to Charles Waldstein. Location of MS. unknown. Typed copy of holograph formerly owned by Lord Walston, Cambridge (England).

9 September 1882, London, to Edmund W. **Gosse.** 3 pp. A.l.s. British Library.

21 on *w.o.* an   25 here ⟨at⟩   28 ↑Edwin Booth↓ [*Howells had first marked the insertion after* and, *then canceled the caret and placed it after* Warner]

14 September 1882, London, to Charles E. Norton. 3 pp. A.l.s. MH.

11 Academy *w.o. illeg.*   29 of *w.o.* a   34 ⟨join⟩ children

24 September 1882, Villeneuve, to William C. **Howells.** 3 pp. A.l.s. **MH.**
[*above dateline, presumably in* W. C. Howell's *hand*: Please return]

13 aisle *w.o.* isles   27 ⟨with⟩ against   29 school, ⟨to-mor
40 unite⟨d⟩

4 October 1882, Villeneuve, to Henry James. 3 pp. A.l.s. MH.

8 ↑on↓   8 was *w.o.* is   16 habit *w.o.* happ   18 with *w.o. illeg.*
23 possibilities *w.o.* possibility   24 commonplace *w.o.* comp
24 appealed *w.o.* t   33 day ⟨before⟩   33 we *w.o.* he   36 ↑again↓

7 October 1882, Villeneuve, to William C. **Howells.** 3 pp. A.l.s. MH.

4 in order] order   9 ↑here↓   26 gave *w.o.* give

16 October 1882, Villeneuve, to James R. **Osgood.** 5 pp. A.l.s. NjR.

9 I am] [*partial letter* h *canceled after* I]   14 ↑or supercargo↓
14 ↑with his ship↓   16 be *w.o. illeg.*   21 ⟨carnival⟩ ↑masking↓
22 one *w.o.* in   31 ⟨of⟩ ↑with the↓   42 Republic *w.o.* Republin

17 October 1882, Villeneuve, to Samuel L. **Clemens.** 3 pp. A.l.s. CU.

18–19 companionship *w.o.* compansh   29 worth⟨y⟩

26 October 1882, Villeneuve, to Edmund W. **Gosse.** 3 pp. A.l.s. British Library.

5 ↑it↓   8 I *w.o.* it   12 hero's *w.o.* heroes   13 ↑of↓   17 ↑a↓
21 send *w.o.* sent   27 comfort *w.o.* common   29 house ⟨its⟩
40–44 send . . . . Howells.] [*in margins, first page*]

16 November 1882, Villeneuve, to Edmund W. Gosse. 4 pp. A.l.s. British
Library.

4 ↑not↓   5 ↑number↓   11 always ↑thought↓
12 Thackeray] thackeray'⟨s⟩   20 novelists, *w.o.*~?   21 ⟨I⟩ my
23 further⟨e⟩ about ↑them↓   29 came⟨s⟩   29 ↑together,↓   34 ↑a↓
35 about it is] about it   36 whether ⟨*illeg.*⟩   40 ↑the↓
43 my *w.o.* me   46–49 apostate . . . . Howells] [*in margin and across salutation and text, first page*]

19 November 1882, Villeneuve, to Roswell Smith. 5 pp. A.l.s. MH.

3 get *w.o.* give   6 ⟨of⟩ ↑in↓   9 ↑endorsed . . . Gilder↓
10 lady's *w.o.* ladi   10 saying, ⟨the⟩   11 have *w.o. illeg.*
17 you *w.o.* we   20 ↑third↓   20 like ⟨t⟩   30 I ↑have↓   39 ↑to↓ give
44 Minor-City *w.o.* minor-city

3 December 1882, Villeneuve, to Daniel C. Gilman. Location of MS. unknown. *Life in Letters*, I, 330–32.

16 and 24 December 1882, Florence, to James R. Osgood. 3 pp. A.l.s. MH.

5 wish⟨es⟩   16 goes⟨t⟩   23 1884. ⟨If he must have it early in that
year, I'm afraid I must return home early in the spring of next year.⟩
32 L.'s *w.o.* his   34 allowing *w.o.* allowed   35 ⟨modify⟩ write
35 Venetian *w.o.* I   40–41 *No hurry.*] [*the sketch of a pointing hand
appears before these words*]

17 December 1882, Florence, to James R. Lowell. 3 pp. A.l.s. MH.

23 know *w.o.* knew   26 from *w.o.* of
[*on verso of third page, in another hand*: Howells]

12 January 1883, Florence, to James R. Osgood. 2 pp. A.l.s. MH.

7 ↑from↓

28 January 1883, Florence, to William C. Howells. 3 pp. A.l.s. MH.

7 a⟨n⟩   7 recurrence *w.o.* recurrd   14 but *w.o.* and   20 the⟨re⟩
37–38 Better . . . London] [*in left margin, first page*]

5 February 1883, Florence, to William C. Howells. 3 pp. A.l.s. MH.

   5 if *w.o.* so

9 February 1883, Florence, to James R. Osgood. 3 pp. A.l.s. Location of MS. unknown. Xerox copy at InU.

   6 Pisa, ⟨*illeg.*⟩ ↑Pistoja,↓   6 ↑and Areggo,↓   24 no⟨w⟩
25 awhile, ⟨we're⟩   26 ↑is↓   35–36 ⟨inconst⟩ inconsistent
36 cities, ⟨first⟩

4 March 1883, Siena, to William C. Howells. 2 pp. A.l.s. MH.

4 March 1883, Siena, to Charles D. Warner. 3 pp. A.l.s. CtHT.

   3 self-⟨reproah⟩ reproach   5 spoiled *w.o.* spoiling   17 ↑to hurry↓
17 ⟨to⟩ it ↑was↓   25 part *w.o.* gr   29 ⟨least⟩ leisure

13 March 1883, Florence, to Thomas S. Perry. Location of MS. unknown. *Life in Letters*, I, 337–38.

   6 Homberger] [*Mildred Howells reads* Hamberger; *but elsewhere Howells spells the name correctly*]

26 March 1883, Florence, to William C. Howells. 3 pp. A.l.s. CSmH.

   13 *Deux w.o. illeg.*   19 ⟨sort⟩ situation   33 Winny *w.o. illeg.*
36 since ⟨I⟩   39 Give . . . . soon.] [*in left margin, first page*]

3 April 1883, Florence, to Edmund W. Gosse. 3 pp. A.l.s. British Library.

   10 With ⟨a⟩   25 bag⟨g⟩   34 Tadema *w.o.* D   45 you ↑both↓

5 April 1883, Florence, to Thomas R. Lounsbury. 3 pp. A.l.s. CtY.

   6 have *w.o.* had   17 [*the comma after* day *is written over a semicolon*]
23 ↑of this kindness↓   23 ↑a↓   33 ↑expressing↓   37 and ⟨that⟩
42 Middle-Ages *w.o.* Middle-age   42 their *w.o.* its
42–43 Middle-Ages *w.o.* middle-Ages

20 April 1883, Venice, to James R. Osgood. 3 pp. A.l.s. ViU.

   9 ⟨it⟩ ↑you↓   13 anything *w.o. illeg.*   20 Pennell] [*the sketch of a pointing hand appears before this word*]   24 ⟨make⟩ ↑Do make↓
25 track.] [*the sketch of a left-pointing hand appears after this word*]
27 ↑to-night↓   28 who's *w.o.* whose

22 April 1883, Venice, to William C. Howells. 3 pp. A.l.s. MH.

4 ↑to↓ the letters   7 ⟨night⟩ afternoon   22 starved] starved/starved
30 ↑head↓   31 But *w.o.* "but   32 ↑a book↓   40 would ⟨not⟩
41–42 ⟨a princely⟩ ownership

22 April 1883, Venice, to Samuel L. Clemens. 3 pp. A.l.s. CU.

14 ↑with↓   15 Prince *w.o.* No   20 had] had had   25 here *w.o.* t
30 ↑been↓   31 ↑air↓   31 she takes *w.o.* we do   35 don't *w.o.* did

20 May 1883, Verona, to William C. Howells. 3 pp. A.l.s. MH.

6 wrote *w.o.* sent   10 impos⟨s⟩-/-sible   14 I will ⟨I will⟩ come
16 ↑cob-↓   17 Of *w.o.* of   20 this] [*followed by these cancelled and
inverted words*: Hotel Riva San Lazzaro]   23 ↑business↓
28 life. ⟨The⟩

3 June 1883, Paris, to William C. Howells. 4 pp. A.l.s. MH.

7 ↑the↓   15 7.30.] 7.30   18 Hotel ⟨Rue⟩   25 ↑whereabouts↓
26 to *w.o.* Jo

21 June 1883, Hay (Wales), to William C. Howells. 8 pp. A.l.s. MH.

7 on *w.o.* and   9 stone⟨,⟩   11 ↑local↓   14 ↑I told↓
15 ⟨wife⟩ owner   20 ⟨style⟩ size   25 nice *w.o.* *illeg.*   28 sharp⟨,⟩
29 ↑her↓   36 ↑the↓ information   53 ⟨l⟩ earliest   59 ⟨t⟩ Lowell
64 that] thatt   65 all.] ~   64–67 I'm . . . . Will.] [*across text, page
five*]

24 June 1883, London, to William C. Howells. 4 pp. A.l.s. MH.

11 Boar" ⟨s⟩   23 ⟨fars⟩ machinery   27 ↑the↓ corner
29 Mrs *w.o.* her   29 Blaney's *w.o.* m   34 fine *w.o.* *illeg.*   45 ⟨h⟩ 'im
46 ⟨*illeg.*⟩ I got   49 the family.] [*in margin, fourth page*]
50–51 Your . . . Will.] [*in margin, first page*]

26 June 1883, London, to Edmund W. Gosse. 2 pp. A.l.s. British Library.

6 talk *w.o.* *illeg.*   14 ⟨*illeg.*⟩ sure

4 July 1883, London, to "My dear Sir." 3 pp. A.l.s. ViU.

8 ↑&↓

6 July 1883, Moville, Ireland, to James R. Lowell. 2 pp. A.l.s. MH.

5 feeling *w.o.* rece   [*at bottom of second page, in another hand*: Howells]

30 July 1883, Boston, to John Hay. Location of MS. unknown. *Life in Letters*, I, 350–51.

2 August 1883, Boston, to Charles D. Warner, 3 pp. A.l.s. CtHT.

6 could *w.o.* can

5 August 1883, Boston, to William C. Howells. 3 pp. A.l.s. MH.

12 ↑than↓   16 sure *w.o. illeg.*   24 ⟨you⟩ write

15 September 1883, Boston, to William H. Ward. 2 pp. A.l.s. CLSU.

11 subject *w.o.* sup   11 pre↑-↓eminently

18 September 1883, Boston, to Samuel L. Clemens. 4 pp. A.l.s. CU.

9 ↑with↓   11 was *w.o. illeg.*   13 ⟨abs⟩ ludicrous   14 an *w.o.* a
14 impartial *w.o.* man   14 ⟨about⟩ ↑critic of↓   14 ↑own↓
15 ⟨admo-⟩ magnanimity   15 **magnanimity** *w.o.* ni

24 September 1883, Boston, to Edmund C. Stedman. 2 pp. A.l.s. VtMM.

13 That *w.o.* This

4 November 1883, Boston, to William C. Howells, 5 pp. A.l.s. MH.

3 Dear *w.o.* M   18 ↑being↓

19 November 1883, Boston, to Samuel L. Clemens. 4 pp. T.l. CU.

4 Mrs. *w.o.* Me   13 ↑week↓   16 with *w.o. illeg.*
16–17 Raymond . . . understanding.] [*Howells first typed*: as you have the type-writer copy; *over that he typed*: Raymond upon this understanding; *finally, he crossed everything out by hand and wrote above the line the phrase as it reads now*]   18 th|e| dialogue   22 Aldriches *w.o.* Aldrich's
23 ↑moment,↓   24 fulfilled] fulfil-/ed   24 ↑me↓
25 pity-/ing *w.o.* pityi/ing   25 know,⟨,⟩   25 Howell↑s↓ sa↑i↓d
29 ↑she↓   30 *spared*⟨d-⟩   31 tol↑d↓

21 November 1883, **Boston, to William C. Howells.** 3 pp. T.l. MH.

   4 ⟨pleas⟩ ↑here↓   13 open⟨ed⟩   15 ↑not↓   18 ↑to↓ tell   18 ↑who↓
25 think ⟨*illeg.*⟩   29 ⟨I⟩ I have   32 perfe↑c↓tly   38 noti⟨j⟩↑c↓es

27 November 1883, **Boston, to Whitelaw Reid.** 3 pp. A.l.s. DLC.

   6 critic⟨s⟩   8 ↑of art↓   8 art;]∼

9 December 1883, **Boston, to Edmund W. Gosse.** 8 pp. A.l.s. British
Library.

   11 confidently *w.o.* confidentfy   11 ↑you↓   14 directly *w.o. illeg.*
33 ↑ago,↓   34 Italy. *w.o.* Italy,   46 ↑her↓

2 January 1884, **Boston, to Edmund W. Gosse.** 10 pp. A.l.s. NjR.

   2 1883.] [1884 *w.o.* 1883 *in another hand*]   8 see,] ∼,,
13 had ⟨*illeg.*⟩   25 be ⟨s⟩   31 Congress *w.o.* we   32 ↑of↓
33 ⟨ap⟩ seeming   38 run⟨s⟩   52 fur-lined *w.o.* furn   53 ⟨bef⟩ behind
54 away from] away for ↑from↓   58 ↑in↓

7 January 1884, **Boston, to John Hay.** Location of MS. unknown. *Life in
Letters,* I, 357–58.

21 January 1884, **Boston, to Charles E. Norton.** 2 pp. A.l.s. MH.

   6 ↑attempted↓   7 for *w.o.* from   18–21 it . . . . Howells.] [*in margin
and across text, second page*]

15 February 1884, **Boston, to Samuel L. Clemens.** 5 pp. A.l.s. NPV.

   3 go ⟨the⟩   5 that *w.o.* this   6 men] men / men   8 name ⟨and⟩
17–18 ↑—not . . . figure.↓   23 is ⟨yours⟩ Sellers   27 ⟨It is⟩ It's
32 Then . . . W.D.H.] [*above dateline, first page*]

23 March 1884, **Boston, to Edmund W. Gosse.** 3 pp. A.l.s. British Library.

   8 written *w.o.* writing   11 ↑on↓   15 From *w.o.* from

4 April 1884, **Boston, to Charles L. Webster.** 2 pp. A.l.s. NPV.

   1 April *w.o.* March   3 play ⟨by⟩

6 April 1884, **Boston, to William C. Howells.** 3 pp. A.l.s. MH.

   11 has *w.o.* is

10 April 1884, Boston, to Samuel L. Clemens. 2 pp. A.l.s. CU.

   3 read *w.o.* m   8 much ⟨struck⟩   9 the *w.o.* it   10 ⟨t⟩ an

16 April 1884, Boston, to Edgar W. Howe. Location of MS. unknown. Joseph R. Kathrens, "The Story of a Story," *Kansas City Star Magazine,* 1 March 1925, p. 9.

30 April 1884, Boston, to Whitelaw Reid. 2 pp. A.l.s. DLC.

12 May 1884, Boston, to James R. Osgood. 4 pp. A.l.s. MH.

   8 I *w.o.* to   20 ↑the↓ assurance   27 like *w.o.* as

14 May 1884, Boston, to Belton O. Townsend. 2 pp. A.l.s. E. N. Zeigler, Florence, S.C.

   8 not *w.o.* k   9 smallest *w.o.* smallesf

19 May 1884, Boston, to John Augustin Daly. 2 pp. A.l.s. DFo.

20 May 1884, Boston, to Edmund W. Gosse. 2 pp. A.l.s. British Library.

   10 reading] written

8 June 1884, Boston, to William C. Howells. 4 pp. A.l.s. MH.

   5 produce ↑it↓

18 June 1884, Boston, to Richard W. Gilder. 2 pp. A.l.s. OOxM.

   3 Letter *w.o.* letter   5 ↑mock-↓

Ca. 20 June 1884, Boston[?], to Hugo Erichsen. 2 pp. A.n.s. NHi.

31 July 1884, Wolfeborough, New Hampshire, to Richard W. Gilder. 3 pp. A.l.s. NN.

   11 somewhere *w.o.* somewhat   14 expect] ex-/expect   18 I . . . away.] [*in margin, first page, next to* the main idea]

7 August 1884, Boston, to Charles E. Norton. 3 pp. A.l.s. MH.

   6 Mother *w.o.* mother   15 love⟨ly⟩

10 August 1884, Boston, to William C. Howells. 3 pp. A.l.s. MH.

   3 Monday *w.o.* S   20 inquiry ⟨order⟩

10 August 1884, Boston, to Elinor M. Howells. Location of MS. unknown. Typed copy at MH.

10 August 1884, Boston, to Samuel L. Clemens. 3 pp. A.l.s. CU.

    4 ↑even↓   16 'love-part'] 'love-part   17 contemporary.⟨"⟩
18 fifteen *w.o.* fifty   25–26 What . . . . elected.] [*in margin and across salutation and dateline, first page*]

15 August 1884, Kennebunkport, Maine, to Thomas S. Perry. 4 pp. A.l.s. MeWC.

    4 Phelps *w.o.* Phepps   4 others *w.o.* an   4 and *w.o.* are
9 a⟨n⟩ son   13 even *w.o.* in   15 ↑generally↓   21 Democrat⟨ic⟩↑;↓
21 power *w.o. illeg.*   21 is *w.o. illeg.*

22 August 1884, Kennebunkport, Maine, to Henry James. 12 pp. A.l.s. MH.

    8 ↑some↓   12 possibly *w.o.* possible   27 to *w.o.* in   28 resort⟨s⟩↑,↓
43 ⟨to⟩ in   45 triumph⟨,⟩   47 with the *w.o.* with this
47 sincere⟨, second hand⟩   57 Osgood *w.o. illeg.*   63 pitfall]~.
63 ↑with another play.—↓   74 numbers ⟨that⟩

7 September 1884, Boston, to William C. Howells. 3 pp. A.l.s. MH.

    9 for *w.o.* to   18 ⟨the⟩ Raymond

19 October 1884, Boston, to William C. Howells. 4 pp. A.l. MH.

    4 ⟨B⟩ New   6 better *w.o.* well   12 set-/-tle *w.o.* the
12 ↑the↓ house   15 outing ⟨at⟩   17 weather⟨,⟩—   20 ⟨I wish⟩ He

9 November 1884, Boston, to William C. Howells. 2 pp. A.l.s. MH.

    2 9 *w.o.* 7   6 A ⟨cycl⟩   16 ⟨Y⟩ Except   16 Uncle *w.o.* uncle

24 December 1884, Boston, to Edmund W. Gosse. 4 pp. A.l.s. Brotherton Library, Leeds (England).

    20 ↑has↓   24 *Mrs. w.o. Miss*   32 ⟨Mrs⟩ Mr.

18 January 1885, Boston, to William C. Howells. 4 pp. A.l.s. MH.

    1 1885 *w.o.* 1884   3 ⟨kno⟩ now   10 ↑early↓

8 March 1885, Boston, to William C. Howells. 3 pp. A.l.s. MH.

   8 a *w.o.* to   8 others to lunch] other lunch   11 has *w.o.* was

9 March 1885, Boston, to Edmund W. Gosse. 8 pp. A.l.s. British Library.

   1 ⟨3⟩ 302   7 inconsolable] inconsable *w.o.* incol   9 ↑almost↓
16 the⟨m⟩   19 ↑take↓   24 in an] in a/an   24 ↑⟨*illeg.*⟩↓ Gosse
50 S *w.o.* L   59 ↑in↓

13 March 1885, Boston, to Joseph W. Harper, Jr. 2 pp. A.l.s. MH.

   10 assume⟨d⟩

27 March 1885, Boston, to James Parton. 3 pp. A.l.s. MH.

   10 ↑for the Century and↓

5 May 1885, Boston, to Samuel L. Clemens. 3 pp. A.l.s. CU.

   14 ⟨you⟩ thing   16 ↑not↓   19 ⟨*illeg.*⟩ ↑lord↓

11 May 1885, Boston, to Clarence C. Buel. 2 pp. A.l.s. OOxM.

   6 ↑in N. Y.↓

28 May 1885, Boston, to J. H. Haulenbeck. 2 pp. A.l.s. MH.
   5–6 I might *w.o.* as might

10 June 1885, Great Barrington, Massachusetts, to Benjamin H. Ticknor.
2 pp. T.l.s. NjP.

   6 ⟨no⟩ reason   6 ⟨not⟩ now   22 told] [tlod *hand-corrected by*
Howells]   22 ⟨st⟩ stood   24 ↑hinted↓

12 June 1885, Great Barrington, Massachusetts, to Aurelia H. Howells,
2 pp. T.l. MH.

   7 ⟨f⟩ from   8 ⟨wo⟩ *work*   18 ⟨Gre⟩ Great

17 July 1885, Old Orchard, Maine, to Cyrus L. Sulzberger. Location of
MS. unknown. C. L. Sulzberger, " 'Silas Lapham' and the Jews," *American
Hebrew*, 4 September 1885, pp. 50–51.

19 July 1885, Wells Beach, Maine, to Horace E. Scudder. 2 pp. A.l.s. MH.

   5 we are in] we in   8 ⟨vulgar⟩ plebeian   10 tops *w.o. illeg.*

4 August 1885, Wells Beach, Maine, to Thomas B. Aldrich, 2 pp. A.l.s. MH.

9 though⟨t⟩

9 August 1885, Bethlehem, New Hampshire, to Samuel L. Clemens. 2 pp. T.l. CU.

4 it in] it i / in   9 vari↑a↓tion   13 ↑in.↓   16 ↑if↓   23 sits ⟨an⟩

11 August 1885, Bethlehem, New Hampshire, to James R. Osgood. 2 pp. A.l.s. MH.

4 Harper⟨'⟩s

11 September 1885, Bethlehem, New Hampshire, to Thomas Donaldson. Location of MS. unknown. Transcription by W. M. Gibson at InU.

1 [*no dateline on Gibson transcription, but information about place and date provided in commentary. Gibson misread 1888 for 1885; correction based on internal evidence*]

12 September 1885, Bethlehem, New Hampshire, to Benjamin H. Ticknor. 3 pp. A.l.s. NjP.

13 September 1885, Bethlehem, New Hampshire, to William C. Howells. 2 pp. A.l.s. MH.

14 October 1885, Boston, to James R. Osgood. 3 pp. A.l.s. MB.

20 October 1885, Boston, to S. Weir Mitchell. 3 pp. A.l.s. PU.

11 ⟨*illeg.*⟩ conclusion   19 ↑very↓   22 what *w.o.* that

26 October 1885, Auburndale, Massachusetts, to Edmund W. Gosse. 4 pp. A.l.s. British Library.

13 ↑⟨near⟩↓ Wellesley   13-14 gymnasium⟨⟩⟩

28 October 1885, Auburndale, Massachusetts, to Edwin D. Mead. 2 pp. A.l.s. RPB.

8 ⟨t⟩ and   8 at 1 *w.o.* or 1

30 October 1885, Auburndale, Massachusetts, to Thomas S. Perry. Location of MS. unknown. *Life in Letters*, I, 372–73.

18 November 1885, Auburndale, Massachusetts, to Helen Walter. 2 pp.
A.l.s. MH.

22 November 1885, Auburndale, Massachusetts, to Thomas R. Lounsbury.
3 pp. T.l.s. CtY.

    1 Lee's Hotel,] [*in Howells' hand*]   8 ⟨H⟩ "Here   12 ↑he↓ was
16 do↑ing↓   28 ⟨ho⟩ however   28-29 characters so] characters s / so
30 use *w.o.* yoe   30-31 you merely] your merely   31 ↑your↓

5 December 1885, Auburndale, Massachusetts, to Samuel L. Clemens.
4 pp. A.l.s. CU.

    [*in upper left corner, third page, in another hand*: Grant War]
13 ↑we↓   14 &] [*added in margin*]

19 December 1885, Auburndale, Massachusetts, to George W. Curtis. 2 pp.
A.l.s. MB.

    8 ↑with↓

26 December 1885, Auburndale, Massachusetts, to William C. Howells.
5 pp. A.l.s. MH.

    4 berries *w.o.* berry   8 too *w.o.* two   26 up⟨o⟩

18 January 1886, Auburndale, Massachusetts, to Samuel L. Clemens.
2 pp. A.l.s. CU.

    5 Mackley *w.o.* Mackey

23 January 1886, Auburndale, Massachusetts, to William C. Howells.
4 pp. T.l.s. MH.

    16 something *w.o.* soyething   17 ↑to↓   26 seen *w.o.* sent
33 ⟨t⟩ this   49-51 tell . . . . it.] [*in Howells' hand*]   50 ⟨you⟩ ↑her↓

24 January 1886, Auburndale, Massachusetts, to Edmund W. Gosse. 4 pp.
A.l.s. British Library.

    5 see you⟨r⟩   9 since *w.o.* said   15 ↑soul↓
25-27 to . . . . Howells] [*in margin, fourth page*]

28 January 1886, Auburndale, Massachusetts, to Thomas S. Perry. Location of MS. unknown. *Life in Letters*, I, 378.

3 February 1886, Auburndale, Massachusetts, to James R. Lowell. 2 pp. A.l.s. MH.

   3 it⟨'⟩s

9 May 1886, Boston, to John Hay. 2 pp. A.l.s. RPB.

   7 p. ⟨g⟩   9 regret⟨s⟩   15-17 both . . . . Howells.] [*in margin and across salutation, first page*]

23 May 1886, Boston, to Samuel L. Clemens. 3 pp. A.l.s. CU.

   12 all *w.o.* is

2 June 1886, Boston, to James R. Osgood. 6 pp. A.l.s. MH.

6 June 1886, Boston, to William H. Smith. 5 pp. A.l.s. OHi.

   17 ⟨your⟩ his   27 see *w.o. illeg.*

27 June 1886, Boston, to William C. Howells. 2 pp. T.l. MH.

   14 don't know what] don't what   17 the|e| 20 month] mo / month

13 July 1886, Boston, to Charles E. Norton. 4 pp. A.l.s. MH.

   6 here *w.o.* his   9 ↑then↓   13 the *w.o.* I   16 ⟨literary⟩ encyclopedia 22 except *w.o. illeg.*

18 July 1886, Boston, to William C. Howells. 3 pp. A.l.s. MH.

   4 think⟨ing⟩   12 finds *w.o.* for

23 July 1886, Boston, to William C. Howells. 3 pp. A.l.s. MH.

   9 you ↑will↓   10-11 the trade *w.o.* this trade 25-26 Remember . . . judgment.] [*in margin and across salutation, first page*]

19 August 1886, Ashfield, Massachusetts, to Elinor M. Howells. 3 pp. A.l.s. MH.

25 August 1886, Boston, to Gertrude Van R. Wickham. 1 p. A.l.s. OClWHi.

   3 am⟨*illeg.*⟩

31 August 1886, Boston, to Thomas W. Higginson. 2 pp. A.l.s. NN.

  7 apple⟨'⟩s   7 because now] because now because   16 eight.]∼
14-18 that . . . . Howells.] [*in margin and across text, second page*]

2 September 1886, Boston, to Charles D. Warner. 2 pp. A.l.s. CtHT.

  7 I could] I / I could   12 friend⟨s⟩

19 September 1886, Boston, to William C. Howells. 3 pp. T.l. MH.

  5 ↑a↓   7 come↑s↓   7 their] thir   12 ⟨the⟩ there's
15 confess, but] confess, / fess, but   18 ⟨$⟩ $1000
21 surprised *w.o.* sprprised   34 Winny's] Winny'w   36 get *w.o.* geat

12 October 1886, Boston, to Albert M. Palmer. 3 pp. A.l.s. MH.

  11 ⟨or else *w.o.* or⟩ ↑or else↓

26 October 1886, Boston, to James R. Lowell. 2 pp. A.l.s. MH.

31 October 1886, Boston, to William C. Howells. 3 pp. A.l.s. MH.

  1 Oct. *w.o.* Nov.   18 ↑can↓

7 November 1886, Boston, to Edmund W. Gosse. Location of MS. unknown. Typed copy by R. Jay Friedman at InU.

  17 Middlemores] [*Friedman copy reads* Midthornes; *emendation based on Howells' reference to the Middlemores' visit in his letter to W. Higginson, 6 November 1886 (NPV)*]

16 November 1886, Boston, to Achille Fréchette. 3 pp. A.l.s. CSmH.

  6 ↑closing episodes of↓   11 send, ⟨I⟩

21 November 1886, Boston, to William C. Howells. 2 pp. T.l. MH.

  5 danger] dang/ger   6 ↑you↓

9 December 1886, Jefferson, to John W. De Forest. 6 pp. A.l.s. CtY.

  7 pen ⟨the when⟩   9 Americans *w.o.* americans
9 a] [*added in margin*]   10 always ⟨a⟩   10 ⟨novel⟩ man
18 in *w.o.* w   22 robust ⟨mak⟩   23 Modern *w.o.* modern
26 might ⟨mgh⟩   29 W. D. Howells.] W. D. H.owells.

15 December 1886, Boston, to Charles E. Norton. 3 pp. A.l.s. MH.

18 December 1886, Boston, to Richard W. Gilder. 2 pp. A.l.s. KyU.

1 18 *w.o.* 2

19 December 1886, Boston, to William C. Howells. 3 pp. A.l.s. MH.

8 this trial *w.o.* the trial   12 both *w.o.* be
12 how much] how / how much

23 December 1886, Boston, to James R. Lowell. A.l.s. MH.

25 December 1886, Boston, to Henry James. 8 pp. T.l.s./A.l.s. MH.

9 ⟨h⟩ had   10 ⟨th⟩ thank   him *w.o.* tim
24 ↑except . . . ignorance.↓   26 ⟨g⟩ gone   27 is⟨t⟩   27 told ⟨m⟩
31 neve|r| 32 ⟨oth⟩ outside   32 and *w.o.* ind
32 indefeasi-/bly *w.o.* indefeasib/bly   33 made *w.o.* madh ⟨i⟩ it
38 character|s| 39 Olive ⟨Cha⟩   43 because ⟨jg⟩
48 litera-/ture *w.o.* literat/ture   50 fel-/low *w.o.* fello/low
53 English] Engli/lish   55-56 ↑to Cambridge;↓
56 for-/ward *w.o.* forwa/ward   60 ↑first↓ ⟨d⟩   62 spend *w.o.* spent
63 be-/tween *w.o.* bet/tween   63 we] w/we   67 |g|reat
67 —I'm sick] [*from here on in Howells' hand*]
69 several times to] several to   69 ⟨a⟩ gay   71 ↑me↓   72 ↑amazed↓
78 reso/↑-lute↓   81 heard *w.o.* heart

26 December 1886, Boston, to William C. Howells, 3 pp. A.l.s. MH.

14 her, ⟨*illeg.*⟩   19 is here *w.o.* are here   19 is here] is here / is here
25-28 get . . . . Will.] [*in margin and across salutation, first page*]

9 January 1887, Boston, to Aurelia H. Howells. 3 pp. A.l.s. MH.

4 ⟨for⟩ ↑and↓   10 the *w.o.* your ↑family↓   25 gratifying⟨,⟩ ↑for us,↓
26 ear⟨th⟩   29 ↑for you↓

1 February 1887, Boston, to John W. De Forest. 3 pp. A.l.s. CtY.

11 a *w.o.* m

6 February 1887, Boston, to Marie M. Fréchette. 4 pp. A.l.s. MH.

26-28 Papa . . . . Will.] [*in margin, first page*]

9 February 1887, Boston, to Thomas W. Higginson. 2 pp. A.l.s. NN.

14 February 1887, Boston, to Samuel L. Clemens. 2 pp. A.l.s. CU.

   3 ↑been↓   6 speech] speech / speech

20 February 1887, Boston, to William C. Howells. 3 pp. A.l.s. MH.

   3 Elinor *w.o.* I   3 after⟨s⟩   4 days *w.o.* weeks   4 and *w.o.* ca
4 as] [*added in margin*]   6 ↑so↓

27 February 1887, Boston, to George W. Curtis. 2 pp. A.l.s. MB.

   10 the *w.o.* a

27 February 1887, Boston, to William C. Howells. 3 pp. A.l.s. MH.

28 February 1887, Boston, to Charles E. Norton. 3 pp. A.l.s. CSmH.

   6 ⟨studies⟩ letters

3 April 1887, Boston, to William C. Howells. 3 pp. A.l.s. MH.

   5 Aurelia *w.o.* V   12 ↑bridges↓   13 ↑the↓

17 April 1887, Boston, to William C. Howells. 3 pp. A.l.s. MH.

   22 The *w.o.* We

2 May 1887, Auburndale, Massachusetts, to Whitelaw Reid. 2 pp. A.l.s. DLC.

   [*above dateline, in another hand*: W. D. Howells]

1 June 1887, Auburndale, Massachusetts, to John W. De Forest. 2 pp. T.l. CtY.

   8 him *w.o.* them   12 the other] t the other   18 write *w.o.* writt

28 June 1887, Lake George, New York, to Edward E. Hale. 3 pp. A.l.s. MNS.

   5 Cupples *w.o.* Couples   8 ⟨*illeg.*⟩ Que

28 June 1887, Lake George, New York, to William H. Rideing. 2 pp. A.l.s. NjP.

   11 ⟨exalted⟩ ↑ideal↓   11 ⟨and⟩ ↑or↓   14 ⟨verities⟩ ↑obvious facts↓
15 ↑vagarians↓

14 July 1887, Lake George, New York, to Charles E. Norton. 3 pp. A.l.s. MH.

　5 has *w.o.* had　　16 year's⟨'⟩　　17 coming] coming / coming
27-30 The family . . . . Howells.] [*in margins, first and second page, and across salutation*]

29 July 1887, Lake George, New York, to Charles D. Warner. 2 pp. A.l.s. CtHT.

　10 ⟨ret⟩ review　　10 My *w.o.* my　　10 Religion.] ∼
14-16 What . . . . Howells.] [*in margin and across salutation, first page*]

18 August 1887, Lake George, New York, to George W. Curtis. 4 pp. T.l.s. MoSW.

　9 ↑though . . . condemned,↓　　10 history ⟨*illeg.*⟩　　11 |n|ecessarily
13 and I] and / and I　　17 inflam↑m↓atory　　19 ↑how↓ distinctly
22 suffer ⟨*illeg.*⟩　　28 ↑But↓　　30 necessarily] ncessarily
36 af-/ford *w.o.* aff/ford　　37 mis-/take *w.o.* mist/take

2 September 1887, Lake George, New York, to John W. De Forest. 3 pp. T.l.s. CtY.

　4 ⟨2⟩ 20th　　6 ⟨or six⟩ or six　　9 ↑shall↓　　15 ↑in Boston,↓
25 Reviews *w.o.* Reviewe　　26 good many] good man　　26 I↑'ve↓
29 not *w.o.* nkt　　32 wo↑m↓an-rid　　37 reciprocity *w.o.* aeriprocity
39 texts *w.o.* temts　　43 little *w.o.* litte⟨s⟩　　48 Excuse . . . pieces.]
[*in Howells' hand*]

7 September 1887, Lake George, New York, to Edward Abbott. 2 pp. A.l.s. MeB.

　4 ⟨matter⟩ ↑case↓　　12 documents. *w.o.* ∼,　　12 ↑as . . . Tolstoi.↓

25 September 1887, Dansville, New York, to Roger A. Pryor. 2 pp. A.l.s. MH.

　4 Anarchists *w.o.* ar　　10 Mead's *w.o.* Meads'　　13 success *w.o.* suct

1 November 1887, Dansville, New York, to John G. Whittier. 3 pp. A.l.s. MSaE.

　10 ↑may↓　　16 know⟨s⟩

4 November 1887, Dansville, New York, to the Editor of the New York *Tribune*. Location of MS. unknown. *Tribune*, 6 November 1887, p. 5.

11 November 1887, Dansville, New York, to Francis F. Browne. Location of MS. unknown. *Life in Letters*, I, 401–2.

12 November 1887, Dansville, New York, to the Editor of the New York *Tribune*. 21 pp. Author's autograph draft with typed sections. MH.

[*at top of first page, in Howells' hand*: A WORD FOR THE DEAD.]
3 called ⟨with others who desired mercy for the m⟩   3 ⟨day⟩ day
4 yesterday ⟨by⟩   6 me. ⟨I will not call you names, am willing· to leave the question to the readers of my books.⟩   7 ↑of course,↓
8 blood ⟨that is⟩   8 ⟨a⟩ thousands   10 noise *w.o. illeg.*
10 cannot ⟨see print to⟩
12-13 ⟨your⟩ ↑the↓ *Te Deum*. ¶ [*Howells' paragraph sign*] By
13 ↑not↓ have ceased ⟨and⟩ ↑but↓
13-14 ↑at least↓ begun.⟨;and⟩ All *w.o.* all   15 ⟨will be⟩ ↑are ↑even↓ now↓
15 ⟨Why ↑For what what↓⟩ ↑For what, really,↓   15 men ⟨really⟩
16 ↑other↓   16 inexorably? ⟨Why were two others sent to the lone By that time⟩ ↑Next week↓   17 ⟨answ⟩ theory   20 answer⟨s⟩
22 ⟨turn⟩ cover it ↑up↓   22 up,] ~   22 ⟨y⟩our   26 responsible⟨th⟩
28-29 ↑apparently↓ been done ⟨by⟩ ↑with↓ the ⟨ignorant public opinion ↑impulse↓⟩ ↑approval↓   29 nation. ⟨If it had been patient⟩
29 ⟨mutel⟩ accuse   30 ⟨have⟩ perished   31 ⟨*illeg.* energy⟩ means
32 ↑by the people↓   34 ⟨a⟩ passion   35 the⟨se⟩ ↑minority↓
36 ↑ignorant↓   38 ⟨but⟩ except   39 ⟨piece⟩ ↑that↓
40 surprises⟨,, its wild disproportion⟩
40 ⟨It seems as if the⟩ ↑But perhaps the↓   42 ⟨murder⟩ ↑men↓
42 conspiracy ⟨while⟩   43 ⟨qu⟩ at home   46 except ⟨for⟩
46 ⟨one⟩ ↑a single,↓ notoriously ⟨truthless⟩ ↑untruthful↓
49 ⟨conceive⟩ imagine this, [*followed by cancelled caret*]
49-50 ↑dream↓ yesterday to ⟨its⟩   51 ↑State's↓ Attorney ⟨General⟩
53 ⟨office⟩ ↑duties↓ of ⟨public⟩ ↑official↓ advocate ⟨of⟩ ↑in↓
54 commonwealth.] [*end of Howells' autograph*]
55 ⟨As for Mr. Grinnell,⟩ It *w.o.* it
56 ⟨the official advocate of a free commonwealth⟩ ↑such an officer↓
56 truth ⟨against⟩   57 than ↑to↓ seek   57 He ⟨brough⟩ brought
59 ⟨starting⟩ eyes of ⟨the⟩ ↑a↓   60 against ⟨the⟩
61 the↑se↓ ⟨accused men⟩ ↑Anarchists↓   61 ↑already↓
62 he said] he / he said   62-63 he ⟨|s|howed the tin cans and bits of gas-pipe ⟨↑claimed to have been↓⟩ found in the Arbeiter-Zeitung office, and⟩ ↑he . . . but he↓   65 guilty ⟨c⟩   65 ⟨these potential⟩ bombs would not ⟨fill the receptacles of tomatoes and sweet-corn with dynamite and⟩ explode
66-67 ↑and . . . saved.↓   69-70 Savior ⟨o⟩ of Society⟨; it was a⟩ ↑—the↓
72 his] [*underlining cancelled by Howells*]

72 ⟨Mr. Grinnell, if not the whole court,⟩ ↑He↓

73 the better *w.o.* tee better   73 bet-/ter *w.o.* bett/ter

75 accus-/ed *w.o.* accuse/ed   76 throw-/ing *w.o.* throwi/ing

78 ↑partly↓   78 ↑some of whom↓ ⟨wh↑o↓m⟩   79 crimes ⟨wa⟩

80 Sheridan's *w.o.* Sheirdan's   82 ⟨finds⟩ located *w.o.* locates

83 ⟨bom⟩ bomb   83-84 ⟨finds⟩ ↑found↓ him ↑doubly↓

84 conception *w.o.* concettion [*end of typescript*]   85 ⟨credit⟩ ↑honor↓

85 ⟨credit—⟩ ↑an honor—↓   86 ⟨men⟩ ↑Anarchists↓

87 ⟨stretch ↑appl↓⟩ ↑interpretation↓   87 do *w.o.* a

88 ⟨itself⟩ ↑its kind↓ . 90-91 ↑⟨it . . . logic⟨s⟩ . . . Ballad"⟩↓

91 were ⟨suf⟩   91 when ⟨sentenced⟩ .

91 sentence. ⟨↑It is like a "Bab Ballad" in its logic.↓⟩   94 ↑Gary↓

95 ⟨under⟩ when   96 be *w.o.* a

97 ⟨aba⟩ commuted. ⟨↑It is like a Bab Ballad.⟩

97-98 ⟨When he ↑Judge Gary↓ asked⟩ ↑He *w.o.* His himself . . . . asked↓

99 reasons,] [*end of Howells' autograph*]   100 ↑long↓ protest, and ⟨p⟩

102 ↑or↓   103 pr↑o↓secution   103 newspapers.] [*end of typescript*]

105 Anarchists, ⟨in⟩] [*end of Howells' autograph*]   105 alone *w.o.* along

105 he *w.o.* we   106 ↑have↓   107 he *w.o.* we

108-9 and ⟨it⟩ ↑he↓ may have ↑thought it had↓

110 ⟨strikes⟩ ↑always struck↓   111 ⟨W⟩ With

112 mel-/odramatic *w.o.* melo/odramatic   113 ⟨strong)⟩ strong⟩

114 but *w.o.* and   115 ↑seven↓   116 ⟨It w⟩ Possibly

117 court ⟨of justice⟩   119 him.] [*end of typescript*]

122 ⟨you⟩ ↑we↓ realize this, ⟨Messrs. Able Editors,⟩

122 ⟨you and for your readers.⟩ ↑us.↓   122 ⟨We committed⟩ By

123 ⟨has⟩ brought   123-24 published] [*end of Howells' autograph; at top of MS. page 18, in Howells' hand:* ⟨—by such a stretch of law, Garrison who published⟩]   124 ↑a↓ compact   127 ⟨because⟩ ↑if↓ a slave ↑had↓

128 ↑Emerson, ⟨and⟩↓   128 and Howe] [and *crossed out but marked by stet. dots*]   128 Giddings *w.o.* Giddins

129 who ⟨applauded armed resistance to⟩ ↑encouraged the war *w.o.* fight against↓ slavery ⟨in Kansas,⟩ in Kansas   131 ⟨Ri⟩ rifles ↑could↓ ⟨*illeg.*⟩

132 ↑John↓   132 Missourians ⟨⟨the mystical number again!⟩⟩

133 ⟨sh⟩ shot them. ⟨in cold blood.⟩   133 Thoreau, ⟨and Sanborn,⟩

134 ⟨John⟩ Brown   135 ↑to↓ death   136 ⟨seven⟩ Anarchists to th|e|

136 Chicago.] [*end of typescript*]

140 dead. *w.o.* ~; ⟨and it only remains for me to pr⟩   141 ⟨but⟩ ↑or↓

144 ⟨bet⟩ beyond   145 ↑them.↓   146 ⟨simpl⟩ selfish

147 poor. *w.o.* ~;   148 ↑this,↓   149 ↑I dread . . . Courts,↓

150 the⟨ir⟩ ↑dead Anarchists'↓   152 ⟨followers⟩ fellow

152-53 ↑I believe↓ they *w.o.* there never ⟨was⟩ ↑were part of↓

153 ⟨B both States Attorney⟩ Judge   155 I⟨n⟩

156 ⟨for⟩ ↑from↓ ⟨in⟩ the ⟨marring of his poetic⟩   157 to⟨r⟩ realize
159 ⟨live to⟩ ↑yet↓ wish that ⟨none⟩ ↑none↓

13 November 1887, Dansville, New York, to William C. Howells. 3 pp.
A.l.s. MH.

    15 crime⟨–⟩   18 ⟨liberty o⟩free

18 November 1887, Buffalo, to Anne H. Fréchette. Location of MS. unknown. *Life in Letters*, I, 403–5.

    23 I] In

20 November 1887, Buffalo, to William M. Salter. 2 pp. A.l.s. IGK.

1 December 1887, Buffalo, to William M. Salter. 3 pp. A.l.s. IGK.

    7 have *w.o. illeg.*   19 ⟨*illeg.*⟩ asked   21 ⟨had⟩ paid
28 condemned] condemed

1 December 1887, Buffalo, to Benjamin H. Ticknor. 2 pp. A.l.s. CtY.

    [*in upper right corner, first page, rubber stamped*: B. H. Ticknor / Bos-
ton / Dec / 3 / 1887]

7 December 1887, Buffalo, to Courtlandt Palmer. 3 pp. A.l.s. KyU.

    6 ⟨*illeg.*⟩ wished   9 weighed upon] weighed upon / upon
11 ⟨are⟩ ↑is↓   22 ↑Tribune↓

25 December 1887, Buffalo, to William M. Salter. 3 pp. A.l.s. IGK.

    15 ↑as I have↓ always ⟨written⟩   18 victims⟨s⟩   19 things *w.o. illeg.*
20 is *w.o. illeg.*   25 haven't *w.o. illeg.*   27 ↑is to↓ prevail⟨s⟩

8 January 1888, Buffalo, to George Bainton. 2 pp. A.l.s. NBu.

    4 something ⟨g⟩

14 January 1888, Buffalo, to James Parton. 2 pp. A.l.s. MH.

    13 ⟨us⟩ bitter

15 January 1888, Buffalo, to Hamlin Garland. Location of MS., except for
1 p., T.l.s., CLSU, unknown. *Life in Letters*, I, 407–8.

    24 of wrong] [*beginning of extant author's typescript*]
25 |and insure| 26 ag|a|inst

22 January 1888, Buffalo, to William C. Howells. 3 pp. A.l.s. MH.

4 February 1888, Jefferson, to Edmund C. Stedman. 3 pp. A.l.s. OKentU.

    11 ↑all↓   11 than *w.o.* that   19 econo|m|ic   24 ⟨k⟩now

26 February 1888, New York, to William C. Howells. 3 pp. A.l.s. MH.

3 March 1888, New York, to George W. Curtis. 3 pp. A.l.s. MH.

    10 oldest ⟨↑for↓⟩   10 quality⟨,⟩ and ↑this↓   11 ↑alloy of↓
16 in ⟨on⟩ one   24 myself ⟨also⟩ ↑a↓

11 March 1888, New York, to Hamlin Garland. 3 pp. A.l.s. CLSU.

    8 ↑made↓   11 in⟨to⟩

1 April 1888, New York, to William C. Howells. 3 pp. A.l.s. MH.

    2 April *w.o.* March   7 her *w.o. illeg.*

5 April 1888, New York, to Samuel L. Clemens. 3 pp. A.l.s. CU.

    11 ↑safely↓   12 than *w.o.* that

14 April 1888, New York, to Thomas S. Perry. Location of MS. unknown.
Life in Letters, I, 413–14.

    38 Boyesen] Boyeson

29 April 1888, New York, to William C. Howells. 3 pp. A.l.s. MH.

27 May 1888, to Madison J. Cawein. 3 pp. A.l.s. KyLF.

    14 is before *w.o.* if before

8 July 1888, Little Nahant, Massachusetts, to William C. Howells. 3 pp.
A.l.s. MH.

    10 ⟨po⟩ bad

9 August 1888, Little Nahant, Massachusetts, to Thomas W. Higginson.
3 pp. A.l.s. NN.

    7 ↑aspects↓   13 singing ⟨it⟩   18 when *w.o.* was   22 ↑grateful↓

30 August 1888, Little Nahant, Massachusetts, to Edward E. Hale. 3 pp. A.l.s. MNS.

13 suppose⟨'⟩   18 blunder,] [*Howells wrote the comma over a semi-colon*]

28 September 1888, Little Nahant, Massachusetts, to Thomas W. Higginson. 2 pp. A.l.s. NN.

5 ↑even↓

29 September 1888, Little Nahant, Massachusetts, to William C. Howells. 3 pp. A.l.s. MH.

14 ↑be↓   15 year's *w.o. illeg.*

10 October 1888, Little Nahant, Massachusetts, to Henry James. 6 pp. A.l.s. MH.

3 house- *w.o.* home-   9 clumsy *w.o.* clumsier   12 to a] to a to a
13 ⟨of⟩ ↑with↓   17 optimistic] optimismistic   17 content ⟨I've⟩
19 ⟨right⟩ wrong   24 helpless↑ness↓   24 ↑for her↓   25 we ⟨g⟩

28 October 1888, Little Nahant, Massachusetts, to Edward E. Hale. 3 pp. A.l.s. MNS.

18 have *w.o.* had   26 ⟨New⟩ new

6 November 1888, New York, to Hamlin Garland. 2 pp. A.l.s. CLSU.

2 Nov. *w.o.* O   6 parson *w.o.* pardon

18 November 1888, New York, to William C. Howells. 3 pp. A.l.s. MH.

1 330 *w.o.* 17   4 had *w.o.* has   5 ↑to Philadelphia↓
11 ⟨work⟩ carry   16 ↑had↓

23 November 1888, New York, to the Editor of the New York *Sun*. 17 pp. Autograph draft signed. MH.

[*at top of first page, in Howells' hand*: A Letter from W. D. Howells.]
4 ⟨To⟩ ↑But↓ that *w.o.* That   5 prime⟨ary⟩   6 ⟨because I think⟩ chiefly
7 ⟨paper⟩ article   8 ⟨deplorable⟩ regrettable   13-14 half, ... people;]
[*Howells' revision from* half of the American people, at least;]
14 still greater *w.o.* even more   16 legitimate, or not] [*appears at top of*

third page circled and marked tra, *in another hand; in the same hand, at bottom of second page*: legitimate or not?]   18↑legal↓

19 ↑of the Anarchists↓   20 ↑news↓papers   20 ⟨when so a⟩ I

24 just.] [*followed by* (Insert A.) ⟨⟨over⟩⟩]   22-28 The laws . . . . Priest.] [*on separate sheet marked* A3]   22 ⟨was⟩ ↑are↓   22 ⟨on⟩ only

23 ↑or↓   24 Justice ⟨which all we know in our ⟨So⟩ souls and judge of there, and above⟩   26 ↑and . . . Churches.↓   30 me⟨,⟩

33 joy ⟨and a heart grateful to God⟩

33 those who ⟨asked mercy, even for those men⟩

35 ↑the eminent journalist↓   36 ↑attorneys like↓

38 ⟨Are⟩ Did they *w.o.* their   39-40 ⟨ask⟩ virtue of that *w.o.* the

41 ⟨But if apart from this [¶] Perhaps it is only I who am a sentimental-ist⟨s⟩ in your view, however, and but from which of my books do you infer that You also call me a n [¶] As for myself,⟩ ↑If neither, then↓

42 sentimentalist⟨s⟩   44 ↑you say↓   46 ↑called↓

50 ⟨I am a man now past fifty, and ⟨all⟩ ↑most of↓ my life has been spent in observing the conduct and scanning the motives of men. Some people are so ⟨good⟩ ↑obliging↓ as to say that I have got some skill in it; but whether this is so or not⟩ I must   52 ↑-minded↓   52 ⟨of⟩ even

53 ⟨it⟩ my   53-54 ⟨abhor⟩ abhor sentimentality: ⟨It was that which which made the hysterical blood thirsty⟩   57 ⟨any⟩ your

58 any⟨thing⟩ ↑facts↓   58 ⟨wife⟩ well-known   61 ⟨heart⟩ ↑conscience↓

61 ↑of↓   62 other *w.o.* man ⟨kind⟩ ↑men.↓   63 a⟨n⟩ positive

67 ⟨al⟩ insane   68 things;] [*followed by* ⟨over⟩ *at bottom of page*]

68-70 and . . . thing.] [*on verso of page nine*]   69 ⟨the⟩ ↑in↓ ⟨to⟩ hopeless

71 England; ⟨are go⟩ and ⟨*illeg.*⟩   72 ↑even↓

73 and production *w.o.* in production   74 ⟨is no⟩ ↑⟨with us, the people⟩↓

75 kind. ⟨For instance,⟩ The *w.o.* the   77 ⟨the⟩ ↑army↓

77-78 ⟨for *w.o.* to⟩ ↑for↓ contractors, ⟨who *illeg.*⟩ ↑to fatten on,↓

79 ↑why↓   81 this ⟨perhaps⟩   87 ↑like . . . dog↓

90 ⟨hotel⟩ ↑watering place↓   91 ↑made↓   92 ⟨corrupt⟩ made

92 ⟨↑man's↓⟩ poverty of the *w.o.* his ↑man's↓   92 ⟨corruptly⟩ gave

94 ⟨but⟩ it   95 ⟨burst into tears⟩ broke   96 ⟨ex-⟩ sorrowful

97 ↑for charity↓   101 thought ⟨again⟩   101 ⟨nation⟩ ↑community↓

102-3 ↑—not alms—↓ and ↑by which,↓   103 here, ⟨by which⟩

103 ⟨carried⟩ ↑sent↓   105 ↑I suppose.↓

106 ⟨must be *w.o.* was a⟩ ↑must be↓   107 ⟨it⟩ ↑my "sentimentality"↓

108 ⟨abhor⟩ ↑deplore↓ all violence⟨,⟩   108 ↑that↓   110 ⟨blo⟩ most

110 ⟨sort of Anarchists.⟩ criminals.   111 ↑your↓ reasoning

111 subject] [*following this word*: ⟨W. D. Howells. New York, Nov. 23, 1888.⟩]   113 ⟨app⟩ applies   115 ↑be↓

7 December 1888, New York, to Theodora Sedgwick. 3 pp. A.l.s. MH.

16 December 1888, New York, to John G. Whittier. 2 pp. A.l.s. CLSU.

  17 for⟨t⟩

23 December 1888, New York, to William C. Howells. 3 pp. A.l.s. MH.

  12 Their *w.o.* their   13 ↑story.↓

10 January 1889, New York, to Thomas B. Aldrich. 3 pp. A.l.s. MH.

  6 family *w.o. illeg.* 7 the *w.o.* to 16 address is] [*followed by* (inside) *to indicate continuation on verso*]

13 January 1889, New York, to William C. Howells. 3 pp. A.l.s. MH.

  9 quiet⟨s⟩

27 January 1889, New York, to Richard H. Newton. Location of MS. unknown. C. and R. Kirk, "Howells and the Church of the Carpenter," *New England Quarterly* 32 (1959), 193.

15 February 1889, New York, to Hamlin Garland. 3 pp. A.l.s. CLSU.

  2 15 *w.o.* 25

24 February 1889, New York, to Edmund W. Gosse. 4 pp. A.l.s. British Library.

  25 forth *w.o. illeg.* 37 Your⟨s⟩

4 March 1889, New York, to William C. Howells. 2 pp. A.l.s. MH.

  3 girl *w.o. illeg.* 6 Cambridge *w.o.* B

7 March 1889, Boston, to S. Weir Mitchell. 3 pp. A.l.s. PU.

  9 ↑so↓ 12 there *w.o.* this 13 may *w.o. illeg.* 15 shall ⟨to the st⟩ 17 ↑in↓ 19 this *w.o.* these

10 March 1889, Boston, to William C. Howells. 3 pp. A.l.s. MH.

  6 the Shalers *w.o.* The Shalers 19 framework] famework

22 March 1889, New York, to William C. Howells. 3 pp. A.l.s. MH.

  3 can] [*Howells cancelled a long upward swooping line, as if he had begun to write* cant] 13 ↑that↓

5 April 1889, New York, to Edward E. Hale. 3 pp. A.l.s. MNS.

11 exists *w.o.* is   13 ↑wish to↓   23 groans ⟨of⟩   24 and⟨t⟩

7 April 1889, New York, to Moncure D. Conway. 3 pp. A.l.s. NNC.

15 intelligence *w.o.* intellect   21 the *w.o.* us   22 ↑so dreadful as↓

26 April 1889, New York, to Alice James. 6 pp. A.l.s. MH.

6-11 It .... loss.] [*enclosed in square brackets, probably not by Howells*]
11-20 And .... his.] [*enclosed in square brackets, probably not by Howells*]   13 ↑somewhere else↓   13-14 ↑and ... morrows.↓
14 with ⟨e⟩   21 ↑to↓ [*probably in another hand*]   22 ⟨w⟩helpless
25 fact *w.o.* is

26 May 1889, Cambridge, to William C. Howells. 3 pp. A.l.s. MH.

18 but ⟨I sup⟩   24-25 Don't .... moods.] [*in margin and across salutation and dateline, first page*]

7 June 1889, Cambridge, to Henry James. 4 pp. A.l.s. MH.

7 offends *w.o.* was   8 ⟨p⟩fond   18 happiness ⟨has⟩
29 ⟨wh⟩ worthier   29 tell⟨s⟩   34 language *w.o.* langug
39-43 on whose shores .... Howells.] [*in margin and across salutation and dateline, first page*]

15 June 1889, Cambridge, to John M. Howells. 4 pp. A.l.s. MH.

6 is *w.o.* in   8 ⟨l⟩ nearer   2150 *w.o.* 2050
9 10,500 *w.o.* 10,000   10 10,200 *w.o.* 10,000   14 worth *w.o.* *illeg.*
19 $⟨1⟩6000   25 1,500⟨0⟩

23 June 1889, Cambridge, to Arthur G. Stedman. 2 pp. A.l.s. NNC.

[*in upper right corner, first page, in another hand*: W. D. Howells.]
10 miss⟨;⟩ ↑us;↓

14 July 1889, Cambridge, to William C. Howells. 3 pp. A.l.s. MH.

15 ↑full↓

4 August 1889, Cambridge, to Francis W. Crowninshield. 3 pp. A.l.s. CtY.

7 promotion *w.o.* progre   8 ↑ano↓ther *w.o.* this   8 Putnam⟨'⟩s
17 publish⟨ed⟩

26 August 1889, Cambridge, to Burt G. Wilder. 2 pp. A.l.s. NIC.

23 September 1889, Cambridge, to Harper & Brothers. 5 pp. A.l.s. MH.

   5 suggest *w.o.* pro   7 I will] I'will   12 II *w.o.* III
26 sketches *w.o.* sce   27 ↑whole↓   28 ↑in two years↓   30 possible,⟨.⟩

17 October 1889, Cambridge, to Samuel L. Clemens. 2 pp. A.l.s. CU.

   2 17 *w.o.* 27   8 ↑mean↓

17 October 1889, Cambridge, to Harper & Brothers. 2 pp. A.l.s. MH.

30 October 1889, Cambridge, to Charles D. Warner. 2 pp. A.l.s. CtHT.

   12 of] of / of

24 November 1889, Cambridge, to William C. Howells. 4 pp. A.l.s. MH.

1 December 1889, Cambridge, to William C. Howells. 3 pp. A.l.s. MH.

   2 Dec. *w.o.* Nov.   10 heart *w.o.* any

22 December 1889, Boston, to William C. Howells. 3 pp. A.l.s. MH.

   8 Annie,] ~.   16 First *w.o.* first

25 December 1889, Boston, to Charles E. Norton. 4 pp. A.l.s. MH.

   5 interest⟨ing⟩   7 ↑wreathed↓   7 what *w.o.* g   12 ⟨t⟩her mother
15 word *w.o.* way

29 December 1889, Boston, to Samuel L. Clemens. 3 pp. A.l.s. CU.

   8 Money-bags *w.o.* money-bags   10 ruin ⟨*illeg.*⟩

30 December 1889, Boston, to Hjalmar H. Boyesen. 3 pp. A.l.s. NRU.

   13 live⟨d⟩   21 join ⟨l⟩

31 December 1889, Boston, to John S. Wood. 2 pp. T.l.s. PSt.

   9-10 boy] boy i   10 is *w.o.* iq   13 ⟨th⟩ the warmest
15 intelligent *w.o.* intellighnt

3 January 1890, Boston, to James Parton. 3 pp. T.l.s. MH.

   5 so↑me↓thing   11 beg⟨g⟩garly   15 heed it] heed i it

17 out *w.o.* but   19 an⟨"⟩   27 see *w.o.* she   28 largely⟨x⟩
34 If ⟨t⟩   39 I . . . it.] [*in Howells' hand*]

5 January 1890, Boston, to Aurelia H. Howells. 4 pp. T.l. MH.

12 in-/stance *w.o.* insta/stance   15 here⟨'⟩,   16 girl⟨'⟩,
16 ⟨tha⟩ that   19 hope she] hope s she   20 ⟨w⟩ want   21 ⟨wh⟩ when
21 work *w.o.* wook   21 ⟨mus⟩ must   24 ⟨ha⟩ have   32 and I] and I I
33 by, . . . start] [*Howells had typed this phrase and then accidentally typed over it* I dream of Winny, *which necessitated handwritten clarification of the original phrase*]   38 ⟨illeg.⟩ than

17 January 1890, Boston, to Charles D. Warner. 2 pp. T.l.s. CtHT.

4 years *w.o. illeg.*   7 writers *w.o.* writhers   8 which ⟨i⟩
10 save *w.o.* savh   12 Golden *w.o.* golden   12 Senate *w.o.* Sentte

2 February 1890, Boston, to William C. Howells. 3 pp. A.l.s. MH.

6 all ⟨Hartford⟩   9 it is *w.o.* is is   12 artists, the] artist ⟨↑was↓⟩ the
12 he came] he he came

4 February 1890, Boston, to Annie A. Fields. 2 pp. A.l.s. CSmH.

7 February 1890, Boston, to Samuel L. Clemens. 2 pp. A.l.s. CU.

3 Dear *w.o.* Cl   8 couldn't *w.o. illeg.*

9 February 1890, Boston, to William C. Howells. 4 pp. T.l.s. MH.

6 and ⟨t⟩ the   9 is ⟨a⟩ a   10 That is ⟨now⟩   12 ↑were↓
13 leisur|e| 17 if you] if y you   20 ⟨vry⟩ clearly   37 Pil⟨'⟩,

18 February 1890, Boston, to James R. Lowell. 2 pp. A.l.s. MH.

8 love, ⟨l⟩

5 March 1890, Boston, to Moncure D. Conway. 2 pp. A.l.s. NNC.

5 War *w.o.* Care   11 How ⟨y⟩   17 Kiss . . . me!] [*in margin, first page*]

27 March 1890, Boston, to Horace E. Scudder. 2 pp. T.l.s. MH.

12 Charybdis *w.o.* Charydiis

1 April 1890, Boston, to Elizabeth S. Phelps Ward. 2 pp. A.l.s. OOxM.

6 April 1890, Boston, to William C. Howells. 4 pp. A.l.s. MH.

16 ⟨did⟩ don't

19 April 1890, Boston, to Harper & Brothers. 3 pp. Autograph draft un-signed. MH.

5 but ⟨I cannot regret it now since it has brought me the pleasure of⟩ your latest⟨. It is perfectly⟩ ↑has . . . perfectly↓   7 ↑an↓
8-9 explained ⟨↑to you↓ fully⟩ my obligations ⟨to you⟩
11 what ⟨your⟩ ↑if you had any↓ wish⟨es were⟩   12 ↑in . . . then↓
13 seeming ⟨desirous⟩   13 pressure ⟨to bear⟩   15 but I ⟨do not feel easy in the renewal of our agreement concerning it from year to year. It takes from the pleasure and spirit of writing it to know that practically it is still an experiment, with no promise of permanency. In fact I⟩
16 about ⟨↑going on with↓⟩   16 see you ⟨about the middle of⟩ ↑early in↓ May.⟨, when we can also arrange for the publication of the two novels I have engaged to write, so that ↑I↓ shall not be driving ↑them↓ abreast, one in the magazine and the other in the newspaper⟨s⟩. I tell you of ⟨the⟩ ↑my↓ arrangement with the Sun in confidence.⟩

27 April 1890, Boston, to William C. Howells. 3 pp. A.l.s. MH.

11 will ↑be↓   14 but ⟨if⟩   15 C. S. *w.o.* S. S.
19 farmer⟨'⟩s ↑money↓ from the⟨ir⟩

6 May 1890, Boston, to Edward E. Hale. 3 pp. A.l.s. MNS.

6 May 1890, Boston, to Madison J. Cawein. 2 pp. A.l.s. CLSU.

15 June 1890, Boston, to William C. Howells. 3 pp. A.l.s. MH.

4 hope⟨d⟩   7 while] white

15 June 1890, Boston, to John De Forest. 3 pp. A.l.s. CtY.

6 article⟨s⟩

19 June 1890, Boston, to James R. Lowell. 3 pp. MH.

11 it] ∼.

6 July 1890, Willsborough Point, New York, to William C. Howells. 3 pp. A.l.s. MH.

5 please⟨s⟩

11 July 1890, Willsborough Point, New York, to Sylvester Baxter. 3 pp. A.l.s. CSmH.

15 ↑and a . . . win↓   16 ↑boarder↓   16 Harold *w.o. illeg.*

17 July 1890, Lake Placid, New York, to Laurence Hutton. 2 pp. A.l.s. NjP.

5 ⟨of⟩ using   8 a *w.o.* i   15 regards *w.o.* rigards
19-20 cottages . . . friends.] [*in margin, second page*]

17 August 1890, Saratoga, New York, to Anne Whitney. 2 pp. A.l.s. George Arms, Albuquerque, N.M.

5 own⟨,⟩

24 August 1890, Saratoga, New York, to William C. Howells. 3 pp. A.l.s. MH.

13 Republican *w.o.* Republicat

27 August 1890, Saratoga, New York, to Hamlin Garland. 3 pp. A.l.s. CLSU.

9 September 1890, Lake Luzerne, New York, to Thomas S. Perry. 3 pp. A.l.s. MeWC.

3 this *w.o.* a   4 have *w.o.* are   6 ⟨Lake⟩ Plattsburg   21 This ⟨V⟩

17 September 1890, Lynn, Massachusetts, to William Archer. 4 pp. A.l.s. British Library.

[*in upper right corner, first page, in another hand*: D-W Howells]
18 gravies *w.o.* gravy   26 our *w.o.* own

25 September 1890, Lynn, Massachusetts, to Henry James. 8 pp. A.l.s. MH.

4 you⟨r⟩   31 ↑mine↓   31 mine.] ~   34 McIlvaine *w.o.* McItvaine
38 ↑could↓   42 console ⟨by⟩   56 ↑young↓ man   61 Just ⟨ye⟩

26 October 1890, Boston, to Theodore Roosevelt. 2 pp. A.l.s. DLC.

28 October 1890, Boston, to Mabel Loomis Todd. 2 pp. A.l.s. MA.

11 ↑better↓   15-17 little . . . . Howells.] [*in margin, first page*]

9 November 1890, Boston, to William C. Howells. Location of MS. unknown. *Life in Letters*, II, 8–9.

16 November 1890, Boston, to William C. Howells. 3 pp. A.l.s. MH.

  6 shall *w.o.* will   13 Nationalists *w.o.* nationalists   18 had *w.o. illeg.*

25 November 1890, Boston, to Mabel Loomis Todd. 2 pp. A.l.s. CtY.

  4 level *w.o.* lines   4 so⟨r⟩   6 ↑in↓

22 December 1890, Boston, to Howard Pyle. Location of MS. unknown. *Life in Letters*, II, 9–11.

9 January 1891, Boston, to Henry M. Alden. 4 pp. A.l.s. OFH.

  4-5 ↑an↓ antislavery   8-9 The ... Jesuitism] [*underlined, but probably not by Howells*]   15 ⟨But⟩ *w.o.* and   16 be-/↑tween us↓ 19 about *w.o. illeg.*   24 n't *w.o.* it   30 the *w.o. illeg.*

11 January 1891, Boston, to William C. Howells. 4 pp. A.l.s. MH.

  14 slid down] slid did [down *inserted in another hand after* did] 26 strike *w.o. illeg.*   27 about] above

29 January 1891, Boston, to Charles A. Dana. 4 pp. A.l.s. NjP.

  9 ↑(exclusive)↓   10 ↑had↓   10 at *w.o.* it   16 especially *w.o. illeg.* 17 ↑will↓   21 ⟨*illeg.*⟩ serve

30 January 1891, Boston, to Thomas W. Higginson. 3 pp. A.l.s. NN.

  8 criticism *w.o.* praise   12 ↑not↓

1 February 1891, Boston, to Sarah Orne Jewett. 3 pp. A.l.s. MH.

  [*on verso of third page, in another hand*: To be kept. / *To keep—*]

8 February 1891, Boston, to William C. Howells. 3 pp. T.l.s. MH.

  6 comfortable *w.o.* comfohtable   6 The *w.o.* THe 11 and be *w.o.* anp be   12 through.]∼..   12 The *w.o.* THe 14 well.]∼..   14 without] with-   17 wo↑r↓k   19 must ⟨te⟩ 19 old ⟨C⟩   24 Victoria *w.o.* victoria   27 or *w.o.* on   29 her] har 31 of *w.o.* if   32 ⟨p⟩ pleasures   32 reach⟨.⟩   35 need ⟨o⟩ 37 the] thh   37 children *w.o.* childreo   41 Don't *w.o.* Donht 44-46 to all ... Will.] [*in Howells' hand*]

15 February 1891, Boston, to William C. Howells. 3 pp. A.l.s. MH.

15 suited.]∼

25 February 1891, Boston, to Sylvester Baxter. 3 pp. A.l.s. CSmH.

5 ⟨find⟩ learn   11 gossip- *w.o. illeg.*

1 March 1891, Boston, to William C. Howells. 3 pp. A.l.s./T.l.s. MH.

2 March *w.o.* Feb'y   4 ↑⟨three⟩ four↓   15 my scheme] [*begin author's typescript*]   15 scheme *w.o.* sgheme
15-16 before him] before him before him   19 He *w.o. illeg.*
23 ⟨ve⟩ very   23 outlandish] oullndish   24 bird's *w.o.* birdhs
27 him ⟨i⟩   28 and *w.o.* anp   28 ⟨c⟩ cannon-cracker   32 hot *w.o.* hob
34 dinner *w.o.* dinnne   39 punch him] punch hi him
42 ⟨pha⟩ phantasm   47 Your *w.o. illeg.*

3 March 1891, Boston, to Samuel L. Clemens. 2 pp. T.l.s. CU.

3 into *w.o.* inti   4 answer *w.o.* answes   6 ears,] ⟨eyes⟩ ↑ears,↓,
6 ⟨wro⟩ wrote   7 mistake] miistake   7 the⟨e⟩ink   8 ⟨chee⟩ cheek
8 dictate the] dictate *w.o.* dictata the the   9 fatigue *w.o.* fategue
9 ⟨t⟩ talk   9 I *w.o.* t   11 ex⟨pe⟩pense   15 for *w.o. illeg.*
17-18 it was a fonograf] it w was ↑a↓ fonofraf

19 April 1891, Boston, to Wendell P. Garrison. 2 pp. A.l.s. NjP.

20 April 1891, Boston, to Robert U. Johnson. 3 pp. A.l.s. NRU.

10 ↑fare↓   13 Hauer *w.o.* Bauer   17 Hauer *w.o.* Bauer

30 May 1891, Boston, to William C. Howells. 3 pp. A.l.s. MH.

1 30 *w.o.* 2   8 it,]∼,,   20 that *w.o. illeg.*   22 I've] Ive

11 June 1891, Boston, to Henry M. Alden. 3 pp. Autograph draft signed. MH.

1 June *w.o.* Jul   3 ⟨I wish to call your attention to the fact that⟩ At
5 and ⟨that⟩ ↑if . . . this↓   6 ⟨therefore⟩ have ⟨justly⟩   7 ↑had↓
9 ⟨I wish also to remind you that⟩ My *w.o.* my
12 ⟨therefore⟩ ↑regard↓ ⟨allow⟩ that *w.o.* this consent ⟨to be regarded⟩
17 closed. ⟨I mentioned the 10 per cent. rate for the paper edition of *The World of Chance*, when I agreed with Mr. Harry Harper, of my own motion, but the motive I had ↑then↓ does not actuate me in this case.⟩

14 June 1891, Boston, to William C. Howells. 4 pp. A.l.s. MH.

12 ↑as I know↓   14 the *w.o.* this   22 that *w.o.* than

23 June 1891, Boston, to Richard W. Gilder. Location of MS. unknown.
Typed copy at InU.

19 ⟨up⟩ very

17 July 1891, Intervale, New Hampshire, to Aurelia H. Howells. 3 pp.
A.l.s. MH.

6 ↑to↓

25 July 1891, Intervale, New Hampshire, to Samuel S. McClure. 3 pp.
A.l.s. ViU.

[*pasted in the upper left corner of the first page is a clipping from a
magazine print of a photograph of Howells*]

9 August 1891, Intervale, New Hampshire, to William C. Howells. 3 pp.
A.l.s. MH.

16 ↑who↓   22 ↑they are↓

4 September 1891, Intervale, New Hampshire, to Robert U. Johnson. 3 pp.
A.l.s. NRU.

3 that *w.o.* the   10 which frequently *w.o. illeg.*   13 ↑no↓

6 September 1891, Intervale, New Hampshire, to Aurelia H. Howells.
4 pp. A.l.s. MH.

20 September 1891, Intervale, New Hampshire, to William C. Howells.
3 pp. A.l.s. MH.

17 say ⟨he's⟩   18 father! *w.o.* father,   20 on *w.o.* in

18 October 1891, Boston, to William C. Howells. 3 pp. A.l.s. MH.

13 Sunday *w.o. illeg.*

21 October 1891, Boston, to James R. Osgood, 3 pp. A.l.s. NjR.

[*below dateline, first page, in another hand*: ans / Nov. 13]
4 the *w.o.* a   7 tell *w.o.* state   13 that ⟨if hereafter⟩
14 desirable *w.o.* worth

22 October 1891, Boston, to Brander Matthews. 3 pp. A.l.s. NNC.

   2 1891 *w.o.* 1899   7 treated ↑me↓   7 those *w.o.* the   15 over⟨"⟩

24 October 1891, Boston, to "My dear Sir." 2 pp. A.l.s. George Arms, Albuquerque, N. M.

25 October 1891, Boston, to William C. Howells. 3 pp. A.l.s. MH.

   14 life ↑in,↓   19 house⟨s⟩ ↑horrors,↓

5 November 1891, Boston, to Thomas W. Higginson. 3 pp. A.l.s. NN.

22 November 1891, New York, to William C. Howells. 3 pp. A.l.s. MH.

   16 though⟨t⟩

12 December 1891, New York, to Charles E. Norton. 3 pp. A.l.s. MH.

   25 literature *w.o.* literar   29-32 me . . . . Howells.] [*in margin and across letterhead, first page*]

13 December 1891, New York, to William C. Howells. 3 pp. A.l.s. MH.

   4 than *w.o.* that   18 ↑you↓   19 boy *w.o.* p   20 ↑like↓

20 December 1891, New York, to Hamlin Garland. 2 pp. A.l.s. CLSU.

   6 in the⟨ir⟩   9 old *w.o. illeg.*

Word-Division

In the two lists below, entries are keyed to the line numbers of the letter texts; the line-count includes all lines of type of a letter proper, beginning at the internal address or dateline. List A records compounds and possible compounds hyphenated at the end of the line in the authorial document or extant transcription used as copy-text for the present edition, and indicates how these end-line hyphenated forms have been resolved. If the compounds occur in consistent form elsewhere in the authorial document or in other such materials of the same general period in time, including literary manuscripts, then resolution was made on that basis; if these other occurrences are inconsistent, resolution was based on the form in closest proximity in time to the possible compound in question. If neither of these resources was sufficient, then resolution was based on the evidence of published texts of Howells' works or on the prevalent usage of the period. List B is a guide to transcription of compounds or possible compounds hyphenated at the end of the line in the present text: compounds recorded in this list should be transcribed as given; words divided at the end of the line and not listed should be transcribed as one word.

LIST A

18 April 1882, to S. L. Clemens	7	self-accusation
18 April 1882, to S. L. Clemens	19–20	half-success
31 July 1882, to W. C. Howells	16	washroom
9 September 1882, to E. W. Gosse	38	churchyard
14 September 1882, to C. E. Norton	30	horse-cars
4 October 1882, to H. James	15	fellow-boarders
7 October 1882, to W. C. Howells	5	church-fair
26 October 1882, to E. W. Gosse	32	note-book
4 March 1883, to C. D. Warner	2	self-reproach
5 April 1883, to T. R. Lounsbury	35	pound-cake
21 June 1883, to W. C. Howells	4–5	birthplace

21 June 1883, to W. C. Howells	18	printing-office
21 June 1883, to W. C. Howells	32	resting-place
21 June 1883, to W. C. Howells	34	to-morrow
24 June 1883, to W. C. Howells	31	linsey-woolsey
21 November 1883, to W. C. Howells	29	type-writer
2 January 1884, to E. W. Gosse	57	to-morrow
21 January 1884, to C. E. Norton	18	sick-room
12 May 1884, to J. R. Osgood	16–17	life-like
22 August 1884, to H. James	28	well-dressed
24 December 1884, to E. W. Gosse	28	rail-road
9 March 1885, to E. W. Gosse	22	glove-trade
12 September 1885, to B. H. Ticknor	8	banker-creditors
9 May 1886, to J. Hay	10	love-marriages
23 May 1886, to S. L. Clemens	7	under-foot
23 May 1886, to S. L. Clemens	10	to-morrow
9 December 1886, to J. W. De Forest	22	love-making
25 December 1886, to H. James	4	type-written
25 December 1886, to H. James	51	Paris-born
6 February 1887, to M. M. Fréchette	18	goings-on
6 February 1887, to M. M. Fréchette	23	dancing-school
14 February 1887, to S. L. Clemens	4	air-holes
14 February 1887, to S. L. Clemens	5	air-holes
20 February 1887, to W. C. Howells	14	bluebirds
27 February 1887, to G. W. Curtis	6	commonplace
3 April 1887, to W. C. Howells	6–7	snow-shovels
3 April 1887, to W. C. Howells	7	sidewalks
2 September 1887, to J. W. De Forest	14	dancing-class
12 November 1887, to Editor, *Tribune*	88	masterpiece
4 February 1888, to C. E. Stedman	10	sugar-coat
27 May 1888, to M. J. Cawein	11	"betting-house"
9 August 1888, to T. W. Higginson	24	health-search
10 October 1888, to H. James	30	where-abouts
4 March 1889, to W. C. Howells	6	to-morrow
15 June 1889, to J. M. Howells	7	paid-up
26 August 1889, to B. G. Wilder	6	health-certificate
23 September 1889, to Harper & Brothers	18	piecemeal
1 December 1889, to W. C. Howells	17	greenhouse
29 December 1889, to S. L. Clemens	7	aristocracy-loving
3 January 1890, to J. Parton	14	under-much
5 January 1890, to A. H. Howells	4	New-Year's
5 January 1890, to A. H. Howells	6	college-room
6 April 1890, to W. C. Howells	9	type-writer
11 January 1891, to W. C. Howells	27	mid-winter

| 25 February 1891, to S. Baxter | 11 | gossip-exchange |
| 22 October 1891, to B. Matthews | 16 | classrooms |

LIST B

2 March 1882, to A. A. Reade	5–6	self-defensive
7 March 1882, to G. W. Cable	6–7	snow-petals
18 April 1882, to S. L. Clemens	19–20	half-success
16 October 1882, to J. R. Osgood	24–25	love-making
16 November 1882, to E. W. Gosse	6–7	re-imburse
19 November 1882, to R. Smith	44–45	semi-historical
9 February 1883, to J. R. Osgood	13–14	story-writing
4 March 1883, to W. C. Howells	8–9	grape-scissors
5 April 1883, to T. R. Lounsbury	42–43	Middle-Ages
9 August 1885, to S. L. Clemens	11–12	well-meaning
5 December 1885, to S. L. Clemens	17–18	title-page
6 June 1886, to W. H. Smith	11–12	news-gathering
15 December 1886, to C. E. Norton	9–10	last-August
9 February 1887, to T. W. Higginson	6–7	hard-running
14 February 1887, to S. L. Clemens	3–4	wall-paper
3 April 1887, to W. C. Howells	6–7	snow-shovels
14 July 1887, to C. E. Norton	5–6	re-named
2 September 1887, to J. W. De Forest	15–16	good-deal
12 November 1887, to Editor, *Tribune*	64–65	ninety-three
10 October 1888, to H. James	3–4	house-hunt
7 June 1889, to H. James	13–14	twenty-five
6 April 1890, to W. C. Howells	12–13	type-writer
6 July 1890, to W. C. Howells	8–9	home-house
1 March 1891, to W. C. Howells	40–41	home-house

List of Howells' Correspondents

The following alphabetical list of Howells' correspondents provides page references for (1) letters written by Howells TO others and (2) letters FROM others addressed to Howells. Page numbers in italic type indicate letters appearing in full or as fully as the source permits; page numbers in roman type indicate letters cited in footnotes, with "cited' used broadly to mean quotation from a letter, description of part of its contents, or mention of it whether printed in this edition or not. The few cited letters *about* Howells, e.g., to Alden from J. W. Harper, Jr., appear not in this list but in the main index.

Abbott, Edward, TO *196-97*
Alden, Henry M., TO *300, 313*; FROM 37, 47, 86, 128, 135, 231, 300-1, 313-14
Aldrich, Thomas B., TO *126*, 126, *242*
Allen, Charles, FROM 206
Anonymous, TO *73*, 272-73, *324*
Archer, William, TO *290-91*

Bainton, George, TO *213*
Balestier, Wolcott, FROM 293-94
Barrett, Lawrence, FROM 284
Baxter, Sylvester, TO *285-86*, 286, 289, 295, *307-8*, 315
Bellamy, Edward, FROM 227
Bellew, Frank W., FROM 206
Blake, James V., FROM 206
Boyesen, Hjalmar H., TO 51, 57, 267
Browne, Francis F., TO *200*, 200, 205; FROM *200-1*
Browne, Katherine (Mrs. C.), FROM 67
Brush, George D., FROM 245
Buel, Clarence C., TO *121-22*; FROM 122
Bumstead, S. J., FROM 206, 212

Cable, George W., to *11*, 11; FROM 11-12
Cawein, Madison J., TO *225-26*, 226, *281*; FROM 226, 282
Clarke, Robert, & Co., FROM 151
Clemens, Olivia L. (Mrs. S. L.), FROM 19
Clemens, Samuel L., TO 8, *18-19*, 20, *27-28*, 28, 31, 37, *38*, 39, 53, 54, 56, *65*, 66, *78-79*, *81-82*, *82-83*, 86, *91-92*, 94, *95*, 99, 101, 105, 106, *106-7*, 107, 108, 111, *120-21*, *126-27*, 131, *136-37*, 137, *149-50*, 152, *154-55*, 155, 157, *181*, 188, 222, 224, *256*, 260, 260, *262*, *266*, 273, 273, *310*, 313; FROM 8, 19,

28, 92, 107, 121, 127, 137, 155, 157, 182, 222, 260, 266, 273, 274, 310
Conway, Moncure D., TO *250*, *276*; FROM 276
Crowninshield, Francis W., TO 257
Curtis, George W., TO 32, *137*, 176, *183*, *193*, 194, *219*, 224; FROM 183, 192, 194

Daly, John A., TO *99*; FROM 100
Dana, Charles A., TO *303*
Dean, Dune, TO 278
De Forest, John W., TO *169-70*, 179, 179, *187-88*, 188, *194-95*, 196, 231, *283*; FROM 170-71, 179-80, 283-84
Donaldson, Thomas C., TO *128-29*
Douglas, David, FROM 322

Erichsen, Hugo, TO *102*; FROM *102-3*

Fairchild, Charles, TO *7-8*, 20, 28
Fields, Annie A. (Mrs. J. T.), TO 93, 269, 272, 305
Fréchette, Achille, TO *168*
Fréchette, Anne H. (Mrs. A.), TO 20, 145, *207-8*
Fréchette, Marie M., TO *180*, 208

Garland, Hamlin, TO *214-15*, 215, 220, 234, *244*, 245, 289, 289, *329*, 329
Garrison, Wendell P., TO 99, 302, 303, *311*
Gilder, Richard W., TO 44, *102*, *103*, *172*, 172, *315*; FROM 44, 48, *63*, 76, 102, 103
Gilman, Daniel C., TO *45-46*, 47, 49, 50; FROM 46
Godkin, Edwin L., TO 254

377

Index

This index records all names of persons, organizations, monuments, ships, public buildings, and titles of magazines and books (the last recorded under the names of their authors, if known). It excludes the names of relatives of Howells' correspondents when they are mentioned for the primary purpose of sending love or minor information; the titles, journals, or publishers of post–1920 criticism and scholarship; and geographical names and government divisions. Some topics are listed as independent entries, but most can be found under Howells' name, where information is divided into two major lists: WORKS and TOPICS. The TOPICS section is further subdivided.

Within entries, the general order of information is: brief and/or general references; citation of correspondence other than that with Howells (e.g., J. W. Harper, Jr., to Alden); works by that person, including reviews and presumably unpublished work; and descriptive modifications, arranged in ascending page order. Finally, the frequent occurrence of some dozen entries has required the use of "passim" (e.g., "Harper & Brothers, WDH's connection with and publications by, 119–327 passim").

Italic numbers designate pages on which significant biographical information is given. An asterisk preceding an entry indicates that a full record of correspondence between Howells and the person or institution so marked is provided in the separate "List of Howells' Correspondents," pages 377–79, the headnote of which explains its arrangement.

Harrison, William H., 227

Hart, Tony, *Dan's Tribulations* (with E. Harrigan; WDH on), 97

Harte, Bret, 28, 30; "The Luck of Roaring Camp" (play with M. S. Van de Velde), 38, 39

Hartford *Courant*, 19

Harvard College (or University), 109; and Class Day, 101; and Dyer, 118; and John M. Howells, 148, 158, 159, 164, 191, 195, 218, 219, 241, 245, 251, 267, 268, 314, 316; and WDH, 173; and Longfellow portrait, 155-56; and A. McKenzie, 246; and Norton, 104; and G. Pellew, 220; and J. Royce, 159; and Tolstoi Club, 189, 229; and Yale games, 262, 263, 326

*Haulenbeck, J. H., *122*

Haver, 311-12

Hawley, Joseph R., 27, 83

Hawthorne, Julian, letter to Lowell cited, 166; Lowell interview (WDH on), 165-66, 167, 175; replies to Lowell, 166

Hawthorne, Nathaniel, 27, 118, 166, 276

Hawthorne, Mr. and Mrs. Nathaniel, 118

Hawthorne, Sophia (Mrs. N.), 276

Hay Castle, 68, 69, 71

Hay, Clara S. (Mrs. J.), 13

Hay, Helen, *154*

*Hay, John, 19, 28, 38, 39, 60, 107, 157; *Abraham Lincoln* (with J. G. Nicolay; reviewed by WDH), 300, 301; *The Bread-Winners* (reviewed by WDH), 74, 75, 89, 90; on *Dr. Breen's Practice*, 13; on *A Modern Instance*, 13; on Daudet's novel, 14; on James, 14; at Osgood's London dinner, 30; on *A Woman's Reason*, 74, 75; on *A Little Girl Among the Old Masters*, 89-90; appears in *Tuscan Cities*, 154; on political chicanery, 294

Hay, Mr. and Mrs. John, see WDHs in Italy, 12, 13, 14, 16-17, 56; meet WDHs in London, 27

Hayes, Rutherford B., 242, 243

Haymarket Affair, 289; WDH on, 145-46, 193-215 passim

Healy, George, Longfellow portrait, *156*

Heard, John, 175, 176

Hearn, Lafcadio, 143

Heath, D. C., & Co., 8; publishes Norton textbooks, 171

Heath, Daniel C., 7, *8*

Heine, Heinrich, 73, 213; *Reisebilder*, 79

Heinemann & Balestier, 293

Heinemann, William, 293

Hellman, George S., 304

Hendricks, Thomas B., *137*

Henschel, Georg, *A Sea Change* (comp.), 88, *89*, 93, 95, 100, 110

Hereford, Cathedral of, 71, 72

Herkomer, Hubert von, 27, *28*

Herne, James A., 273-74

Herrick, Robert, 255

Hibbard, George, 319; *The Governor*, 320; *Induna*, 320

*Higginson, Thomas W., 181, 186, 311; "Americanism in Literature," 304; *A Larger History of the United States* ...,17, 18; *The New World and the New Book*, 304, 326; *Poems by Emily Dickinson* (1890, 1891, ed. with M. L. Todd; reviewed by WDH), 295, 326; *Poems by Emily Dickinson, Second Series* (ed. with M. L. Todd) 295, 326; on *A Modern Instance*, 17, 18; on *Annie Kilburn*, 146, 227-28; on *The Minister's Charge* and WDH's literary theory, 162-63; and J. Brown, 206; invites WDH to speak on Tolstoy, 229-30; on *A Hazard of New Fortunes* and WDH's criticism, 304-5; on *The Quality of Mercy*, 325

Hillebrand, Carl, 56, 57

Hill, Lucille E., 132, *133*

Hinton, Richard J., 235-36; "The Howells Family," 178, 236; "Organization of Labor," 236

Hoar, Ebenezer R., *108*

Holmes, John, 91

Holmes, Oliver W., 86, 114, 117, 129, 186; "Astraea," 174, 176

Holt, Henry, and Co., and Conway book, 25; and Gosse book, 88; and Crowninshield, 257

Homberger, Heinrich, 51; review of "Private Theatricals," 56; "William Dean Howells" (review of *A Foregone Conclusion*), 56

Homer, 183; *Iliad*, 290

Hong Kong blue books, 39, 40

Hooper, William, 77

Hopkins, Lemuel, 98, *99*

Hôtel Dieu, Quebec, 185

Hough, Sabin, 80, 81

Houghton, Lord. *See* Milnes, Richard M.

*Houghton, Mifflin & Co., publishes "American Men of Letters," 17, 163; publishes "Niagara Revisited" in *Their Wedding Journey* (1887 ed.), 63; and V. W. Cupples, 189; WDH's royalties from, 255; publishes James novel, 294

Housatonic Railroad, 124

*Hovey, William A., 206

Meader, Elizabeth C. (pseud.). *See* Walter, Helen.
Melrose (ship), 88
Merrill, Ginette de B., 8
Merrimac Mills, 183
Meserve, Walter J., 106, 110, 165, 169
Methodism. *See* WDH: Religion.
Metropolitan, 257
Middlemore, Maria T. H. S. (Mrs. S. G. C.), 60, 167, 168
Middlemore, Samuel G. C., 60, 167, 168
Mill, James S., 9
Miller, Ezra, 33, 34
Millet, Francis D., 35, 155, 156
Millet, Mr. and Mrs. Francis D., 272
Millgate, Michael. *See* Mattheisen-Millgate.
Milnes, Richard M., 74
Milton, John, 41; *Paradise Lost*, 67
Minerva Hotel, Florence, 48, 50
Missouri Compromise, 239
Missouri Pacific Railroad, 298
Mitchell, John K., 247, 253
*Mitchell, S. Weir, *In War Time* (reviewed by WDH), 131-32; considered for Winifred, 131, 229; treatment of Winifred, 147, 235, 239, 253; calls on WDHs, 241, 243; thanked by WDH, 247; and Elinor, 249
Mitre Tavern, Oxford, 27
Moffett, Annie. *See* Webster, Annie M. (Mrs. C. L.).
Monnigo, Countesses of, 67
Monroe, Harriet E., "Stateman and Novelist" (interview), 258
Montenegro, Princess of, 67
Moore, H. Humphrey, 271-72
Moran, Thomas, 237, 239
Moretti's, 224
Moreys, 307, 309
Morley, John, 32; "English Men of Letters" (ed.), 31
Morse, Robert M., Jr., 123
Morton, Levi P., 227
Moser, Charles A., 302
Most, Johann, *Revolutionäre Kriegswissenschaft*, 210, 211
Mulholland, John, 178
Mulligan, James, 112
Municipal Woman Suffrage Bill (Massachusetts), 220
Munsey's, 257
Murfree, Mary N., 117, 180, 228; *The Prophet of the Great Smokey Mountains* (reviewed by WDH), *116*
Mutual Life Insurance Co. of New York, 254

Napoleon III, of France, 202, *205*
Nation, 224, 291; reviews *The Minister's Charge*, 184
Nationalists, meetings attended by WDH, 227, 264, 268; and Christian Socialists, 280; and Garland play, 289; and Baring failure, 297; and H. G. Wilshire, 326. *See also* Bellamy, Edward, *and* WDH: Reform.
National League, Ireland, 206
National Observer (London), reviews *Criticism and Fiction*, 318
Natural Gas Jubilee, 188
N., D., letter to Reid, 97
Neebe, Oscar E., 200, 202, 205
New Church Society, Newtonville, 318
New Church Theological School, Boston, 318
New England Conservatory of Music, 244
New Englander and Yale Review, publishes W. W. Patton article, 192
New England Magazine, 229; publishes M. L. Todd sketch, 296
New England Phonograph Co., 310
New England Trust Co., 254
New Princeton Review, publishes Norton article, 159
New Review, publishes Archer essay, 291
*Newton, Richard H., "Is Poverty Providential or Perpetual?" (WDH on), 243-*44*
New York Central Railroad, 281, 288-89
New York *Dramatic Mirror*, publishes Archer essay, 291
New York *Herald*, 182
New York Stationers' Board of Trade, 182
*New York *Sun*, and W. M. Laffan, 28, 316-17, 319; publishes articles on WDH, 236, 239; publishes *The Quality of Mercy*, 279, 303, 313, 316, 319, 320, 325; publishes S. M. Kravchinski articles, 303
New York *Times*, publishes W. W. Phelps letter, 108; publishes C. Schurz speech, 108; reviews *A Foregone Conclusion* (play), 165, 169; publishes Lowell speech, 224; reports R. H. Newton sermon, 244
*New York *Tribune*, alleged attack on Clemens, 8; publishes news item on WDH, 76; reviews *A Little Girl Among the Old Masters*, 84-85, 90; offered drama review by WDH, 97; and Haymarket Affair letters, 145, 198; publishes "Mr. Howells on Realism" (interview), 196; publishes Haymarket Af-